CW00832337

'An ambitious tome which explores India's various dietary conventions and religions through the ages . . . The early history of natives, travellers and migrants and evolution of regional diets is erudite and fascinating.'
— *The Independent*

'The most comprehensive and thorough on the subject so far . . . The book is beautifully designed as well. Its range, from prehistory to the food of the Indian diaspora, is impressive and she even includes clear, easy recipes so that we can taste the food mentioned . . . Feasts and Fasts is a fascinating book, packed with information and one that should stand as the definitive work for some time.'
— *Petits Propos Culinaires*

'A comprehensive one-volume introduction to Indian food, embedded in a narrative that gains texture from history and cultural anthropology, and is attractive for the specialist and non-specialist alike.'
— *TLS*

'The book is not merely a collection of recipes or listings of the country's diverse cuisines, but delves much deeper into the supremely aromatic world of Indian food, right from the time of the Vedas and ancient empires to the 21st century. So what you have is an engaging book on the impact of history, trade and foreign influences on Indian food and its evolution in the social, moral, scientific and religious context . . . painstakingly researched.'
— *Discover India Magazine*

'Although a rich variety of Indian foods has been enjoyed over the ages by countless generations in India and later the rest of the world, there have been few historical, cultural, and scholarly studies on the subject. This book amply fills that void . . . The book offers readers an in-depth narrative at once interesting, informative, and insightful. Well researched with abundant notes and references, and interspersed with colorful pictures, this book will prove fascinating to Indian and non-Indian readers alike. Recommended.'
— *Choice*

FOODS AND NATIONS is a new series from Reaktion that explores the history – and geography – of food. Books in the series reveal the hidden history behind the food eaten today in different countries and regions of the world, telling the story of how food production and consumption developed, and how they were influenced by the culinary practices of other places and peoples. Each book in the Foods and Nations series offers fascinating insights into the distinct flavours of a country and its culture.

Already published

Al Dente: A History of Food in Italy
FABIO PARASECOLI

Beyond Bratwurst: A History of Food in Germany
URSULA HEINZELMANN

Cabbage and Caviar: A History of Food in Russia
ALISON K. SMITH

Delicioso: A History of Food in Spain
MARÍA JOSÉ SEVILLA

Feasts and Fasts: A History of Food in India
COLLEEN TAYLOR SEN

Gifts of the Gods: A History of Food in Greece
ANDREW AND RACHEL DALBY

Rice and Baguette: A History of Food in Vietnam
VU HONG LIEN

A Rich and Fertile Land: A History of Food in America
BRUCE KRAIG

Savoir-Faire: A History of Food in France
MARYANN TEBBEN

True to the Land: A History of Food in Australia
PAUL VAN REYK

Feasts and Fasts

A History of Food
in India

COLLEEN TAYLOR SEN

REAKTION BOOKS

In memory of my mother,
Kathleen Gilbert Taylor

Published by Reaktion Books Ltd
Unit 32, Waterside
44–48 Wharf Road
London N1 7UX, UK
www.reaktionbooks.co.uk

First published 2015, reprinted 2021

Copyright © Colleen Taylor Sen 2015

All rights reserved

No part of this publication may be reproduced, stored in a retrieval system,
or transmitted, in any form or by any means, electronic, mechanical,
photocopying, recording or otherwise, without the prior permission
of the publishers

Printed and bound in India by Replika Press Pvt. Ltd

A catalogue record for this book is available from the British Library

ISBN 978 1 78023 352 9

CONTENTS

INTRODUCTION

> [India] was like some ancient palimpsest on which layer upon layer of thought
> and reverie had been inscribed, and yet no succeeding layer had completely
> hidden or erased what had been written previously . . . Though outwardly
> there was diversity and infinite variety among our people, everywhere there
> was that tremendous impress of oneness, which had held all of us together
> for ages past, whatever political fate or misfortune had befallen us.
> Jawaharlal Nehru, *The Discovery of India* (1946)

India has been called a universe, not a country. It is the second most populous country in the world after China and the seventh largest in area; no other country has such a diversity of climate and soil, race and language, religion and sect, tribe, caste and class, custom – and cuisine.[1] Sometimes India is compared with Europe in its multitude of languages and ethnic groups – but imagine a Europe with eight religions (four of them born on its own soil), each with its own prohibitions and restrictions. As Mark Twain observed, 'In religion all other countries are paupers; India is the only millionaire.'[2]

From ancient times, foreign travellers have marvelled at the country's agricultural bounty. Plants indigenous to India include lentils (such as urad, mung and masur dal), millet, aubergines, many tubers, pumpkins, melons and gourds, mangoes, jackfruit, citrus fruit, ginger, turmeric, tamarind, and black and long pepper. India is also the home of domesticated chickens. Today these foodstuffs are still central to the diet of a great many Indians.

But India was also one of the world's first global economies. From the time of the Indus Valley civilization in the third millennium BCE, it was the centre of a vast network of land and sea trade routes that were a conduit for plants, ingredients, dishes and cooking techniques from and to Afghanistan, Persia, Central Asia, the Middle East, Africa, China, Southeast Asia and the Indonesian archipelago. The spread of Buddhism from India to China, Southeast Asia, Korea and Japan changed the dietary habits of those countries. Later, Europeans brought plants from the western hemisphere and elsewhere, including tomatoes, pineapples, cashews, potatoes and chillies. All these added layer upon layer to what, paraphrasing Nehru, we might call the palimpsest of Indian cuisine, in which no layer ever hides or erases what has gone before.

In light of this diversity, it is intriguing to unearth what makes Indian food recognizably Indian and how it came to be that way, and to investigate whether there is a gastronomic culture common to all Indians. This book addresses these questions by tracing the history of Indian food from prehistoric times to the present in the context of historical, social, religious and philosophical developments. It is organized more or less chronologically, although with certain liberties, since many old Indian works can be dated only over a span of centuries or even millennia. As one leading scholar wrote, 'One of the rarest gifts to those who study the vast corpus of epic and mythological literature in India is a date.'[3]

The religious, moral and philosophical significance of food is an important theme of the book, since in India, more than in any other part of the world, food has been invested with meaning as a marker of identity. The corollary of 'You are what you eat' is 'You eat what you are.' Buddhists, Jains, Hindus, Sikhs, Muslims and those adhering to other religions have their own food prescriptions and proscriptions. Feasts to celebrate festivals and life transitions and fasts for spiritual and medical reasons are universal on the subcontinent.

Another important theme is the unbreakable connection between diet and health. Diet was the prime treatment in Ayurveda (Indian medicine) and Unani (Islamic medicine). Modern scientific research is now confirming the efficacy of many Ayurvedic treatments and ingredients.

My sources for this book include reports on archaeological discoveries for the earliest period; scripture, philosophical writing and treatises or books of rules (*shastras*); Ayurvedic texts; Kautilya's (Chanakya's) *Arthashastra*; the Hindu epics; the Tamil Sangam literature and other poems; the accounts of foreign travellers from the time of Alexander the Great onwards; and memoirs. The first rudimentary 'cookbooks' – the *Manasollasa*, the *Lokopakara*, the *Supa Shastra* and the brilliantly illustrated *Ni'matnama* of the sultans of Mandu – began to appear only in the twelfth century. While all these works give a general idea of what and how people ate, what is missing is detailed information about exactly how dishes were prepared. The anthropologist Arjun Appadurai wrote:

> Recipes, the elementary forms of the culinary life, are missing in the great tradition of Hinduism . . . While there is an immense amount written about *eating* and feeding, precious little is said about *cooking* in Hindu legal medical or philosophical texts . . . Food is principally either a moral or medical matter in traditional Hindu thought.[4]

Because of this physical and cultural diversity, there are not one but *many* distinctive Indian cuisines based on regional, religious and social differences – too many to enumerate in this or perhaps any work. Indian regional variations and the domestic consumption of food were largely ignored by British administrators and writers and have received relatively little attention from historians. The study of food has been left largely to anthropologists, who, as one member of the profession put it, have developed a 'large and impressive conceptual apparatus for talking about food abstracted from its historical context'.[5]

The most comprehensive study of Indian foodways to date is Professor K. T. Achaya's brilliant *A Historical Companion to Indian Food* (and its companion volume, *A Historical Dictionary of Indian Food*, 1998), which first appeared in 1994. One of my regrets is that I never met Professor Achaya during my visits to India. Students of Indian food also owe a debt of gratitude to Professor Om Prakash for his compilation and translation of passages from Sanskrit works in *Food and Drinks in Ancient India: From Earliest Times to c. 1200 AD* (1963). A list of other useful sources is given in the Select Bibliography.

A NOTE ON TRANSLITERATION

Sanskrit, Urdu, Hindi and other languages of the Indian subcontinent are written in non-Roman scripts, and the English letters rarely correspond exactly to the sounds of the original language. Scholars use diacritical marks to indicate the correct pronunciation; for example, ā indicates a long vowel and ṣ a sibilant. When words have common English transcriptions (for example, Krishna instead of *Kṛṣṇa*), these are used in the text; diacritical marks are retained in the bibliography.

ONE

Climate, Crops and Prehistory

The starting point for an understanding of any nation's food is its physical features, its environment, climate and weather, its soil and its landscape. India is a country of astonishing geographical diversity, with virtually every climate imaginable: the frigid peaks of the Himalayas, the cedar woodlands of Kashmir, the lush tropical forests of Kerala, the bone-dry deserts of Rajasthan and the flood plains of Bangladesh and Bengal, as well as 7,500 miles of coastline and ten major river systems.

THE PHYSICAL ENVIRONMENT

For hundreds of millions of years, the Earth's land made up a single continent called Pangaea, which floated in a giant ocean. About 200 million years ago parts of Pangaea began to drift away, and it eventually broke into two land masses: Laurasia and Gondwana. (The latter name comes from a region of India inhabited by a tribal people called Gonds.) Gondwanaland was the precursor of modern-day Antarctica, South America, Africa, India and Australia. The Indian subcontinent broke away from Gondwanaland some 90 million years ago and drifted north before colliding with the Eurasian Plate. It smashed into what is now Central Asia with such violence that it squeezed the earth's surface 8 km (5 miles) upwards, forming the Himalayas.

In the north, the Himalayan range (from the Sanskrit word *himalaya*, 'abode of snow') extends 2,400 km (1,500 miles) from Pakistan and Afghanistan to Burma (Myanmar). Some of the world's highest mountains, including Everest and K2 – both nearly 9,100 m (30,000 ft) high – are here. These ranges have often been called a barrier that isolates India from the rest of Asia, but in reality there has always been continuous communication between India and Western and Central Asia through passes and valleys, including the famous Khyber Pass. Transhumant pastoralists with their flocks and merchants from Central Asia, Iran and Afghanistan came here thousands of years ago. In the northeast, high snow-covered peaks made communication more difficult, but there was always trade with Tibet and China.

Melting snows from the Himalayas and seasonal rains feed the mighty river systems of the subcontinent: the Indus, which drains into the Arabian Sea, and its five tributaries, the Jhelum, Chenab, Ravi, Sutlej and Beas (called *panj ab*, 'five rivers' in Persian and Urdu); the Yamuna-Ganga (Ganges in English); and the Brahmaputra, which flows southeast through Assam into the Bay of Bengal. Their basins form the 3,200-km-long (2,000-mile), 240 to 320-km-wide (150 to 200-mile) Indo-Gangetic plain, the cradle of North Indian civilization.

The northern and eastern parts of this plain form India's most productive agricultural region because of the rich sedimentary soil deposited by the rivers and the large reserves of underground water that have been supplemented by extensive irrigation systems. The Indian states of Punjab and Haryana and the Pakistani province of Punjab produce wheat, barley, rye and other grains. Bengal, Bangladesh and Assam produce two, sometimes three, crops of rice each year.

The Indo-Gangetic plain was once covered with dense forests that are now much depleted, notably in the barren wasteland of Rajasthan's great Thar Desert. The only staples that grew here before irrigation were the so-called coarse grains: sorghum and millet.

Much of the southern part of India is occupied by the Deccan Plateau, a dry, rocky region bordered to the north by the Vindhya and Satpura mountain ranges and the Narmada River. These mountains have served as a partial barrier to communication between northern and southern India, and fostered the development of distinct cultures, languages and cuisines in the four southern states, Kerala, Karnataka, Tamil Nadu and Andhra Pradesh. The three major rivers of South India, the Kaveri, the Godavari and the Krishna, flow into the Bay of Bengal. Their deltas are the rice bowls of southern India.

Between the Western Ghats, an ancient mountain range running down the west coast of India, and the Indian Ocean lies a narrow coastal strip, the lush, green Malabar Coast. Thanks to abundant rainfall, it is one of India's most fertile regions and the historical centre of India's spice trade. This was the first part of India to be visited by Europeans in the late fifteenth century.

THE CLIMATE

The last glacial period, which ended about 12,500 years ago, was not as severe or extensive in northern India as in Eurasia and North America, and southeastern India escaped it entirely. Its end made the gathering of food easier and contributed to an increase in population.

India comprises a very wide range of weather conditions and climatic regions: tropical in the south, temperate and alpine in the north. The Himalayas serve as a barrier to cold winds from the north, keeping the subcontinent warmer than other countries at similar latitudes. Many regions have their own unique microclimates. The traditional Indian calendar has six seasons:

> Vasanta (spring), mid-March to mid-May (during which
>   many festivals are held)
> Grishma (summer), mid-May to mid-July
> Varsha (rainy or monsoon), mid-July to mid-September
> Sharad (autumn), mid-September to mid-November
> Hemant (winter), mid-November to mid-January
> Shishir (cool season), mid-January to mid-March

Today the Indian Meteorological Department designates four official seasons: winter (December–early April), summer/pre-monsoon (roughly April–June), rainy/monsoon (June–September) and post-monsoon (October–December). In Ayurveda, the seasons determine diet, with cooling foods recommended in the hot months, drying foods in the wet seasons, and so on.

India's climate, agriculture and entire economy have been dominated by the monsoons, or tropical rain-bearing winds. The southwest monsoon blows from the Indian Ocean across the Indian land mass between June and September, bringing rains to western, northeastern and northern India. More than 75 per cent of India's rainfall occurs during this period. Later in the year the wind reverses direction and, as the northeast monsoon, carries rain to southern India. From ancient times, Indian merchants used these winds to power their sailing ships westwards across the Arabian Sea to the Arabian Peninsula, the Middle East, the

A field of millet, a traditional Indian grain.

Roman Empire and Africa, and eastwards across the Indian Ocean to Southeast Asia and China.

The timing of the monsoons and the amount of rain they bring are critical for food supplies. Before modern methods of irrigation and the Green Revolution (see pages 273–4), the failure of the monsoon resulted in devastating famines.[1] The heaviest rainfall (more than 2 m/80 in. a year) occurs in northeastern India and along the western coastal strip, allowing the cultivation of rice, which requires a lot of water. The northern plain receives moderate rainfall – between 1 and 2 m (40 and 80 in.) annually – but many crops, including wheat, can be grown without irrigation. Wheat, a winter crop that is the dietary staple in northern India and Pakistan, is sown at the end of the rainy season and ripens in December. Barley also grows in northern India. Much of India has two growing seasons: winter and summer. Winter crops, called *rabi*, are sown in winter and harvested in summer, while summer crops, or *kharif*, are sown in summer and harvested in winter.

Areas of low rainfall (50–100 cm /20–40 in.) are home to dry-zone crops, including varieties of millet that can be grown without irrigation even when rainfall is scanty. Corn flourishes on the plains and in the hills and can thrive in both dry and moderately damp regions. Sugar cane grows nearly everywhere, but is mainly cultivated in the irrigated lands of the Upper Ganges Valley and the Punjab.

The Development of Agriculture

A prevailing theory used to be that European and Central and South Asian agriculture originated in a 'core area' in southeastern Turkey, where all major groups of crops were domesticated at the same time. More recent evidence suggests that crops were domesticated at different times in different places. In South Asia, the domestication of native crops may have developed independently at as many as six sites: southern India, the Ganges plain, Orissa, Saurashtra in Gujarat, the Indo-Gangetic Divide and Baluchistan.[2] They were spread by the movement of hunter-gatherers or farmers from one area to another or by contact between different areas (a process known as cultural diffusion).

The two core crops common to every major agricultural civilization are cereals (annual grasses grown for their grain) and pulses (the edible seeds of leguminous plants). Both are relatively rich in carbohydrates and protein, so that together they contribute to a balanced human diet. The rotation of crops or the mixing of legume and cereal crops also enhances soil fertility. Every culture has had its own combination of staple cereals and companion legumes: in the ancient Middle East, it was wheat or barley and various legumes and beans; in Central America, corn and beans; in China, rice or sorghum and soy beans; and in India, barley, wheat, rice, millet or sorghum with lentils. Today the most widely consumed grains on the subcontinent are rice and wheat.

Pulses

An emblematic feature of Indian cuisine is the consumption of pulses. *Dal*, a Hindi word that means both raw and prepared lentils, may be the closest India has to a national dish. India is by far the world's largest producer of pulses, and the average Indian gets nearly four times as much nutrition from pulses as do Americans or Chinese.[3] The protein content of pulses is on average equivalent to 20–25 per cent of their weight. Pulses are hardy, grow in most soil and climatic conditions, and add nitrogen to the soil.

Indian pulses have four separate places of origin. Urad and mung dal were cultivated in the grasslands of South India starting in the early to mid-third millennium BCE, together with two local millets.[4] Chana dal (also called chickpea, garbanzo bean or Bengal gram), masur dal, green peas and grasspeas came from Western Asia to the Indus Valley in the fourth millennium BCE, probably around the same time as wheat and barley, since they are found together at most archaeological sites. Since all are winter crops, they were later adopted in North India as part of a two-season cropping system.

Hyacinth bean and cow peas plus sorghum and millet most probably came from the savannas of Africa to the grasslands of South India early in the second millennium BCE and were easily assimilated into existing agricultural systems. The plants may have been carried by coastal pastoralists and fishermen in small craft.[5] Another common lentil, pigeon pea,

THE MAIN PULSES IN PREHISTORIC SOUTH ASIA
AND THEIR REGION OF ORIGIN

LATIN NAME	ENGLISH NAME	HINDI NAME	PROBABLE REGION OF ORIGIN
Cajanus cajan	red gram	arhar, tuvar	India: Orissa, Northern Andhra Pradesh, Chhattisgarh
Vigna mungo	urad, black gram	urad	South India: forest–savanna margin
Vigna radiata	mung, green gram	mung	South India: forest–savanna margin
Macrotyloma uniflorum	horse gram	kulthi	India: savannas, peninsula(?)
Cicer arietinum	chickpea, Bengal gram, garbanzo beans, chana dal	chana	Southwest Asia, Levant
Lathyrus sativus	grass pea	khesari	Southwest Asia, Levant
Lens culinaris	lentil	masur	Southwest Asia, Levant
Pisum sativum	pea	matter	Southwest Asia, Levant
Lablab purpureus	hyacinth bean	sem	East Africa
Vigna unguiculata	cow pea	chowli, lboia	West Africa, Ghana

Source: Dorian Q. Fuller and Emma L. Harvey, 'The Archaeobotany of Indian Pulses: Identification, Processing and Evidence for Cultivation', *Environmental Archaeology*, XI/2 (2006), p. 220.

Soy beans in India

Soy beans came to India from China some time after 1000 CE, either via the Silk Route or through Burma and Assam. They were then cultivated in northeastern India, where they were fermented and prepared in stews or chutneys (freshly ground relishes of vegetables, fruits, nuts and other ingredients). The British tried to develop a commercial soy-bean industry elsewhere in India, but their efforts failed. Interest was revived in the 1930s when Mahatma Gandhi advocated soy beans as a cheap source of high-quality protein, and the Maharaja of Baroda promoted their use and cultivation. But soy beans never caught on, perhaps because, by treating them as dal, Indians undercooked the whole beans, which led to digestive problems.

During the Green Revolution, American varieties proved to be ideal for growing in Central India. It was at first thought that they would be used to make high-protein dairy products, such as soy-bean milk, cheese and yoghurt. In 1972 the Seventh Day Adventists opened the first soy dairy in Poona and several cookbooks on the use of soy products were published.

In the 1960s and '70s India was facing a new problem — a shortage of cooking oil. Soy beans were the ideal solution. Oil extraction plants were built throughout the country, production increased dramatically, and today about 90 per cent of the soy beans grown in India are used to make cooking oil.[6]

appears to have originated in Orissa and northern Andhra Pradesh and migrated south.

GRAINS

Wheat and barley are two of the world's oldest cultivated cereals and once grew wild over much of Western Asia. The complex process of domesticating wild wheat grasses began in the mountains of southern Turkey in about 10,000 BCE, spread to the rest of Southwest Asia and into

Major Grains in South Asia and their Regions of Origin

Latin name	English name	Hindi name	Probable region of origin
Triticum spp.	wheat	gehun	Euphrates Valley
Hordeum vulgare	barley	jau	Euphrates Valley
Oryza sativa	rice	dhaan (paddy)	Yangtze Valley
Paspalum scrobiculatum	kodo millet	kodra	India
Sorghum bicolor	sorghum	jowar	Africa
Pennisetum glaucum	pearl millet	bajra/bajri	Africa
Eleusine coracana	finger millet	ragi	Africa
Panicum sumatrense	little millet	kutki	Western India
Panicum miliaceum	broomcorn, common millet	cheena	Manchuria
Setaria italica	foxtail millet	kangni	probably China
Brachiaria ramosa	browntop millet	pedda-sama	India
Echinochloa frumentacea	barnyard millet	jahngora	unknown
Fagopyrum esculentum	buckwheat	kuttu/koto	Central Asia

Source: Steven Weber and Dorian Q. Fuller, 'Millets and their Role in Early Architecture', based on the paper presented at 'First Farmers in Global Perspective', seminar of Uttar Pradesh State Department of Archaeology, Lucknow, India, 18–20 January 2006.

Mesopotamia, then travelled to Europe, North Africa, Egypt and Central Asia. By 6500 BCE wheat was grown in Baluchistan, India.

The two main varieties are bread and durum (hard) wheat. Durum has a high gluten content, which gives it elasticity, so the dough can be rolled very thin. Today 90 per cent of the wheat grown in India (and worldwide) is durum. Finely ground, it makes a flour called *atta* in Hindi that is used to make parathas, puri and other delicious Indian breads. Atta contains both the germ (the embryo of the wheat kernel) and the endosperm, the nutritious tissue surrounding the germ. The Green Revolution greatly increased India's wheat output, and today it is the world's second largest wheat producer, after China. Wheat is mainly grown in northern India and the Pakistani province of Punjab.

Barley was domesticated in the Fertile Crescent about 12,000 years ago, and came to the Indus Valley via settlements in Baluchistan. During the second millennium BCE barley was the main cereal in India, and it is the only one mentioned in the *Rig Veda* (see chapter Two). Because it can grow in fairly dry, poor soils in marginal areas, it came to be considered a poor man's food. Today India ranks only 28th in the world for barley production. But like other ancient ingredients, such as sesame, barley still plays a role in some Hindu religious ceremonies, including the *shraddha* (a ceremony performed to honour one's ancestors).

Millet Bread
500 g (5 cups) millet flour
90 g (6 tbsp) ghee
pinch of salt

Sift the millet flour into a bowl and gradually add warm water to make a semi-soft dough. Knead for five minutes. Divide the dough into balls 8 cm (3 in.) in diameter. Flatten the balls with your palms until they form discs 13–15 cm (5–6 in.) in diameter. Heat a heavy pan and cook each disc for 2 minutes on the first side and 30–40 seconds on the other, turning until both sides are crisp and golden brown. Using tongs, hold it over a flame to make it crisp. Smear ghee on the bread before serving.

Bakers preparing bread in Kashmir, 19th century.

Millet and sorghum, the so-called coarse grains, grow in arid, semi-arid or mountainous areas with marginal fertility and moisture. They have a short growing season, so during years of scarcity they can provide quick nutrition. Their protein content ranges from 6 per cent to 14 per cent, similar to wheat, and they contain no gluten. The main millets grown in India and their origins are shown in the table on p. 17.

India was home to several native millets which were later supplemented by imported varieties from sub-Saharan Africa and perhaps China in the second millennium BCE. After processing, millets can be ground into flour and prepared as bread or boiled to make a porridge.

Domestic consumption of coarse grains has fallen sharply since the Green Revolution of the 1970s because of a preference for wheat, which is softer, easier to use and considered more 'modern'. But recently there has been a resurgence of interest in these grains, driven by health concerns (see chapter Thirteen). India leads the world in millet production, most of it grown in the western part of the country.

The origin of rice has been the subject of considerable research and controversy. The latest theory (at March 2012) is that it was first domesticated in the Pearl River valley in China between 10,000 and 8000 BCE, after which the two main varieties – *indica* (long grain) and *japonica* (short grain) – were cultivated in central China. In the third millennium BCE rice cultivation expanded into Southeast Asia and west across Nepal and India.[7] However, it appears that a wild progenitor of rice (*Oryza nivara*) grew on the Ganges plain much earlier, and archaeological finds at Lahuradewa in Uttar Pradesh date rice use and its associated pottery to as long ago as 6400 BCE.

Today India is the world's second-largest rice producer, after China. The main growing areas are along the eastern and western shoreline areas, the northeast, and the Ganges basin. In eastern and southern India, rice is the staple and wheat is eaten only as a supplement in the form of bread.

FRUIT AND VEGETABLES

Fruit and vegetables that are probably indigenous to India include some varieties of pumpkins, melons and gourds, including members of the Curcumis and Citrullus families. The cucumber, ash gourd, parwal, snake

Bael is a sour fruit used in Ayurveda to cure gastrointestinal and other ailments. It also plays a role in Hindu religious rituals.

Jackfruit, which
originated in
India, is used
in many different
preparations.

gourd and bitter gourd are very ancient and play an important part in the Indian diet. (The Cucurbita species, which include pumpkin, squash and marrow, originated in the New World. Some varieties may have reached India thousands of years ago by seeds floated across the Pacific,[8] but most were introduced during the Columbian Exchange, notably pumpkin.) Other indigenous plants include aubergine (eggplant); green leafy vegetables collectively known as *shaka* in Sanskrit; amla, the Indian gooseberry; ber, the Indian jujube; myrobalan, a plum-like fruit; jamoon, a sweet, astringent fruit; bael, a hard-shelled fruit with a yellow aromatic pulp; jackfruit; and one of India's great culinary gifts to the world, the mango.[9] In the early stages of their domestication 4,000 years ago, mangoes were very small and fibrous, but they were later improved by selective breeding, especially by the Mughals and the Portuguese. India is also the original home of many varieties of citrus fruit. Two indigenous nuts are the chironji, the seeds of which are used to flavour sweet dishes, and the chilgoza, the nut of an evergreen tree. Although okra (lady's fingers; *bhindi* in Hindi) most likely originated in Africa, it was probably domesticated in India.

The coconut palm (*Cocos nucifera*) was likely domesticated independently in two locations: around the Pacific Ocean/Southeast Asia and the Indian Ocean. Linguistic evidence indicates that coconuts were cultivated in South India 2,500–3,000 years ago. The plant has myriad uses as a source of fuel, drink and food. Today India is the world's third-largest producer, and coconut plays an important role in the cuisine of Kerala. The origin of bananas and plantains, members of the *Musa* genus, is also problematic. They probably originated in New Guinea, but they were grown in India very early on. Onions and garlic were grown in Southwest Asia and Afghanistan from ancient times but are not mentioned in the earliest Indian texts. When the onion first appeared, it was as a food of the despised tribal population and foreigners, which may explain later taboos.

Sugar cane is a perennial grass that was first domesticated in New Guinea in about 8000 BCE and quickly spread to Southeast Asia, China and India. Its stems are filled with a sappy pulp that is up to 17 per cent sucrose. The stems are crushed to extract the juice, which is boiled down to make a solid piece of dark brown sugar, called gur or jaggery.

A fruit stand in New Delhi selling both imported and local fruits.

In the third century BCE Indians discovered the technique of refining the juice into crystals. Sugar has always played an important role in the Indian diet, and its consumption per capita is one of the highest in the world.

Grapes, peaches, plums, apricots, pomegranates, saffron, spinach, rhubarb, apples and marijuana (*Cannabis sativa*) came to India from China and Central Asia, Afghanistan and Persia at different times. Indigenous nuts were supplemented by almonds, pistachios and walnuts from West and Central Asia, and later peanuts and cashews from the Americas. Starting in the sixteenth century, when the Portuguese established trading posts throughout the subcontinent, a wave of fruit and vegetables arrived from the New World, among them papayas, guavas, chayote, sapodilla, avocado, potatoes, tomatoes, pineapples, cashews and chillies, all of which thrived in India's tropical climate (see chapter Ten).

SPICES

The quintessential feature of Indian cuisine is the use of spices. Spice is a broad term, covering different parts of a plant: bark (cinnamon, cassia), seeds (cumin, coriander, cardamom, mustard), underground roots or stems, called rhizomes (ginger, turmeric), stigma (saffron) and flower buds (cloves). The International Organization for Standardization (ISO) has registered 109 spices, of which 52 are supervised by the Spice Board of India.

Spices indigenous to India are ginger, turmeric, tamarind, black (also called round) pepper (*Piper nigrum*), curry leaves (*Murraya koenigii*), pippali or long pepper (*P. longum*), green and black cardamom (which grew wild in the Western Ghats, sometimes called the Cardamom Hills) and holy basil or tulsi (*Ocimum sanctum*), although the last is not used as an ingredient, perhaps because it is sacred to the deity Vishnu and worshipped by many Hindus. Sesame seed (*Sesame indicum*), one of the oldest oilseed crops, was domesticated very early. Other spices arrived from Western Asia very early on, including cumin, fenugreek, mustard seed, saffron and coriander. Asafoetida (hing), the dried gum from an underground rhizome (widely used by orthodox Hindus and Jains as a substitute for garlic), originated in Afghanistan, which is still a major producer. Cinnamon from Sri Lanka, cassia from South China, and cloves and nutmeg from Indonesia reached India from the third century CE onwards. Cloves were not grown in India until about 1800.

Long pepper, which has a pungent, almost earthy taste, was once the most popular form of pepper, but has largely been replaced with black pepper and chillies and today is used mainly in Ayurvedic medicine.

The betel vine (*Piper betle*) and betel nut (*Areca catechu*) may have initially been domesticated in Southeast Asia, but soon became part of Indian culinary and social life as the main ingredients in paan (betel quid). Chillies (the fruit of plants from the genus *Capsicum*, which also includes sweet or bell peppers) were brought from the New World in the sixteenth century and quickly became assimilated into the cuisine as a replacement for long pepper. In Indian languages, the word is an extension of the word for pepper; for example, in Hindi, *kali* or *hari mirch*, meaning black or green pepper. Most of the spices used in India today have Sanskrit names, indicating their ancient provenance.

Many explanations have been offered for the intensive use of spices in India, Mexico and other hot countries – and most are myths. Hot spices do not, for example, induce enough perspiration to cool the body. Nor have they been used to mask the flavour of tainted meat, since those who ate such food would still be likely to become ill and even die. Spices do provide nutrients, such as vitamins A and C, but in very small amounts. The latest theory, backed by a body of scientific evidence, is that a taste for spices evolved over the centuries in hot climates because they contain powerful antibiotic chemicals that can kill or suppress the bacteria and fungi that spoil foods. Some spices can kill or stop the growth of dozens of species of bacteria; the most potent are garlic, onion, allspice, cinnamon, cumin, cloves and chillies. The antibiotic effects are even stronger when ingredients such as chillies, onions, garlic and cumin are combined. Turmeric has been used for thousands of years in India and China to combat infection and reduce inflammation. Recent research has shown that spices, especially turmeric, are powerful antioxidants that can reduce inflammation, enhance the absorption of the protein in grains and chickpeas, lower cholesterol and even slow the progress of cancer.[10] Frying in oil before cooking, a common technique, enhances the therapeutic properties of turmeric and other spices.

From a gastronomical point of view, the purpose of spices is to add flavour, texture and body to dishes. They also provide flavour and excitement at low cost for poor people whose diet is otherwise bland and unvarying. In preparing simple vegetable dishes, cooks may use just two or three spices, whereas more complex meat dishes are made with a dozen or more. Spices may be added once, twice, even three times during the cooking process. They may be ground into a powder or masala

A seal from the Indus Valley showing a bull, *c.* 2450–2200 BCE.

('mixture' in Hindi), used whole (especially peppercorns, cardamom and cloves), or ground with water, chillies and onions, yoghurt or tomatoes to make a paste. Spices are generally dry-roasted or briefly fried first to intensify their flavour.

People often equate the use of spices with heat. The burning sensation in the mouth associated with 'hot' food is produced by black pepper and chillies. The pungency of pepper is due to the volatile oil piperine and resin, which together increase the flow of saliva and gastric juices. Chillies' heat is produced by capsaicin, an alkaloid found mainly in the membranes lining the pod (not in the seeds, as is generally believed). Generally speaking, food in South India tends to be hotter than that in the north, although Pakistani food can also be quite mouth-searing.

ANIMALS

Animals native to the Indian subcontinent include the water buffalo (*Bubalus bubalis*), which was domesticated in about 4000 BCE; the zebu, or humped cattle, also known as Brahman cattle (*Bos indicus*); and the chicken (*Gallus gallus*), which was probably originally raised for fighting, not food. Sheep and goats, which originated in Afghanistan and Central Asia, were being raised in India by the third millennium BCE. Because they graze on natural vegetation, they are useful in rural economies where crop and dairy farming are not feasible. Genetic data implies that pigs were domesticated from wild boar in India several millennia ago.

The other common breed of cattle (*B. taurus*) originated in the Fertile Crescent and may have been brought to India by the Indo-Aryans, where it interbred with local breeds. Both the cow and the zebu are thought to share a common ancestor in *B. primigenius*, the wild cattle or aurochs that roamed Eurasia at the end of the last ice age.

India's once-vast forests abounded with game, including wild boar, quail, partridge, hare and many varieties of deer, including antelope, spotted deer and blue deer (*nilgai*), but these have largely disappeared.

PEOPLE

As with plants and animals, it is difficult to categorize which people are indigenous and which are alien, especially in the remote past. The historian Romila Thapar wrote:

The game of 'who was there first', played by those claiming to speak on behalf of Aryans, or Dravidians, or Austro-Asiatics, or whatever, is historically not viable. Not only are the claims to these identities as being historical and having an immense antiquity untenable but the paucity of the required evidence to prove this makes it impossible to give answers with any certainty.[11]

There is now genetic evidence that the subcontinent's earliest inhabitants migrated from Africa between 70,000 and 50,000 BCE along the coast of Arabia. Tools found at Jawalapuram, a 74,000-year-old site in southern India, match those used in Africa in the same period. From there people migrated to other parts of Asia, Indonesia, Australia and Europe. DNA testing has indicated links between some groups in South India and Australian aboriginals (although the aboriginals bear an ancient DNA called Denisovan, while Indians do not).[12] In India, the descendants of these earliest peoples are sometimes called Munda, the name of an Austro-Asiatic language related to the national languages of Vietnam and Cambodia.

These original inhabitants were hunter-gatherers who ate fruit, nuts, tubers and the meat of various animals. From about 10,000 BCE they began to settle in or near rock shelters and to domesticate dogs, cattle, sheep and goats. Large animals were used for transportation and traction, smaller ones for meat. They cultivated wheat, barley and millet as well as peas, chickpeas, green gram and mustard. Excavations in northern Rajasthan indicate that forests were cleared and grain seeds planted as early as 8000 BCE. At first they used stone tools to grind wild grains and plants; these were later supplanted by the wooden plough.

Our knowledge of these early people was enhanced by the discovery in 1974 of the village of Mehrgarh on the Kachi Plain of Baluchistan. Excavations revealed that the residents lived in mud-brick houses, made tools out of locally mined copper ore, produced terracotta pottery and seals, and lined their basket containers with bitumen. As early as 6500 BCE they were cultivating primitive forms of barley and wheat. Over the following millennia, they developed higher-yielding strains of wheat and barley and cultivated jujubes, grapes, red lentils, field peas, chickpeas, linseed and dates, and domesticated wild sheep, goats and cattle. Their main cooking fuel was juniper wood. In eastern Baluchistan, rice was cultivated in summer, perhaps a sign of contact with regions to the east.

Mehrgarh was abandoned in 2500 BCE for unknown reasons, and by 2000 BCE the region had become desert. One theory for this is that its inhabitants moved to the more fertile Indus Valley, and Mehrgarh is now regarded as a precursor of the Indus Valley civilization.

In southern India, the valleys of the Godavari, Krishna, Kaveri and other rivers were settled as early as the third millennium BCE. The people spoke Dravidian languages, which are unrelated to any other language family in the world. Today some twenty Dravidian languages are spoken in southern and central India, with a small pocket of speakers of Brahui in Pakistan and Afghanistan.[13] By 2000 BCE they had spread over a very wide area, including present-day Maharashtra, Andhra Pradesh, Kerala and Tamil Nadu.

By reconstructing the language of these ancient inhabitants, called Proto-Dravidian, and comparing it with the remains of plants, tools and artefacts found in archaeological excavations, scholars have formed a picture of how they lived, farmed and ate.[14] In the Neolithic period (2800–1200 BCE), their dietary staples were two pulses and two millets. Cereals were ground into flour and mixed with pulse flour to make what may have been the ancestors of such typical South Indian foods as idli, vadai and dosa.[15] The discovery of large open bowls and open pots suggests the boiling of flour-based porridges and gruels and communal dining.

Throughout the second millennium BCE there was a selective uptake of new crops (wheat, barley, rice) from the northwest. New vessels in-cluded perforated bowls, some with spouted lips, which archaeologists speculate may have been used for steaming, as colanders, to extrude a sorghum flour dough boiled in milk, or to strain yoghurt. Ceramic platters were later used, perhaps indicating that people were eating flat-breads or rice, over which other dishes would be poured.

THE HARAPPAN OR INDUS VALLEY CIVILIZATION, 3000–1500 BCE

Together with Mesopotamia and ancient Egypt, the Harappan or Indus Valley civilization is one of the early cradles of Old World civilization and one of the most fascinating stories in the history of archaeology. In the 1920s the British archaeologist Sir Mortimer Wheeler began exca-vating the remains of ancient cities of vast proportions in what is now Sindh, Pakistan. Archaeological digs have continued to reveal the extent

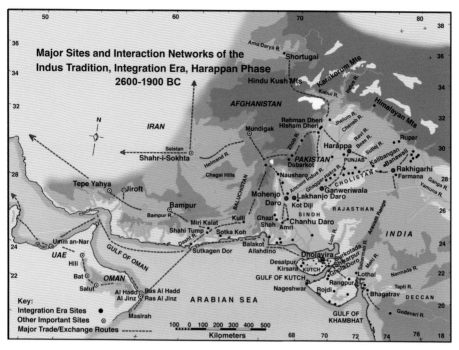

Major sites of the Indus Valley civilization, 2600–1900 BCE.

and sophistication of this vast civilization, whose citizens knew the arts of writing, town planning, metallurgy, architecture and drainage.

At its peak, the civilization extended over more than 1 million sq. km (386,000 sq. miles) in the Pakistani provinces of Baluchistan, Sindh and Punjab and the Indian states of Punjab, Haryana, Rajasthan, Gujarat and Uttar Pradesh, almost to the outskirts of New Delhi. Archaeologists have discovered more than 1,500 villages and small cities and five large cities. The most famous are Mohenjo Daro in the south, which covered more than 200 ha (500 acres) and had 40,000 inhabitants, and Harappa in the north (150 ha/370 acres). These cities flourished between 2500 and 1600 BCE.

Today much of the land is desert, but in ancient times it was fertile and forested, allowing the production of surplus wheat and barley and the technological competence to develop an urban civilization. A ploughed field at Kalibangan in Rajasthan has been dated to as early as 2800 BCE. It has a grid pattern of furrows, placed about 30 cm (12 in.) apart running east–west, with others spaced about 190 cm (75 in.) apart running north–south. This allows the planting of two crops (such as mustard and chickpeas) in the same field, a practice still followed in the region.

The Indus Valley civilization was an affluent commercial society, with merchants engaged in trade by land and sea with Central Asia, Mesopotamia and the Arabian Peninsula. Technology allowed the construction of seagoing ships that were mentioned in Akkadian texts. Seals from the civilization have been found in Oman and Iraq. The merchants exported barley, cotton and cotton goods, sesame and linseed oils, wood, iron, gems, lapis lazuli from Afghanistan, copper and gold. Some merchants lived in special quarters in Mesopotamian cities, so there was probably some exchange of food customs between the two civilizations.

Artefacts found in excavations in the Indus Valley include ceramics, stone, copper and bronze statues and jewellery, especially bangles, whose elegance indicates a high level of sophistication. Clay seals and pottery depict elephants, tigers, the Indian humped bull and a horned deity seated in a yogic posture that some people interpret as a prototype of the Hindu god Siva. Excavations reveal well-planned urban centres with streets in a grid pattern, brick houses, water and sewage systems, and what may be brick granaries with raised platforms and ventilated floors. A room in a building excavated on one of the main streets of Mohenjo Daro has five conical pits and places to hold large jars and may have been a public restaurant. A central feature of Mohenjo Daro is a large pool, called the Great Bath, which could have been used for ritual bathing – a sign of a concern for personal cleanliness that characterized later Indian civilization. There is little evidence of military conflict or warfare or the palace of a powerful ruler, such as those found in Egypt and the Middle East. Some scholars theorize that the Indus cities were ruled instead by powerful elites, such as landowners, merchants and ritual specialists.

No one is sure where these early urban dwellers came from, or what language they spoke. Their script has not yet been deciphered, although one theory is that they spoke a Dravidian language.

The civilization grew up beside rivers that were fed by the melting snows of the Himalayas and emptied into the Arabian Sea near present-day Karachi. During the monsoons these rivers flooded, leaving a rich, fertile silt. Their tributaries provided links to other towns and regions along the coast and inland, and access to such resources as copper, semi-precious stones, minerals and timber. One of the main rivers was the Indus; another was the Saraswati, which features in many ancient Vedic hymns (and is the name of a Hindu goddess). The Saraswati had disappeared by around 2000 BCE, leading some to believe that it was a myth or an underground river. Modern scientists have been using satellite photography and other technology to attempt to identify its possible location.[16]

Agricultural operations included ploughing, furrowing, building channels and dams, and irrigating. The main crops were wheat and barley, planted in autumn and harvested in spring or early summer. Archaeologists have found the remains of West Asian winter crops and South Asian summer crops, including millet, wheat, barley, black and green lentils, peas, chickpeas, grass peas, sesame, melon, cucumber and mango.

Bread was a staple of the Indus Valley diet. More than 200 varieties are listed in ancient Mesopotamian tablets, and we can speculate that a similar variety existed in the Indus civilization. A collection of Mesopotamian recipes from about 1600 BCE indicates that unleavened dough made from flour and water was rolled out and then stuck on the very hot surface of a clay oven, called a *tinuru*, with an opening on the bottom to add fuel and let in air – just like modern Indian tandoors. To make leavened bread, a little beer or leftover sour soup was added to the dough, which was shaped into a loaf and baked in a domed container at the bottom of the *tinuru*.[17] The most basic way of cooking meat was to grill it directly on a fire, perhaps skewered on sticks. This was a precursor of

Cooking pot from the Indus Valley, 3300–2800 BCE.

the modern kebab; in fact, one theory of the origin of that word is that it comes from an Akkadian root meaning 'to burn, to char'.

Analysis of the residue in cooking pots and human and bovine teeth (then, as now, bovines were fed leftovers) at Farmana, 60 km (37 miles) from New Delhi, confirms that between 2500 and 2000 BCE cooks in the Indus Valley were using turmeric, ginger and garlic as flavourings – the ingredients for a 4,000-year-old north Indian curry. (Throughout this book the word 'curry' denotes a meat, fish or vegetable stew served with rice, bread or another starch.[18]) A charred lump of sesame seed was found in Harappa, together with wheat and peas. Bananas appear at three widely dispersed sites. Even rice, long assumed to be a late addition, has turned up as the main grain in at least one village in the third millennium BCE.[19] Roasted barley, boiled lentils, chickpea flour and baked tubers were other foodstuffs. Common people probably ate a simple diet of wheat or barley with lentils, a few vegetables and occasionally a little meat or fish – just as they do in India today.[20]

Sugar cane was not known to the Indus Valley people; the main sweeteners were honey, dates, palm sugar and such fruit as jujube, jamun and mango. Pomegranate, grapes, apples, plums, apricots, pistachios, walnuts, almonds and pine nuts were available from the highlands, and coconut, bananas, jackfruit and citrus fruit were grown in the eastern regions. Sea salt and rock salt were available. Cooking oil was made from butter, mustard and sesame seeds, and perhaps cotton seed and linseed.

In addition to settled agriculturists, the Indus Valley was home to pastoral nomads wandering with their herds of water buffalo. Selective breeding produced varieties adapted to such tasks as pulling ploughs and ox-carts and carrying goods. Buffaloes were an important source of milk. (Even today, the region around Sahiwal near Harappa is famous for its grazing and the excellent quality of its milk.[21]) Buffalo's milk has a higher fat content than that of cows, and is good for making ghee, clarified butter and yoghurt. Goats and sheep were raised as pack animals, as a source of meat and dairy products and for their wool or hair.

The diet of the Indus Valley people was supplemented by game, including deer and wild boar. The bones of wild pigs have been found at many sites, but pigs were probably not domesticated. Cows were not known.

Given the long coastline and many rivers, fish and seafood played an important role in the diet of the Indus Valley people. Fish are the most common symbol on the civilization's seals, and large quantities of seashells and fish bones (including those of freshwater and marine catfish, carp, eel and shad) have been found. Often the fish was dried and sold as far away as Mesopotamia.

It was once commonly thought that the Indus Valley civilization was suddenly wiped off the face of the earth by an invasion of Indo-European hordes from the north, who destroyed the cities. This theory has been discounted, however, and scholars now believe that the civilization disintegrated gradually over hundreds of years (perhaps between 1900 and 1300 BCE) as its people dispersed and formed new political entities at the eastern and northern edges of the region. The cause may have been desertification, a natural calamity such as an earthquake or flood, the sedimentation of rivers or some combination of the above.

Another explanation is that extensive flooding (perhaps similar to the Indus Valley floods that devastated Pakistan in the summer of 2010) and shifting rivers destroyed the agricultural foundation of the Indus cities, forcing the inhabitants to develop new agriculture strategies or move to more stable regions. The cultivation of summer crops such as rice, millet and sorghum made possible an expansion into the Ganga-Yamuna-Doab region and Gujarat.

As the cities of the Indus declined, refugees may have merged with other groups to form small city states or chiefdoms in Afghanistan and Central Asia and near the Ganges and Yumuna river systems. In the first millennium BCE, these new polities formed the basis of a second major urban civilization. There was no significant break between the two urban civilizations, but rather a gradual transition from one to the other. Much of the continuity reflects not only similar environments, but also subsistence practices, raw materials and some symbols. As the prominent Indus Valley archaeologist Jonathan Mark Kenoyer wrote:

> Even today, in the modern cities and villages of Pakistan and India, we see the legacy of the Indus cities reflected in the traditional arts and crafts as well as the layout of houses and settlements [to which we would add food customs]. These remnants of the past do not represent a stagnation of culture but rather highlight the optimal choices made by the Indus people.[22]

TWO
The Age of Ritual, 1700–1100 BCE

THE INDO-ARYANS

The second millennium BCE saw the appearance of the Indo-Aryans, who planted the seeds of what were to become some of the most unique features of Indian society: the caste system, the veneration of the cow, and the central role of milk and dairy products in food customs and rituals.

The Indo-Aryans were speakers of Indo-European languages, a family that includes Sanskrit, Greek, Latin, Hittite (a language once spoken in Anatolia) and most modern European and north Indian languages. Some scholars place the origin of these languages in the general region of the Pontic Caspian steppe – a vast grassland stretching from north of the Black Sea eastward to the Caspian Sea to western Kazakhstan, the eastern Ukraine and southern Russia – between the fifth and fourth millennia BCE.[1] Another theory is that Proto-Indo-European languages originated in Anatolia before the rise of agriculture and spread with Neolithic migrants into all parts of Europe and the Pontic steppes, beginning in the eighth millennium BCE.

The Indo-Aryans formed a semi-nomadic society consisting of small kinship groups who raised cattle and sheep and practised some settled agriculture and cereal cultivation. They domesticated the horse and used carts with wheels. Constantly looking for arable land and greener pastures for their flocks, they branched out from Asia Minor and Anatolia into the Middle East, Armenia, Europe, Iran, Afghanistan and eventually the Indian subcontinent, which they entered between 1700 and 1300 BCE. The old theory that hordes of Indo-Aryans 'invaded' India has been discounted; rather, it is most likely that small groups trickled in through the mountain passes over the centuries. One of their earliest settlements was in the Punjab, near the current Indo-Pakistani border. As they moved

Bawarchi (cook)
preparing food
over a *chula* (stove).
Varanasi, *c.* 1850.

eastwards, they fought and subjugated the local inhabitants, called *dasas*, whose origin is problematic. They may have been Mundas, Dravidians, survivors of the Indus Valley civilization or Indo-European migrants who arrived even earlier. There is linguistic evidence that these earlier inhabitants were already farmers, since the Sanskrit word for plough (*langala*) is not Indo-European.

Obtaining and raising cows was the main occupation of the Indo-Aryan elite. People counted their wealth in cattle, and the verb 'to fight', *gavishthi*, means 'to search for cows', implying that cattle raids were the source of conflict. Even today, the word for clan is *gotra*, meaning 'cowshed'.

Although we know who the Indo-Aryans were and where they came from, our knowledge of their material culture is less than for the Indus Valley civilization, because their homes and villages were made of wood and other natural materials and did not survive. However, some idea of their food habits and lifestyles can be gleaned from an extensive body of written texts, the Vedas (from a Sanskrit word that means 'knowledge'). Composed in northwestern India in the second millennium BCE, the Vedas were memorized and passed on orally for centuries, and finally written down in the first millennium CE. Even today they are revered by Hindus as the most sacred of all Indian texts. Although few people read them in their entirety, verses are recited during important Hindu ceremonies, making them one of the world's oldest religious texts in continuous use. English translations in the mid-nineteenth century made an enormous impression on Western intellectuals, including the writer Henry David Thoreau and the philosophers William James and Arthur Schopenhauer, the latter of whom said that they laid the foundation of his philosophical system.

The oldest of these texts, composed between 1700 and 1100 BCE, is the *Rig Veda* (*rig* means 'song of praise'), a collection of hymns and paeans to the gods, incantations, chants, prayers for life and prosperity, and philosophical speculations.[2] The *Rig Veda* consists of 1,028 poems or hymns organized into ten books (*mandalas*). Although centuries elapsed between their composition and transcription, scholars believe they are very close to the original because of the elaborate mnemonic techniques that were developed and the care with which they were transmitted from father to son or from teacher to student.

The gods were forces of nature, with counterparts in the mythology of classical Greece and Rome. Indra, the equivalent of Zeus and Jupiter, was the main deity in the Vedic pantheon and ruled over the sky and heavens. Agni was the god of fire, Varuna, thunder, Rudra, lightning, Vayu, the wind, and Surya, the sun. Minor deities included Vishnu, who centuries later became one of the three major Hindu gods.

Life and nature were uncertain, and the way of placating the gods and winning their favour was by rituals, *yajna* in Sanskrit – a word that can mean worship, prayer, offering, praise, oblation or sacrifice. Vedic Indians did not have temples; *yajnas* were conducted either in the home, where each family had a sacred hearth, or in the open air around a fire. Fire was considered the purest of elements, and still plays an important role in Hindu ceremonies; for example, in the marriage ceremony, the couple walks around a fire seven times. Agni, the god of fire, was considered the mouth through which the gods eat the sacrifices; he was both the priest of the gods and the god of the priests. One of his favourite foods was ghee (clarified butter), a divine substance exalted in many of the hymns of the *Rig Veda*:

Ode to Ghee

They pour over the fire, smiling,
Like beautiful women on their way to a festival.
The streams of butter caress the logs,
And Jatavedas [meaning obscure], taking pleasure in them,
   pays them court.

I watch them eagerly; they are like girls,
Painting themselves to go the wedding
There where the soma juice is pressed, where sacrifice is made,
The streams of butter run down to be clarified (IV.58)

The formulae and rituals were the monopoly of the priests, called *brahmins*, and paid for by the *yajamanas*, the patrons of the sacrifice. There were three kinds of *yajna*: cooked food offered on the domestic hearth; public sacrifices; and the soma ritual. The sacrifices entailed killing animals and offering the meat to the gods, after which it was eaten by the patrons and their guests and later by the person performing the sacrifice.[3] (Similar rites took place in classical Greece and Rome, and in Persia.) The meat was cooked in a cauldron or baked in a *chula*, a U-shaped mud fireplace with an opening for inserting firewood, still used today. The animals sacrificed included goats, sheep, oxen, castrated bulls, horses and barren cows. Some sacrifices were bloody; the most important sacrifice of Vedic times, the horse sacrifice, required the killing of more than 600 animals and birds.

Although cows were the mainstay of the Vedic economy and were held in high regard, there is textual evidence that they too were sacrificed. Some argue that this evidence stems from mistranslation, and that the ancient Indians never ate beef.[4] The subject is politically contentious in present-day India.

Later, as we shall see, there was a reaction against sacrifice, expressed in the doctrine of *ahimsa*, or non-injury. Some scholars see the seeds of this reaction in the Vedas themselves, which state that any animal killed is not really killed at all but 'quieted', and where the people performing the slaughter turn away from it – 'lest we should become eyewitnesses'. Occasionally a figure made of flour (*pista*) was substituted for animal victims. This ambivalence becomes even more apparent in later texts, as is discussed in chapter Five.

A traditional stone for grinding spices.

The sacrificial ritual required a great many specialized utensils, including devices for straining and filtering the soma juice (see below), large earthenware pots for heating milk and ghee, mortars and grinding stones, pots for boiling meat, clay ovens for roasting, wooden skewers for grilling organs, pottery shards on which to bake bread, ladles and spoons to hold butter, milk and water, and leaf cups and plates.[5]

SOMA

Many rituals, especially those honouring Indra, involved the use of an intoxicating, perhaps hallucinatory substance called soma. Soma (a word borrowed by Aldous Huxley for the drug in his novel *Brave New World*) is the name of three things: the plant, the drink made from it, and a deity. The identity of soma is one of the great unsolved mysteries of culinary history. The *Rig Veda* contains hundreds of references to soma, including an entire chapter of 114 hymns dedicated to it. During rituals, soma is offered to the gods and ingested by the priests and worshippers, who are inspired with confidence, courage, faith, even a feeling of immortality. Soma's effects appear to be both stimulating and hallucinogenic:

Like impetuous winds, the drinks have lifted me up, like swift horses bolting with a chariot . . . One of my wings is in the sky; I have trailed the other below. I am huge, huge! Flying to the cloud. Have I not drunk soma? (x.119)

We have drunk the soma; we have become immortal; we have gone to the light; we have found the gods . . . The glorious drops that I have drunk set me free in wide space. (viii.48)

The plant, which is described as yellow with long stalks, grew in the mountains and was collected by women, who extracted juice from its stalk by pressing it between two stones or pounding it in a mortar. The juice was filtered through lamb's wool and stored in jars or wooden tubs. It was brown or tawny in colour. Before being drunk, it was mixed with milk or yoghurt. From various references, we know that soma became increasingly difficult to obtain – one prayer even apologizes to the gods for the use of a substitute – and after 800 BCE no references to it survive at all. It has been suggested that the need for a substitute for the conscious-altering soma may have led to the development of other ways of creating unusual psychic states, such as yoga, breath control, fasting and meditation.[6]

Some writers think soma was a leafless shrub called *somalata*, which means soma leaf or branch (*Sarcostemma acidum*), a stimulant used as a bronchodilator in Ayurvedic medicine. Another candidate is the plant *Ephedra sinica*, which was used by Iranian Zoroastrians in their rituals as late as the nineteenth century. It contains the alkaloid ephedrine, which is a stimulant similar to amphetamine but is not hallucinogenic. Another, less likely, possibility is *Cannabis sativa* (hemp), a plant native to Central Asia that today grows all over India. The leaves and flowers of the female cannabis plant make bhang, which nowadays is mixed with milk and drunk during the spring festival Holi. Another candidate is the fly agaric mushroom (*Amanita muscaria*), which produces hallucinogenic effects and is used by Siberian shamans in their rituals.[7] The debate remains open.

A popular beverage of the time was an intoxicating liquor called sura, made by fermenting barley or rice. There are many references to sura in later works. But unlike soma, drinking sura was frowned on by the priestly compilers of the Vedas, who listed the consumption of alcohol as one of seven sins, along with anger and gambling.

After soma, the item most frequently mentioned in the *Rig Veda* is the cow, the subject of more than 700 references and three hymns. There is textual evidence that cows were occasionally killed in ceremonies honouring ancestors (*shraddhas*) or to honour distinguished guests. But at the same time the cow was venerated as a cosmic symbol, the universal mother and the source of life and nourishment:

> The Cow is Heaven, the Cow is Earth, the Cow is Vishnu,
>   Lord of Life
> Both Gods and mortal men depend for life and being on
>   the Cow
> She hath become this universe; all that the Sun surveys is she.
>   (x.10)

This quasi-religious attitude was the starting point for what later became the veneration of the cow, an end to its role as a sacrificial victim and, indeed, a ban on eating its meat at all. The cow's products – milk, ghee and yoghurt – became part of religious rituals since they were pure foods that could be offered to the deities. Starting in the nineteenth century, the protection of cows became a symbol of Hindu identity, and today many states ban the slaughtering of cows.

WHAT THE VEDIC INDIANS ATE

Hymn 187 of the *Rig Veda* is a charming if somewhat obscure address to food. At the beginning and end of the hymn, the poet praises food as the essential support of both gods and men, and compares the juices of fruit dispersed throughout the realm to the life-giving rains. The rains in turn produce food in the form of plants and animals and are returned to heaven by ritual offerings. The waters and plants mentioned in Verse 8 become the milk and grain mixed with soma in Verse 9, and are asked to 'become just the fat', which is clearly considered the choicest part of the food substance.

Although wheat was grown and consumed in the Indus Valley, there are no references to wheat in the *Rig Veda*. Barley was the main grain. It was ground in mortars and pestles or between two stones, then sifted to make flour and kneaded into a dough. Several texts mention apupa, a kind of cake made of barley or sweetened with honey and fried in ghee over a slow fire. Professor Achaya speculates that it could be a precursor of

Hymn 187 of the *Rig Veda* (Food)

Now I shall praise food, the support and power of the
   great . . .
O sweet food, honeyed food, we have chosen you: for us
   be a helper.
Draw near to us, food – kindly with your kindly help
Joy itself, not to be despised, a very kind companion
   without duplicity.
These juices of yours, food, are dispersed throughout the
   realms, adjoined to heaven like the winds.
These [juices] are those that yield you, O food, and they
   also are part of you, sweetest food.
Those who receive the sweetness of your juices press
   forward like strong-necked [bulls]
On you, food, is the mind of the great gods set.
A deed was done at your signal; he smashed the serpent
   with your help.
When yonder dawning light of the mountains has come,
   O food,
Then you should also come here to us, honeyed food, fit
   for our portion.
When we bite off a full share of the waters and plants,
O you friend of the winds – become just the fat.
When we take a share of you when mixed with milk or
   mixed with grain, O Soma,
O you friend of the winds, become just the fat.
Become the gruel, O plant, the fat, the steaming suet
O you friend of the winds – become just the fat
We have sweetened you with words, O food, as cows' milk
   does the oblations
You as feasting companions for the gods, you as feasting
   companions for us.[8]

the modern appam, a South Indian bread made of fermented rice flour, and the Bengali malpoa or malpua, a fried pancake soaked in sugar syrup.[9] Although sugar cane was grown and apparently chewed, the technology had not been invented to convert the juice into sugar.

Ripened barley seeds were parched in fire and eaten with soma juice, fried in ghee, or ground into a gruel mixed with yoghurt, ghee, soma, water or milk. Barley seeds were also pulverized into a powder called saktu, the forerunner of sattu or chhattu, a dish still widely eaten by poor people in eastern India. Although rice (*vrihi* in Sanskrit) was apparently known in the Indus Valley, it is not mentioned in the Vedas (nor was cotton, another Indus Valley crop).

Milk from cows and buffaloes, and its products, played an important role in the Vedic Indians' diet and, indeed, in the Indian diet generally from this time onwards. Milk, raw or boiled, was drunk, or cooked with parched barley meal to make a porridge called odana. Since milk left out in a hot climate quickly ferments and coagulates, it was converted into yoghurt. The process can be speeded up by heating the milk and adding a starter, which could be more yoghurt, certain barks, or fruit. Yoghurt was eaten by itself, flavoured with honey, mixed with barley (a dish called karambha, similar to modern curd rice) or folded into fresh milk.

The widespread consumption of milk distinguishes South Asia from Southeast Asia and China, where milk and its products are rarely consumed. This reflects not just differences in regional agricultural economies, but also the prevalence of lactose intolerance (the inability by adults to digest lactose, a sugar, in milk). An estimated 90–100 per cent of east Asians and 70 per cent of south Indians are lactose intolerant, but this falls to just 30 per cent of north Indians and 5–15 per cent of people of northern European ancestry.[10] However, yoghurt made with active and live bacterial cultures can be consumed by lactose-intolerant people, and this is the way that most Indians consume milk today, especially in the south and west of the country.

Yoghurt was and is churned to make butter (unlike in Europe, where butter is made from cream), and the leftover liquid became buttermilk – a favourite drink in rural India, sometimes flavoured with cumin or pepper. If butter is boiled to evaporate the water so that the milk solids fall to the bottom, the melted butter becomes translucent ghee (clarified butter), the most valued of all Indian condiments. When the impurities are filtered out, ghee can be stored for six months or more, an important quality in a hot climate.

> ### Sattu
>
> Bring water to the boil, add chana dal and mix well. Cook for 2 or 3 minutes. Drain the water and keep the pot covered for several hours. Drain through a cotton cloth and let it cook. Heat a kadhai (a wok-like iron pot), add sand, and dry the chana dal together with the sand, adding a little at a time. Use a sieve to separate the dal from the sand, and grind it into a fine powder.

Scholars disagree over whether the ancient Indians made cheese by separating solids from milk with a souring agent. The Vedic texts contain a single reference to something called *dadhanvat*, which some translate as cheese and others as 'abundance of curds'. But *panir*, the Hindi word for curds or farmer's cheese, is Persian in origin and probably arrived much later.

Today, milk, butter and ghee are used in many Hindu rituals, since only cooked food can be offered to the deities and milk was considered by its

Sattu is a simple dish of ground cooked chickpeas served with onion and chilli, and is often eaten in the state of Bihar by poor people.

Til Pinni (Sesame-seed Balls)

400 g (14 oz) grated gur/jaggery
(available at Indian grocers)
400 g (14 oz) brown sesame seeds

Grate the jaggery by hand. Dry-roast the sesame seeds over a
low heat until they start to crackle. Put the warm sesame seeds
into a food processor with the jaggery and pulse several times
until the mixture does not move, then scrape the sides and
pulse again several times. Transfer the mixture to a bowl and
make small balls (around 5 cm or 2 in. in diameter). Store in
an airtight container.

nature to have been cooked in the stomach of the cow. These products
were also considered to be intrinsically pure, and to have purifying powers.
The supreme purifying material, *panchagavya*, combined five products of
the cow: milk, yoghurt, ghee, urine and dung.

Flavourings used in Vedic times included mustard seeds, turmeric,
black and long pepper, bitter orange and sesame seeds. The *Atharaveda*, a
collection of spells and remedies against diseases, mentions black pepper
as a cure for infections caused by wounds. Sesame is mentioned in many
texts, both as a food and as a ritual item that was part of every major life
event. Sesame-seed balls (pinda) were offered to one's ancestors during
the Hindu rite called *shraddha*. The seeds were boiled with rice and milk
to make a porridge, cooked with vegetables, or roasted and pounded to
make a crispy bread. The seeds were also crushed in an animal-powered
device to produce an oil that remains a common cooking medium in
southern and western India.

Fruit and vegetables mentioned in the *Rig Veda* include three varieties of jujube, bael, dates, Indian gooseberry, mango, cucumber, lotus
stalks and roots, bottle gourd, bitter gourd, water chestnut and other
aquatic plants. Archaeological excavations have found charred or cut
bone fragments of sheep, deer, pigs, fish, river turtles, dogs and such
wild animals as leopard and blue deer (*nilgai*). Relatively little is known
about the cooking techniques of the time. Meat was roasted on spits,
perhaps over charcoal, or was cooked in liquid in a clay oven. Cooking
vessels were made of clay, wood, stone or metal. Some scholars speculate

that the use of oil as a cooking medium may have been adopted from the non-Aryans.

A verse in the *Rig Veda* indicates that people ate their meals sitting on the ground. Men did not eat with their wives, nor did women take their food in the presence of their male relatives. Hospitality was considered a prime virtue, and feeding a guest was as meritorious as performing a sacrifice or even worshipping God.

THE EMERGENCE OF CASTE

Originally the Vedic Indians were divided into two classes: their own, which they called *arya* ('noble'), and the people they conquered, the *dasas* (servants or slaves). Internally they were organized as clans under a *raja*, or chief. His leadership was legitimized by his patronage of the sacrifice, a tradition that continued for centuries.

By about 1000 BCE, however, social divisions had become sharper, and there gradually emerged one of the most distinctive and controversial features of Indian society, the caste system. The English word caste (from the Portuguese *casta*, 'pure') is rather confusedly used to refer to two separate, although related, institutions: *varna* ('colour' in Sanskrit), which refers to four basic divisions of society and may be translated as 'class', and *jati* (birth), a more narrowly defined group related by occupation or ancestry.[11]

The earliest mention of the fourfold division is a hymn in the *Rig Veda* that gives a mythical sanction to its origin (x90):

> When the gods made a sacrifice with the Man as their
> victim . . .
> When they divided the Man, into how many parts did they
> divide him?
> What was his mouth, what were his arms, what were his
> thighs, and his feet called?
> The brahmin was his mouth, of his arms were made the
> rajanya
> His thighs became the vaisya, of his feet the sudra was born.

The brahmins were priests, the rajanya (later called ksatriya) were warriors and rulers, and the vaisya were the providers of wealth through herding, agriculture and trade. Those in the fourth category, the sudra, were artisans and service providers. Later a fifth category was added for people who did jobs that no one else would perform, such as tanning hides, collecting rubbish and burying the dead. They may once have been dasas. Today these communities are officially known as Scheduled Tribes but prefer to call themselves dalit (from a Sanskrit word meaning suppressed, crushed or broken in pieces).

In the centuries that followed its inception, the caste system came to have many ramifications, especially for the two most fundamental human activities: sex and eating. People could not marry, accept food from or eat with someone outside their caste under pain of ostracism, banishment or even death. Caste became closely associated with ideas of purity and pollution, with the brahmin being the purest of the pure and the dasa the least pure. For a brahmin to dine with a dasa or a non-Aryan was considered a sin. In Vedic times the priests shared in the fruits of the sacrifice (it was not until later that many brahmins, although not those in Kashmir and Bengal, became vegetarian). Vegetarianism as a widespread ethical and moral idea came with two movements, Jainism and Buddhism, and later became central to some branches of Hinduism – a subject that will be fully explored in subsequent chapters.

THREE

The Renunciant Tradition and Vegetarianism, 1000–300 BCE

Around the beginning of the first millennium BCE the Vedic Indians began to move into a region called the Doab ('two waters') between the Ganges and Yumuna rivers, near the site of present-day Delhi. From there they migrated eastwards to what is now the state of Bihar and westwards into Gujarat. Their earliest form of political organization was the *gana-sangha* (people's assembly), a clan headed by a chief who governed with the help of an assembly. The members of these political entities, sometimes called proto-republics, belonged to a single clan or a confederacy of clans and were mainly *ksatriyas*. From the *gana-sanghas* emerged the founders of two major reform sects, Jainism and Buddhism, both of them the sons of clan chiefs.

The most powerful of these political entities were the sixteen *mahajanapadas* (kingdoms or republics), which ranged from Afghanistan in the northwest to Bihar in the east and as far south as the Vindhya mountain range. Their rise was driven by the discovery of iron deposits, especially in Bihar, and the manufacture of iron weapons, ploughs, nails and other objects from about 800 BCE. Iron axes made it easier to clear forests, while iron hoes and ploughshares increased agricultural production. Tools were developed for digging wells, canals and ponds for irrigation. New farming techniques included double cropping and crop rotation.

Rice cultivation, which originated in China, came to northern India in the third millennium BCE, expanded through Orissa and Bengal and reached Andhra Pradesh and Tamil Nadu by 300 BCE. Although labour-intensive, it gave high yields, making it possible to grow two or even three crops each year.

The dietary staple in the western Doab (modern-day Punjab, Haryana, Rajasthan and Western Uttar Pradesh) was barley. Wheat was grown –

perhaps brought by people from the Indus Valley, since some varieties are the same as those found there – but it still played a relatively minor role in the local diet. Excavations have unearthed kodon and pearl millet, chickpeas and other pulses. Oil seeds included mustard, sesame and linseed. Seeds were ground in a large mortar and pestle driven by an ox, a device still used in Indian villages. There is evidence of the use of bhang (*Cannabis sativa*).

The development of agriculture led to a rapid increase in population and migration into new areas. In what historians call 'the second urbanization' (the first being the Indus Valley civilization), towns and cities were built, many on rivers or the coast. The most important were Champa in West Bengal; Kashi (modern-day Varanasi); Mathur and Kaushambi in Uttar Pradesh; Pataliputra (Patna), the capital of the Magadha kingdom in Bihar; Taxila in the Punjab; and the port of Bharuch on the west coast. Urban craftsmen and artisans made textiles, pottery, ceramics, glassware and metal artefacts and tools for domestic use and export. Merchants traded local products for horses and woollen goods from Afghanistan, Persia and Central Asia. Outside the towns, most people lived in small and medium-sized villages.

By the sixth century BCE Magadha had emerged as the most powerful kingdom. Its ruler Bimbisara (558–491 BCE) created India's first standing army and expanded his empire eastward. His inspiration may have been Cyrus the Great (580–529 BCE), founder of the Persian Achaemenid Empire, which conquered parts of Afghanistan, Pakistan and north India. Two centuries later, Alexander the Great (356–323 BCE), having conquered Persia, invaded India, lured by tales of its fabulous wealth. After a hard battle he defeated King Porus in the Punjab, but in 326 BCE he was forced to turn back when his men, weary of decades of fighting, insisted on returning home. Reports of the strength of the armies massed against him may have been another reason.

After Alexander's death, his generals became rulers of independent kingdoms, among them the Indo-Greek or Hellenistic kingdom of Gandhara in Afghanistan. Some of the rulers converted to Buddhism, and the region became home to a brilliant syncretic Greek-Indian culture. Gandharan coins and sculptures combine elements of Greek and Indian art; for example, Buddha is depicted as a classical Greek deity. The brahmins called the Greeks *yavanas* (from Ionians), a term that came to mean 'barbarian'.

According to the first-century BCE Greek historian Plutarch, while in India Alexander met a 'young stripling' named 'Sandrocottus', who was probably Chandragupta (340–298 BCE), the founder of India's first nation-wide dynasty, the Maurya. In 321 BCE the twenty-year-old Chandragupta defeated the armies of the short-lived Nanda dynasty (345–321 BCE), sometimes referred to as India's first empire, which stretched from Bengal to Punjab and as far south as the Vindhya mountain range. His advisor and later chief minister was Kautilya (*c.* 370–283 BCE), who is also known as Chanakya and sometimes called the Indian Machiavelli. Chandragupta took advantage of a power vacuum in the territory ruled by Alexander's generals to absorb the Punjab, Gandhara and most of Afghanistan, and also expanded his domain west to Gujarat and the Indian Ocean. In 298 BCE he abdicated to live as a Jain ascetic in the south of the country. He was succeeded by his son Bindusara (320–272 BCE), who conquered land as far south as Karnataka.

The Maurya emperors were in close contact with their Greek neighbours and relatives. Chandragupta had a Greek wife and Greek ambassadors served his court. However, there appears to have been little Greek influence in India, whereas they were deeply influenced by the Persian Empire, at the time the mightiest the world had known. The customs at Chandragupta's court are believed to have been purely Persian; like the Great King, he lived in seclusion, appearing only for religious festivals.

Bindusara's son Ashoka (304–232 BCE) inherited the throne following a succession struggle. In 260 BCE he defeated the armies of Kalinga (present-day Odisha), the last to be holding out in northern India, in a bloody battle that resulted in hundreds of thousands of deaths. Ashoka expanded his empire by conquest and alliances until at its height, in 250 BCE, it covered the entire subcontinent except for the southernmost tip, and incorporated present-day Pakistan, Kashmir, southeastern Iran, much of Afghanistan and probably Nepal – an area of 13 million sq. km (5 million sq. miles). It was the largest empire in the world at the time and the largest in Indian history, surpassed by neither the Mughals nor the British. Agriculture, trade and other economic activity flourished, thanks to a well-organized administration and decades of peace and security. To this day Ashoka is considered by many to be the greatest of all Indian rulers, and is revered for his efficient administration and his tolerance.

CHANGES IN INDIAN SOCIETY: THE GREAT MOOD SHIFT

The period from the eighth to the sixth century BCE was one of great intellectual ferment throughout the civilized world, with Pythagoras, Empedocles, Heraclitus and other philosophers in Greece; the major Hebrew prophets; Confucius and Lao Tze in China; and Zoroaster in Persia.[1] In India, new beliefs, attitudes and practices emerged that would become central to Indian culture. The breakdown of the old tribal culture, rapid social change and the growth of urban centres engendered pessimism, a pervasive feeling of angst and scepticism about the value of worldly existence. One scholar wrote of a 'passionate desire for escape, for unison with something that lay beyond the dreary cycle of birth and death and rebirth, for timeless being, in place of transitory and therefore unsatisfactory existence'.[2] One explanation is that the surplus economy, based on agriculture, booming trade and the rise of a middle class, supported the emergence of a class of economically unproductive people, including philosophers, religious mendicants and hermits.

The new ideas were defined in a collection of philosophical texts called the *Upanishads*, sometimes known as *Vedanta* (the end of the Vedas), which were composed from about 500 BCE. Two central concepts posited in these texts are *atman* (the individual self) and *brahman* (the universal spirit). One of the goals of life is to obtain knowledge of the *atman* and to recognize its identity with *brahman*, an idea expressed in the Sanskrit phrase *Tat tvam asi* – that's what you are.

Many definitions for this self were proposed, including *prana* (breath) and food. Food, eater and *brahman* are one and the same: one cannot exist without the others. An eater becomes the food of another eater, which in turn becomes the food of a third, until the whole of creation is linked in a vast food chain. Food is the central element of creation, a source of immortality and an object of worship. One of the *Upanishads* contains the ecstatic utterance:

> Oh wonderful! Oh wonderful! Oh, wonderful!
> I am food! I am food! I am food!
> I am an eater of food! I am an eater of food! I am an eater of food!

Another concept is that the self is faced with an endless cycle (*samsara*) of birth and rebirth. From this emerged the law of *karma*, a word that means 'action' or 'deeds'. Our actions determine what we become in the

> ## Ode to Food (from the Taitiriya Upanishad)
>
> From food, verily creatures are produced
> Whatsoever creatures dwell on the earth.
> Moreover, by food, in truth, they live
> Moreover, into it also they finally pass
> For truly, food is the chief of beings;
> Therefore, it is called a panacea
> Verily, they obtain all food
> Who worship Brahma as food
>
> From food created things are born.
> By food, when born, do they grow up
> It is both eaten and eats things
> Because of that it is called food [3]

future, and the best way to escape this cycle, to attain liberation (*moksha*), is to neutralize *karma* altogether. The laws of *karma* are not divinely ordained, since God is absent from this world view, but inherent in the nature of reality.

One way of release was renunciation (*sannyasa*) – leaving a worldly existence to live in forest retreats, called ashrams. Some renouncers, or *sannyasi*, practised austerity (*tapas*), such as fasting and breath control, to eliminate *karma*.[4] Meditation and yoga appeared at this time. The word *ahimsa*, translated as non-injury, non-violence or harmlessness, is used for the first time in the *Upanishads*. It became one of the most important terms in Indian philosophy and culture and, in recent times, was central to the political philosophy of Mahatma Gandhi, Martin Luther King and other advocates of non-violent political action.

The link between *ahimsa* and vegetarianism is complex. While the *Upanishads* do not overtly advocate vegetarianism, compassion for all living beings tops the list of the virtues to be cultivated by renouncers. For example, the texts state that when gathering his food, the ascetic should not take any part of a plant unless it has already fallen; he should avoid the destruction of seeds and eat only the meat of animals already killed by beasts of prey.[5] Ascetics who were mendicants could not produce, store or even cook their own food, but had to obtain it by begging. Those who lived as hermits in the forest could eat only food that was wild and uncultivated – a practice that survives to this day in the Hindu fast called *phalahar*. Indeed, many contemporary practices have their roots in very ancient times. Such developments were accompanied by a downgrading of the importance of sacrifice and other ritual activities and with it the role of the brahmin caste as the administrators of the sacrifice.

The ascetic lifestyle attracted many young people: the historian Romila Thapar even compares the movement to the counterculture of the 1960s.[6] Some ascetics attracted followers, who formed small groups that became sects and then orders or congregations called *sanghas*. Audiences gathered to hear these leaders preach and debate in the parks and forests on the outskirts of cities; some settlements even had assembly halls where such debates took place. The best known and most influential of these *sanghas* were Jainism and Buddhism.

JAINISM

Vardhamana Mahavira (possibly 540–468 BCE), possibly considered to be the founder of Jainism, was the son of the ruler of a small kingdom in Bihar. The word *Jain* means 'a follower of *jina* (conqueror)', *jina* being the name bestowed on Mahavira because of his self-control. Mahavira married and had children, but left home in search of enlightenment. (At the time he was not considered to be the founder of a new religion but the most recent of twenty-four *jinas*, called *tirthankaras* – omniscient teachers who attained enlightenment and showed others the way to liberation.) According to legend, Mahavira initially converted eleven brahmins, who became leaders in his organization.

Jains did not and do not accept the authority of the Vedas or the brahmins. They see the goal of human existence as being to free oneself from attachment and aversion in order to attain a state of perfect omniscience and ultimate release from the body; they believe that people are prevented from doing this by the bondage of *karma*. Jains came to view *karma* not as a spiritual or intangible element, but as a physical substance – a superfine matter that clings to people's souls and conforms to mechanical laws of cause and effect. We attract *karma* particles when we do or say something wrong, such as telling a lie, stealing or killing another living being. These bad actions cause our souls to attract more *karma*, creating a vicious circle.

Mahavira rejected caste, although he appears to have recognized four classes of people, based on their activities rather than their birth. Jainism has temples but traditionally no priests. Some Jains became monks and nuns (called respectively *sadhus* and *sadhvis*), who did not own any possessions and wandered barefoot from place to place begging for their food. The sight of an itinerant monk, a mask over his mouth to prevent him from breathing in insects, sweeping the ground in front of him with a broom, is still a common one on Indian roads.

A central doctrine of Jainism is that all nature is alive. Everything, from rocks and plants to gods, has an eternal soul, or *jiva*, although some souls are more powerful and complex than others. Related to this is *ahimsa*. Mahavira's 'pure unchanging eternal law' was that 'all things breathing, all things existing, all things living, should not be slain or treated with violence' – a clear repudiation of the Vedic sacrifice. The prohibition against taking life was so extreme that Jains were forbidden from being farmers, since agriculture meant destroying insects in the soil.

With regard to food, the rules of Jainism are the most stringent of any religion. 'To say that Jains are strictly vegetarian hardly begins to convey either the rigour and severity of the rules which some Jains put themselves under or the centrality of such practices to Jain religious life', writes one scholar.[7] Five things are absolutely forbidden: meat and meat products, fish, eggs, alcohol and honey. Alcohol is reviled because the process of fermentation multiplies and destroys living organisms and because it clouds one's thinking and may lead to violence. Jain monks are not allowed even to stay in a place where alcoholic drink is stored. Honey is banned because its removal from the comb kills bees.

Monks and nuns and other observant Jains avoid many other foods, including fruit and vegetables with many seeds, such as figs, aubergines, guava and tomatoes (because seeds contain the germ of life); vegetables that grow underground, such as potatoes, turnips, radishes, mushrooms, fresh ginger and turmeric (because pulling them up kills the plant as well as millions of *jivas* in the soil); onions and garlic (believed to inflame the passions); foods containing yeast and fermented foods; cauliflower and cabbage (insects live within their leaves); and buds and sprouts.

The abundance of fruit, vegetables and dairy products in India clearly facilitated a vegetarian diet – it is hard to imagine vegetarianism emerging in a cold climate. Jain food is largely regional and, despite the restrictions, can be delicious.[8] As in much of India, the dietary staples are grains and legumes. Hing, or asafoetida, is a common replacement for garlic. Spices are essential in daily cooking, although they may be given up during fasts. Gujarat and Maharashtra, home to most of India's Jains, are fertile regions where a wide array of fruit and vegetables is available all year round. There are no restrictions on dairy products, sugar or ghee, and affluent Jains are known for the amount of these substances they use in their cooking. Most Jains are not vegans. (In general, veganism is rare in India.) However, some Jains living in the West avoid dairy products because of the violence involved in producing milk by machines, and the fact that cows are killed when they stop producing.

Jain writings contain detailed rules about how and when food can be taken. Jains must not eat after sunset, lest they accidentally ingest an insect. All water must be boiled and reboiled every six hours, and all liquids strained before drinking. Milk must be filtered and boiled within 48 minutes of the cow being milked; yoghurt should not be more than one day old unless it is mixed with raisins or other sweetening agents; flour is to be kept for only three days in the rainy season and seven days in winter; and sweets must be consumed within 24 hours. Jain monks are not allowed to eat food sold at a roadside stand. Although these rules may no longer be relevant because of modern refrigeration, they reflect an awareness of hygiene and the risk of infection.

An important way of removing *karma* is by fasting, which Jains elevated to an art form. The ultimate fast, called *smadhi maran* or *sallekhna*, entails giving up all food and water and starving oneself to death. This practice is undertaken by someone who is in the final stages of a fatal illness or is very old and feels they have fulfilled their duties in this life. They must be given permission to do so by a senior monk.[9]

According to legend, the Maurya emperor Chandragupta was a practising Jain who fasted to death. Early on, the Jain community broke into branches descended from specific teachers who moved from the Ganges basin to other areas. Unlike Buddhists, Jains did not actively proselytize. In the south, the religion was patronized and, paradoxically, even espoused by militaristic kings who admired its emphasis on striving, discipline and self-control. In urban areas Jainism was patronized by merchants, artisans, jewellers and even courtesans, and today some of India's wealthiest business families are Jains. Some Jain kings later returned to the traditional Vedic fold and even persecuted the Jain community. Today, there are only around 4 million Jains in India, mainly in the state of Gujarat and in the Indian diaspora, plus an estimated 300,000 Jains living abroad. But some of their beliefs and customs were absorbed into the mainstream religious practices of what later came to be called Hinduism.

BUDDHISM

Siddhartha Gautama (563–483 BCE), later known as the Buddha ('enlightened one'), was, like Mahavira, the son of the ruler of a small kingdom, in northeastern India. He led a protected life in his palace until he reached his twenties, when he encountered for the first time the suffering of ordinary people. This led him to begin a spiritual quest, during which he joined the ascetics where he practised austerity and almost starved to death. But in a moment of enlightenment, he rejected this approach in favour of what he called the Middle Way, a path of moderation between the extremes of self-indulgence and self-mortification. Its purpose is to put an end to the suffering that is intrinsic in existence. Suffering is caused by greed, desire, ignorance and hatred, and can be eliminated by following the eightfold path: right understanding, right intention, right speech, right action, right livelihood, right effort, right mindfulness and right concentration. The concept of *ahimsa* is central to Buddhist doctrine, although it was not taken to the extremes of Jainism. Gautama Buddha also accepted the idea of *karma*, the idea that one's actions in a previous life determine how one will be reborn. The ultimate goal is to attain *nirvana*, freedom from the cycle of birth and death.

Gautama preached the equality of all castes, which gave his religion a universal appeal. An excellent organizer, he founded monasteries for both men and women (although he was suspicious of the latter) and substituted congregational meetings for rituals. What distinguished Jainism and especially Buddhism from earlier practices was the institutionalization of ascetic practices. In keeping with the principle of *ahimsa*, the Buddha unequivocally rejected animal sacrifice. According to legend, the king of Kosala planned a great sacrifice of 500 oxen, 500 male calves, 500 female calves and 500 sheep, but abandoned it on the advice of the Buddha.

When it came to food, the Middle Way prevailed. Early Buddhism placed no restrictions on the diets of laypeople, but on many occasions the Buddha urged moderation, so as to avoid excessive attachment to the pleasures of the table. In one of his sermons, he told of a king whose love of eating meat was so great that he even ate human flesh. This so alienated his subjects and family that he had to abandon his throne and suffered great hardships. Alcohol and other intoxicants were also prohibited by the Buddha.

Monasteries had huge and complex kitchens and, like royal courts, their own food-processing equipment, such as oil presses and sugar mills. The food served at Buddhist monasteries was vegetarian. Monks were supposed to eat only what was necessary to sustain life, and to consume solid foods only between sunrise and noon. Their diet consisted of rice and milk in the morning, rice with cooked vegetables at lunch, and a little ghee, oil, honey or sugar in the afternoon. Outside the monasteries, where monks begged for food, they had to accept anything that was given to them, even meat or fish, provided the food was 'blameless'; that is, not slain on purpose for the monk and killed out of the sight, hearing and even suspicion of the recipient (leaving the animal's death to be the responsibility of the person who donated the food). Unless a monk were ill, he was not to ask specifically for meat, fish, ghee, oil, honey, sugar, milk or yoghurt. Only a few substances were absolutely forbidden to all Buddhists: alcohol, for example, and certain meats, including elephant, horse, dog, snake, lion and tiger. Venison and other game were allowed.

Buddhism, unlike Jainism, was a proselytizing religion. The third Buddhist Council, in 250 BCE, reportedly convened by Ashoka himself, made a decision to send missions to other parts of the subcontinent and beyond. Starting then and continuing until the thirteenth century CE, Buddhist emissaries, as well as brahmin priests, went to South and Southeast Asia, including Sri Lanka, Burma, Cambodia, Thailand and southwestern China. In the seventh century CE another wave of missionaries went to Tibet. They took with them Buddhist dietary and monastic rules, including vegetarianism. Later, however, when Buddhism split into various sects, the propriety of eating meat because a subject of doctrinal dispute. In Southeast Asia and Sri Lanka today, monks eat meat if it is given to them, whereas in China, Korea and Vietnam they are strictly vegetarian. In Tibet, a cold country where vegetables are scarce, vegetarianism is rare and even the Dalai Lama eats meat.[10]

Buddhism has almost disappeared in the land of its birth since, like Jainism, many of its tenets and practices were absorbed into Hinduism. (The Buddha is often considered the tenth avatar of the deity Vishnu.) The Indian census in 2001 showed only 8 million Buddhists (0.8 per cent of the population), the majority of whom were dalits who converted en masse to Buddhism starting in the 1950s to escape the strictures of caste.

THE SUCCESS OF THE NEW MOVEMENTS

Many people found the moral and ethical teachings of the new movements an attractive alternative to the esoteric and expensive rituals of the brahmins. Some sacrifices required hundreds of animals, which placed a great burden on the farmers who had to donate their livestock, and the rulers' growing administrative and military costs competed for the funds demanded by the brahmins for their increasingly elaborate rituals. In addition, both the new religions welcomed women and members of oppressed castes.

Like Mahavira, Gautama Buddha was successful in attracting political patronage. Buddhism became the official religion of a number of states, including Magadha, Kosala and Kaushambi. An important and enthusiastic supporter of Buddhism and Jainism was the Emperor Ashoka. According to Buddhist sources, Ashoka had once led a life of self-indulgence and cruelty. In 260 BCE he waged a violent war against the state of Kalinga. The terrible suffering and destruction that ensued caused him great remorse and led him to question the value of military action. Influenced by the teachings of Buddhism, Ashoka renounced violence. He built and supported Buddhist monasteries and sent missionaries all over the subcontinent and even further. He built thousands of *stupas* (semicircular mounds) to house the Buddha's relics, constructed roads and rest houses, planted trees for shade and founded hospitals for both humans and animals.

The central tenet of Ashoka's philosophy and practice was *dharma* (in Sanskrit; *dhamma* in Pali), a word that has been translated as duty, social order, righteousness or universal law. He expounded it in fourteen edicts posted on rock surfaces or sandstone pillars in more than 30 places in India, Nepal, Pakistan and Afghanistan. For Ashoka, *dharma* was essentially a moral concept, encompassing compassion, liberality, truthfulness, purity, gentleness and goodness.[11]

Ashoka also expressed concern for the well-being of animals. An inscription in his first edict reads: 'Our Lord the king kills very few animals. Seeing this, the rest of the people have also ceased from killing animals. Even the activity of those who catch fish has been prohibited.'[12] The most famous inscription shows that Ashoka practised what he preached:

> Formerly, in the kitchens of the [emperor], several hundred thousand animals were killed daily for food, but now at the time of writing only three are killed– two peacocks and a deer,

though the deer not regularly. Even these three animals will not be killed in future.

(Perhaps peacock and venison were exempt because they were very popular meats, especially at banquets and feasts, and also were considered healthy by Ayurvedic physicians.) The edict lists other animals that are not to be killed, including parakeets, swans, pigeons, bats, ants, tortoises, boneless fish, porcupines, squirrels, cows, rhinos, pigeons, nanny goats, ewes and sows with young, and animals less than six months old. Cockerels were not to be castrated, and one animal should not be fed to another.

Unfortunately, there is no record of the food served at the Mauryan court. The food historian Rachel Laudan speculates that since the Mauryan emperors emulated the Achaemenid rulers of Persia (550–330 BCE) in many areas, including their writing system, roads, art and architecture, their cuisine is also likely to have followed the Persian model, which in turn was based on the high cuisine of Mesopotamia developed over thousands of years.[13] Lavish banquets featured hundreds of dishes, including breads made from wheat and barley flour of various grades; the meat of geese and other birds; fresh, fermented and sweetened milk; garlic, onions; fruit juice; and date and grape wine. An army of cooks toiling in vast kitchens at the Achaemenid court specialized in certain dishes: stews, roasts, boiled fish, a particular kind of bread, and so on.

Ashoka did not impose an outright ban on the killing of male goats, sheep and cattle for food or sacrifices (although an inscription on one of the pillars rules that 'no animal should be killed as a sacrifice here'). His position was one of compromise and won over many of his subjects. He insisted that all beliefs be respected, and invited Buddhists and non-Buddhists to conferences. Nearly 2,000 years later the Mughal emperor Akbar adopted a similar stance by becoming a virtual vegetarian and patronizing different religions. In India, food and politics are inseparable.

On Ashoka's death, the Mauryan Empire began to disintegrate and broke into regional states. But the memory of Ashoka's empire, which stretched from sea to sea and from the mountains to the peninsula, remained alive. Ashoka's symbol, the wheel, representing the wheel of law, is at the centre of the modern Indian flag, while the symbol of India is four lions at the top of the pillar Ashoka erected at Sarnath, near Varanasi.

Feast at a hermitage: a scene from the *Ramayana* (1712).

What People Ate

Compared with earlier periods, we have much more information about Indian food customs from this time, thanks to the reports of Greek travellers, Buddhist and Jain texts, and the *Arthashastra* (*Science of Wealth*) by Chanakya (Kautilya).

Like later travellers, the Greeks were fascinated by what they saw in India, and painted a somewhat idealistic picture of Indian society. The Greek ambassador Megasthenes (*c.* 350–290 BCE) recorded his observations in a work called *Indika*. Although the original is lost, passages have survived in the works of the Greek geographer Strabo (64/63 BCE–*c.* 24 CE) and the Graeco-Roman historian Arrian (86–*c.* 160 CE). Megasthenes was impressed by the country's prosperity:

> India has many huge mountains which abound in fruit trees of every kind and many vast plains of great fertility . . . inter-sected by a multitude of rivers. The greater part of the soil, moreover, is under irrigation and consequently bears two crops in the course of the year. It teems at the same time with animals of all sorts.[14]

Thanks to this abundance, he continued, the inhabitants 'exceed . . . the ordinary stature and are distinguished by their proud bearing. They are

Sugar in India

The conversion of sugar cane to products was first carried out in India, probably during the first millennium BCE. The cane was crushed in a machine called a yantra, a large mortar and pestle turned by oxen, still used in rural India. The juice was filtered and cooked slowly in a large metal pot over a low fire fuelled by the sugar-cane stalks. The thickened juice, called *phanita*, was similar to molasses. It was further concentrated and dried to make solid pieces of brown sugar, known as *jaggery* or *gur* (perhaps from Gaura, the ancient name for Bengal, which was famous for its superior varieties of sugar cane). *Jaggery* can also be made from the juice of palm trees; its distinctive flavour makes it the preferred flavouring for certain sweets. The removal of more liquid yielded sandy solids called *sarkara* (Sanskrit for sand or gravel, and the origin of the English word 'sugar').

In 326 BCE the Greeks described 'stones the colour of frankincense, sweeter than figs or honey'. This may have been pieces of crystallized sugar called khand (the origin of the English word 'candy'). Exactly how this was made is not clear.

Further refinements came from Persia in the eighth century CE. In 1615 a Mughal governor presented the English diplomat Sir Thomas Roe with a loaf of sugar 'as white as snow'.

The discovery that sugar cane could grow in the New World led to the rapid growth of plantations and the migration of millions of Indians to the Caribbean in the late

also found to be well skilled in the arts, as might be expected of men who inhale a pure air and drink the finest water.'

Wheat was sowed in winter and summer, rice and millet in summer. Fruit grew spontaneously and vegetables thrived on riverbanks and in marshes. Because of this abundance, famine never visited India, nor had there ever been a scarcity of nourishing food. Megasthenes was particularly struck by 'tall reeds which are sweet both by nature and by concoction' – sugar cane, still unknown in Europe.

nineteenth century. In the face of this competition the Indian sugar industry declined, and by the early nineteenth century it was almost forgotten. Sugar was imported into India from China (white sugar is called *chini* in Bengali and Hindi), Egypt (crystallized sugar is called *misri* in Hindi, from the name of Egypt) and Java at considerable expense. In 1912 the Sugar Cane Research Institute was created to develop hybrid sugar canes using New World plants that were thicker and more resistant to insects and had a higher sugar content than Indian varieties. Production increased dramatically, and today India is the world's second-largest producer after Brazil.

Making sugar by boiling molasses in water, late 19th century.

Megasthenes was intrigued by the division of society into seven classes. of which the most pre-eminent were the 'philosophers' (brahmin priests) who performed sacrifices and rites for the dead in return for gifts and privileges. Second were farmers, who were regarded as 'sacred and inviolable', since even during times of warfare their fields were left untouched. Other classes were shepherds who live in tents in the forests and rid the country of noxious birds and beasts; artisans; soldiers; overseers; and government administrators. He observed that no one was allowed to marry outside his caste or follow any profession except his own.[15]

Elsewhere Megasthenes is quoted as saying that the Indians lived frugally, never drank wine except as part of sacrifices, and ate mainly a mixture of rice and a thick stew, perhaps some form of dal or curry. A group of philosophers, the Brachmanes (brahmins), lived a simple life, abstained from sex and listened to serious discourse. They ate meat but not that of working animals, and abstained from highly seasoned food.[16] Other ascetics, called Sarmanes (*shramans*), lived in the woods, where they wore clothes made of bark and ate only acorns and wild fruit. Megasthenes also writes of physicians whose diet consists of rice and barley meal, and who effect cures by regulating diet rather than administering medicine – one of the earliest foreign references to Ayurveda.

Another source of information about Indian agriculture and food is the *Historia Plantarum* (*History of Plants*) by the Greek philosopher Theophrastus (371–*c.* 287 BCE), who based his writings on the reports of Alexander's soldiers. Of Indian rice, he wrote:

> More than anything they grow the so-called oryzon, which is their boiled cereal. It is similar to emmer [a type of wheat] and, when bruised, similar to hulled emmer grains and is easy to digest. When growing it looks like darnel [a thin Eurasian grass], though standing for most of its life in water, but it fruits not into an ear but into a sort of plume, like millet.[17]

One result of Alexander's sojourn in India was that rice entered the classical world, where, like spices, it was originally valued as a medicine. The chicken, first domesticated in India, reached Greece by the early sixth century BCE via the Persian Empire. Wine made from grapes came to Persia from Greece at about the same time, and from there went to Afghanistan and eastern India.[18]

According to Buddhist and Jain texts, summarized in Om Prakash's *Economy and Food in Ancient India*, rice was the staple grain in northeastern and central India.[19] The two main varieties were *sali*, which was grown from transplants and harvested in winter, and *vrihi*, a more ordinary variety grown by scattering seed harvested in autumn. Both were sown at the beginning of the rainy season. The most valuable variety was *mahasali*, which had large, fragrant, shiny grains and has been identified with basmati rice. Black and red varieties of rice were

A rice paddy.

also cultivated and are still eaten today in parts of northeastern and southern India.

Odana was a general term for a porridge-like dish made from rice and other grains. Rice cooked with yoghurt, honey or ghee was called payodana; made with sugar and milk it was known as kshiraudana (the modern kheer); and with meat, mamsaudana, an early version of pilau. Rice was heated in hot sand until it swelled up. Today muri (puffed rice) is a common breakfast dish and snack in Bengal. Puffed rice could be sweetened with honey or sugar. Soaked husked rice cooked in ghee was a popular offering to the gods. Puri-like breads were made from rice flour, ground lentils and wheat and sometimes coated with sugar.

Barley pearls were boiled in water or milk to make gruel that could be drunk or licked. Ground parched barley flour (sometime mixed with wheat flour) was used to make bread. Yavagu, a salty or sweet gruel of rice or barley flavoured with long or black pepper and ghee, was popular in western India and became a standard Ayurvedic remedy for digestive problems.[20] Poor people ate kulmasha, a thick porridge of grains or

Salty Yavagu (Rice Porridge)

200 g (I cup) long-grain rice
1.5 litres (6 cups) water
½ tsp grated fresh ginger
pinch of freshly ground black pepper
salt, to taste

Bring the water to the boil, add the rice and cook until soft.
Add the other ingredients and stir well.

Sweet Yavagu

200 g (I cup) long-grain rice
1.5 litres (6 cups) water
120 ml (½ cup) milk
120 g (½ cup) sugar
3 or 4 green cardamom pods

Prepare as above.

lentils cooked with a little water and flavoured with jaggery or oil. They often carried a ball of dried kulmasha with them to eat in the fields while they worked – a practice still followed in rural India. The most widely eaten lentils were mung, masur and horse gram. They were boiled to make a thin dal called supa, which was eaten with rice or any other solid or dry food. Lentils were ground, formed into balls, fermented and fried in ghee.

Cows and buffaloes were milked morning and evening. Rice was boiled in milk and mixed with fragrant spices and sugar to make a rice pudding called payasa (modern Bengali payesh, Tamil payasam). Sikharini, a mixture of yoghurt with crystallized sugar and pepper and other spices, is like the modern shrikhand. Sweetened rice flour or lentils were shaped into balls called modaka, one of present-day India's most popular sweets at festivals.

Seasonings for modaka included five kinds of salt (sea, black, rock, kitchen and red), black pepper, long pepper, cumin, asafoetida, myrobalan, ginger, turmeric and mustard seeds. The most important oil seed was sesame, which was made into cakes, used as a seasoning or ground to make cooking oil. A Buddhist monk was said to be so fond of a sweet called saskuli (a large ear-shaped sweet made of rice flour, sugar and sesame, fried in ghee) that he asked a householder to make it for him – and had to apologize for this breach of the rules before an assembly of monks.

According to Prakash, 'the general feeling of the time about meat eating seems to be that it should be used in extending hospitality to guests, as [an] offering to gods and ancestors, but animals should not be killed otherwise.'[21] Buddhist texts contain many references to meat: venison, pork and chicken were popular but sheep, goats and even buffaloes were also eaten. Meat was roasted on spits, boiled in soup, mixed with spices, ghee and yoghurt to make curry, or fried in oil and seasoned with salt and pepper. By the middle of the first millennium BCE the notion of clean and unclean meat was well developed. The consumption

Modaka

120–480 ml (½–1 cup) water
1 tsp vegetable oil
120 g (1 cup) rice flour
110 g (1 cup) grated coconut
2 tsp ghee (or melted butter)
½ tsp ground cardamom
90 g (½ cup) brown sugar
pinch of salt

Bring the water to the boil, add the salt and oil, then the rice flour, and stir until it forms a smooth dry paste. Set aside. Fry the grated coconut in the ghee. Add the ground cardamom and the sugar, mix well, and fry until the mixture thickens. When cool, roll the coconut mixture into small balls. Take a small piece of the rice flour mixture, flatten it on your palm into a circle about 8 cm (3 in.) in diameter, insert a coconut ball and wrap into a little package, squeezed at the top so that it looks like a head of garlic. Continue until all the ingredients are used up. Place in a steamer or colander over boiling water and steam for 7–10 minutes.

Four women selling food, Patna, *c.* 1850.

of dogs, village cockerels, carnivorous animals, village pigs, cows and other animals was discouraged, although such meat could be eaten if it were a matter of life or death.

Items that had stood overnight, had turned sour or had been cooked twice were also considered unfit to eat, perhaps because of the risk of infection. Anything touched by a dog or a crow could be eaten if the defiled part was removed and the rest sprinkled with water. There were some restrictions on accepting food from people of different castes, but they were not as rigid as they would later become. These restrictions and prohibitions were codified in the texts called the *Dharmashastras* (see chapter Four).

In his Sanskrit grammar *Asthadhyahi* (*Eight Chapters*), the great linguist Panini (considered to be the father of modern descriptive linguistics) described the food-related habits in northwestern India where he lived around the fourth century BCE.[22] He divides food into three categories: meat; *supa*, a word that means dal or perhaps a thin soup similar to the south Indian rasam; and vegetables. Vegetables were prepared with salt, yoghurt and churma (wheat flour fried with ghee and sugar), and could be flavoured during the meal with jaggery, sesame oil or ghee.

Both men and women worked as professional cooks. Some specialized in certain dishes; others were known for the amounts of food they could prepare, and were paid accordingly. Cookware was made of copper, iron, stone and clay. Bread was baked on pottery shards; meat was roasted on spits over live charcoal or fried in oil. Metal pots and utensils were cleaned with ashes, wooden ones by scraping. The main cooking techniques were roasting, boiling, sautéing and frying in sesame oil, ghee or mustard oil.

Domestic servants were given food as part of their wages. They also had the right to eat leftovers, although who ate which leftovers was carefully prescribed: leftovers from the serving dish were given to the family barber, food left in the cooking pot was given to the cook, while food on a plate from which rice had been served was given to dogs, crows or other scavengers.

Another valuable source of information is the *Arthashastra*, a manual of how a kingdom should be organized and run.[23] Government superintendents were responsible for departments of agriculture, weights and measures, tolls, alcoholic drink, slaughterhouses, warehouses, even prostitutes and elephants. One superintendent had to inspect the preparation of foods sold in the market to make sure that customers were not cheated. For example, when barley was cooked as a gruel, it was supposed to swell to twice its original size, millet three times, ordinary rice (vrihi) four times and expensive rice (sali) five times. Rules were established for the preparation of flour, and any adulteration was punished with a fine. Cities had to have ample stores of dried meat, fish and other commodities in case of famine.

Food prepared in a large cauldron over a fire: a scene from the *Ramayana* (1712).

The dietary staple of the kingdom was rice, and the *Arthashastra* specifies how much should be consumed by the various categories of person, perhaps indicating some kind of rationing system. The meal of an *arya* (a man belonging to one of the three upper castes) was to consist of one *prastha* of rice (one *prastha* is equal to 48 handfuls, or approximately 2 kg, or 4½ lb), one-quarter of a *prastha* of dal (½ kg, or just over 1 lb), and one-sixteenth of a *prastha* (1/8 kg, or ¼ lb) of clarified butter or oil. Women were allotted three-quarters and children half of the men's allowance. Members of the lower castes were to have one-sixth of a *prastha* of dal and half as much oil. There were even allocations for animals: dogs were supposed to be fed one *prastha* of cooked rice, and geese and peacocks half as much. Rice and dal were supplemented by other dishes, including meat and fish curries, but the amounts of those were not specified.

Spices and herbs mentioned in the *Arthashastra* include long pepper, black pepper, ginger, cumin seeds, white mustard, coriander, kiratatikta (*Agathotes chirayta*, a bitter herb grown in the Himalayas), choraka (angelica), damanaka (*Artemisia indica*), maruvaka (*Vangueria spinosa*, a kind of basil) and sigru (*Hyperanthera moringa*, drumstick tree). Today the last five items are used only in Ayurveda.

All animals, including domesticated animals, birds, game and fish, were under state protection. Butchers were supposed to sell the boneless meat of animals that had just been killed. If they included bones or used false weights, they had to compensate the customer by giving him or her eight times as much meat as the original order. Calves, bulls and milk cows could not be killed, and a large fine was imposed on those who did so. It was forbidden to sell meat from animals killed outside a slaughterhouse or which had died a natural death.

Poaching was subject to heavy fines. One-sixth of all wild animals were supposed to live unharmed in state-run forest preserves, although this may in reality have been a way of protecting the rulers' hunting preserves. Other animals protected from 'all kinds of molestation' included elephants, horses, animals 'having the form of a man' (perhaps monkeys), geese, brahmany ducks, partridges, peacocks and parrots.

The production and sale of alcoholic beverages were a state monopoly under the superintendent of liquor. The description of his duties indicates the existence of a lively pub scene. Every village had at least one state-supervised shop that was a combination of shop and tavern. The shops had rooms with beds and chairs and were decorated with flowers. To

A container for storing home-made rice beer in Meghalaya.

prevent unruly behaviour, alcoholic drink was sold only in small amounts and had to be drunk on the spot, although people known to be of good character could take it out of the shop. Government spies were stationed in taverns to make sure that customers were not spending more than they could afford or concealing stolen goods. Special attention was paid to foreign customers who 'acted like *aryas*' but lay in a drunken stupor with their beautiful mistresses. If customers lost anything while drunk, the shopkeeper had to make good the loss and pay a fine as well.

On special occasions, families could make certain kinds of alcohol for their own use. For festivals, fairs and pilgrimages, they could make it for four days, giving the state a share of the proceeds. Alcoholic drinks were made from rice, barley, grape, palm, mango, wood apple, sugar cane, the flowers of the mahua tree (*Madhuca longifolia*), jasmine or the bark of certain trees.[24] The fermenting agent was originally honey, but later treacle, yeast and other ingredients were used. Digestion techniques included putting the ingredients in a jar and burying it in the earth, covering it with manure or grain, or exposing it to the sun. A popular fermenting and flavouring agent was sambhara, a mixture of cinnamon, long and black pepper and other spices. Sukta was a mixture of treacle, honey, fermented rice water and whey placed in an earthen pot and left on a pile of rice for three days in summer.[25]

In the *Arthashastra*, Kautilya lists the ingredients of five kinds of alcoholic drink:

Medaka. Water, fermented rice and a mixture of ground spices
and herbs, honey, grape juice, panic seeds, turmeric, black
pepper and long pepper.
Prasanna. Flour, various spices and the bark and fruit of a tree
called putraka.
Asava. Wood apple (*Feronia limonia*), sugar and honey. (It can
also be made from sesame and sugar-cane juice.) It is flavoured
with ground cinnamon, Ceylon wort (*Plumbago zelanica*),
coco grass, lodh tree, betel nut and mahua flower.
Aristha. Water, treacle and medicines are placed in an earthen
pot coated with a mixture of honey, butter and ground long
pepper. The pot is put in a mass of barley and the mixture
allowed to ferment for at least seven nights.
Maireya. A wine made from various ingredients, including grapes.

Maireya was so popular that Buddha explicitly banned his followers from drinking it. It was sold in taverns and sweetened with sugar, jaggery or thickened sugar juice. One of the most prestigious drinks was a wine made from grapes from Kapisi in northern Afghanistan, an ancient centre of wine-making, where excavations have found glass flasks, fish-shaped wine jars and drinking cups.

Other texts of the time contain many references to alcohol, which appears to have been very popular despite brahmin, Buddhist and Jain disapproval. Characters in later Sanskrit plays drank spirits and coconut wine (perhaps toddy) to the point of intoxication. Alcohol was seen as enhancing the charm of a woman by making her complexion rosier and her behaviour more amorous.

From ancient times, Indian attitudes towards alcohol have been ambivalent. Despite disapproval by respectable people (even today, several states have prohibition or 'dry' days), there has always been a rich tradition of making alcoholic beverages from available materials.

Toddy drawers.

Toddy tapper and his wife, Tamil Nadu, 1830–35.

FOUR

Global India and the New Orthodoxy,

300 BCE–500 CE

D uring the period discussed in this chapter, India was part of a world economy, exchanging goods with Africa, the Middle East and China. New ingredients entered the Indian culinary repertoire, including cloves and betel nuts, while Indian merchants may have introduced tamarind, garlic, ginger, turmeric and pepper to Southeast Asia. According to Rachel Laudan, in the period between the first and fifth centuries CE, 'India was as pivotal to the wider Asian sphere as Greece and Rome were to the Mediterranean, North Africa and Europe.'[1] Although the term 'Hindu' was not used until much later, some beliefs and practices that came to be associated with Hinduism were codified at this time, especially with regard to food.

THE GOLDEN AGE

The last Mauryan emperor was assassinated in 184 BCE, and until the establishment of the Gupta Empire in 324 CE, India was politically fragmented. The Mauryas' immediate successor in the northeast was the Shunga dynasty, which lasted only 100 years. In the northwest, Greek Bactrians (descendants of Alexander the Great's generals) took over Afghanistan, and by the end of the second century BCE had conquered the entire Punjab.

Northern India was invaded by various groups from Central Asia: the Scythians or Sakas, the Pahlavas and the Kushans (from the second to the third century BCE). Over time many of the invaders adopted Indian names and the caste rank of *ksatriya* and supported the *brahmins'* rituals to sanction their kingship. In Rajasthan and central India, some became the ancestors of the Rajputs.

72

The Guptas (324–550 CE) started life as rulers of small kingdoms in Bihar. Through marriage, alliances and warfare they expanded their rule over much of northern India. The Gupta period is sometimes called the Golden Age of Indian civilization, since at that time India enjoyed relative peace, order and prosperity. It was one of the richest regions in the world, thanks to thriving agriculture and extensive overseas trade. Unlike Ashoka, the Gupta emperors performed Vedic sacrifices, but they also made endowments to both Buddhist and brahmin establishments. However, the two communities were physically separated, with the monasteries located outside the cities and the brahmin schools in the cities, close to the court.

The study of science, art, mathematics, literature, logic, philosophy and religion flourished. The positional number system, the notion that the Earth revolved around the Sun, and the game of chess were all conceived during this period. The plays of Kalidasa, who probably lived in the fourth century CE, are still performed today. The world's first university, at Nalanda in Bihar, was founded in the fifth or sixth century CE. It had more than 10,000 students and 2,000 teachers, and attracted scholars from as far away as China, Persia and Greece.

The south of India was ruled by independent chieftains and dynasties: Cheras and Pandyas in the southeast, Cholas in the west, and the Satavahanas, also called the Andhra dynasty, who for more than 450 years controlled a large expanse of western, southern and central India.

India was the centre of a vast network of foreign trade routes. A Greek maritime geography of the mid-first century CE, *The Periplus*, lists more than fifty ports and routes on the Red Sea and twenty posts on the east and west coasts of India. Located at the mouths of rivers, these ports were major emporia for the exchange of goods with the Roman Empire, the Arabian Peninsula, Western and Southeast Asia. Each year a fleet of 120 Roman ships left Egypt (then part of the Roman Empire) for the west coast of India, a trip that could take just 40 days if the winds were favourable; later they were able to sail around the southern tip of India to reach the ports on the east coast. Three major ports were Muziris in Kerala, Arikamedu near Pondicherry, and Puhar in Tamil Nadu.[2] The streets of these bustling cities were lined with merchants' mansions and warehouses. Trade continued into ports further north, including Bharuch, and may have been a continuation of the trade routes of the Indus Valley civilization.

Many Indian merchants were Buddhists, in part because of the prohibitions against sea travel by upper-caste Indians because of the risk

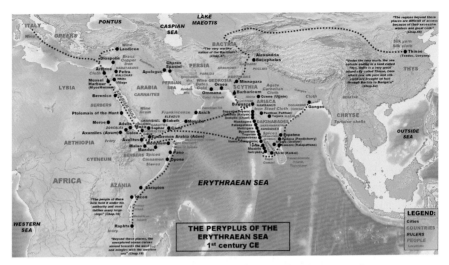

The Periplus of the Erythraean Sea.

of contamination. Most of the merchants who bought goods for Rome were Arabs, Egyptian Jews and Greeks. They came to India for aromatic oils, ivory, agate, muslin and cotton cloth, silk trans-shipped from China, precious stones, apes, parrots and peacocks, salt from the Punjab, saffron and musk from the Himalayas, cloves and nutmeg from Southeast Asia, and cardamom, long pepper and black pepper from Kerala. The last was much in demand in the Roman Empire both for its flavour (pepper is an ingredient in two-thirds of the 468 recipes in *Apicius*, a Roman cookbook written in the late fourth or early fifth century CE) and as a status symbol, since it was very expensive.[3] Recent archaeological evidence indicates that the Romans may also have imported medicinal plants from a region in Karnataka.[4]

In exchange for their goods, the Indians received mainly gold and silver coins, hoards of which have been discovered along the coasts. Luxury goods included wine (those from southern Italy and the Greek islands were much valued), women for the rulers' harems, and horses from the Middle East and Central Asia. Mediterranean amphorae recently discovered near Pondicherry contain the remains of olive oil, garum (fermented fish sauce) and apples.[5]

Such contact had other consequences. According to an apocryphal version of the New Testament Acts of the Apostles, in 52 CE the Apostle Thomas sailed to India to spread Christianity, and was martyred near Chennai. Some members of Kerala's Syrian Christian community claim descent from his converts. Jews came to southwest India in 68 CE to escape religious persecution, and centuries later were joined by Jews from the Middle East. Most have since emigrated to Israel, but a small number remain in Cochin today.

As the Roman Empire began to crumble in the third century, its trading declined, but Indian trade with Southeast Asia and Indonesia expanded. Black pepper was exchanged for cloves, nutmeg and mace, which at the time grew only in the Malaccan Islands. An intriguing question is when these spices entered Indian cuisine. The Sanskrit word for clove, *lavanga*, comes from the Malay word *bungalavanga*. References to nutmeg are found in Buddhist and Jain texts composed a few centuries BCE. The earliest reference to cloves (as a flavouring for meat and paan) appears in Tamil works written between the third and sixth centuries CE. The betel palm (*Areca catechu*) and the leaf of the betel vine (*Piper betle*), components of paan (betel quid), reached South India from Southeast Asia by the late fifth century. Indian merchants may also have introduced tamarind, garlic, ginger, turmeric and pepper to Southeast Asia and Indonesia, and disseminated such spices as lemongrass and galangal.

Indian merchants, accompanied by priests, also brought Indian religious beliefs and practices, dance, sculpture, music and their concepts

These fishing nets in Cochin may have been introduced
by the Chinese in the 14th century.

of statecraft to Southeast Asia. Local rulers enlisted the service of *brahmins* to support their political authority, married Indian women and adopted Hindu ceremonies and rituals. The two great epics of the *Ramayana* and *Mahabharata* are central to the cultures of the region, especially Thailand and Cambodia, where the stories are immortalized in the temples of Angkor Wat. So-called Hinduized kingdoms flourished in Thailand, Vietnam, Cambodia and Indonesia until the eighteenth century, and Hinduism is still practised in Bali. Almost uniquely in the history of the world, this cultural expansion was brought about by peaceful means and did not involve political hegemony or an attempt by Indian rulers to build an overseas empire.

Trade with China was conducted by sea and land via the Silk Road, where Buddhist monasteries provided a link between South and East Asia. Chinese merchants established posts along India's coasts and brought silk, porcelain and musk, the last of which became highly valued as a flavouring. En route they stopped in Malacca for nutmegs, mace, cloves and aloes, and Sri Lanka, where they bought cinnamon, all for resale in India, Persia and Arabia. Remnants of the Chinese presence are the Chinese-style fishing nets and wok-like cooking pots used in Kerala to this day. (Other theories are that they were introduced later by the Chinese explorer Zheng He (1371–1433) from the court of Kublai Khan or by Portuguese settlers from Macau.)

The Sanskrit names of several Indian foods contain the element *chini*, indicating their Chinese origin, including peaches (chinani), pears (chinarajaputra), lettuce (chinisalit), camphor (chinakarpura) and cinnamon (dalchini, or Chinese bark). Indian Buddhist travellers may have introduced sugar-refining to China, where the earliest reference to processing dates from 286 BCE.

THE NEW ORTHODOXY

In the middle of the first millennium BCE brahmin priests wrote a series of prose texts called *Dharmasutras*, which can be viewed as extensions of the ritual prescriptions of the Vedas. Their central purpose was to define *dharma*, a term that has been called 'the most central and ubiquitous concept in the whole of Indian civilization'.[6] Originally, *dharma* referred to rules of correct ritual procedure for such occasions as funeral ceremonies and purification rites, but the concept was later extended to include definitions of correct behaviour in the public sphere, such as in marriage and inheritance, and even in private activities, such as bathing, brushing one's teeth, sexual conduct, general etiquette and diet.

The *Dharmasutras* told people what to do, but probably did not reflect what people actually did, especially since they contain contradictory statements and opinions. The very diversity of the instructions 'belies the common assumption that ancient Indian society was uniform and stifling under an orthodoxy imposed by the Brahmins', writes Patrick Olivelle. If even the experts disagreed so vehemently, 'the reality on the ground must have been even more chaotic and exhilarating'.[7] The content of the *Dharmasutras* is elaborated on in the *Dharmashastras*, composed somewhat later. The earliest and most famous of these is the *Manu Smriti*, translated as the *Code* or *Lawbook of Manu*. Composed in verse between 200 BCE and 200 CE, it was written by a conservative brahmin ('Manu') in northern India, or perhaps more probably by several authors living at different times. It is still considered by some to be the most authoritative code of Hindu customs.[8]

The writing of these works may have been motivated by a desire (especially by those in power) for stability and the establishment of social norms, caused by the period of political and social uncertainty that followed the disintegration of the Maurya and Shunga empires. The brahmins' status and power had been weakened by the spread of Buddhism and Jainism, by the royal support for these movements and by Ashoka's restrictions on animal sacrifice. To retain their position of superiority and their royal patrons, the brahmins had to steal a march on non-brahmin ascetics by presenting themselves as the 'ultimate exemplars of the canons of proper asceticism'.[9] The sutras represented an attempt to restore and consolidate their position and also to rationalize the myriad social groups that had emerged. The following is a summary of the main ideas in this literature, with a focus on dietary prescriptions and proscriptions.

Manu reiterates the concept of four castes (*varnas*), with brahmins at the pinnacle. Brahmins studied and taught the Vedas, offered and officiated at sacrifices, and gave and received gifts. Ksatriyas studied the Vedas, offered sacrifices, gave gifts to the brahmins and protected their subjects by arms. The vaisyas also studied the Vedas, offered sacrifices and practised agriculture, trade, animal husbandry and lending money on interest. These three castes were called 'twice born' because they underwent an initiation ceremony that represented a second birth. The job of the fourth caste, the sudras, was to serve the first three.

Twice-born men were supposed to live in a certain region, called Aryavarta or the region of the *aryas* (although by then this was not very feasible because of population growth). It was located between the Himalaya and Vindhya mountains and the eastern and western oceans, a region that coincides with the natural range of the black antelope. If a *sudra* did not have a means of livelihood, he could live anywhere at all. Beyond the Aryavarta was the land of the *mlecchas*, a word sometimes translated as 'foreigners' or 'barbarians' and applied to individuals and groups outside mainstream society.

Brahmins and ksatriyas were supposed to avoid farming, since farmers harm living beings in the soil – an idea perhaps adopted from the Jains. If hard-pressed a brahmin could engage in trade, but he could not sell meat, cooked food, salt, alcohol, milk or certain other items under pain of losing his caste status. A man who practised the profession of a higher caste was theoretically banned from society.

However, this fourfold taxonomy did not account for the thousands of clans, professions and tribes, called jatis, so the writers of the *dharma* literature came up with the ingenious solution of attributing the origins of the jatis to intercaste unions (an explanation that has little historical justification). Outcastes were said to be the children of sudra men and brahmin women. This abhorrence of the mixing of castes became the driving force of other prescriptions, including those relating to food.

DIETARY PROSCRIPTIONS AND PRESCRIPTIONS

The *dharma* literature has a lot to say about what, when and how a man could eat at different stages of his life, how his food should be prepared, from whom he could accept food and with whom he could eat. The term 'man' is used deliberately, since the readers were assumed to be men. Women were not supposed to study or even read the Vedas and *dharma* literature. However, while men were the arbiters of social norms, it was the women who inculcated and enforced these norms in the domestic sphere. Even today, in traditional Hindu households it is women who look after the ritual purity of the food and the kitchen and undertake fasts, often for the benefit of their husbands and children.

A twice-born man ideally passes through four stages, called *asramas*: student, householder, hermit or forest-dweller (*vanaprastha*) and ascetic or renunciant (*sannyasi*). In an interesting transformation, the practices and even the names (*asrama*, *sannyasi* and so on) from an earlier era were incorporated into the mainstream of life. Each stage had its own dietary rules. Students, who lived in their teachers' homes, led an ascetic existence in which they abstained from sex, honey, meat, spices, onion, garlic, acid dishes and other foods believed to stimulate the passions (practices still followed in Hindu ashrams). They also had to beg for food on certain days.

Householders had to follow the dietary rules appropriate to their caste. After their hair turned grey, they had the option of retiring to the forest and living as a hermit. They were to wear clothing made of bark and animal skin, could not enter a village or step on ploughed land, and had to avoid eating cultivated grains (*anna*), a practice still observed in Hindu fasts called *phalahar*. During these fasts, breads and snacks were made of water-chestnut or lotus-seed flour instead of wheat, while onions, turmeric, garlic, ginger and urad dal were also banned.

One category of hermit did not cook their food, and ate only raw fruit, vegetables, leaves and roots. 'To move around with animals, to dwell with them alone, and to sustain oneself just like them – that is the visible token of Heaven', proclaims one of the *Dharmasutras*. 'Having embarked on this splendid path far away from wicked men and undertaken the forest life, a Brahmin never comes to ruin.'[10]

In the final stage of life, as a man prepares for death, he abandons attachment to all worldly things. He wanders around without a fixed dwelling, practises yoga and meditation, lives by begging and avoids injuring any living creature. This lifestyle guarantees freedom from re-birth after death. Today most Hindus are familiar with the idea of this life cycle, although very few put it into practice.

For householders, the literature enjoins moderation in food: 'A sage's meal is eight mouthfuls, a forest-dweller's sixteen, a householder's twenty-two, and a student's an unlimited quantity.'[11] It was considered improper to eat early in the morning, late in the evening or between meals, or to eat too much. A person should wash before and after eating, wear at least two garments, remove his hat and shoes, sit on the floor facing east and dine in privacy without talking. Before eating, a householder should offer some food to the gods and then give it to children, old men, newly wed girls, sick people and pregnant women. He should also set aside food for dogs, outcastes, people who are ill, birds and insects. Rules of etiquette forbid one from cracking one's joints or striking one's nails, tapping one's eating bowl, drinking water from cupped hands, splashing water or throwing pieces of food at other diners. Indian meals must have been lively events if such proscriptions were necessary!

The *dharmic* literature contains lists of foods that must not be eaten by twice-born men. They fall into two categories: those that are always forbidden because of their intrinsic nature (*abhaksya*), and those that could normally be eaten but have been made inedible because of contact with someone or something that is impure (*abhojya*).[12]

Foods that are always forbidden for twice-born men include the following:

Garlic, leeks and onions
Mushrooms and all other plants springing from impure substances
Red juices flowing from incisions on trees
The thickened milk of a cow after calving or the milk of an animal within ten days after calving
Rice boiled with sesame, wheat mixed with butter, milk rice and flour cakes unless they were prepared for a sacrifice
Meat that has not been sprinkled with water while sacred texts were recited
The milk of camels, one-hoofed animals, sheep, a cow in heat or one that has no calf with her, all wild animals except buffaloes
All substances that have turned sour, except sour milk and food prepared from it
Meat from a slaughterhouse (as opposed to meat obtained by hunting)
Dried meat
Village pigs
Most fish
Alcohol, especially distilled spirits
Certain categories of animal and bird (see below)

Although onions are native to Central Asia and Afghanistan and grew in India at a very early date, they are not mentioned in the Vedas, perhaps because they were associated with the despised indigenous people or because of their odour. Onions and garlic were reputed to have aphrodisiac properties, which is why they were forbidden to students and widows. (Later, the ban may have been reinforced by their association with

> *Singhare ki Puri (Puris made with Water-chestnut Flour)*
>
> 2 medium-sized potatoes, boiled
> 150 g (1 cup) water-chestnut flour (kuttu)
> ¼ tsp black pepper
> oil for deep frying
> salt, to taste
>
> Peel and mash the potato, and mix it with the flour, salt and pepper. Slowly add a little water (about 60 ml/¼ cup) until the dough is smooth and fairly hard. Form it into 12–15 small balls and very gently roll each one into a disc about 8 cm (3 in.) in diameter. Deep-fry in the oil until puffy.

Islamic cuisine.) Even today, Jains, orthodox brahmins, widows, ascetics and some Hindus avoid onions and garlic, and they are *never* used in religious ceremonies.

Mushrooms are banned because they grow in dirty soil. The ban on red sap may be because of its association with blood. (According to legend, the god Indra once killed a brahmin; his guilt was assumed by trees and became their sap.) Avoiding the milk of newly calved cows can be seen as protecting the young.

As for the ban on alcohol, the justification is that a brahmin, stupefied by drunkenness, might fall on something impure, mispronounce Vedic texts or commit some other sin. The punishments are dire: if he deliberately drinks alcohol he must drink a liquid from a boiling-hot glass. If he drinks alcohol by accident, he must live on hot milk, hot ghee, hot water and hot air for three days each. If he even smells the breath of a man who has drunk alcohol, he must practise yoga, control his breath and eat ghee. A brahmin woman who drinks alcohol becomes a leech or pearl oyster that lives in water in her next life.

The classification of animals in the *dharma* literature challenges that of Leviticus in complexity. Eating animals with five-nailed paws and single hoofs is forbidden, but those with cloven hoofs are acceptable. Animals with incisor teeth on both jaws are not allowed; those with a single row of teeth are permitted. The only animals that meet both criteria of acceptability are goats, wild oxen, sheep, deer, antelopes and pigs. Dogs are not even mentioned because they are particularly abhorred as food, perhaps because of their association with *chandalas*, a tribal people who were sometimes called 'dog-cookers'. Another forbidden category is birds that scratch with their feet, have webbed feet or are carnivorous.

Overriding all these taxonomical categories is habitat: animals and birds living in villages are forbidden, while those living in the wild or raised as farm animals are allowed. Thus the meat of a wild boar is acceptable, but not that of a village pig. A village chicken is banned but wildfowl can be eaten. Perhaps animals that live in villages were considered unclean, since they ate waste. Other blanket taboos are on carnivores and animals that lead solitary lives. The rules are silent about eggs, which could mean that they were rarely eaten at the time.

Regarding fish, the older literature assumes that all fish may be eaten except those that are grotesque or misshapen. Later writers, however, forbid all but a few fish, reflecting a belief that fish were carnivorous. 'A man who eats the meat of some animal is called eater of that animal's meat, whereas a fish-eater is an eater of every animal's meat,' says Manu.

The anthropologist Mary Douglas explains the origins of such classifications by defining forbidden and impure animals as those that are 'out of place' and deviate in some way from others in their category. For example, birds without feathers, fish without scales or cloven-footed animals that do not chew the cud are forbidden to the Jews because they are anomalies and therefore unclean. Pollution occurs when a category boundary is violated. Holiness requires that individuals conform to the class to which they belong, and that different classes of things not be confused. 'To be holy is to be whole, to be one: holiness is unity, integrity, perfection of the individual and of the kind. The dietary rules merely develop the metaphor of holiness on the same lines', Douglas wrote.[13]

As for eating meat in general, and the topic of vegetarianism, the *Code of Manu* devotes an entire section to the pros and cons. The anti-meat verses (of which there are 25) far outnumber pro-meat verses (three), and could have been written at different times, perhaps in an attempt to reconcile renunciant ideals with traditional views on the value of the sacrifice. On the side of eating meat, Manu quotes Prajapati, the creator of the universe:

The immobile are food for the mobile, the fangless for the fanged, the handless for the handed, and the timid for the brave. The eater is not defiled by eating living beings suitable for eating even if he eats them day after day.

God himself created domestic animals for sacrifice for the prosperity of the entire world, and killing for sacrifice is, therefore, not killing. Plants, trees, cattle, birds and other animals that are killed for sacrifice are reborn into higher existences.

On the other hand, Manu dictates that while the consumption of meat for sacrifices is a rule made by the gods, to persist in using it on other occasions is demonic, and if a twice-born man eats meat in violation of this law, he will be eaten after death by his victims. A brahmin should not eat meat out of desire, but only for lawful reasons. If he has a craving for meat, he should make an animal out of clarified butter or flour and eat that; otherwise, he will suffer a violent death in future lives. Manu even gives a forced etymological explanation: 'Me he (*mam sa*) will devour in the next world whose meat (*mamsa*) I eat in this world – this, the wise declare, is the real meaning of the word "meat" (*mamsa*).'

Manu further states that a man who abstains from meat and a man who offers the horse sacrifice every year for 100 years gain the same merit: 'Even by living on pure fruits and roots and by eating the food of sages, a man fails to obtain as great a reward as he would by abstaining completely from meat.' Manu remains firmly on the fence by finally declaring: 'There is nothing wrong in eating meat nor in drinking wine nor in sexual union, for this is how living beings engage in life, but abstention bears great fruit.'

Another category in the texts is that of unfit food (*abhojya*) – food that can normally be eaten, but which has been rendered impure by coming into contact with someone or something that is considered un-clean. Some prohibitions are probably based on hygiene and display an understanding of the principle of infection; for example, people should not eat food that has been touched by a dog or smelled by a cow; contains mouse droppings or an insect; looks disgusting; is stale (except vege-tables or fried food); has been touched by someone's foot or the hem of a garment; has been sneezed on; or is served by a sick person or someone who has had a death in the house.

Other foods are rendered unfit by caste distinctions, personal preju-dice or perhaps just pure snobbery, including food given by a physician, a drunkard, a blacksmith, a goldsmith, a prostitute, a woman made impure by childbirth or menstruation, a hunter, a sudra, a law-enforcement agent, a thief, a eunuch, a miser, a liquor dealer, a carpenter, a woman without a husband, a washerman, the lover of a married woman, a man who keeps dogs, a man married to a sudra woman, or even a man who is bossed around by his wife. Some of these people (physicians and hunters, for example) were in contact with diseased or dead bodies, which in a hot climate could be a source of infection. But others – such as goldsmiths, eunuchs or hen-pecked men – were not, and the explanation must be sought elsewhere, notably in the correlation between perceived 'purity' and status.

As the anthropologist Louis Dumont stated in his classic *Homo Hierarchicus*, the Indian 'classification of foods is essentially related to the classification of people and to relationships between human groups. It is not a primary datum resulting from a universal classification of pure and impure.'[14] Mary Douglas argues that the restriction on eating out-siders' food was a way of protecting one's group from threats from below, especially since the higher a caste's status, the more of a minority it must be. Then there is the 'Primrose Path' theory: eating with someone from outside one's group could be the first step towards sleeping with them, a concept summed up in the Hindi phrase 'roti-beti': bread = daughter-in-law.

One of the main sources of food contamination is bodily fluids, including saliva, and this concern dictates, if only subconsciously, many modern practices in India.[15] Some people do not sip water from a glass but pour it into their mouths, since even one's own saliva can be pollut-ing. To this day, many Indian women do not taste food while they are cooking it. An orthodox Hindu takes a bath before entering the kitchen, and wears freshly washed clothes.[16] Food is eaten only with the right hand, the left being reserved for bathroom practices. Sampling food from another diner's plate, except that of a close relative, is unacceptable.

Leftover food was the subject of complex rules. A person could eat the leftovers of his superiors only, which for a brahmin meant only God (that is, the food offered as a sacrifice or offering); for a ksatriya, the leftovers of a brahmin; for a vaisya, those of a ksatriya or brahmin; and for a sudra, those of the three castes above him. A student could eat his teacher's leftovers. A twice-born man could not eat food left by a woman.[17]

But these barriers may not have been as rigid as they sound. According to the *Dharmashastras*, a brahmin could eat the food of a sudra as long as the sudra in question was a tenant farmer, a friend of the family or his own cowherd or slave (perhaps because he would be familiar with his hygiene and habits). The attitude of the person giving the food was equally important: the gods once compared the food of a miserly brahmin and a generous usurer and proclaimed them equal. However, no leniency was given to chandalas, who had to live outside villages, and were not even allowed to cook their own food but had to receive it from other people, who gave it to them in broken dishes.

Changing one's eating habits could be a way of upward mobility. By emulating the ritual and customs of higher castes (or sometimes by an outright bribe), individuals or groups were able to rise in the caste hierarchy, a process the anthropologist M. N. Srinivas called Sanskritization:

> The caste system is far from a rigid system in which the position of each component caste is fixed for all time. Movement has always been possible, and especially in the *middle regions of the hierarchy*. A caste was able, in a generation or two, to rise to a higher position in the hierarchy by adopting vegetarianism and teetotalism, and by Sanskritizing its ritual and pantheon. In short, it took over, as far as possible, the customs, rites and beliefs of the Brahmins, and adoption of the Brahminic way of life by a low caste seems to have been frequent, though theoretically forbidden.[18]

Although some prohibitions and restrictions remained in force well into the twentieth century and beyond, they are now breaking down, especially in cities where a neighbour's or colleague's caste may be unknown or a matter of indifference. More than twenty years ago, Srinivas wrote:

> In the big cities of India there are small numbers of rich people who are educated and have a highly Westernized style of life. These may be described as living minimally in the universe of caste and maximally in class. The occupations practised by them bear no relation to the traditional occupations of the caste into which they were born. They ignore pollution rules, their diet includes forbidden foods, and their friends and associates are drawn from all over India and may even include foreigners. Their sons and daughters marry not only outside caste but occasionally also outside region, language and religion.[19]

What People Ate

These prescriptions and proscriptions fascinated the Chinese Buddhist scholars who travelled to India to visit monasteries and collect and translate texts. The monk Faxian (337–c. 422 CE) wrote:

> Throughout the whole country the people do not kill any living creature, nor drink intoxicating liquor, nor eat onions or garlic. The only exception is that of the *chandalas* [outcastes]. That is the name for those who are (held to be) wicked men, and live apart from others. When they enter the gate of a city or a market-place, they strike a piece of wood to make themselves known, so that men know and avoid them, and do not come into contact with them. In that country they do not keep pigs and fowls, and do not sell live cattle; in the markets there are no butchers' shops and no dealers in intoxicating drink . . . Only the *chandalas* are fishermen and hunters, and sell flesh meat.[20]

Such observations were probably the result of the commentators seeing the world through Buddhist-coloured glasses, since other texts indicate that meat and even alcohol were consumed. A similar picture of a segregated society was painted by Xuanzang (Hsuan-tsang, 602–664 CE), a scholar and translator who travelled throughout Central Asia and large swathes of India for seventeen years and recorded his impressions in his book *Great Tang Records on the Western Regions*. According to Xuanzang, 'butchers, fishermen, actors, executioners, scavengers and so on have their dwellings outside the city. In coming and going these persons are bound to keep on the left side of the road until they arrive at their homes.'[21] He reported that people were divided into four castes with different degrees of ceremonial purity, and could marry only within their own caste. He admired the prestige assigned to austerity and simple living, while those who 'lead idle lives, abounding in food and luxurious in their dress', are met with shame and disgrace.[22] He was impressed with the cleanliness of the people who wash before every meal and never use leftover food or dishes a second time.

Xuanzang observed a certain culinary democracy, inasmuch as the sudras and people born of mixed castes ate the same food as everyone else, the only difference being the material of the cooking vessels. But beverages differed: the ksatriyas drank alcoholic drinks made from grapes and sugar cane, the vaisyas drank strong, fermented drinks, while brahmins drank a kind of alcoholic syrup made from grapes or sugar cane.

Noting that it was impossible to list all the fruit grown in India, Xuanzang wrote that the most common were mango, tamarind, mahua (*Madhuca longifolia*), melon, jujube, wood apple, myrobalan, fig, coconut, jackfruit, pomegranate, pumpkin and sweet orange. Dates, loquat and persimmon were unknown. Peaches, pears, apricots and grapes grew only in Kashmir. Among the edible items were ginger, mustard and kunda (*olibanum*, an aromatic resin sometimes confused with frankincense). Onions and garlic were rarely eaten, and those who did eat them were ostracized.[23] The most widely consumed foods were milk, butter, cream, soft and crystallized sugar, mustard oil and various breads. Fish, mutton and venison, served in joints or slices, were sometimes eaten, but the meat of the ox, ass, elephant, horse, pig, dog, fox, wolf, lion, monkey and ape was forbidden.

Xuanzang was surprised that although Indians used varied cooking equipment, steaming was unknown. Dishes were made from earthenware and everyone ate from a separate plate, mixing all the ingredients together and eating with their fingers, not chopsticks or spoons (except when they fell ill, when they used copper spoons).

The most detailed description of Indian food customs at this time is given in the writings of Yijing (635–713 CE), a Tang Dynasty Chinese Buddhist monk who left a record of his 25-year travels throughout Southeast Asia and India, including a stay at Nalanda University.[24] In a Buddhist monastery, he wrote, the basic meal consisted of wet and soft food such as rice, boiled barley and peas, baked flour (perhaps meaning bread), meat and cakes. If a monk were still hungry, he could partake of another course, comprising hard and solid food that is chewed or crunched: roots, stalks, leaves, flowers and fruit. Milk, cream and other dairy products were served at every meal.

In the north, Yijing reported, wheat was the dietary staple, in the west rice or barley, and in Magadha (Bihar) and the south, rice. Dairy products and oil were eaten everywhere, and there were so many kinds of bread and fruit that it was difficult to name them all. Because of this bounty, he wrote, even lay people rarely needed to eat meat.

Yijing was surprised by the absence of foods popular in China, including glutinous rice, glutinous millet, millet and edible mallow (the soft shoots and leaves of *Malva verticillata*). Indian mustard seed was different from the Chinese variety. No one in India ate onions or raw vegetables; onions were forbidden because they caused pain, spoiled the eyesight and weakened the body.

The drinking of alcohol was apparently common. The plays of the fifth-century dramatist Kalidasa, which depicted all levels of society, contain innumerable allusions to alcohol and to intoxication, even among women, to whom it was supposed to lend a special charm. In Kalidasa's epic *Raghuvamsa*, the queen of Aja receives wine directly from the mouth of her husband, while Raghu's entire army drinks wine made from coconuts. The upper classes scented their wine with mango flowers or orange peel to remove the smell of drink and sweeten their breath.

Moreover, as Hashi and Tapan Raychaudhuri write, 'Contrary . . . to another stereotype. Hindu spirituality and the supposed normative objections to worldly pursuits have never precluded culinary delights.'[25] A seventh-century Sanskrit poem, Dandin's *Dasakumaracharita* (What Ten Young Princes Did), contains vivid pictures of how both men and women lived, not how they should live, including a two-page detailed description of how a woman cooks and the pleasure it gives to her guest:

She stirred the gruel in the two dishes which she set before him on a piece of pale green plantain leaf. He drank it and felt rested and

A seller of dried fruit, nuts and spices in Delhi's Chandni Chowk market.

A vegetable seller
in Patna, Bihar, 1826.

happy, relaxed in every limb. Next she gave him two ladlefuls
of the boiled rice, served with a little ghee and condiments. She
served the rest of the rice with curds, three spices, and fragrant
and refreshing buttermilk and gruel. He enjoyed the meal to the
last mouthful . . . [The water] was fragrant with incense, the smell
of fresh trumpet flower, and the perfume of full blown lotuses.
He put the bowl to his lips, and his eyelashes sparkled with
dewdrops as cool as snow; his ears delighted in the sound of
the trickling water . . . his nostrils opened at its sweet fragrance;
and his tongue delighted in this lovely flavour.[26]

South India

Scenes from daily life are depicted in the Sangam literature – anthologies
of Tamil poetry compiled and written down between 600 BCE and 300
CE. The poems are set in six distinct areas: the dry hill or forest region,
pastureland, forests, coastal areas, barren areas, and fertile land in the river
valleys. Originally the inhabitants of these areas practised shifting cultivation and raised cattle, but later agriculture became more settled and

more productive, especially after the introduction of iron ploughs and irrigation. The staple crops were pulses and millet; later rice cultivation began in the river valleys, where the land was so fertile that, it was said, the space in which an elephant could lie down could support enough crops to feed seven people. Forest products that were brought under cultivation included bamboo, jackfruit, honey, black pepper and turmeric. Kerala was famous for its black-pepper farms.[27]

Boiled rice was flavoured with tamarind or sesame seeds and sugar or cooked with lentils, meat or ghee. Rice was also soaked, heated in hot sand and pounded until it was flat, or heated until it puffed up, then was eaten with milk – like the modern poha (Hindi) and aval (Tamil). Cooked rice or rice gruel left overnight to ferment produced a beverage that even brahmins consumed (although this violated proscriptions against stale food and alcohol, indicating that perhaps such rules were not yet widespread in the south).[28] Other items mentioned in the literature were idi-appam, noodles made from rice flour; aval, flattened or beaten rice soaked in milk; and bamboo rice, made from the seeds of bamboo plants, a dish today found in Kerala and parts of Karnataka. There are many references to coconut and cloves. The latter were used to flavour meat and pickles, mixed with bhang (cannabis) or chewed.

A passage from a third-century Sangam poem describes the meals served to a wandering minstrel. The hunters gave him red rice and lizard meat on the leaf of a teak tree; the shepherds fed him sorghum and beans

Flattened rice is dehusked rice that is beaten to form dry, light flakes that can be lightly fried with nuts and spices to make a snack.

and millet boiled in milk; agricultural labourers offered him a meal of white rice and roast fowl; the fishermen on the coast gave him rice and fish in dishes made of palmyra leaves; the brahmins served him fine rice with mango pickle and pomegranate cooked with butter and curry leaves; while the farmers feted him with sweetmeats, jackfruit, banana and coconut water.[29]

A sweet shop in Vrindaban.

FIVE

New Religious Trends and Movements: Feasting and Fasting, 500–1000 CE

From about 500 CE new forms of belief and worship started to appear. Although Vedic sacrifices remained essential for the consecration of kingship, they no longer had much following among the general population. Many people began to worship at home or in temples in rituals called *pujas*. Temples were built, especially in South India; some housed statues of a single deity, while others honoured many gods. The patrons of the temples were rulers and wealthy merchants. These temples became the sites of royal ceremonies and initiations, as kings came to seen as deputies of particular deities.

The new movements were called Puranic, as opposed to the Shramanic, or ascetic, religions of Jainism and Buddhism. The name comes from a series of texts called the *Puranas*, collections of stories about the myths, legends and genealogies of gods, heroes and saints as well as descriptions of cosmology, philosophy and geography. They were composed in Sanskrit over a very long period of time, perhaps between the fourth century BCE and 1000 CE. They were translated into vernacular languages and disseminated by brahmins who read from them and told their stories at local temples. In effect, they became the scriptures of the common people.

The main gods were Vishnu and Siva, who had been minor gods in the Vedic pantheon, and mother goddesses who embodied the primordial energy or *shakti*. Today most Hindus in India and Nepal are Vaishnavs, followers of Vishnu; Saivites, devotees of Siva; or Shaktas, who worship Durga, Kali and other forms of the mother goddess. Over time the gods became more humanized and acquired wives, children, musical instruments, weapons and 'vehicles' (*vahana*) – animals that served as both companions and mounts. Siva, for example, is married to Parvati; their children are Ganesh (who has a human body and an elephant's

What is Hinduism?

The term 'Hindu' was first used in the ninth century CE by people living outside India to describe the inhabitants of the subcontinent. The word came from the Persian Sindh, meaning the land on the banks of the Sindhu (the Indus River). It was originally a secular term applied to all the residents of the subcontinent, but it was later applied, first by Muslims and then by the British, to Indians who followed indigenous religions (as opposed to Islam or Christianity). In the nineteenth century the term was adopted by some Indians in the context of establishing a national identity.

Throughout most of history, Hindus have not called themselves Hindus. Even now, they tend to identify themselves by the name of their sect (Vaishnava, Shaiva) or sub-sect. Sometimes the term *sanatana dharma* is used, meaning the eternal or absolute set of duties (*dharma*) that are incumbent on all Hindus.

Unlike Islam or Christianity, Hinduism does not have a founder, a single set of scriptures (although many traditions revere the Vedas as revelation), a creed or a centralized authority.[1] What is called Hinduism incorporates many strands and traditions, a diversity of beliefs, practices, world views and sometimes contradictory ideas and ideals about such things as caste, renunciation and the worship of one or many gods. The idea that there are many ways of reaching God may in fact be the defining feature of Hinduism; as one ancient text puts it, "all these paths, O Lord, Veda Samkhya, Yoga, Pasupata [worship of Siva], Vaishnava, lead but to Thee, like the winding river that at last merges into the sea.'[2]

head) and Kartikeya, god of war. Siva's vehicle is the bull Nanda, whose statue always sits outside temples dedicated to Siva. The deities also had their own temperaments and culinary preferences. Siva, for example, who has a rather violent, angry (*rajasic*) nature, is said to like spicy, hot and pungent food, especially green chillies. Vishnu, who is of a serene

As a mischievous child, Krishna steals butter from the house of a neighbour, a popular scene in Indian art, *c.* 1750.

disposition, prefers mild ghee and milk-based foods, and avoids chillies. Vaishnavs in western India were mainly vegetarian, and affluent Vaishnav merchants there donated large sums to charity to promote vegetarianism. Food offerings are part of many Vaishnav *pujas*.

Vishnu came to be worshipped as the divine saviour of mankind, whose nine (ten, if the Buddha is counted) avatars or incarnations come to save the world whenever it is threatened with disaster. His two most popular incarnations are Rama, hero of the epic *Ramayana*, and the dark-skinned Krishna, originally a local pastoral deity.[3] Krishna's stories are told in the *Bhagavata Purana*. This text describes his life as a young cowherd in the village of Vrindavan in northern India (about 160 km or 100 miles south of Delhi), today a major pilgrimage centre. Krishna is worshipped in many forms: as the divine herdsman (Govinda), as a mischievous child who stole butter, as the playmate and lover of Radha and other *gopis* (milkmaids), and as a teacher of philosophy. Some of the legends associated with his various forms repudiate the stern moral code of the *Dharmashastras*, since Radha and the other *gopis*, lured by Krishna's charms, leave their husbands to sport with him. Their love can be interpreted as mirroring the worshipper's love of the divine.

Late 18th-century
painting from the
Nathdvara temple in
Rajasthan depicting
the offering of food
to Krishna in the
Annakuta festival.

The worship of Krishna is often expressed in culinary metaphors; for
example, 'I hunger after the sweet nectar of devotion.' One of the world's
most spectacular food-related events is the Annakuta, or Mountain of
Food, held annually at a temple in Mount Govardhan near Vrindavan
at the end of the rainy season.[4] It commemorates an event in Krishna's
childhood when he persuaded the local cowherds to make their annual
offerings of harvest grains and pulses to Mount Govardhan instead of to
the god Indra. Angered, Indra punished the people by sending a violent
rainstorm. To commemorate this event, which is often depicted in Indian
paintings, worshippers build a large mound of rice, sometimes weighing
thousands of kilos, in the temple courtyard, facing the sanctum where
the deity resides. They surround it with hundreds of dishes of sweets,
savouries, vegetables and grains, all vegetarian and containing no onions
or garlic. Pilgrims come to Govardhan to view these displays and enjoy
the food, which is later distributed to devotees.

A similar food festival is organized every year by members of a sect
called the Vallabhites or Pushti Marga, founded in Gujarat in the fifteenth
century. They worship Krishna in his infant form, depicted with one arm
upraised, a ball of butter in his hand. This sect lavishes so much attention
on food that one scholar has called them 'the undisputed gourmets of
Hinduism'.[5]

At the Vallabhite temple in Jatipura, the image representing baby Krishna is fed eight times a day. The food, an amalgam of Gujarati, Rajasthani, South Indian and local cuisines, is always sweet or bland, because salt and spices are injurious to a child's sensitive palate. Pusti Marga holds large food festivals, the showpiece of which is always *chappan bhoga* (56 dishes). Fifty-six categories of vegetarian food are each prepared five or six ways and 56 baskets of each dish are made. The dishes are displayed in a temporary enclosure on the side of a hill. A similar, though often scaled-down, version of the festival is celebrated at Pushti Marga temples in India and abroad.

Some scholars claim an early version of Siva was worshipped in the Indus Valley civilization because of the discovery of a seal depicting a figure in a yogic posture surrounded by animals. (Ancient pictures of figures in a similar position have, however, been found in other places, including Scandinavia and Western Asia.) His origin has also been traced to Rudra in the Vedas. Siva is worshipped in different forms: as Lord of the Creatures, Lord of the Dance and Lord of Creation. While many Saivites are vegetarians, others eat meat. The animal, most commonly goat, must be slaughtered by a method called *jhatka*, which entails killing the animal with a single stroke of the knife or sword.

Annakuta festival at a Swaminarayan temple in Wheeling, Illinois, in which 2,000 dishes are offered to the deity.

Ganeśa.

A statue of Ganesh, holding a modaka in his hand, Patna, early 19th century.

The consorts of the deities may originally have been local fertility deities. Parvati, Siva's wife, is worshipped in her incarnations Durga and Kali, especially in eastern India. Kali, regarded as the primary reality, is worshipped by the sacrifice of goats, especially at the Kalighat temple in Kolkata (perhaps a continuation of a pre-Aryan practice.) More benign is Saraswati, the goddess of learning, sometimes considered the wife of Brahma or, in eastern India, the daughter of Durga. Lakshmi, the goddess of prosperity and the wife of Vishnu, is worshipped mainly in northern and western India.

One of the most beloved deities throughout India is Ganesh, the pot-bellied elephant-headed son of Siva and Parvati, who is revered for his ability to remove obstacles. (According to one story, Parvati once asked him to guard the door while she bathed. Siva, unaware of his son's identity, cut off his head for refusing him entry. When Siva learned who he was, he promised to restore him to life with the head of the first creature that passed by, which happened to be an elephant.) Ganesh is famous for his love of sweets, and is always depicted holding a modaka (a steamed or fried flour dumpling filled with coconut, nuts, jaggery and

98

Sundal

2 cups (580 g) dried chickpeas that have been soaked
overnight and boiled, or 2 cups of canned chickpeas,
drained and washed
½ red onion, chopped
1 tbsp finely chopped ginger
1 tsp finely chopped green chillies, or to taste
a few curry leaves
salt
3 tbsp grated coconut (fresh or frozen)
2 tbsp vegetable oil

Heat oil and sauté onion, green chillies, ginger and curry
leaves until tender. Add cooked chickpeas. Add salt to taste.
Sprinkle with grated coconut and lemon juice.
Toss and serve hot.

Courtesy of Nalini Saligram

spices). He is said to have once cursed the moon for making fun of him for eating so many sweets, which is why the moon waxes and wanes, regularly losing its beauty and sometimes vanishing altogether.

During this period, the main form of worship for the common people became the *puja*: a ceremony in which the devotee offers incense, flowers, leaves, sweets and fruit to the image of the deity while reciting *mantras* (Sanskrit verses). A *puja* can be a simple offering of food at a home altar or an elaborate ceremony conducted by priests in a temple. The ritual may include bathing the statue in milk or ghee, clothing it and making a food offering called *naivedya*, a practice that probably started in about the eleventh century. This offering is always *sattvic*, which means it is strictly vegetarian and never contains onions, garlic or, at some temples, tomatoes, potatoes, red lentils, carrots and cauliflower – perhaps because of their colour, which resembles blood, or their foreign origin. Sweets are almost always part of the offering: some temple manuals list recipes for over 200 sweet dishes. However, curdling milk with a souring agent to make chhana (the basis of many Bengali sweets) is not common, since it is thought to destroy the purity of the milk.[6] The food for these offerings is usually cooked in ghee, which is considered ritually pure and auspicious.

The priest brings the food close to the idol's mouth and then consumes it on the god's behalf. After the deity has tasted the food, his leftovers, called *prasad* (a word that can be translated as 'grace'), are given to the devotees, who eat it on the spot or take it home to share with family and friends. The food is highly valued because it has been processed by the deity. One writer describes the experience this way:

> Many devotees feel spiritually uplifted simply by offering and receiving Prasad. It can be thought of as the grace of a god . . . [which] energizes, invigorates and induces devotion to the lord. . . . The consuming of Prasad is the most exalted divine intimacy, an intensely personal experience, the saliva of deity and devotee being mixed through the sharing of food. At this spiritual level, the food, the deity and devotee become coextensive – the essence of this experience being expressed in the saying 'You are what you eat and you eat what you are.'[7]

A Hindu priest makes an offering of coconut, flowers and sweets to Ganesh.

Palani Pancamirtam for a Temple

100 plantains
10 kg (22 lb) unrefined sugar
1 kg (2¼ lb) seedless dates
500 g (1 lb) crystallized sugar
500 g (1 lb) raisins
25 g (1 oz) whole cardamom pods
250 g (8¾ oz) ghee

Crush the plantains with your hands and mix with the unrefined sugar. Add the dates, crystallized sugar and raisins,
then the cardamoms and ghee. Stir the mixture, using only
the right hand, until it becomes thick. Before consuming,
let it rest a few hours to become slightly fermented.[8]

While food offerings are essential in Vaishnav ceremonies, generally worshippers of Siva avoid contact with the god's leftovers, which are eaten by his priests.[9]

Some temples have enormous kitchens where brahmin cooks prepare food for worshippers and pilgrims.[10] For example, the Sri Venkateswara temple in Tirupati, Andhra Pradesh (the most visited temple in India, and the world's second most visited holy place after the Vatican), is visited by 60,000 pilgrims each day and up to 200,000 during festivals. Its speciality is laddus, sweet balls made of lentils, sugar, nuts and spices, including a giant version called kalyana laddu.

The Jagannatha temple in Puri, Odisha, dedicated to Lord Krishna, serves more than 100 dishes, all cooked in ghee. The gods are served ritually five times a day, and pilgrims can either eat in a large dining hall or buy *prasad* at a market within the temple walls. The Murukan temple in Palani, Tamil Nadu, is famous for its palani pancamirtam, a thick, dark red, jelly-like substance sold in the temple's shops. It is offered with milk to the deity at night and then distributed as *prasad* the next day.

India's most famous temple food comes from the town of Udupi in Karnataka, the site of a famous Krishna temple, many smaller temples and eight monastic institutions. The temple kitchens are staffed with brahmin cooks. In the twentieth century, some of these cooks opened their own restaurants serving similar vegetarian food – first locally, then all over the country and eventually abroad. Standard dishes on the menus of these South Indian restaurants, which sometimes have the word *Udupi* or *Udipi* in their names, are sambar, rasam, idlis, dosas, vadai and coconut chutney. The Mysore Woodlands and Dasaprakash restaurant chains started in this way. The latter's original outlet, in Madras, has statues of Indian deities in the halls and porticos, and even a small worship room. (So ubiquitous are South Indian restaurants that when Sir Edmund Hillary and Tenzing Norgay reached the top of Mount Everest, they are said to have discovered that someone had arrived before them – a South Indian restaurant owner!)

At first many Udupi hotels had separate dining rooms for brahmins or barred Muslims and dalits from entering (or sometimes took both precautions), but this ended in the 1950s. The practice of hiring only brahmin cooks has likewise ended, in part because fewer brahmins want to enter the profession.[11]

TANTRISM

A more extreme rebellion against brahmanical norms was the Tantra movement, which emerged between the sixth and eighth centuries CE in eastern and northeastern India. Tantra promised release from existence and the attainment of *nirvana* by liberation *through* the body rather than *from* the body. Those wanting to join a Tantric sect were initiated by a *guru* in a secret ritual, sometimes held at a cremation ground, which required partaking of the Five Ms: *madya*, alcohol; *mamsa*, meat; *matsya*, fish; *mudra*, parched or fried grain; and *maithuna*, sexual coupling.[12] Some rituals required the ingestion of five bodily fluids, called the Five Jewels. Some Tantrics worship a mother goddess; others (the Kaula and Kapilika sects) Siva.

A major Tantric text, the *Mahanirvana Tantra*, describes the Five Ms in more detail.[13] Alcohol can be made from sugar, rice, honey or palm-tree juice by someone of any caste. The best fish are those without bones, although those with lots of bones can be offered to the deity provided they are very well roasted. The best parched grains are shali rice (a fine winter variety) and barley, which are especially delicious when fried in butter.

But even Tantra imposed certain restrictions. According to the *Mahanirvana Tantra*, killing animals should be avoided except for ritual purposes, and only meat sanctified by Tantric rituals can be eaten. People who consumed meat at other times were subject to penances.

A Tantric rite at a cremation ground, the frequent
site of Tantric rituals, *c.* 1790, illustration.

In *Mahanirvana Tantra*, alcohol is called

> Tara [the mother goddess] herself in liquid form, the Saviour of
> beings, the mother of enjoyment and liberation . . . Mortals who
> drink wine with their minds well under control are immortals
> on earth and become like Siva himself. (XI.105)

But there is also a warning against drinking too much, because it can lead
to harm to oneself and to others.

Tantra was open to all castes and included women in its rituals.
There were no restrictions on eating with outcastes or taking food from
them. 'A chandala versed in the knowledge of [Tantric] doctrine excels a
brahmin and a brahmin who is wanting in such knowledge is beneath
even a chandala', says a Tantric scripture. Some of the concepts were incorporated into hatha yoga, including the idea of *kundalini*, the latent energy
believed to lie coiled like a serpent at the base of the spine.

FESTIVALS AND FEASTS

Events in the lives of the deities are celebrated with festivals, fasting,
feasting and sometime both. Some festivals are local or regional; others,
notably Holi and Diwali, are celebrated throughout India and in countries
with Indian diasporas. Some are family-based; others are occasions for
visiting temples and pilgrimage sites, sometimes with millions of other
devotees.

Sweets are an intrinsic part of many celebrations, perhaps because
they were a rare luxury for poor people and also because, since they were
vegetarian and fried, everyone – regardless of religion and caste – could
enjoy them. Sweets were traditionally made at home, but today most are
purchased from professional confectioners.

Because most festivals are determined by the lunar calendar, they
are not celebrated on exactly the same day every year. The year starts with
harvest festivals: Makar Sankranti in north India, Lohri in the Punjab,
Pongal in Tamil Nadu and Sankranthi in Andhra Pradesh. Pongal is the
name of both a festival and a dish. Married women boil newly harvested
rice in milk with jaggery, cashews, ghee and coconut. When it starts to boil,
they shout 'Pongal!', 'It is boiling over.' Some of the mixture is offered to
Ganesh as *prasad*. In Andhra Pradesh, for Sankranthi, Hindus prepare
a payasam, a rice pudding made with rice, milk and jaggery.

Mahashivratri in mid-March is a pan-Indian festival that celebrates Siva's marriage to Parvati. Devotees fast during the day and spend the night in meditation. The next day, they worship the *lingam*, a phallic stone that is a symbol of Siva. Devotees wash it with water from the Ganges, milk, yoghurt and honey, and make offerings of milk, yoghurt, sugar, honey, ghee, the leaves and fruit of the bael tree, betel leaves and flowers. Sometimes little rivers flow outside the main temples from the excess milk and fruit. Unlike most other festivals, where a feast follows worship, in this case devotees fast throughout the day. At midday they eat a special vegetarian meal consisting entirely of *phalahar* (dishes made without cereals). The fast then resumes, and continues for another 36 hours until the morning of the third day.

The most riotous and colourful of Hindu festivals, Holi is celebrated on the day of the full moon in early spring. Children and teenagers squirt coloured water and throw coloured powder at friends, neighbours and passers-by, so everyone wears old clothes. A special drink prepared at this time is thandai – a mildly intoxicating beverage of bhang (cannabis) mixed with ground almonds and sugar. In western India, popular Holi snacks include puran poli and gurpoli, sweet pancakes stuffed with lentils and jaggery made from the newly harvested sugar.

Observed in August or September, Janmashtami commemorates the birth of Lord Krishna. Devotees fast during the day and celebrate Krishna's birthday at midnight by eating sweets.

Ganesh Chaturthi in early autumn celebrates the birthday of Ganesh. The most spectacular celebrations are in Maharashtra and Mumbai, where clay models of Ganesh are installed in homes and special buildings for ten days, after which they are immersed in a river or the sea. The main sweet served during the festival is Ganesh's favourite, modaka.

Two festivals called Navaratri (nine nights) are devoted to the goddess Durga, one in spring, the other in early autumn. In South India, dishes made from nine grains and pulses are prepared at home, offered to the goddess on consecutive days and distributed to friends and family. Common ingredients, each used in a separate dish, include barley, millet, rice, toor dal, mung dal, black chickpea, hyacinth bean, black sesame, urad dal and horse gram. In West Bengal, the nine-day Durgapuja festival is celebrated with great pomp and show. Neighbourhoods commission artists to build elaborate shrines and clay statues of the goddess. The exchange and consumption of sweets is de rigueur, and restaurants and sweetshops do a booming trade. On the final day a community vegetarian meal is prepared. It might include a special khichri made of rice and lentils; luchis, puffed fried bread made with white flour; vegetables; and many sweet dishes.

In North India, a festival called Dussehra (ten nights) is celebrated in autumn to commemorate the battle between Lord Rama and the demon king Ravana, which is described in the epic *Ramayama* and re-enacted in street plays. The festival begins with the planting of a few seeds of millet, which are watered daily, sprout on the tenth day and are eaten in a salad. In South India, where the festival is more religious in nature, a special vegetarian dish is prepared every day for nine days and offered to the goddesses Durga, Lakshmi and Sarawati in turn.

Diwali, the Festival of Lights (Deepawali in South India) is a family festival that is celebrated nationwide in late autumn. It commemorates the return of Lord Ram to his kingdom, Ayodhya, after fourteen years in exile, and symbolizes the victory of good over evil and light over darkness, represented by the lighting of small lamps. Animals and toys made of pure white sugar are distributed to children. In rural areas, farmers revere cattle by feeding them sweets.

Another religious event is the pilgrimage to sacred places, called *tirthas*, which are usually located on the banks of rivers or in the mountains. People go on pilgrimages to fulfil a vow, ask for a favour, obtain spiritual purification or simply behold the place itself, since the viewing of a sacred place confers spiritual benefits. Often ascetics live in or near the *tirthas* and are believed to amplify the power of the place. The pilgrim also becomes an ascetic of sorts, leaving behind his or her household and dealing with the hardships of the road.[14]

FEASTS IN THE EPICS

Krishna and Rama are central characters in India's two great epics, the *Mahabharata* and the *Ramayana*. They belong to a genre called *itihasa* – a narrative of past events filled with philosophical observations and commentary. Both were passed down orally for hundreds of years. The *Ramayana* was probably written down in the third century CE, while the *Mahabharata* began to be written down earlier and extended much later. It is difficult to date the events of the poems, since many passages were added later.

The *Mahabharata* – the world's longest poem, with more than 200,000 verses – describes a battle between two branches of a family, the

Rama, his brother Lakshamana and his wife Sita preparing
a meal in the forest, 1815–25, illustration from *Ramayana*.

Kauravas and the Pandavas. It is set in the region between the Ganga
and Yamuna rivers, near present-day Delhi, and recounts events that may
have taken place between the ninth and eighth centuries BCE. Intervening
in the narrative is Krishna, a local chief or king with divine powers, who
is both a relative of and advisor to the Pandavas. The story is interspersed
with philosophical and religious discourse, including the *Bhagavad Gita*,
one of the most important texts of Hinduism.

The much shorter *Ramayana* is set further east and may describe
local conflict between the newly emerging monarchies and the forest
tribes in the first millennium BCE. Its authorship is attributed to the poet

Valmiki, who lived in the fifth or fourth century BCE, but there are many versions in Sanskrit and regional languages. It tells the story of Rama, the exiled king of Ayodhya, and his wife Sita, who is abducted by the demon king Ravana and rescued by Rama with the help of the monkey general Hanuman. Rama and Sita are considered by some Hindus to be the ideal man and woman and Rama's kingdom the ideal state.

The heroes of both epics are ksatriyas, for whom hunting is a way of life, and the epics contain many references to hunting and the consumption of meat. For example, in the *Ramayana*, Rama's brother Laksmana kills eight antelopes; after drying the meat in the sun, Sita offers portions to the gods and then proceeds to enjoy the meal. In the *Mahabharata*, the exiled Pandava brothers feed themselves by 'collecting the produce of the wilderness and killing the deer with pure arrows, first dedicating a portion of the food to the brahmins and themselves eating the rest'. This diet was apparently healthy, because no one there 'looked pale or ill or was lean or weak or was melancholy or terrified'.[15] The *Mahabharata* describes a banquet given by Rama's father, King Dasaratha:

Sugar cane, sweets of various kinds, honey, crushed barley, wine and other excellent drinks, hot rice in heaps as high as mountains, milk, a stew, other fare combining the six tastes and countless other dishes with sweets made of jaggery were distributed . . .

The men beheld countless dishes of mutton, pork, venison and other meats cooked in fruit juices and fried in butter, with cloves, caraway seeds and lentils simmering gently in them. Thousand of vessels were filled with spiced rice and garnished with flowers and flags . . . The trees dripped honey and the lakes were filled with the sparkling wine Maireya and banked with dressed viands such as deer, chickens and peacocks. Hundreds and thousands of dishes were provided and myriads of vessels filled with yoghurt, mixed with caraway seeds, ginger and other fragrant spices were served there.[16]

A feast given by the Pandavas' father, King Yudhisthira, is equally lavish:

Clean cooks, under the supervision of diligent stewards, served large pieces of meat roasted on spits; meat cooked as stews and sauces made of tamarind and pomegranate; young buffalo calves roasted on spits with ghee dripping on them; the same fried in ghee, seasoned with sour fruit, rock salt and fragrant leaves; large haunches of venison boiled in different ways with spices and mangoes and sprinkled over with condiments; shoulders and rounds of animals dressed in ghee, sprinkled with sea salt and black pepper powder and garnished with radishes, pomegranates, lemons, fragrant herbs, asafoetida and ginger.[17]

Other passages, however, display reservations about eating meat. In the *Mahabharata*, a brahmin asks a pious butcher how he can follow such a cruel profession. He answers that the animals he kills and whose meat he sells acquire *karma* because their meat feeds gods, guests and servants and propitiates the ancestors. If the sacred fire had not been so fond of animals in ancient times, it could never have become people's food. Moreover, he says, 'whoever partakes of animal food after having first offered it duly and respectfully to the gods and the ancestors is not polluted by the act.'

The butcher also argues that he is following his own profession, his *dharma*, which itself is a meritorious act. Even farmers do great harm to animal life by ploughing the earth where countless creatures are living, while men of wisdom and enlightenment destroy animal life while walking or sleeping: 'The earth and the air all swarm with living organisms, which are unconsciously destroyed by men from mere ignorance.' He concludes that the commandment that people should not do harm to any creature was ordained in the old days by men who were ignorant of the true facts of the case.[18]

Another passage contains a much stronger condemnation:

That wretched man who kills living creatures for the sake of those who would eat them commits great sin. The eater's sin is not as great. That wretched man who, following the path of religious rites and sacrifices as laid down in the Vedas, would kill a living creature from a desire to eat its flesh, will certainly go to hell. That man who having eaten flesh abstains from it afterwards acquires great merit on account of such abstention from sin. He who arranges for obtaining flesh, he who approves of those arrangements, he who kills, he who buys or sells, he who cooks, and he who eats it [acquire the sin of those who] are all considered as eaters of flesh. [Therefore] that man who

Recipes from the Pākadarpaṣa

Aubergine

Cut an aubergine into small pieces and put in hot water for 10 minutes. Remove from the water and set aside in a clean bowl. Take ground cumin, ground coriander and ground black pepper and add fully ripe tamarind, powdered mango and curd. Mix well, and coat the aubergine pieces with the paste. In a frying pan, heat a little ghee and fry the spiced aubergine pieces. Remove from the heat and add flowers and camphor for fragrance. Wrap the aubergine pieces in areca palm leaves and sauté in hot ghee, then remove from the palm leaves and serve.

Bitter Melon

Cut off the ends of a fresh bitter gourd and cut into equal-sized pieces. Place the pieces in a pan, add rock salt and the juice of jambiri nimbu (Indian lemon), and cook, covered (otherwise it will be bitter). Remove from the heat and sauté the pieces in fresh ghee. Toast asafoetida powder in a pan. Make a powder of pepper, cinnamon, bay leaves, cardamom and nagkesar (the dried buds of the tree *Mesua ferrea*), and add it to the asafoetida. Sprinkle the mixture with ground fenugreek, ground cumin, ground coriander and ground box myrtle. Add camphor and kasturi for fragrance. Pour cold water on the spice mix, add the pieces of bitter gourd and cook over a low heat. Deep-fry the cooked pieces in ghee and serve.[19]

wishes to avoid disaster should abstain from the meat of every living creature.[20]

These contradictions may be the result of passages added at different times or by different authors, and incorporate both brahmanical practice and popular views.

The *Mahabharata* contains a great many digressions, some related to food. Bhima, one of the five Pandava brothers, was famous for both his enormous appetite and his cooking prowess. For a time he was forced to disguise himself as a cook at the court of the king of Virata, who was impressed by his mouth-watering dishes.

The mythical Nala, the king of Nishada, is said to be the author of the first Indian cookbook, *Pakasastra* (*The Science of Cooking*). A series of events reduced him to the role of charioteer for the king of Ayodhya. He prepared a meal for the ruler with such success that he became head of the king's kitchen and eventually regained his own throne. His recipes were documented in a Sanskrit text called *Pākadarpaṣa* or *Nalapāka*, a work in 760 verses divided into eleven chapters. Various versions of the text have been printed in Sanskrit and some regional languages, although whether they are based on the original is a matter of contention. Even today, cooks in North India are called 'maharajah', perhaps in his honour, and the term 'Nalapaka' (Nala's cuisine) refers to food of excellent quality. It is also the name of several restaurants and a popular television cooking show.

THE *BHAGAVAD GITA*

One of the most famous texts in Indian literature is the *Bhagavad Gita*, or *Song of the Lord*, a dialogue in the *Mahabharata* between Krishna, who is serving as Arjuna's charioteer and advisor, and Arjuna, on the eve of a battle against his cousins (the Kauravas). Arjuna is paralysed by doubt: on one hand, it is his duty as a warrior to fight; on the other, that would entail killing his friends and relatives. Krishna's message is that liberation from suffering and repeated rebirth lies in disciplined action (*karma-yoga*) in conformity with one's *dharma*, without concern for the results. Thus it is Arjuna's duty to fight.

In his discussion of *dharma*, Krishna defines three basic qualities (*gunas*) that are still central to Indian thinking about food: *sattvic*, which is often translated as lucid, pure, dispassionate; *rajasic*, translated as passionate, restless, energetic; and *tamasic*, slothful, dull, lethargic, ignorant. These qualities define a person's nature, which determines what he eats; in turn, his taste expresses his nature. Brahmins, *yogis*, meditators and students who have *sattvic* dispositions should eat *sattvic* foods; ksatriyas, who needed to be energetic and warlike, *rajasic* foods; while *tamasic* foods are associated with outcastes. Krishna says:

> Foods that please lucid men
> Are savoury, smooth, firm and rich

They promote long life, lucidity
Strength, health, pleasure and delight.

Passionate men crave foods
That are bitter, sour, salty, hot
Pungent, harsh and burning
Causing pain, grief and sickness.

The food that pleases
Men of dark inertia is stale,
Unsavoury, putrid, and spoiled,
Leavings unfit for sacrifice.[21]

Other texts, especially those associated with hatha yoga, define the different categories of food in more detail.[22] *Sattvic* foods include rice, barley, wheat, fresh fruit and vegetables (especially green leafy ones), green dal, milk, fresh yoghurt, almonds, seeds, crystallized sugar, dry ginger, cucumber and ghee. *Rajasic* foods include fermented foods that have not been freshly made, cheeses, some root vegetables, fish, eggs, salty, sour and hot foodstuffs, white sugar, spices and (in modern texts) coffee and tea. *Tamasic* foods include leftovers more than a day old, preserved foods, fried foods, meat, alcohol and other intoxicants and (in modern texts) fast food and canned food.

FASTING

An important feature of Hindu dietary practices that became common during this period is fasting. The *Bhavishya Purana* (first composed in 500 BCE and added to over the centuries) prescribes nearly 140 fasts every year. The eighth and eleventh days of the first half of the lunar month were cited as fast days, while other days were sacred to various deities. The Sanskrit word for fasting, *vrata*, means 'vow'. Today, Hindus undertake a fast for many reasons. It can be a mandatory part of a religious festival, a form of worship, out of gratitude for a blessing, a petition to a god for a favour, an instrument of self-discipline or a method of physical cleansing. Women generally fast more than men and have special fast days on which they pray for blessings for their husbands and family, including an annual fast, *karva chauth*, observed in North India. Children are not expected to fast.

Often, fasting does not connote total abstention from food but rather a restricted way of eating. The dishes are always vegetarian. At its least rigorous, it may mean cooking dishes in pure ghee instead of oil, or replacing sea salt with rock salt. Sometimes only *kaccha* ('uncooked', but including boiled) foods are permitted. Meals might be taken only once a day, in the morning. At the most rigorous, no food at all is eaten, and only sips of water are allowed. Some Hindus fast on a certain day of the week, often Tuesday, or on the eleventh day of the lunar fortnight, called Ekadashi. Communal fasts are associated with religious holidays such as Ram Navami, Mahashivratri and Janamasthami. Hindu astrologers recommend daily fasts for warding off problems caused by the planetary bodies, with certain food prescribed to keep negative influences at bay.

Today even the most secular Hindu follows traditional funeral rites when a parent or other close relative dies. All eating and cooking activities in a household stop until the body is cremated, which is done as soon as possible. The eldest son of the deceased, the chief mourner, symbolically lights the crematory fire. A household's normal food patterns are suspended for ten to thirteen days, depending on the community. What is eaten and prepared during this period varies widely. In an orthodox Hindu family, only one meal a day may be eaten, frying is prohibited and spices are eliminated, especially turmeric (a symbol of auspicious events). The chief mourner may have to cook his own food, which might consist of boiled white rice, dal and bread. Families that normally eat meat may take only vegetarian dishes during this period. According to an ancient custom, on the thirteenth day family members feed rice balls to cows and then to crows, who, it is believed, will carry the soul of the deceased to heaven. The fast then ends, and a lavish feast is held for family and friends. Every year on the anniversary of the death a ceremony is held and special vegetarian dishes may be eaten. Hindu widows traditionally become vegetarian, and in times past were expected to lead very austere lives.

A common form of fasting involves a category of food called *phalahar*. Foods are divided into two categories: *anna* – those that are harvested with the help of special equipment, such as rice, wheat, barley and lentils – and *phala*, those that grow without special cultivation, for example, wild grains, vegetables, fruit, certain roots and tubers, leaves and flowers. Only the latter are permitted in a *phalahar* meal. This division can be traced back to the practices of the ascetics. Breads and snacks are made of water-chestnut flour or lotus-seed flour instead of wheat and other grains. Other prohibited foods include onions, turmeric, garlic, ginger, sea salt, urad dal (perhaps because it is black and resembles meat) and spices. Milk, ghee and water are allowed, as are tea, coffee and soft drinks.

Jains share many festivals with Hindus, but these are often marked by abstinence from food, rather than by feasting. The major Jain festival is Paryusanan, an eight- or ten-day period in August or September during which all Jains are supposed to emulate the austere practices of monks and nuns as closely as they can. Some people fast totally for the entire period, drinking only boiled water; others fast only on the final day. On the last day they ask forgiveness of those they have offended. During Siddha Chakra, which is observed twice a year, Jains take only water and one food, which is boiled, each day. In April, Jains observe Akshyatriya, a day on which sugar-cane juice is offered to those who have fasted throughout the year.

LIFE TRANSITIONS

Food is central to life transitions, including marriage, pregnancy and the birth of a child. All communities spend a great deal of time, energy and money arranging and celebrating marriages for their children. Every stage of the marriage process is celebrated by entertaining. The festivities – which can last for days and involve thousands of guests – drive less affluent families into lifelong debt. The banquet, rather than the ceremony, is the focal point of weddings. The bride's and groom's families jockey for position and status, and the amount and quality of the food served at wedding meals becomes symbolic of prestige and respect. People freely discuss the meals they are served and compare them with those at other weddings they have attended.[23]

Events before the wedding include the settlement of the terms of the marriage, the announcement of the engagement, the betrothal ceremony, and so on. These occasions are associated with offering snacks and sweets or a full meal, sending food to the other family, and the exchange of auspicious foods, especially sweets. In South India, the conclusion of the marriage negotiations is marked by the exchange of paan among the family members making the arrangements. In some regions fish, a symbol of good luck, happiness and prosperity, plays an important part. In West Bengal and Bangladesh, for example, the bride's family presents gifts to the groom's family, including a large carp decorated with flowers and sometimes even made up with lipstick or a bindi (the red dot on a married woman's forehead) to resemble the bride.[24]

The wedding feast is paid for by the bride's family and prepared by professional caterers with their own equipment and ingredients. Traditionally the banquet would be held in a large tent on the family's property or near by. Guests sat in long rows on the floor, and the food was served on banana leaves in front of them. Teams of servers would go up and down the rows carrying large pots from which they ladled food on to the leaves. Copious amounts of ghee were poured over the food, signifying richness and auspiciousness. Among brahmins and orthodox Hindus, the wedding banquet was always vegetarian. Water or butter-milk were served as beverages, rarely alcohol. Today tables and chairs are becoming more common, although banana leaves may still be used as plates; wealthy and even middle-class people hold receptions at clubs or luxury hotels. The meal may be served buffet-style and include a few Thai, Mexican and Continental dishes, as well as cocktails.

Birth and pregnancy are also accompanied by special foods. According to Ayurveda and folk belief, pregnancy is considered a 'hot' condition. As a result, the pregnant woman is not allowed to eat what-ever foods are considered 'hot' in her region, since it is believed that they will cause miscarriage. In Bengal, for example, pineapple and certain fish are considered hot. Cold foods such as milk products, on the other hand,

Early 19th-century South Indian painting depicting the *annaprasana* ceremony, when a child is given his first solid food.

are considered to promote strength and a successful delivery. In parts of North India, the mother's parents send her dried dates, pieces of coconut and wheat bread and laddoos fried in ghee in the fifth month, while in Andhra Pradesh, she is fed spicy and sour dishes to tempt her to eat. For five days after the birth of her child, the mother is given a semi-liquid diet, including semolina cooked in milk, light chicken broth and fruit. On the sixth day, she is fed a large meal consisting of a great variety of rich foods, traditionally served in groups of six. The purpose is to give the nursing child strength and also to expose it indirectly to a variety of foods.[25] When a child is six months old, a ceremony called *annaprasana* takes place in which it is fed solid food for the first time, in the form of a sweet rice pudding.

SIX

Food and Indian Doctors,
600 BCE–600 CE

One of the most valuable sources of information about ancient Indian food is medical texts. In India, food and medicine have always been virtually interchangeable. All foods have properties that exert an influence on the body and the mind – including foods that are otherwise prohibited. Not only did Indian doctors *not* advocate a vegetarian diet for their patients, but also they recommended the consumption of meat, garlic, mushrooms and even alcohol for many conditions. And no apologies were offered. As an eleventh-century physician wrote, 'the recommendations of medicine are not intended to help someone achieve virtue (*dharma*). What are they for, then? They are aimed at achieving health.'[1]

The existence of competing and sometimes contradictory food ideologies is not unique to India. As the food historian Ken Albala points out in his *Food in Early Modern Europe*, an elegant meat pie may have been fashionable among the elite but was banned by the Catholic Church during Lent, while a physician might forbid it because its many ingredients made it impossible to digest.[2] Physicians themselves were anything but united in their opinions about food – a situation that is just as true today as it was 2,000 years ago.

In Vedic times diseases were associated with supernatural forces. The physician of the Vedic gods was Dhanvantari, who in some parts of India is worshipped as a god. The *Atharvaveda*, written around 1000 BCE, is a collection of incantations and spells against disease, demons, wizards and noxious animals, but it also contains a few recommendations of medical treatment. Black pepper, for example, is recommended as a treatment for arrow wounds.

Greek observers commented on the excellent health and physiques of Indians. Alexander the Great was so impressed by Ayurvedic practitioners that he sent several Indian physicians to Greece, where they may have influenced Greek medicine (and perhaps introduced the theory of the humours, although this is a matter of debate). Sanskrit medical works were translated into Arabic and Persian. During the golden period of Arab civilization (749–1258 CE), Greek and Indian physicians competed for prominence at the caliph's court in Baghdad.

In some parts of India, especially Bengal and Kerala, Ayurvedic physicians, known as vaidyas, formed a distinct caste and the profession became hereditary.[3] One branch specialized in surgery. Centuries ago, Indian surgeons had special instruments to perform such procedures as rhinoplasty, cataract removal, amputation and Caesarean sections. In the eighteenth century Europeans went to India to study these procedures. The taboo on contact with human corpses was so strong, however, that Indians' knowledge of internal anatomy was limited.

The main concern of Ayurvedic physicians was the prevention and treatment of illness. They made house calls and also saw patients in their own homes, which had storerooms filled with drugs and medical equipment. Physicians made their own drugs from herbs and other plants, which they either collected or grew in their gardens. The pharmacopoeia was very large: Susruta (see below) mentions more than 700 medicinal herbs, and the number increased over time with the introduction of drugs from Western and Central Asia. The Himalayas were especially famous for their medicinal herbs.

The goal of the more ambitious vaidyas was to enter the service of a king. Large courts had many physicians who reported to the king's personal physician. His duties were not only to treat the king when he fell ill, but also to promote his health, longevity and virility. The vaidya supervised the royal kitchen, ensuring that the king's diet was healthy, and was also responsible for detecting and preventing attempts at poisoning him, which – judging by the amount of attention paid to it in the medical literature – was an ever-present threat.

The main Ayurvedic texts comprise the writings of three men called the Great Triad: Susruta, who may have taught medicine between 700 and 600 BCE at the university in Benares; Caraka, a physician who lived in the second century CE or possibly was a composite of several physicians; and Vagbhata, a physician who may have lived in the Sindh in the sixth or seventh century CE. The principle texts are *Caraka Samhita* (*Caraka's Encyclopedia* or *Compendium*), a monumental work three times as large as any extant texts from Greek medicine, and *Susruta Samhita*, both of which contain chapters on food and diet.[4] Dating these two texts is difficult. There may have been an original text, which was redacted by physicians in the first centuries CE. Vagbhata's *Astangahrdaya*, or *Heart of Medicine*, is considered to be the greatest synthesis of Indian medical thought, and was translated into Tibetan, Arabic, Chinese and other languages. Another important source of information is the so-called Bower Manuscript (named after the British officer who discovered it in 1890), a group of medical texts dating back to the fourth or fifth century CE, which contains among other things a famous treatise on garlic.

The tradition of writing medical texts continued well into the eighteenth century. In about 1300 CE the physician Sarngadhara wrote a popular treatise that included many recipes. Another work written in Sanskrit verse was the *Vaidyajivanam* (A Doctor's Livelihood) by Lolimbaraja, a late sixteenth-century physician who lived near Pune. *Ksemakutuhalam* (Diet and Well-being) by Ksemasarma, which appeared in the mid-sixteenth century, is an interesting work: besides discussing the medicinal properties of various foods, the author is interested in the preparation and flavour of dishes, and even gives quantities and measurements.

THE PRINCIPLES OF AYURVEDA

A central concept in Ayurveda is that everything that exists in the universe – the macrocosm – exists in the microcosm of the human body. All matter is made up of five elements, earth, water, fire, air and ether, which in turn are classified into ten pairs of contrasting qualities: heavy and light, cold and hot, oily/moist and dry, slow and intense, stable and mobile, soft and hard, clear and sticky, smooth and rough, subtle and gross, and solid and liquid.

Body parts such as bone and cartilage are mainly earthy. Fat and vital bodily fluids, such as lymph, blood, semen and mucus, are predominantly watery. Digestive fluids, endocrine secretions, body heat and substances that produce mental awareness are fiery. Everything mobile, including the nervous system, is air. All channels through which things pass – blood and lymph vessels, pores, nerves – are ethereal. In humans, elements manifest themselves in three *doshas* (a Sanskrit word variously translated as 'humours' and 'faults'), which flow within the body. The three *doshas* are *vata* – a product of air and ether, sometimes translated as wind; *pitta* – fire and water, or bile; and *kapha* – made from water and earth, or phlegm.

Vata (located mainly in the large intestine) regulates all physical and mental motion, a concept consistent with recent findings concerning the role of gut flora in warding off diabetes, inflammation and other conditions; *pitta* (in the navel) is in charge of transformations, such as the process of digestion; while *kapha* (in the chest) stabilizes the other processes.[5] Their attributes can be summed up as movement, metabolism and stability, respectively.

The three *doshas* keep the body healthy only as long as they can flow and accumulate in the right places. Under- or overproduction of the *doshas*, or their accumulation in the wrong part of the body, causes irritation or inflammation and therefore disease. Many things can affect the balance of the *doshas*: the season, a person's age and level of physical activity, emotional stress, external heat and cold, and diet. People are especially prone to disease at the junctions of the seasons, and regular purification and fasting help to protect against this. Some of these practices have been institutionalized into holiday rituals and festivals.

There are many ways of controlling and adjusting the *doshas*, including massage, exercise, proper sleeping habits, herbal medicine and especially diet. As Caraka wrote, 'Without proper diet, medicines are of no use; with a proper diet, medicines are unnecessary.'[6] Thus the physician plays an active role in regulating and supervising his patient's diet and food habits. Often the same dish is prescribed for both healthy people and patients, the difference being the addition of medicinal herbs to the latter.

Digestion is extremely important in Ayurveda, since if one cannot digest one's food, it cannot produce the proper effects. The Sanskrit word for digestion (*pacaka*) also means cooking, and the digestive force itself is called fire (*agni*). Once food is cooked by this fire, it turns into a pulpy substance in the stomach, which is then transformed by heat into blood, flesh, fat, bone marrow and finally semen, considered the highest bodily essence. The sperm-producing quality of a food is considered extremely important. (No equivalent is given for women.) Stagnant pools of un-digested food, called *ama*, inevitably breed disease. To eliminate *ama*, an Ayurvedic cure often begins with fasting, considered one of the most important medicines. The source of a body's energy and strength is an essence called *ojas*, which is both the cause and the effect of good digestion. Foods are characterized as light (easy to digest) or heavy (difficult to digest).

There are six basic tastes (*rasas*): sweet, sour, salty, bitter, pungent and astringent. A person's diet should contain all six tastes to maintain balance and promote health, and today most of India's cuisines include at least some of them. However, the astringent taste has all but disappeared, except in Assamese dishes referred to as *khar*, or alkaline. Taste also stimulates the appetite, promotes digestion and affects the *doshas* in various ways. For example, bitter foods reduce *pitta* and *kapha* but increase *vata*; sweet foods increase *kapha* but reduce *pitta* and *vata*.

Ayurvedic texts use dozens of adjectives to describe the medical properties of food, based on the six tastes, the ten pairs of qualities, and so on. For example, food may be described as sweet or acid. Sweet food (which includes most meat and milk) is easy to digest, calms wind and encourages the production of phlegm, while acid food has the opposite qualities. But these descriptions are not to be taken literally. As the anthropologist Francis Zimmermann wrote, 'The adjectives describing the meat – "cold" and "unctuous" – clearly have no descriptive value; they should be interpreted as strictly conventional, as indicating in technical language particular pharmaceutical processes and effects.'[7]

Another classification is the division of plants, animals and people into categories based on their natural habitats. The first category, *jangala*, denotes a dry area with little water, few trees, a lot of wind and abundant sunshine, such as the Indus–Ganges basin; the steppes; the semi-desert and desert of Punjab, Rajasthan and Gujarat; and dry tropical forests stretching from Uttar Pradesh to Tamil Nadu.[8] The opposite category, *anupa*, covers places that are wet and tree-covered, such as marshes, rainforests, mangroves swamps and mountains. This region includes the monsoon forests of the east and west coasts of India and the rainforests of Bengal, Assam and Kerala.

Diseases are said to be rarer in *jangala* areas: people who live there have tough, dry bodies. *Anupa* areas are full of *doshas*, and their inhabitants tend to be soft and delicate. Certain diseases are endemic in both terrains, and a person who wants to avoid falling victim to them must eat food that has opposite qualities to the region in which he or she lives. *Jangala* animals include the many varieties of deer and antelope that once thrived on the subcontinent, and game birds such as quail and partridge.[9] They eat light food and their meat is accordingly light and easy to digest. The meat of creatures that live in *anupa* regions or wallow in mud (pigs, water buffaloes and rhinoceroses, for example) is heavy and hard to digest.

Food Prescriptions

The Ayurvedic texts contain many descriptions of dishes and ingredients and their effects on health. Some items are difficult to identify, because the words have disappeared from modern Indian languages or the same animal is called by a dozen or more names. In the *Susruta Samhita*, the author writes that the intelligent physician determines what food his patient should eat after taking into account several things: the cause and nature of the disease; the season of the year; the attributes of the ingredients; the properties they acquire through flavouring and combination; and the patient's natural longings for a certain food when his *doshas* are deranged. A food's properties depend on the method of preparation and cooking more than on the ingredients, and on the amount more than how it is cooked. For example, boiled rice is heavy to digest, while fried rice is light. A heavy food should be eaten until one's appetite is only half satisfied, while a substance that is light to digest may be eaten to satiety.

Meat is very important in Ayurvedic cures. Caraka lists four *jangala* animals that should *always* be kept on the premises of an Ayurvedic hospital: quail, partridge, hare and antelope. Meat cooked with ghee, yoghurt, sour rice gruel, sour fruit (pomegranate, Indian gooseberry) and pungent spices, such as black pepper and asafoetida, is considered very wholesome. Another method is to cut meat into pieces, fry it in clarified butter, boil it until the water dries up, then sprinkle it with cumin seeds and other spices. Minced meat is shaped into patties that are cooked over charcoal or coated with ghee, threaded on skewers and roasted (similar to modern chapli and seekh kebab). Meat is marinated in mustard oil and aromatic spices, then roasted over charcoal until it is the colour of honey. Although these meat dishes are described as heavy to digest, they also improve the appetite and intellect, build up fresh tissue and increase the production of semen.

A thin meat broth is prescribed for shortness of breath, coughs and consumption; weak memory; and loss of appetite and emaciation arising from fever, endocarditis and other diseases affecting a person's vital energy. Boiled minced meat cooked with treacle, clarified butter, black pepper, long pepper and ginger imparts strength. A broth prepared with pomegranate juice and spices is considered particularly beneficial since it subdues the action of all three deranged humours. But meat whose essence has already been removed, perhaps by overcooking, is useless, and dried meat is especially hard to digest.

Rice is a particularly versatile remedy. A dish of rice prepared with clarified butter, meat, sour fruit or any lentil helps to build new tissue and imparts strength and rotundity. Fried rice alleviates vomiting and dysentery; pulverized, it alleviates vomiting, thirst and a burning sensation of the skin. Immature or newly harvested rice builds tissue. Old or well-matured rice promotes the healing of fractured bones. Old rice is easier to digest than new rice, and raw rice is the least easy to digest.

By far one of the most common methods of preparing rice under Ayurvedic guidance is to boil it into gruel or porridge. (Monier Monier-Williams's *Dictionary of Sanskrit* lists 80 words related to gruel.) Rice gruel is prescribed for invalids or people who have gone through a regimen of purging and emetics. Kanjika is a sour rice gruel made by leaving boiled rice overnight until it ferments slightly, and is drunk hot or cold. (In modern Hindi, *kanji* or *ganji* means the water in which rice is boiled, and is often fed to invalids.)

Manda (today the name of a steamed sweet rice dumpling) was a porridge made by frying rice with long pepper and ground ginger and then boiling it in water. Yavagu, a word that can signify either rice or a thin gruel made from another grain, refers to another porridge-like dish made by cooking grain with meat, fruit and vegetables. It has an extremely coarse texture and is hard to digest, but strengthens the body. Another rice preparation is payasa (modern payesh or payasam), a pudding made from boiled rice, milk and sugar.

According to the old Ayurvedic texts, mung dal has many benefits. Cooked with grapes and pomegranate juice it subdues deranged *doshas*; prepared with snake gourd or neem it cures skin diseases; and boiled with horseradish it relieves coughs, catarrh, fever and diseases of the throat. Dal made from horse gram is a remedy for asthma, catarrh and diseases of the bladder and abdominal glands. Prepared with pomegranate or amla juice, dal pacifies deranged humours and helps to cure epilepsy and obesity. Other ingredients that can be added to boiled lentils are dairy products, rice gruel (kanjika), cumin seeds, black pepper and certain fruit. A soup made from any unhusked lentil is light and wholesome.

Vegetables should sometimes be avoided during therapy, since they are considered astringent and may close the channels. Susruta has little to say about vegetables, other than that green leafy vegetables (shaka) boiled well, thoroughly drained and then cooked in oil, are wholesome, while those cooked in a different manner are not.

> ### *Shrikhand*
>
> 3 litres (5¼ pints) milk
> 1 tbsp yoghurt (as starter)
> 1 tbsp sugar, or to taste
> a few strands of saffron, lightly toasted or soaked in
> a little warm milk
> 5 green cardamom pods, ground
> chopped almonds and pistachios
>
> Boil the milk and let it cool a little. While still warm, add the yoghurt and mix well. Cover and leave in a warm place overnight.
>
> Next morning, pour the yoghurt into a white muslin cloth, tie the four corners in a knot and hang it over a bowl until all the liquid has drained out. (This will take several hours.)
>
> Remove the remaining yoghurt from the cloth and mix with the sugar. Strain the mixture again in the same way.
>
> Add the saffron and ground cardamom and mix well. Garnish with the nuts and serve chilled.

In Ayurveda, ghee is considered a virtual panacea. As an eighteenth-century physician wrote, 'ghee rejuvenates, is tasty, alleviates *pitta* and *vata*, removes poisons, prolongs life, promotes growth, and destroys sins and poverty.'[10] It features in many Ayurvedic recipes both as a cooking medium and as a flavouring, and may be prepared with various spices and herbs.

Sweets fried in ghee, roasted in earthenware pots or cooked over a charcoal fire are light and tonic, and improve the complexion and eyesight, while those that are deep-fried are heavy and pungent and irritate the skin. *Susruta Samhita* lists a large number of sweet and savoury dishes – what today would be termed snack foods – although details of how they are made are scanty. Gaudikas are wheat-flour balls filled with treacle, perhaps similar to Rajasthani choorma. Sattakas are made by mixing yoghurt with jaggery and powdered trikatu (a mixture of ginger, black pepper and long pepper that is sold at Ayurvedic pharmacies), straining it through a piece of cloth and flavouring it with camphor and pomegranate seeds. A phenaka is a deep-fried pastry made from flour, ghee and jaggery and stuffed with spiced mung dal or minced meat (a dish that sounds very like the modern street foods dal puri and kachauri).

In Susruta's view, the best restorative is water mixed with molasses, unrefined sugar and sour fruit, and scented with camphor. Drinks made with pomegranate juice are very soothing and strengthening. An important aid to digestion, especially after a very heavy meal or one that deranges the *doshas*, is an after-dinner drink – an Ayurvedic version of the French *digestif*. Common *digestifs* are cold or warm water, a drink made from mung dal, the juice of sour fruit, sour rice gruel, milk, concentrated meat broth, asava (wine) and madya (spirits.)

Susruta is as assiduous in matching alcoholic beverages with food as any French sommelier. The main categories are *sura* and *asava*, but the precise meaning of these terms is not clear, and translators usually use the generic word 'wine'. He recommends a particular drink for every category of bird and animal, and the long list of alcohol beverages demonstrates the imagination and ingenuity of Indian wine-makers and distillers. This table shows some of Susruta's recommended pairings.

Another beverage recommended by the Ayurvedic physicians is the urine of cows, buffaloes, goats, sheep and other animals that is pungent, hot, light and saline. This stimulates the heart, purifies the blood and stimulates the appetite.[11]

Caraka Samhita is a composite work that may have been written by many authors over centuries. It consists of 120 chapters divided into eight parts covering diet, the causes of disease, anatomy, embryology, diagnosis, therapy and pharmacy. He summarizes the properties of various foods:

> In keeping with its nature, water wets, salt melts, acid digests, honey joins broken parts, clarified butter anoints, milk enlivens, meat causes growth, meat soup nourishes the weak, liquor builds up weakened flesh, wine called sidhu [prepared from the juice of ripe sugar cane] causes scraping of tissue, wine prepared from grape juice stimulates the digestive fire, phanita [thickened sugar-cane juice] causes the accumulation of *doshas*, yoghurt causes oedema, sesame-oil sediment causes fatigue and depression, soup prepared from urad dal produces excess faeces.[12]

Caraka lists 60 oilseeds, including sesame, mustard, safflower, linseed, castor, chironji, bael and kola, plus many kinds of animal fat together

Food and Beverage Pairings
Recommended by Susruta

Dish	Recommended beverage
Oily food	Hot water
Honey, yoghurt, payasa	Cold water
Rice or mung dal	Milk, meat essence
Diet heavy with meat	Wine
Meal with a lot of cereals	Sour soup made from jujubes?
Venison	Wine with long pepper
Seed-eating fowl	Jujube or fig wine
Meat of scavengers	Fig-tree wine
Meat from cave-dwelling animals	Coconut, date-palm wine
Birds of prey	Wine from withania plant (Indian ginseng)
Animal with unbifurcated hoofs	Wine made with triphala (a mixture of three varieties of myrobalan)
Animal that lives in marshy or damp land, molluscs or lizards	Liqueur made from water chestnuts
Sour fruit	Lotus-root wine
Astringent fruit	Pomegranate or rattan(?)-fruit wine
Sweet fruit	Kanda(?) wine with trikatus
Fruit of the palmyra palm	Sour, fermented rice gruel
Pungent fruit	Rattan fruit, kind of millet
Long pepper	Wine from a herb called goat's head
Pumpkin	Tree turmeric or caper wine
Sun creeper, green vegetables, cucumber	Triphala wine
Date-palm tree pith or marrow	Wine from sour fruit

Source: *The Sushruta Samhita: An English Translation Based on Original Sanskrit Texts*, trans. Kaviraj Kunja Lal Bhishagratna (New Delhi, 2006), vol. I, pp. 457–66. While the literature refers to various kinds of alcohol there are no descriptions of the method of production. One scholar argues that, based on linguistic and archaeological evidence, Indians may have distilled alcohol as early as the fourth century and possibly as far back as the Indus Valley civilization. See F. R. Allchin, 'India: The Ancient Home of Distillation?', *Man*, n.s., XIV/1 (March 1979), pp. 55–63.

with their effects on the health. More than 60 fruits and nuts are cited, including apples, almonds, bananas, pistachios, walnuts, four varieties of jujube, two varieties each of grape and pomegranate, the nagaranga (a kind of orange) and the starfruit or carambola, which is native to eastern India and Southeast Asia. A dozen varieties of sugar cane are mentioned, with a description of their medical benefits. In Caraka's view, the whiter and purer the sugar, the 'cooler' it was. Barley was a very common ingredient. It was ground into flour and made into cakes (kulmasa and yavapupa), prepared as a porridge, fried (dhana), or sprouted and fried (viruda-dhana). Other dishes include thin and thick rice gruels (pepa and velepika), rice water flavoured with long pepper and ginger (laja manda), a gruel made of fried rice (laja-saktu) and deep-fried spirals of rice-flour dough (saskuli). Some dishes sound delicious by modern standards: pupalika, a rice- or wheat-flour cake filled with honey or mung dal paste and fried in ghee; rasala, churned yoghurt flavoured with cinnamon leaf, cardamom, ground cinnamon, cumin and ginger; and vesavara, minced meat cooked with long pepper, black pepper and ginger (a dish that appears in later collections of recipes).

In prescribing meat, the physician must take into account the animal's habitat and inherent nature, the part of the animal, the method of cooking and the amount, which depends on the strength of the patient's digestive fire. Caraka warns against eating too much parched rice, dry meat, dry vegetables, lotus roots or nutmeg, because they are heavy. But sali rice, salt, myrobalan, barley, rainwater, milk, ghee, the meat of animals that live in the forest, honey and green gram can be eaten regularly.

For patients with consumption, Caraka recommends chicken soup mixed with sour and pungent ingredients and flavoured with ghee. It is also recommended for piles, fever and wind disorders. Other health-giving preparations are chicken soup boiled with sweet wheat dumplings, and a broth of four birds: sparrow, partridge, chicken and peacock.[13]

An interesting passage in Caraka's *Samhita* indicates an awareness of the dietary habits of other groups in India and beyond:

Bahlikas, Pahlavas, Cinas, Sulikas, Sakas and Yavanas [northern tribes, some of Central Asian origin] are habituated to consuming meat, wheat, mead, [to] fighting and [to] fire. Easterners have an affinity for fish, while the people of Sindh have an affinity for milk. Tradition has it that Asmakas and Avantikas [of central India] have an affinity for oil and sour tastes. The

How to Give up Bad Eating Habits and Lose Weight

Suppose someone wants to give up unwholesome barley in favour of wholesome red rice. On the first day he eats three parts barley to one part rice. On the second day two parts of each; on the third day the same again. On the fourth day one part barley to three parts rice, and the same on the fifth and sixth days. From the seventh day onwards he eats only the wholesome rice.

Cakrapanidatta, an eleventh-century Ayurveda scholar and physician, quoted in Dominik Wujastyk, *The Roots of Ayurveda: Selections from Sanskrit Medical Writings* (London, 2001), p. 43.

inhabitants of Malaya are known for their affinity for tubers, roots and fruit, while southerners have an affinity for milk and northeasterners for churned drinks. In the central region there is an affinity for barley, wheat and cow's milk. One should prescribe medicines that are in harmony with the affinities of these people, since such affinities give rapid strength and do little harm even in excess.[14]

In Ayurveda, garlic is one of the greatest panaceas. According to the Bower Manuscript (a collection of Sanskrit medical texts discovered in eastern Turkistan in 1890 by Lieutenant Hamilton Bower), garlic was created when the king of demons drank the elixir of immortality and Lord Vishnu cut off his head as punishment. The drops that fell to earth became garlic, but because they flowed from a body, the bulbs are forbidden to brahmins.

The author of the Bower Manuscript, whose name and date remain unknown, describes garlic's qualities and curative powers:

It was ordained by the creator to remove all three humours and to subdue all diseases. It vitiates wind because of its sour, hot and oily nature; pacifies choler because it is sweet and bitter; and mitigates phlegm because of its heat, bitterness and pungency. It strengthens the force of the digestive fire and promotes strength and complexion. It drives away pallid skin disease, appetite loss,

Turmeric, an ancient Indian spice, has many medicinal properties.

abdominal lumps, cough, thinness, leprosy and weak digestion. It removes wind, irregular periods, gripes, phthisis [tuberculosis], bellyache, enlarged spleen and piles. It takes away paralysis of one side, lumbago, worm disease, colic and urinary disorders. It completely conquers lassitude, catarrh, rheumatism of the arms or back, and epilepsy.[15]

To obtain these benefits, a person must first purify his body, worship the gods and drink fresh garlic juice strained through cloth, or gargle the juice mixed with one-third an unspecified kind of alcohol. This should be followed by a meal of milk or soup made from lentils or the meat of *jangala* animals. The patient should then drink wine or equal parts of mead, spirits and mead, plum brandy, rum made from molasses, thick rice liquor, blended liquor, or any other liquor that is available – always with water and drunk one glass at a time to avoid inebriation. Teetotallers can drink warm water, sour fermented rice, barley or bean-husk water or fresh whey.

An alternative treatment is to soak peeled garlic overnight in wine, crush and filter it, and mix the garlic with wine, milk or meat broth. For additional benefit, tender garlic bulbs, crushed and mixed with an equal amount of ghee, should be eaten at dawn for at least ten days together with Bengal quince (bael).

Garlic can be threaded with meat on a spit and roasted; mixed with cold pickled and spiced meats; cooked in ghee and oil with barley meal, fermented rice water and vinegar; added to a meat soup thickened with wheat flour; or mixed with powdered mung beans, green herbs, aromatic spices and salt.

A powerful remedy is a mixture consisting of 32 parts garlic juice, 8 parts yeast, 1 part oil and 6 parts ground garlic, left to rest until it becomes liquid. To it is added 16 parts of the juice of the herb *Gymnema sylvestre* and two more parts ground garlic. After 25 days, the mixture acquires taste, colour and aroma, and can be used as an oil. The author of the Bower Manuscript explains: 'The armies of disease beat a retreat from the man who makes diligent use of this as an oil, or as liquor, just as in a battle the opponents retreat from a person who carries bullets.'[16]

Brahmins are not allowed to eat garlic, but if a cow is given almost no grass for three days and then fed a mixture of two parts grass to one part garlic stalks, a brahmin can consume its milk or yoghurt, ghee or buttermilk made from it with impunity.

GENERAL RULES FOR EATING

Caraka makes some general recommendations for healthy eating. It is not advisable to eat a lot of foods with the same taste at the same time, nor to indulge constantly in dishes with various tastes. Eat only one main meal a day. Avoid bread, which is hard to digest; if you must eat it, drink twice as much water as usual. Take only half portions of heavy foods, but eat as many lighter items as you like. Avoid foods that are incompatible with one another, such as dairy products and fish. (This is one of the earliest mentions of a belief that may have originated in India and which gained wide currency in Africa, the Middle East, Europe and North America.[17]) Other rules are as valid today as they were centuries ago:

Eat properly combined food after digesting the previous meal
    to allow a free passage for all substances
Eat in a congenial, quiet place either alone or with affectionate
    people so that the mind is not depressed
Eat neither hurriedly nor leisurely, to appreciate the qualities of
    the food you are eating

Eat without laughing or talking, with concentration, consid-
ering your constitution and what is good and not good for
you as you eat

Do not eat when you are not hungry and do not fail to eat
when you are hungry

Do not eat when you are angry, depressed or emotionally dis-
traught, or immediately after exercise

Keep as large a gap as possible between meals

Sit to eat whenever possible, facing east

Pray, thanking the Creator for the food you are offering your
digestive fire

Never cook for yourself alone; the gift of food is the best gift
at all

Feed all five senses: look at the food and savour its appearance
and aroma; listen to the sounds it makes, especially when
cooking; eat with your hands to enjoy its texture; chew
each morsel many times to extract its flavour

Stroll about a hundred steps after a meal to assist the digestive
process

Do not eat heavy or *kapha*-producing food like yoghurt and
sesame seeds after sunset, and eat nothing within two hours
before going to bed

Never waste food.[18]

Food should be 'alive' in order to give life to the eater. Raw food is
more alive than cooked food. Overcooked, undercooked, burnt, bad-
tasting, unripe or overripe, putrefied or stale food should never be eaten.
Leftovers should be heated as soon as possible or, ideally, avoided all
together.

A traditional Indian belief is that the materials in which food is
prepared and served affect its properties. Silver and gold are considered
the best materials, since they are non-reactive and 'pure'. In the sixteenth century Akbar's physician advised the head cook that rice cooked
in copper destroyed gas and removed spleen disease, and that rice cooked
in gold alleviated poisons and improved vigour and vitality. Even today,
copper, considered a pure metal, is used to make *thalis*, plated with tin
to negate the effects of the acid.[19] In Susruta's description of a palace
meal, clarified butter is served in metal bowls, liquid foods in silver
bowls, and fruit and confectionary on leaves. Meat dishes are served on

golden plates, soups and meat essences in silver bowls, condiments and buttermilk in stone dishes, and cold milk or fruit juices in copper dishes. Other drinks, wines and cordials are served in earthen pots.

According to Susruta, dishes should also be served in a certain order. Sweet substances are eaten first to subdue wind, followed by sour and salty dishes to stimulate digestion, and finally pungent foods to subdue phlegm. During a meal the diner should frequently rinse his mouth or gargle, since a clean palate enhances the flavour. At the end, the diner cleans his mouth with water and removes food stuck to the teeth with a toothpick, and perhaps chews a betel leaf wrapped around areca nut, camphor, nutmeg and clove – one of the earliest references to paan. After resting for a while, he should walk 100 steps, then lie down in a bed on his left side, all the while enjoying 'soft sounds, pleasant sights, sweet perfumes, soft and velvety touch'.

OTHER MEDICAL THEORIES
Hot and Cold

A popular belief is that foods have heating or cooling properties, depending on their effect on the body. This concept probably travelled from India to the Middle East in the sixth century BCE and later to Greece and Europe, where it became widespread in the Middle Ages. A similar idea exists in China.

Defining a food as hot or cold has little to do with its actual qualities. While most Indians can tell you whether a food is hot or cold, the classification varies by region. For example, wheat is considered a hot food in South India but only moderately hot in the north. Most varieties of lentil are considered cold in western India but hot in the north. Papayas are regarded as extremely heating in South India but not in the north. Most spices are considered hot everywhere, although a few, such as cumin and fennel seeds, are thought to be cold. Certain combinations of foods are also considered deleterious to health, including fish with dairy products, while others are considered beneficial; for example, mangoes and papayas followed by milk.

In summer cold foods are recommended, while in winter and monsoon seasons hot foods are desirable. Certain foods are recommended or prohibited for conditions such as pregnancy and a head cold, although again this varies by region. In some parts of the subcontinent, 'cold' foods are to be avoided during pregnancy on the grounds that they could cause death (which is cold) in the womb, while in other parts hot foods are banned as they could cause miscarriage.

The Three Gunas

A key concept in Indian philosophy is *guna*, a word that means 'qualities' or 'tendencies'. As discussed in chapter Four, there are three *gunas*: *sattvic*, lucid, pure or dispassionate; *rajasic*, passionate, extroverted, interested in sensual pleasures; and *tamasic*, lethargic, dull, ignorant. Each quality is associated with certain foods, which are preferred by people with the same qualities and stimulate the *gunas* in those who eat them.[20]

Although attempts have been made to equate the three *gunas* with the three *doshas*, the concepts come from different traditions and cannot be absolutely correlated. However, an Ayurvedic physician is supposed to be familiar with the presence and functioning of the *gunas* in his patient, and to take it into account in his treatment.

Kaccha versus Pukka

Another distinction made by some Hindus is based on the method of preparation.[21] *Kaccha* foods are those prepared in the family kitchen by boiling or roasting, such as rice, dal, khichri, dry-roasted breads (chapatti, naan) and vegetables – the basic everyday food in rich and poor families that can be supplemented with other dishes.

Kaccha foods are also exclusive. Traditionally a Hindu from a higher caste would eat this category of food at home and give it to or accept it from his relatives only. *Pukka* foods, on the other hand, could be shared with outsiders or purchased in the marketplace. Many fried street foods fall into this category. This distinction is largely disappearing with the weakening of caste boundaries, especially among city-dwellers and young people. However, only *pukka* foods are served at temples and at some community festivals and feasts.

Concerns for safety may have motivated this distinction, since cooking oil has a higher temperature than water and thus eliminates more bacteria.[22] As the historian Arthur Llewellyn Basham wrote:

> It is surprising how many of the instructions in the texts would tend to minimize the dangers of infection and food poisoning. Indian society seems unconsciously to have found a means of remaining healthy as far as possible in a subtropical climate, in its efforts to preserve its ritual purity.[23]

133

Chapattis, also called rotis, are a popular North Indian bread made from wholewheat flour and heated over a hot flame until they puff up.

OTHER SYSTEMS OF MEDICINE

Siddha

This system was developed in South India in the seventh or eighth centuries CE, and today is practised in Tamil-speaking regions. The principles are similar to those of Ayurveda: the human body is considered a replica of the universe, as are food and drugs. The main difference is in the extensive use of metals and minerals in treatment, especially sulphur and mercury.

Unani

The Unani system of medicine (Unani Tibbia) is practised by Muslims. The theoretical framework is derived from the writings of the Greek physicians Hippocrates (460–377 BCE), who is considered to be the father of both allopathic (conventional Western) and Unani medicine, and Galen (*c.* 130–*c.* 210 CE). The Arabic word *Unan* refers to Greece.[24] Unani practitioners are called *Hakims*.

When the Mongols invaded Persia and Central Asia in the fourteenth century CE, many physicians and scholars fled to India, where the Delhi sultans and later the Mughal emperors hired them as court physicians.

Delhi became a centre of Unani medicine, which was at its peak between the thirteenth and seventeenth centuries. During the British rule Unani medicine suffered, but official interest returned after Indian Independence in 1947, and today India is the world leader in Unani medicine, which has its own licensed physicians, hospitals and institutions for education and research.

Unani medicine is based on the Greek theory that assumes the presence of four humours in the body: blood, phlegm, yellow bile and black bile. These humours are composed of the four basic elements: earth, water, air and fire. The seasons also have qualities, as does an individual's temperament, which can be one of four kinds: sanguine, choleric, cold or phlegmatic, or melancholic.

Every person is born with a unique humoral constitution. When the balance of the humours is upset because of external or internal change, disease results. Restoring the quality and balance of the humours is the goal of treatment. Diet is one of the therapies, together with surgery, medicines and regimental treatments (such as massage or steam baths). One tenet is that many diseases can be prevented by regular digestion; conversely, poor digestion can cause illness. Foods that cause indigestion are those that putrefy quickly (milk and fresh fish), those that take time to digest (such as beef), stale foods, spices and chillies, alcohol, strong tea, coffee and oily food. However, any food is acceptable in moderation. Aids to digestion include decoctions and teas made from ajwain (carom) seeds, mint, fennel and coriander seeds; pomegranate juice; and other herbs and spices.

Diet therapy treats ailments by regulating the quality and quantity of a patient's food. As in Ayurveda, treatment often starts with a total fast, which gives the patient's system a chance to rest. People are also advised to eat foods that have the opposite quality to the distemper. For example, a person who has too much of the sanguine humour, which increases heat, should eat cold food, such as barley water and fish, and cooling herbs (although cold and hot are again to some extent determined by local and regional beliefs and customs). Some of the cures may be based on folk remedies: for example, a recommended treatment for influenza starts with ground long pepper mixed with honey and ginger juice, followed by milk and turmeric powder. Weaknesses of specific organs are corrected by eating the same organ of an animal. In both Ayurveda and Unani, bitter and astringent foods are prescribed for diabetes.

Bitter melon, often part of the first course in a Bengali meal, is also a treatment for diabetes in Ayurveda. Late 18th or early 19th century.

TODAY Ayurveda, Siddha and Unani together with allopathy are among the schools of medicine recognized by the Indian government and taught in state colleges. In India recently there has been a resurgence of interest in Ayurveda, especially with the rise of such diseases as diabetes. Ayurveda has also gained considerable popularity in the West because of its holistic approach to illness. Many clinical trials are being conducted at universities and medical centres to test the efficacy of Ayurvedic cures, such as the use of bitter melon against diabetes and turmeric for Alzheimer's, cancer and other diseases.[25]

SEVEN

The Middle Ages: The *Manasolassa*, *Lokopakara* and Regional Cuisines, 600–1300 CE

F rom the early seventh to the thirteenth century, the subcontinent was ruled by local and regional dynasties. Drawing an analogy with the West, some historians call this time the Feudal Period or the Middle Ages. Food habits were becoming more sophisticated, and for the first time they were recorded in some detail in the literature, including many distinctive regional dishes that are popular to this day. During this period, texts on food were composed that were neither medical nor religious, notably the *Manasolassa* and the *Lokopakara*. They are not cookbooks in the modern sense, since they lack detailed recipes, but they provide valuable information about the dishes of the time.

At its peak the Buddhist Pala dynasty controlled most of north and central India from its base in Pataliputra. Parts of this empire were taken over by the Hindu Senas, while from the eleventh to the fifteenth centuries the Eastern Ganga dynasty controlled Orissa and parts of West Bengal and Andhra Pradesh. The Gurjara Pratiharas, based in Malwa, ruled over much of northern and western India from the sixth to the eleventh centuries and later fragmented into various states, including the Rajput kingdoms.

Several dynasties contended for control over southern India: the Chalukyas in Karnataka, the Pallavas with their capital in Kanchipuram, and the Chola Empire, which at its peak controlled much of the Indian subcontinent and Sri Lanka. Later South Indian dynasties were the Pandyas and the Cheras. By 1343, the last of these dynasties had disappeared, to be replaced by the mighty Vijayanagar Empire.

During the many power struggles, local rulers were granted land in return for their service and loyalty. The agricultural sector became more organized, and major improvements were made in cultivation, implements, irrigation, the handling of seeds, insect control, the use of manure and weather forecasting. Foreign visitors continued to marvel at the country's prosperity.

In the early eighth century the Arabs conquered Sindh in northwest India, but their main interest was in trade rather than military dominance. Indian merchants benefited from association with the conquering forces, and some became extremely rich. They endowed magnificent temples, including the Jaganath temple in Orissa (now Odisha) and the Jain temples at Mount Abu in Rajasthan. This wealth became a magnet for raiders from the north, and at the end of the first millennium Mahmud of Ghazni (971–1030), leader of a principality in Afghanistan, began raiding northern India for plunder. His successors established the first of the Islamic dynasties that would rule much of the subcontinent for centuries to come. Jains, their numbers diminished, came to be concentrated in the west and southwest of India, while Buddhism, which had once had a foothold in the east, almost disappeared on the subcontinent.

INDIAN FOOD WRITING

One of the challenges of writing about the history of Indian food is the absence of cookbooks. According to Arjun Appadurai,

> While *gastronomic* issues play a critical role in Hindu texts, *culinary* issues do not. That is, while there is an immense amount written about *eating* and feeding, precious little is said about *cooking* in Hindu legal medical or philosophical texts . . . Food is principally either a moral or medical matter in traditional Hindu thought.[1]

Ingredients and raw materials are mentioned in food texts, sometimes in connection with their effect on the *doshas* or their seasonality, but there is little description of the processes that transform them into dishes, except in generic terms. One reason may be that the emphasis on the moral and medical aspects of food prevented it from becoming a source of independent gustatory pleasure. The brahmins, the producers and guardians of the major textual traditions, did not particularly care about the culinary aspects of eating; nor did the affluent merchants, many of whom were strictly vegetarian Jains or Vaishnavs. Restrictions on commensality and concerns about pollution precluded the emergence of a restaurant culture and the kind of gastronomical experimentation that appeared in China around the same time.

A corollary of this was the fact that no pan-Indian Hindu cuisine emerged until modern times. While other social and cultural forms were highly standardized, there was no culinary tradition common to the entire country. Although some fairly elaborate regional and courtly high cuisines developed, Hindu culinary traditions 'stayed oral in their mode of transmission, domestic in their locus, and regional in their scope . . . traditional Hindu cuisine was thoroughly Balkanized'.[2]

One of the first non-medical culinary texts was the *Manasolassa*, a composition in Sanskrit verse by King Somesvara III (ruled 1126–38). Somesvara was the eighth king of the Western Chalukya dynasty, which controlled much of southwest India from the late tenth century to the thirteenth, a region that today includes Karnataka, Goa and parts of Maharashtra, Kerala and Andhra Pradesh. The land was rich and fertile, producing rice, lentils, black pepper, cardamom, betel nuts and leaves, coconut and sugar, and the kingdom had strong commercial ties with Southeast Asia, Central Asia and China.

It was fashionable for rulers of the time to display their learning by writing about various topics. The *Manasolassa* (its name means 'delight' or 'refresher of the mind') covers medicine, magic, veterinary science, precious stones, vehicles, the art of acquiring and ruling a kingdom, elephants, painting, music, dance, literature, women, fish, plants and cuisine. Cuisine is covered in the section called 'Annabhoga', or 'enjoyment of food' (verses 1341–1600; pp. 113–28 in the Arundhati translation).[3] It describes nearly a hundred dishes, many of which exist today, especially in southern and western India. Others are rarely encountered: blood-filled sausages, goat's head in sour gruel, grilled stomach membrane and barbecued river rats.

Somesvara, like most Indian rulers, was a ksatriya, which meant that he did not have to conform to the vegetarian regime of the brahmins.[4] Meat, especially game, was considered an appropriate food for royalty, so there are a lot of recipes for game birds, deer and wild boar. However, chicken and beef are missing.

The most common spice to appear in the *Manasolassa* is asafoetida, often dissolved in water – a practice still followed in Maharashtra and Gujarat. Other flavourings are fresh or ground ginger, turmeric, black pepper, rock salt, mustard seeds, coriander, cumin and occasionally camphor and cardamom. Cloves are mentioned in only one recipe;

cinnamon not at all. Just a few recipes call for onions and garlic, perhaps indicating that, proscriptions aside, they were not in common use in western India. Spices are added both during cooking and afterwards. Citrus fruit, Indian gooseberry (amla), tamarind, pomegranate or yoghurt impart sourness. Coconut is not used as a cooking ingredient, although coconut water is mentioned as a healthy drink.

The six basic flavours (sweet, sour, salty, bitter, pungent and astringent) were combined in individual dishes and in meals. Somesvara writes that meat should be eaten with sour items, milk with sweet ingredients, salt with acidic substances, and astringent foods with acidic or salty items. In keeping with the prescriptions of Ayurveda, food should also be appropriate to the season. Pungent food is eaten in spring, cold and sweet food in summer, sweet dishes in autumn, sweet in winter, salty food in the rainy season, hot and oily items in late autumn, and hot and acidic dishes in the cool season.

Dishes were deep-fried, shallow-fried or cooked in liquid, and sometimes more than one technique was used. For shallow- and deep-frying, the cooking medium was sesame oil or ghee. Grilling over hot coals was common, especially for meat threaded on metal skewers.

A typical royal meal started with hot cooked rice and green lentils mixed with ghee, followed by tender pieces of meat prepared with lentils and then some kind of curry (spiced stew). The next course was meat mixed with sour leaves and seasonal fruit and vegetables flavoured in different ways. Any item could be mixed with rice. Midway through the meal, payasam (rice and milk pudding) and sweet and sour fruit were served. Throughout the meal the king sipped water, fruit juice (panakam) and spiced buttermilk. The meal ended with yoghurt to promote digestion.

The dietary staple was rice, as it is today in the region. Somesvara identifies eight varieties, including red rice (still grown in parts of India, notably the south and the northeast); large-grained rice; fragrant rice; rice produced in Kalinga; thick, coarse rice; small rice; and 60-day rice (rice grown during the hot season and harvested in 60 days). Rice was cooked in a copper or earthenware pot over a slow fire. While still *al dente*, it was removed from the heat, the water drained off and milk or ghee added. The rice water could be flavoured with spices and drunk.

A dish of boiled spiced lentils was served with any kind of rice or with 'less pleasant' grains (that is, those eaten by poor people), such as millet or uncultivated rice. The text lists seven kinds of pulse: mung,

Paratha is a pan-fried unleavened bread that can be plain or filled with vegetables.

hyacinth bean (lablab), chickpea, pigeon pea, urad (black lentils), red lentils (masur) and black-eyed peas. Boiled lentils were flavoured with asafoetida, salt and turmeric powder and topped with slices of fresh ginger. Pieces of aubergine, goat meat or animal marrow could be added to the dal, and black pepper or ground ginger sprinkled on top for extra flavour.

Savouries and sweets were popular, and many were similar to those still eaten today. Discs of white flour 'thin as white cloth' were fried to make a bread called mandakas, similar to modern parathas, and polikas (a word related to the modern *puranpoli*), a sweet paratha stuffed with lentils and sugar. Balls of white flour were baked in hot coals and were especially good if slightly charred – a dish similar to Rajasthani baatis, hard dough balls cooked in ashes and served with dal and churma, a sweet wheat-based pudding. The same dough, mixed with sugar, milk, ghee, black pepper and ground cardamom, was shaped into little balls that were fried in ghee and then stuffed into a wheat envelope to make a dish called udumbara (perhaps from a Sanskrit word meaning 'fig', a reference to its shape).

Lentil or chickpea flour mixed with asafoetida, salt, sugar, ground black pepper, cardamom and water was ground to a paste, formed into little discs and deep-fried to make purika, a forerunner of modern papdi (round crispy wafers used in the popular street food papdi chat). A fermented paste of ground urad dal and black pepper was shaped into balls and deep-fried to make vadika, which was soaked in milk or yoghurt. A modern incarnation of this is the popular Indian street food dahi vada – fried spicy lentil balls smothered with fresh yoghurt and topped with ground cumin, other spices and a sweet-and-sour chutney.

Dhosika was a crêpe made from a paste of ground urad dal, black-eyed peas or green peas flavoured with asafoetida, cumin, salt and ginger, and cooked in a lightly oiled hot pan. Its modern descendant is dosa, which is made from a batter of lentils and rice. According to K. T. Achaya, rice was probably added as an ingredient in the thirteenth century.[5] Deep-fried snacks included the vidalapaka, a blend of five lentils seasoned with turmeric, rock salt and asafoetida; katakarna, patties made of a paste of green peas and cow peas; and iddarika, balls of urad-flour paste dusted with pepper, cumin and asafoetida.

Some of the *Manasolassa*'s many meat recipes are complex and highly aromatic, belying the notion that elaborate meat dishes appeared only with the arrival of the Muslims. Pieces of meat marinated in custard apple and ginger were threaded on to skewers, grilled over red-hot coals and flavoured with ground black pepper and a sour juice. Pieces of meat

Papri chaat, a popular street food, is based on papris – crisp round wafers topped with potatoes, chickpeas and sauces.

142

Recipes from the *Manasolassa*

Barbecued Rat

The strong black rats that live in fields and along riverbanks are called maiga; they are held by the tail and fried in hot oil until the fur comes off. The rat is then washed in hot water, the stomach cut open and the inner parts cooked with Indian gooseberry and salt. The rest of the rat is put on an iron skewer and fried over red-hot coal until the skin is charred. When the rat is well cooked, it is sprinkled with salt, cumin and dried ginger.

Kebabs

Lamb or goat is cut into small pieces, which are mixed with asafoetida, turmeric and ginger and strung on to iron skewers. The kebabs are turned constantly over hot coals, and flavoured with salt and pepper once cooked. This dish is called bhaditrakam; it is tasty, light and wholesome, and stimulates the appetite. In another recipe, the meat is marinated with a sour substance (perhaps citron juice) and asafoetida, and then mixed with ginger juice, coriander, ground fenugreek and ground cumin. The mixture is cooked in ghee until the liquid dries up and then flavoured with pepper.

were beaten until they were as thin as palm leaves, flavoured with ground ginger, sugar, yoghurt and cardamom, and fried.

Meat from the back of an animal was considered the best. It was grilled to make kebabs or made into a curry-like dish. Sheep blood and meat were cooked with a sour juice until the liquid dried up, then seasoned with asafoetida, ground cumin, camphor and black pepper, and fried in ghee. Blood was mixed with water, lemon juice, ginger, cumin, asafoetida, pepper, coriander, salt and fat and stuffed into intestines, which were tied to look like ropes and cooked slowly until they hardened – a twelfth-century black pudding. A dish called panchvarni ('five colours') was made by simmering pieces of intestine with mustard seed, myrobalan, ginger, sour flavouring, salt and asafoetida until the sauce thickened. Intestines were also grilled on skewers until they became hard and crisp.

Kakori kebabs
on a grill.

A part of the animal called the *vapa*, perhaps the stomach membrane, was folded into layers, cut into pieces and fried in oil or grilled on skewers over hot coals. It could also be flattened with a rolling pin, flavoured with citrus fruit and salt, cut into pieces and fried. Goat brain was simmered with a gruel of fermented rice.

In the *Manasolassa*, Somesvara lists 35 varieties of fish together with information on their habitat (fresh or salt water), size, appearance and feeding habits. Fish were raised in large ponds. Some were fed a purely vegetarian diet of sesame-seed balls, chickpea flour or cooked rice; others ate meat, or meat and grains. Large fish were cut into pieces, small ones were cooked whole. After scaling, the fish were smeared with salt and oil to remove the smell, then washed with turmeric water, drained, boiled and seasoned. The roe was cooked until it became hard, cut into pieces, deep-fried and seasoned with salt, pepper and asafoetida water. Tortoise, meanwhile (said to taste like ripe plantain), was prepared by removing the legs and shell and roasting it in oil in a hot pan. Crab meat was roasted in a copper pan.

Fruit, leaves, stems and flowers were served raw or cooked and with or without meat. Leafy vegetables (25 varieties are named by Somesvara) were mixed with yoghurt or citrus juice. Fruit (40 are listed, of which most have no English equivalent), roots, and bamboo shoots and leaves were salted or mixed with ground black mustard seed, sesame oil and salt.

> ## *Huli (Dal)* from *Lokopakara*
>
> For a delicious soup, grind cinnamon, cumin, mustard, black
> pepper, cardamom and coriander seeds with water. Boil any
> type of dal until it reaches the consistency of gruel, add the
> ground spices and cook, stirring. Garnish with mustard seeds,
> cumin seeds, asafoetida and curry leaves fried in a little ghee
> or oil.

A salad of raw mango, plantain, bitter gourd and jackfruit in a sesame
and black mustard-seed dressing sounds like a dish that would be served
in a contemporary upscale Indian restaurant.

Some of the sweet dishes were made with khoya – cow's or buffalo's
milk thickened by being boiled over a slow fire. Sikharini (drained spiced
yoghurt) again makes an appearance. Milk was split by adding a souring
agent and drained through cloth to make curds or chhana; the curds were
blended until smooth, mixed with sugar and fried in small balls.

Drinks called panaka were prepared from various fruit, sometimes
mixed with buttermilk. People also drank fresh coconut water, diluted
molasses sprinkled with pepper, and *majjika* (churned buttermilk flavoured
with black pepper and mustard seeds). Alcoholic drinks include gaudi, a
rum-like drink made from sugar or molasses, and madhvi, made from the
flowers of the mahua tree.

A somewhat earlier work from the same region describes a more
down-to-earth cuisine. *Lokopakara*, which means 'for the benefit of the
people', was written in the local language Kannada (not Sanskrit, like the
Manasolassa) in about 1025 by Chavundaraya II, a Jain poet and scholar
at the court of Jaisimha II (ruled 1015–42), one of the Western Chalukya
kings. In addition to discussing food, it contains chapters on astrology,
architecture, omens, perfumes, water divining and veterinary and human
medicine.

The chapter called 'Supa Shastra', or 'The Art and Science of Cooking',
gives 57 rudimentary recipes, all for vegetarian dishes without onion or
garlic. Many are for sweet dishes and snacks, perhaps because these
are the most complicated to prepare. The very first recipe describes the
correct method of cooking rice, which should be washed three times
before being boiled in a lot of water, which is drained off at the end
(still the preferred way of cooking rice in India).

Barley (which by then had almost been replaced by rice as the staple grain) is an ingredient in only two dishes. After being soaked in milk, it was dried and roasted, ground into a flour, flavoured with ground saffron, cinnamon, cinnamon leaves and cardamom, and mixed with sugar and ghee to make a porridge. A similar dish, called rave unde, made with wheat or semolina flour, is still served at festivals and ceremonies in Karnataka. Alternatively, a paste of barley and milk was formed into balls and fried in ghee. Today kajjaya, a similar dish made with rice, is served on special occasions.

The most commonly used lentils were mung, urad and chana dal. The lentils were cooked in water until thick, then mixed with a paste of cardamom, cumin, coriander, black pepper and mustard seed. The dal was flavoured with tamarind or lemon juice and garnished with mustard and cumin seeds, asafoetida and curry leaves fried in a little oil, a mixture called oggarane.[6]

A few sweet dishes were made by curdling hot milk to make chhana, which was mixed with sugar, ghee, ground cinnamon and ground cardamom and formed into balls. Laddus, one of the most popular Indian sweets (see chapter Five), were made by mixing savige – vermicelli made from a dough of rice flour, yoghurt and ghee – with ghee and a sugar syrup, forming it into balls and frying it in ghee. Tamarind or jujube juice was added for flavour. A mixture of finely grated coconut, dates and sugar was stuffed into pieces of dough that were fried in ghee – the modern Karnataka sweet sajjappa.

The most complex recipe is for sikharini. Yoghurt was mixed with cinnamon, dried ginger, black pepper, rock salt, jaggery, nutmeg, zedoary (white turmeric), the flowers of *Mesua ferrea* (ironwood), myrobalan, honey and sugar-cane juice, and finally with edible camphor.

A gruel made from rice and flavoured with cassia extract, ground barley, sesame seeds, urad dal, asafoetida and turmeric powder was formed into balls that were dried in the sun and stored. When deep-fried, they swelled into large balls called sandige, still a popular snack in Karnataka, especially during the rainy season. A paste of ground urad dal soaked in water drained from yoghurt and flavoured with asafoetida, cumin seeds, coriander and black pepper was used to prepare idlis. However, the recipe does not include rice, nor is it fermented. According to Achaya, rice was probably not adopted as an ingredient until the fifteenth century.[7] It is said that fermentation was introduced by the cooks of Indonesian Hindu kings who visited South India in search of brides between the eighth and twelfth centuries, but a more likely explanation is that it was a natural process that was discovered independently in India, since nearly all cultures use fermentation in some form.

Unlike the Chinese, Indians rarely attempt to make vegetarian dishes that resemble meat or fish. There is an exception in *Lokopakara*, however: a dough of parched chickpea flour is pressed into fish-shaped moulds, then fried in mustard oil.

A large section of *Lokopakara* covers methods of preserving various foods by using yoghurt, salt and jaggery, and ways of removing toxicity and bitterness from fruit, vegetables, shoots and leaves that grew in the wild – an indication of the importance of economy in the diet of common people. For example, unripe mangoes are cut into pieces, smeared with black pepper and jaggery and dried in the sun, while ripe mangoes can be preserved for days in sugar syrup or honey.

EMERGING REGIONAL CUISINES

North India

According to a poet at the court of the last independent Hindu king of Delhi, Prithviraj Chauhan (1149–1192), meals at the royal palace included meat flavoured in various ways; five kinds of sag (green vegetables); fruit; vegetables flavoured with the six tastes; pickles and condiments; buttermilk; and yoghurt.[8] Sweet dishes included kheer, a rice pudding flavoured with cardamom, other spices and nuts; payesh (payasam), rice cooked slowly in milk and sugar; rabari, milk thickened by boiling and mixed with sugar; and kesara, a ball made of flour, sugar and ghee. Savoury dishes include khirora, a steamed rice-flour ball; bara, small deep-fried lentil balls; khandvi, a savoury made from chickpea and wheat flour; and lapsi, cracked wheat boiled in milk and eaten with sugar and spices. The wealthy enjoyed khichri, mixed rice and lentils prepared with ghee, spices and vegetables.

The food of the common people lacked richness and variety. The Arab geographer al-Idrisi (1099–1161) wrote: 'Their food consists of rice, chickpeas, beans, haricots, lentils, peas, fish and animals that died a natural death.'[9] Other staples were the ancient sattu and khichri without ghee. Milk, milk products and sugar were reserved for the upper classes. Another Arab traveller commented that Hindus disapproved of the drinking of wine both by themselves and others, not on religious grounds but because of its intoxicating effect.[10]

Laddoos, balls made of chickpea flour, semolina or other ingredients,
are perhaps the most popular Indian sweets.

East India

Eastern India (modern West Bengal and Bangladesh) is one of the most
fertile areas in the subcontinent. Barley and rice were staples from early
times, since little wheat grew there. Other common foods were fruit (including citrus), roots, leafy green vegetables, the stalks and flowers of vegetables
(a characteristic feature of modern Bengali cuisine), milk and milk products, jaggery, crushed fried barley and chickpeas. At least twelve varieties
of sugar cane are mentioned in the literature. Popular vegetables included
patola, a small member of the gourd family, aubergine, radishes and bitter
gourd. Typical flavourings included turmeric powder and paste, mustard

seeds, dried ginger, cumin seeds, long pepper, cloves, coriander seeds and asafoetida. Both betel creepers and betel-nut trees were cultivated, and the chewing of paan was common. Coconut trees were ubiquitous, and both the kernel and the water of the nut were consumed.

With exception of some orthodox brahmins, widows and Jains, most Bengalis were not vegetarians. Law-writers of the Middle Ages found it necessary to sanction the eating of fish (provided it had scales) and meat, except on certain days each month.[11] Dried fish was not considered fit for human consumption, although it was eaten by poor people along the coast. Although alcohol was prohibited, songs written in the twelfth century show that there were many taverns in Bengal selling not just intoxicating beverages but also cannabis. A poem by an eighth-century Buddhist mystic reads:

> There is a woman winemaker who enters two rooms
> She ferments wine with fine barks.
> Hold me still, Shahaja, then ferment the wine
> So that your shoulders are held strongly and your body is free
> from age and death.[12]

A series of epic poems called *Mansamangal*, written between the thirteenth and eighteenth centuries, depicts the daily life of the affluent.[13] They

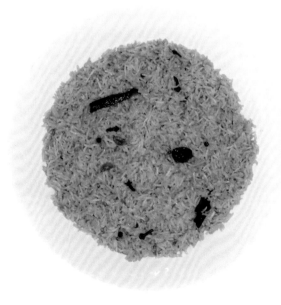

Khichri, a dish of rice and lentils, is one of the oldest Indian dishes, with many variations.

ate aubergines fried in oil, green vegetables cooked with cumin seeds, pepper, fresh ginger, various kinds of lentils and fish, especially rohu (carp) and ilish (*Tenualosa ilisha*), goat and duck meat, various pitha (a kind of pancake made with rice flour and jaggery) and many varieties of rice.

In a poem describing a meal at the home of a rich merchant, the dishes and the order in which they are served are nearly identical to those that would be served as the midday meal of an upper-middle-class Hindu family in Bengal today: a bitter dish (sukhta); a liquid dish (jhol); mixed vegetables (ghanta); green leafy vegetables (saka); boiled lentils (dal); fish served whole, in pieces or as balls; meat; a sour dish (ambala); rice-flour sweets (pitha); thickened milk-based sweets (ksira); and yoghurt.[14]

A twelfth-century description of a marriage feast indicates the skill of the cooks. The boiled rice was white, fragrant and delicious, each grain separate from the others. It was mixed with ghee. Dishes of yoghurt with black mustard seeds made guests scratch their heads because of their pungent taste. Delicious broths were made from venison and fish. The dishes were so skilfully made that guests could not distinguish between those that were vegetarian and those that were not.[15]

The diet of ordinary people consisted of boiled rice, yoghurt, vegetables and gourds, served on banana leaves. Boiled rice was dried in the sun to make muri, or puffed rice, a popular dish in eastern India and Bangladesh.

South India

Returning home to Italy from China in 1292 CE, the merchant traveller Marco Polo landed on the Coromandel Coast and spent a year in South India. He called the kingdom of the Tamil Pandyas near modern-day Tanjore 'the richest and most splendid province in the world', and noted the abundance of pepper, ginger, cubebs (Java pepper), nuts and turmeric. Although most people avoided alcohol, he reported, many were addicted to chewing a leaf called *tambur* (paan), sometimes mixing it with 'camphor and other spices and also, with lime . . . They go about chewing this leaf and spitting out the resulting spittle.' They also used paan to express disdain by targeting the spittle at another person's face, which sometimes led to violent clashes. The people 'worship the ox', did not eat beef (except people of low social status) and daubed their houses with cow dung. Polo reported that a group of their holy men, the Yogis, ate frugally and lived longer than most, some as long as 200 years (a typical example of his tendency to exaggerate). The men belonging to one religious order –

probably the Jains – wore no clothes and led 'a harsh and austere life'. They believed that all living beings have a soul, and took pains to avoid hurting even the tiniest creatures.[16]

West India

Vegetarianism was prevalent in Gujarat from ancient times. The Jain presence was and still is strong in the region, and in the twelfth century CE King Kumarapala (ruled 1143–72) supported Jainism and banned the slaughter of animals in his kingdom. Many merchants who converted to Vaishnavism from the sixth century onwards were vegetarians.

Jain literature composed between the seventh and fifteenth centuries mentions many Gujarati vegetarian dishes that are still eaten today, including dukkia (dhokla, a steamed cake made of chickpea flour), vedhami (also called puranpoli, a bread stuffed with sweet spiced lentils), kacchari (kachori, a puffy deep-fried bread stuffed with lentils), kosamri (a lentil salad spiced with mustard seeds), sarkara (dudhpeda, a round sweet made of khoya – thickened milk – and sugar) and ghrtapura (thevara), a sweet soaked in sugar syrup.[17]

EIGHT

The Delhi Sultanate: *Ni'matnama, Supa Shastra* and *Ksemakutuhalam*, 1300–1550

THE ARRIVAL OF ISLAM

For centuries Arab merchants sailed to the west coast of India to buy spices and luxury goods. In 664 CE an Arab general defeated the local Hindu king at Hyderabad in Sindh, and made it part of the Umayyad Empire, which was based in Damascus. In 738 an alliance of Hindu kings defeated the Arabs. In the eighth and ninth centuries Arab merchants, now converted to Islam, settled permanently on the west coast of India, where they married local women.

Founded in Saudi Arabia by the prophet Muhammad in the year 622 CE, Islam is a monotheistic religion whose central tenet is that there is one God, Allah, and that every Muslim must surrender himself to Allah's will ('Islam' means 'surrender'). This message was revealed to Allah's prophet Muhammad through the archangel Gabriel and recorded in the sacred text, the Quran. All Muslims are considered equal and united in a brotherhood, called the *ulama*. The five basic tenets (called 'pillars') of Islam are to affirm the credo 'There is but one God, Allah, and Muhammad is his prophet'; to give alms to the poor; to pray five times a day facing Mecca; to fast during the ninth lunar month (Ramadan); and to make a pilgrimage (*hajj*) to Mecca.

Islam is a proselytizing religion that spread quickly under the caliphs of Medina and the Umayyad Empire. Within a century it had extended across North Africa, Spain, the Middle East, Central Asia, Persia, Kashmir and Afghanistan. One consequence of the Arab conquest of Persia in the mid-seventh century was the flight of Zoroastrians to western India, where they became known as Parsis. They were to play an important role in Indian trade and commerce, and created a distinctive food culture.

Dietary Rules and Restriction in Islam

Islam has relatively few food restrictions, but they must be observed strictly. They are derived from both the Quran and the Sunna, the recorded words of Muhammad. Pork, carrion, blood, alcohol and other intoxicants, termed *haram*, are forbidden to believers. Animals must be slaughtered according to the Islamic method by a person appointed to the task. They must be handled with mercy and kindness and killed swiftly with a sharp cut across the neck, severing the windpipe and the jugular veins, while 'Allah Akbar' ('God is great') is said three times. All blood is drained, since it is considered unclean. Such meat is called *halal*.

Fasting, one of the five pillars of Islam, commemorates the revelation of the Quran to Muhammad, and is a way of purifying oneself physically and spiritually. A mandatory fast is the holy lunar month Ramadan (Ramazan in Urdu), during which Muslims refrain from eating, drinking, smoking and sex during daylight hours. (Exceptions are made for travellers, sick people and pregnant women, who have to make up the fast later.) The fast is broken at sunset with a small snack called iftar, which includes dates (because the Prophet ate them to break his fast), sweet and salty snacks, and fruit. It is followed by a large meal. The end of Ramadan, called Id-ul-Fitr or simply Id (also spelled Eid), is celebrated by communal feasts and the serving to guests of sweet dishes, especially sawaiyan, a dish of vermicelli, milk and sugar.[1]

The second major Muslim festival is Edi-ul-Zuha or Bakrid, which commemorates Abraham's offering of his son to God, who at the last moment replaced him with a ram. On this day Muslims are expected to sacrifice a ram or goat if they can afford it and distribute one-third of the meat to friends, one-third to family and one-third to the poor. Every subsequent meal includes meat dishes until the animal is eaten up. All these festivals signify piety, hospitality and charity. Indian Muslims who belong to the Shia sect fast for one or more days during the month of Muharram, a period of mourning to remember the death of Husain, the Prophet's grandson, who was murdered by Muhammad's enemies. Mourners march barefoot in procession, beating their chests, crying out the name of Husain and even whipping themselves.

A Muslim wedding banquet is a lavish affair featuring as many meat dishes as the bride's family can afford. It traditionally included at least one biryani (chicken was considered the most prestigious meat, because it was the most expensive); zarda, a sweet rice with candied fruit dyed bright yellow with saffron; mutton korma; lal roti (bread saturated with ghee); shami kebab; fish curry or fried fish (among Bengalis); and many desserts, including rice pudding (kheer) in clay pots, gulab jaman and sheer korma of vermicelli, milk, sugar, dates and sometimes nuts, saffron, raisins and rosewater.[2] Separate vegetarian dishes are prepared for Hindu guests.

INVADERS FROM THE NORTH

Attracted by stories of the fabulous wealth of India, which they called Hindustan, Central Asian and Afghan tribes regularly invaded the northwest of the country between the eighth and twelfth centuries, in search of booty and converts. In 962 CE Alptigin, a general in the Persian Empire, seized the Afghan fortress of Ghazni. His grandson Mahmud used it as a base from which to invade India and plunder its cities. Some Hindus converted to Islam, and thousands of Buddhists fled to Nepal and Tibet.

The Ghaznavid dynasty ruled much of Persia, Central Asia and northern parts of India from 975 to 1186. Although Turkish in origin, they were entirely Persianized in language, culture, literature and habits. They were succeeded by the Ghorids, who ruled over parts of Afghanistan, Iran and Pakistan until the early thirteenth century.

By 1225 all of northern India was under Islamic rule. Collectively called the Delhi sultanate (although the capital was not always in Delhi), various Turkish, Afghan and Central Asian dynasties held sway for more than 300 years. They included the Mamluks or Slave dynasty (1206–90), the Khiljis (1290–1320), the Tughlaqs (1321–98), the Sayyids (1414–51) and the Lodis (1451–1526).

To rule their empire, the sultans needed judges, scholars, administrators and military officers. They offered high salaries and lavish gifts, and their courts became a magnet for people from all over the Islamic world, including the Middle East, North Africa, Turkey and Central Asia. (According to some estimates, up to 60 per cent were of Turkish origin).[3] One was the famous Moroccan traveller and chronicler Ibn Battuta (1304–c. 1368), who served Sultan Mohammad Tuqhlaq as a judge for seven years and left an account of his experiences in his *Tahqiq-i-Hind* (History of India). In the thirteenth century, a Mongol invasion of Central Asia and Persia drove many Islamic scholars and jurists into North India, where they were welcomed by the sultans. While the newcomers no doubt originally intended to make their fortunes and return to their home countries (like the eighteenth-century English *nabobs*), many stayed. The official language of the court and government was Persian, and many Arab scientific works were translated into that language. As the bureaucracy grew, Hindus were co-opted into the administration and became the North Indian kayastha caste. Hindu cooks entered the royal and aristocratic kitchens.

Entertaining on a grand scale was a mark of prestige, and in this the sultans sought to emulate the traditions of the shahs of Persia.[4] They had their own private kitchens, called *matbakhs*, managed by an officer called the *chashnigir*. They usually dined in the company of their nobles and courtiers from a common *dastarkhan* – a Persian word that meant both an elaborate tablecloth and a lavish meal of many dishes – and often from the same plate. A royal banquet given by the pleasure-loving Delhi sultan Kaiqubad (ruled 1287–90) began with sharbat, a drink made from fruit juice or extracts of flowers or herbs, combined with sugar and water.[5] Breads included nan-i-tanuri – a wheat bread filled with a sweet paste and dried fruit and baked in a *tanur*, a clay oven – and kak, a ring-shaped crispy bread of Arab origin. Rice dishes included plain rice and surkh biryani (the word comes from the Turkish *biryan*, meaning roasted, boiled, grilled or baked), rice fried in ghee and coloured red. There followed meat and cereal dishes: roast kid, goat's tongue, leg of lamb, skinned and stuffed goat, the tail (*dhumba*) of a type of sheep bred specially for the purpose, chicken, partridge, quail and other birds.

A popular dish was sambusa or samosa, a triangular pastry filled with minced meat and nuts. Arab cookbooks dating back to the tenth and eleventh centuries call these pastries sambusak, a word still used in the Middle East. (It may come from the Arabic *se*, 'three', referring to the triangular shape, and *ambos*, a kind of bread.) A thirteenth-century Baghdadi cookbook, *Kitab al-Tabikh* (*The Book of Dishes*), has recipes for three versions.[6] One is filled with meat flavoured with coriander, cumin, pepper, cinnamon, mint and pounded almonds; the second with halwa (halva); and a third with sugar and almonds. A characteristic feature of this and other medieval Arab recipes is the lavish use of spices, including pepper, ginger, saffron, cinnamon, galangal, cumin and coriander (but not garlic). This may be a product of thousands of years of trade reaching back as far as the Indus Valley civilization. In any case, the newcomers' encounter with the highly spiced dishes of Indian cuisine would not have represented a dramatic break with their own culinary tradition and tastes.

Sweet dishes were served both during and at the end of a meal. They included sabuniya, a soft nut brittle; lauz (known today as firni), a pudding made of rice boiled in milk and mixed with almonds, pistachios, raisins and saffron; and different types of halwa, made by cooking carrots, squash and other vegetables with nuts, sugar, ghee and saffron. Carrot halwa was a popular winter dessert. A favourite of the sultan was tutmaj, a preparation of milk, rice, nuts and sugar, usually containing some small squares of cooked dough (*tutmač* in Turkic languages).[7] The names of these dishes are Arabic, and they are probably of Middle Eastern origin.

A detailed account of royal banquets was left by Ibn Battuta. Meals started with thin, round breads (perhaps chapattis or parathas), followed by roast meat cut into large pieces, served with round dough cakes made with ghee, stuffed with sabuniya and topped with another sweet called khisht, made from flour, sugar and ghee. Meat cooked with onions, ghee and green ginger was served in large porcelain bowls, and followed by four or five sambusak for each person. Next came a dish of rice cooked in ghee with a roast chicken on top, and finally sweet items were served, such as halwa and al-qahirya, an almond pudding named after a tenth-century Baghdadi ruler.

A private dinner at the sultan's palace was attended by twenty or so specially chosen relatives, nobles and distinguished foreign visitors. Each person had his own plate, instead of sharing dishes as was the Arab tradition. A public dinner was held every day for religious leaders, jurists, nobles and relatives of the sultan. It consisted of various kinds of bread, including round bread filled with a sweet paste (perhaps a stuffed paratha or naan), roast meat, chicken and rice dishes, both plain and cooked with meat and served with sambusak. Ibn Battuta notes that courtiers had adopted the Indian habit of eating khichri – rice and mung dal topped with ghee – for breakfast. This simple dish (the parent of the English kedgeree) was later a favourite of the Mughal emperors. Another breakfast dish was nihari (also nahari), a beef stew with a rich aromatic gravy that simmered overnight and was eaten with bread. It remains a popular breakfast dish in Hyderabad, Delhi and Lahore.

The sultan and his nobles had large kitchen staffs that included cooks, bakers and dishwashers. The officer in charge was the *chashnigir*, or taster, who had to make sure the food was properly cooked and free from poison. Rich people maintained public kitchens, *langars*, to feed the poor. Large public kitchens supported by such endowments were maintained by Sufis (Muslim holy men).

Chef making naan, a baked, slightly leavened bread.

Shami kebabs are small
patties of minced meat
and ground chickpeas
that are a popular snack.

Although the success of a meal among the elite was determined by the number and variety of meat dishes, as their residence in India lengthened, they developed more of a taste for vegetarian food. At a banquet at the court of Sher Shah (ruled 1540–45), the Muslims dined on naan; meat kebabs; yakhni (a spiced meat broth); roast lamb and khasi, castrated goat; red and yellow mutton shorbas, or soups;[8] chicken and partridge; and several kinds of halwa. Their Hindu guests enjoyed puris, various vegetable preparations, lentils, suhali (a round, crisp flatbread), gulguli (little cakes soaked in sugar syrup), yoghurt and baris and baras, little fried lentil dumplings. On another occasion, Hindus were served fragrantly spiced rice dishes, jhala (a ribbon-shaped bread), manda (a steamed ball of ground rice and coconut), sohari (a kind of puri described as 'exceedingly soft'), baris and various achars (pickles).

Another very popular dish, shami kebab – light patties made of ground meat, split peas (chana dal) and spices – may have been introduced at this time, although its origin remains uncertain. The name comes from *sham*, the Arabic word for Syria or the Levant, and similar dishes exist in Afghanistan and Iran.

Meals always ended with the chewing of paan, a local custom that caught on like wildfire among the elite.[9] Although betel nuts and leaves originated in Southeast Asia, the two were combined in India some time before 500 BCE. The consumption of paan was widespread among rich and poor alike. Its three basic ingredients are areca nut (betel nut), betel leaf and lime (calcium hydroxide), which can be made from limestone or by burning and crushing seashells and mixing the powder with water to make a paste. Another ingredient is kaththa, a sticky paste made from the astringent dark-brown extract of the core of the areca tree. Cardamom, cloves, camphor, nutmeg, black pepper, cinnamon, coriander seeds, ambergris, ginger, saffron, sugar syrup and in modern times tobacco (*gutka*) can be added to taste.[10] The very rich added ground pearls and shells to the lime paste and commissioned elaborate bowls (called *bargdan*), boxes and trays made of silver and gold and inset with precious stones to hold the ingredients. The pastes are spread on the leaf, the spices added and the leaf folded into an elegant little triangle, sometimes held together with a clove. The eater carefully places it in his mouth and chews until it disappears or spits out what is left.

To this day, paan serves many purposes. At the end of a meal it stimulates saliva and gastric flow and freshens the mouth. Paan has a mild stimulant effect, so it is used to stay awake. Exchanging paans was

Ode to Paan (Amir Khusro)

A chew of betel bound into a hundred leaves,
came to hand like a hundred-petaled flower.
Rare leaf, like a flower in a garden,
Hindustan's most beautiful delicacy,
sharp as a rearing stallion's ear,
sharp in both shape and taste,
in sharpness a tool to cut roots,
as the Prophet's words tell us.
Full of veins with no trace of blood,
yet from its veins blood races out,
wondrous plant, for placed in the mouth,
Blood comes from its body like a living thing.[11]

sometimes regarded as equivalent to a contract or oath of loyalty, and done to seal a marriage engagement. It became a symbol of hospitality and the focal point of elaborate aristocratic rituals. How one served and ate paan was a marker of sophistication and affluence. A fourteenth-century visitor wrote:

> The Indians think the most respectable way to entertain the guest is with betel leaf. If a person entertains his guests with various kinds of eatables, sharbats, sweetmeats, perfumes and flowers and does not offer betel leaf to them, it means he has not been a good host and guests have not had honour done to them. Similarly, when an important man has to oblige some acquaintance, he offers him a betel leaf.[12]

The custom never became popular in Central Asia or Persia, however. The poet Amir Khusro (1253–1325), who was born in India and wrote in Persian and Hindustani, noted: 'The Persians are so sluggish as not to be able to distinguish between paan and grass. It requires taste to do so.'[13]

Caterers, bakers and butchers set up shop in urban areas, along roads where caravans passed, and in places where a Sufi holy man lived or where a Sufi's tomb was located. Some sold snacks – street food – while others offered more expensive dishes, such as whole roast kids or chickens, which could be eaten on the spot or bought to take away. Urban centres had a flourishing catering profession that served all classes of society. According to Ibn Battuta, the common people ate a porridge of pounded millet and water or buffalo's milk. Domestic animals and birds were plentiful and cheap, and food in general was much less expensive than in Egypt or Syria.[14]

Central Asians and Persians, who longed for the fruit, plants and flowers of their homelands, grew grapes, pomegranates, dates and melons. Ibn Battuta noted the availability of delicious melons grown in or around Delhi (although a century later the first Mughal emperor, Babur, complained about the lack of good melons in India). Khusro wrote that in Delhi you could find not only all the fruit grown in India and in Khusrasan/Khorasan (a region that covered parts of modern-day Afghanistan, Iran and Central Asia), but also fruit from even further afield. Since the fruit could not be delivered fresh to India because of the distance, it was cut into strips and dried in the sun, and sold to the wealthy at a very high price. Merchants in Iran, Bukhara (part of Uzbekistan) and Afghanistan sold yellow plums, fresh melons, grapes, almonds, pistachios and raisins in India. Until the partition of the subcontinent in 1947, Afghan traders peddling nuts and dried fruit were common sights in large cities. Today the same goods are brought in by air.

Many of the herbs used under the Islamic system of medicine were introduced to India, including aniseed, which also entered the cooks' spice

An elegant preparation of paan wrapped in silver foil.

Aristocrats owned elaborate sets for the preparation of paan,
often made of precious metals and jewels.

boxes. As early as the late fourteenth century the court used ice, which was
carried from the Himalayas in winter and buried underground where it
could be preserved for years. In summer the merchants dug it up and sold
it at the market to cool sharbats.

DISINTEGRATION OF THE DELHI SULTANATE

In 1398 Timur (known in the West as Tamerlane), a Turkic leader who
was a descendant of Genghis Khan of Mongolia, invaded India and sacked
Delhi, with great bloodshed. He had already conquered much of Central
Asia, Iran and Afghanistan, and later he extended his empire as far east as
Turkey. His reign of terror lasted sixteen years and accelerated the fragmen-
tation of the central power of the sultans. But Timur was also a patron of
artisans and artists, and he transformed his capital city, Samarkand, into the
most magnificent city in Central Asia. His entourage included many Iranian
artisans, artists and cooks, some of whom stayed in India after he left.[15]

By the beginning of the fifteenth century the Delhi sultanate had
broken into separate kingdoms. For a period, northern and western India
was divided into several powerful kingdoms, but they too broke up into
smaller political units. The Rajputs founded kingdoms in Rajasthan, ranging in size from small principalities to large states such as Mewar, Jaipur
and Marwar. By the middle of the fifteenth century they were a major
political force in northern India. In the south a great Hindu kingdom

arose, with its capital at Vijaynagar. As the control of Delhi weakened, some of the sultans' generals and governors established their own independent kingdoms, the most famous of which – from a culinary point of view – is Malwa.

The *Ni'matnama* of the Sultans of Mandu

In 1401 the governor of Malwa, Dilawar Khan, declared himself sultan and set up his capital at Mandu. His grandson Ghiyath Shahi ascended the throne in 1469 and ruled for 30 years. In 1500 he deputized the the ruling of the kingdom to his son Nasir Shah (ruled 1500–11) in order to devote the rest of his life to the pursuit of pleasure. He filled his palace with musicians, cooks, painters and thousands of women, many of whom were taught an art or a skill, such as wrestling and cooking. Five hundred female Abyssinian slaves, clad in armour, formed his personal bodyguard. During his reign, Mandu became known as Shadiyabad, or 'city of joy'.

To document his luxurious lifestyle, Ghiyath Shahi commissioned the *Ni'matnama*, or *Book of Delights*. Composed between 1495 and 1505, it consists of several hundred recipes written in a mixture of Urdu and Persian and illustrated by 50 paintings depicting the preparation of various dishes. Ghiyath Shahi himself, recognizable by his splendid

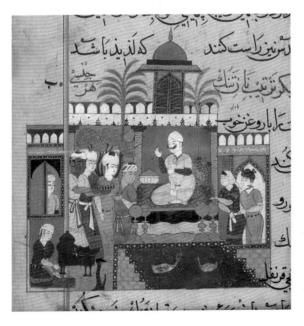

Food prepared for the Sultan Ghiyath al-Din: a scene from the *Ni'matnama* (1495–1505).

moustache, is usually present, watching and supervising the operations, enjoying his food, or hunting and fishing. The book was completed by Nasir Shah.

The *Ni'matnama* opens with a charming invocation: 'King of cockroaches! Please do not eat this, my offering to the culinary world – recipes of cooking food, sweetmeats, fish and the manufacture of rose-water perfumes.' The recipes are for the shah's favourite dishes, and many be accompanied by such comments as 'This is delicious' or 'This is a favourite of Ghiyath Shahi.' They are not arranged in any particular order, and there is a lot of repetition. Recipes for sharbat, for example, are suddenly interspersed with those for soup, as if the thought of a liquid had jogged the compiler's memory, while a recipe for fish may be followed by one for an aphrodisiac. Most of the recipes are simply lists of ingredients; quantities and cooking methods are missing. There are also recipes for perfumes, salves and pastes, medicines and aphrodisiacs. As in earlier texts, there are warnings about the dangers of eating certain foods and food combinations, including milk with fish, radishes, mung dal, green vegetables, sour fruit, salt or meat.

The *Ni'matnama* may owe its inspiration to the recipe collections of the Persian court, which focused on refined, luxurious and special-occasion dishes; and the shah's court did include Persian artists and cooks. However, while the earliest paintings in the manuscript are Persian in style, the illustrations become increasingly Indianized towards the end. This mingling of Persian and Indian styles is apparent in the recipes as well, although it is difficult to chart a progression.

Many of the dishes have Persian or, in a few cases, Turkic names: shorba (soup), paliv (broth or soup), qima (minced meat, from the Turkic verb *kiymak*, meaning to finely chop), baghra (a stew to which pieces of baked dough are added), dugh (a yoghurt drink), naan (baked bread), yakhni (meat stew), kebabs or seekh (skewered meat), burani (a vegetable dish with yoghurt, often made with aubergine), halwa (a generic word for sweetmeats), sakba (a dish of meat, wheat flour and vinegar), harisya (harissa, a mixture of grains, usually wheat and barley, with meat), kash (a very thick porridge of milk and flour), ashsham (supper food: from the Persian *ash*, 'food', and *sham*, 'evening'), baranj (rice), kofta (meat balls), sambusa (samosas), biryan (a general term for baked food), khashka (plain boiled rice), mahicha (slices of lentil dough added to a stew), paluda (a drink made of water thickened with flour and honey; also a noodle), pihiya (meat gruel), *tutmač* (small squares of dough), thuli

Recipes from the *Ni'matnama*
Saffron Meat

Wash the meat (goat or lamb) well and, having put sweet-smelling ghee into a cooking pot, put the meat into it. When the ghee is hot, flavour it with saffron, rosewater and camphor. Mix the meat with the saffron to flavour it, and when it has become well marinated, add a quantity of water. Chop cardamoms, cloves, coriander, fennel, cinnamon, cassia, cumin and fenugreek, tie them up in muslin and put them with the meat. Cook almonds, pine nuts, pistachios and raisins in tamarind syrup and add them to the meat. Put in rosewater, camphor, musk and ambergris, and serve it. By the same method cook partridge, quail, chicken and pigeon.

A Spice Mixture That Can Be Added to Any Dish
4 parts rosewater, 10 parts white hibiscus, 20 parts cardamom, 1 part cloves and 4 parts mace.

(a dish of spiced cracked wheat), qaliya (a stew) and sharbat (a cold drink made from various ingredients).

A characteristic Persian feature (although it is also found in earlier Indian writings on food) is the flavouring of stews with sour fruit, fruit juice and green herbs, including sweet and sacred basil, orange, citron and lime leaves, and mint. For example, in one recipe parboiled rice is cooked with the leaves of sour orange, limes, citrons and basil; the leaves are then removed and cardamom and cloves added, imparting an Indian flavour. In another, rice is boiled with an orange stuffed with cloves, cardamoms, musk, camphor, saffron and rosewater. Green vegetables are fried with asafoetida, salt and ghee and then topped with sweet and holy basil, mango leaves, fresh lime leaves, sour orange leaves and mint, each tied in a separate bunch. The vegetables are steamed briefly with the leaves, which are then thrown away.

Although there are several dozen recipes for rice, oddly there is no mention of pulao, which *The Oxford Companion to Food* defines as 'a Middle Eastern method of cooking rice so that every grain remains separate'. Pulao or pilaf is usually flavoured with meat or vegetables and cooked in ghee. Its origin is uncertain. Descriptions of the basic technique appear in thirteenth-century Arab cookbooks, although the name *pulao* is not used. The word itself is medieval Farsi, and the dish may have been created in the early sixteenth century at the Safavid court in Persia. The earliest reference to pulao in English is in the writings of Edward Terry (the chaplain to Sir Thomas Roe, English ambassador to the Mughal court) in 1616: 'Sometimes they boil pieces of flesh or hens, or other fowl, cut in pieces in their rice, which they call pillaw.'[16] Although dishes combining rice, meat and spices were prepared in ancient times, the technique of first sautéing the rice in ghee and then cooking it slowly to keep the grains separate probably came later with the Mughals.

From linguistic evidence, other dishes in the *Ni'matnama* are of indigenous origin, and many are vegetarian. They include bara or bari (also spelled vada or vadi), deep-fried balls made from ground grain or lentils; bhat (plain boiled rice); bhuji (fried vegetables); dal (lentils, both raw and cooked); ghee; khichri (rice and lentils); khandvi (swollen parched grain); lassi (a yoghurt drink); laddu (a round sweet); karhi or kadi (a stew of yoghurt and lentils); lapsi (a bulgar-wheat porridge) and raita (yoghurt with vegetables or fruit). Both puri (deep-fried puffy bread) and chapatti (an unleavened flatbread) are mentioned, although not parathas, which may have been a later invention.

A few dishes are called *ganvari* or *gharib*, which means rustic or poor man's food.[17] These are very simple dishes – even kings sometimes want

Ambergris

One of the world's rarest and most expensive substances, ambergris is a waxy secretion produced in the intestine of the sperm whale. Lumps that are excreted by the whale may wash up on beaches. Aged by oxidation and seawater, it develops a sweet, earthy, animal-like marine aroma. Ambergris was highly valued by the ancient Chinese, who referred to it as 'the flavour of dragon's saliva', and it was used in the Middle East and Persia as an aphrodisiac, medicine and flavouring for coffee and confectionery. Ambergris has been a crucial ingredient in perfume. However, today many countries prohibit its sale and trade as part of a ban on the hunting of sperm whales.

Preparing halwa for
Sultan Ghiyath al-
Din. Illustration
from the *Ni'matnama*
(1495–1505).

a break from elaborate dining. An example is green vegetables boiled
in water or dal, flavoured with vegetable oil, asafoetida (a spice associated
with Hindu cuisine), ginger, onions and black pepper, and served with
millet bread. Millet, a locally grown grain, features in a dozen or so recipes,
boiled as rice, parched or made into bread. Another *gharib* recipe calls for
cooked meat to be covered with dough, wrapped in a leaf and baked on
hot coals.

Techniques in the shah's kitchens include shallow-frying in ghee or
oil, deep-frying, steaming, boiling, grilling, roasting on hot stones, baking
on or in hot coals, and roasting in a pit. Sometimes meat is marinated
before cooking. Many recipes call for venison, partridge and other game.
Some dishes are prepared with as many as 50 spices and flavourings,
which are added at different stages of the cooking process.

Nowhere is the lavishness of the shah's cuisine more apparent than
in the extensive use of three flavourings: camphor, ambergris and musk,
valued not only because of their powerful, complex scents, but also
because they were rare and expensive.

Camphor is a crystalline white or transparent solid that comes from
the wood of the camphor laurel, a large evergreen tree that grows throughout Asia. (Dried rosemary leaves contain as much as 20 per cent camphor.)
The word is derived from the Sanskrit *karpura*, which may have come from
the name of a port in Sumatra. Camphor was one of the spices originally

brought by traders from the Spice Islands to India and the Middle East, and it was used as an ingredient as long ago as ancient Egypt. In India, it was one of the five ingredients (together with cardamom, clove, nutmeg and mace) of pancha-sugandha, a paan filling enjoyed by the wealthy. Today camphor is an ingredient in a few sweet dishes. It is also used in Hindu ceremonies, especially in South India, where people burn it to make a flame and a rich aroma that is used in certain rites. (Today camphor is sold in some Indian grocers, but it is important to make sure that it is labelled 'edible' before cooking with it.)

Musk, a wax made in the glands of the musk deer, is another rare ingredient, and is used both as a flavouring for food and as a deodorant. ('Rub musk into smelly armpits', says an instruction in the *Ni'matnama*.) First mentioned in India as a remedy in Ayurvedic medicine, it later came to Europe and the Middle East where the Arabs valued it as a fixative in perfumes and as an aphrodisiac. Like ambergris, its sale is now illegal.

In common with other Indian culinary collections, the *Ni'matnama* contains recipes and prescriptions for many ailments and conditions. Impotence and low sperm production were a priority for the shah. Almost all spices are considered to have aphrodisiac properties. For example, the following ingredients when mixed together and rubbed on the penis 'produce lustful feelings and increase the flow of semen': long pepper, cardamoms, chironji nuts, fresh cow's butter, ghee, sheep's milk, poppy

Preparing qima for Sultan Ghiyath al-Din. Illustration from the *Ni'matnama* (1495–1505).

seeds, cloves, date sugar, pine nuts, dried ginger, dates, roasted chickpeas, almonds, figs, myrobalan, raisins and honey. The following foods, fried in ghee, are said to produce the same effect: veal, mutton, sparrow brains, pigeon, ghee, cow's milk, mace, cinnamon and cardamoms. Combinations of spices and other ingredients are recommended for such ailments as excessive thinness, broken bones, weak eyesight, itchiness and tuberculosis. Many medical benefits are attributed to paan.

In 1562 Malwa was conquered by Akbar and became part of the Mughal Empire. We can only speculate as to whether some of the shah's cooks migrated to the court in Delhi and influenced the development of Indian cuisine.

THE SUPA SHASTRA

A work written or commissioned at about the same time as the *Ni'matnama* is the *Supa Shastra* (The Science of Cooking, *c.* 1508). Its author, Mangarasa III, was the Jain ruler of Kallhalli, a tiny state in Mysore District, Karnataka, that was part of the Vijayanagar Empire. The book was written in verse on palm-leaf manucripts in an old version of Kannada, and contains six chapters consisting of a total of 450 poems. In the introduction, the author emphasizes its roots in Hindu tradition by thanking the mythical figures Bhima, Nala and Gouri (an incarnation of Durga famed for her cooking skills).

The intended readers of the *Supa Shastra* were housewives, albeit affluent ones.[18] Mangarasa does not specify the exact amounts of ingredients, leaving it up to the cook's judgement, but he does provide fairly precise descriptions of cooking techniques, which include roasting, frying, tempering with spices, baking, boiling in a thin or thick gravy, steaming, distilling, grilling and heating in hot sand. While all the recipes are vegetarian, a few use onions and garlic in violation of the usual Jain proscriptions. The flavouring is both basic – coriander, cumin, mustard seeds and fenugreek, still staples of the South Indian spice box – and more aromatic: cardamom, camphor, nutmeg, screwpine, even musk. Often grated coconut is called for.

The first chapter describes 50 snacks, breads and sweet dishes, including nine kinds of roti, ten vatakas (vadas) and stuffed dishes made from wheat, rice or lentil flour. One technique is to make cups out of wheat dough, fill them with a sweet or salty mixture and fry or bake them – a medieval Indian version of a French tart. An unusual recipe calls for

---

Stuffed Aubergine, from the *Supa Shastra*

'This is one of the top preparations of aubergines, with all its aroma, charm, taste, and makes you crave for it whenever memory recalls it.'

Take an aubergine and remove the top with a knife so that it can be replaced afterwards.

Remove the inside and set aside. Take another aubergine, which is already boiled, and remove the inside. Mix the following ingredients with the pulp: grated coconut fried in ghee, pepper, cumin seeds, fenugreek, sesame seeds, chickpeas, urad dal, dried and fried little pieces of bread, turmeric powder, all fried in ghee, ginger, onion, curry leaves, coriander leaves, all chopped finely and then fried in ghee. Stuff the mixture into the unboiled aubergine, then fry it nicely in ghee or oil.

---

mixing bananas, dates, mangoes, jackfruit and grapes with powdered sugar, cardamom, edible camphor and musk (if available), and ghee, then wrapping it in dough and baking it.

The second chapter covers drinks, including milk and its products, and sweet drinks made from fruit, flowers and the water that remains from cooking rice. The third chapter features 20 rice preparations, including several versions of khichri, kanjika (porridge), rice flavoured with tamarind or mustard seeds, and sweet rice pudding.

The vegetables in the recipes are those that are sold today in Indian markets or grow in people's gardens. The fourth chapter contains recipes for aubergines and plaintains; of the 60 vegetable recipes in the *Supa Shastra*, about half are for aubergines and half for plantains or plantain flowers. Aubergines are particularly versatile because of their ability to absorb flavour. In the *Supa Shastra* they are boiled into a soup; fried with spices; baked with yoghurt; steamed, filled with ground spices and simmered in a thick broth; stuffed with green leaves; grilled then mixed with yoghurt and spices or boiled in milk; cut into tiny pieces, mixed with onion and sautéed in ghee and spices; stuffed with panir (farmer's cheese) and spices; roasted, flavoured with tamarind juice and oil and served as a salad; or baked and flavoured with yoghurt and ginger.

Plantain flowers are boiled, squeezed dry and prepared in many ways, some quite elaborate. Pieces of plantain and panir strung on a metal wire are brushed with ghee and grilled over hot coals to make an edible garland. Banana chunks are served in sugar syrup or sprinkled with ghee, mustard or pepper.

The fifth chapter contains recipes for ridged gourds and pumpkin, and 34 recipes for jackfruit, an enormous green fruit (one can weigh up to 36 kg/80 lb) with a prickly skin that grows wild throughout India. After being soaked and drained, pieces of jackfruit may be fried in ghee and spices; boiled with lentils; minced with onions and coconut and shaped into balls; or boiled and served in sugar syrup.

The final chapter offers recipes for amla (Indian gooseberry) and bamboo shoots or sprouts – common ingredients in western Karnataka and northeast India, where they are often pickled. In the *Supa Shastra*, the shoots are cut into chunks or rounds and sautéed with spices; slightly fermented and cooked in a liquid, such as buttermilk; mixed with ginger, onion and grated coconut to form a paste, which is wrapped in betel-leaf cups and steamed; or ground with ginger, onion and curry leaves, steamed, then mixed with rice, urad dal and coconut, and fried.

KSEMAKUTUHALAM

Ksemakutuhalam (*Diet and Well-being*) is a Sanskrit treatise in verse written about 1550.[19] The author, Ksemasarma, was a poet and scholar and possibly physician at the court of King Vikramasena, who most likely was a Rajput ruler, perhaps in the kingdom of Ujjain, just 80 km (50 miles) north of Mandu.[20] The author was a brahmin and the book is filled with references to Hindu gods, albeit in a charming, slightly irreverent manner. For example, a dessert is described as having tasty layers 'that resemble the chapters of the Puranas'; another has such a divine fragrance that 'even men who hanker for liberation long greedily to taste it', while a drink is described as 'a delicacy rarely met with even in paradise'.

The author's concern for the healthy properties of dishes and their effects on the *doshas* is combined with a gourmet's appreciation and love of good food. His personal comments, snippets of poetry, appeals to the gods and metaphors are scattered throughout the text. Some recipes come from medical literature, others from the *Manasolassa*, while still others may be his own creations.

> ┌───┐
> **Culinary Equipment in Sixteenth-century India**
> (from *Ksemakuthuhalam*)

Broom	Pestle and mortar
Big pot	Winnowing basket
Brush	Clod of clay
Grindstone	Ladle
Bamboo vessel	Square piece of cloth
Jar filled with water	Two pairs of tongs
Stones to produce fire	Four pieces of cloth
Pieces of dry wood cut to	Tubular reed
arm's length, not	Knife
old, neither very	Iron spit for roasting
thick nor thin, and	Frying pan
free from worms and	Long ladle-like piece of
insects	iron to move fire
Sieve	Wooden or iron pot for
Strainer	storing ghee

The *Ksemakutuhalam* consists of twelve chapters, or *utsava*, each dealing with a separate topic, including the royal kitchen and its equipment; the qualities of a good physician and head cook (he should be both an expert in Ayurveda and a good manager); healthy daily routines; seasonal diets; and recipes. The recipes list ingredients but, with a few exceptions, do not give quantities or cooking times. They reveal a rich and diverse cuisine with few restrictions, although onion and garlic are used very sparingly. Except for beef, almost every kind of meat is consumed by the king, including boar, lamb, castrated goat, venison, rabbit, lizards, wild and domesticated pig, game birds, peacocks and tortoises. (Being a brahmin, the author notes that he has not personally tasted the meat dishes, but describes only what he has learned about their preparation.) Ksemasarma writes that meat should be freshly killed and animals that have died from natural causes avoided. The best meat comes from an active animal, since it is good for the heart and improves appetite.

The most important factor in preparing delicious meat dishes, however, is the skill of the cook. Ksemasarma writes:

Be it [the meat] of village-bred animals, of forest beasts, of those
that are aquatic or those that live in burrows, be it white, yellow,
green or red in colour, be it floated in oil, roasted on spits, cooked
as broths, boiled or cut in pieces, meat that is prepared by excellent cooks is savoured by man and praised in accordance with
their taste.[21]

Many of the meat and vegetable dishes are flavoured with water
infused with asafoetida. Other common spices are black pepper, ginger
juice, ground ginger, turmeric and, to a lesser extent, cardamom, clove,
camphor, musk and cinnamon. Many recipes call for a spice mixture
called vesavara (which in Ayurvedic texts means a spiced dish of minced
meat) – a blend of asafoetida, fresh ginger, cumin seeds, black pepper,
turmeric and coriander seeds. Trikatu, an Ayurvedic mixture of equal parts
of long pepper, black pepper and ginger, is another common flavouring
for meat. Spices are added at different points in the cooking process, as
they are today: to flavour a sauce, as a rub or marinade, or fried in oil and
sprinkled over a cooked dish to lend extra fragrance (cardamom, clove,
camphor, musk, black pepper and cinnamon are mentioned as ingredients for such a garnish). Sesame oil is a common cooking medium, and
a souring agent such as pomegranate is occasionally added.

Cooking should always be done over a low flame, especially milk,
which should never be cooked over high heat unless it is mixed with rice.
The ratio of water to rice is four to one. Mung dal requires three times
as much water, urad dal slightly more. When frying meat, the ratio of oil
to meat is one part oil to ten parts meat. When cooking fish, the ratio of
oil and spices to flesh is one to four. Still, all amounts have to be adjusted
to the eater's taste.

The best cooking pots are made of clay, since they imbue the food
with healthful qualities, but rich men and kings use gold and silver vessels
since they cure deranged *doshas* and improve the intellect. Boiled rice can
be served in its own cooking pot; other dishes should be transferred to
a serving plate. Ghee is stored in a wooden or iron pot. Milk products
are served only in earthenware containers. Rich people keep deer, swans,
peacocks and other animals in their gardens to test for poison, since
each will react in a specific manner when served a poisoned food.

The king's meal consists of rice, dal, ghee, a dish cooked with coconut
and cucumber, soft and crispy papads (papadums), meat with vegetables,
a dish made with rice flour, and boiled milk mixed with cooked rice and

a sweet juice. Fruit (except for cucumber and banana) is eaten only at the start of a meal. The king should be moderate in his diet, and his meals should be served between three and six hours apart. The author cites a long list of undesirable combinations: milk, for example, should not be taken with tamarind, horse gram, vegetables, certain fish, alcohol, meat, sesame, oil cake, salt or yoghurt.

As for service, a large plate is placed on a platform in front of the diner, who sits on the floor. Cooked rice is piled in the middle of the plate. Dal, ghee, meat, vegetables and fish are placed (in that order) on the right, and broths, water, drinks, food that is sucked and licked, and pickles on the left. Nowhere in this or other texts is it mentioned that food is eaten with the right hand, presumably because this was so well known. The server, who must be a brahmin or come from a respectable family, must have bathed and be anointed with sandalwood paste, have an elegant countenance, and be adept at cooking and tidy by nature.

Meat was prepared in nine ways: deep-fried in ghee, fried, dry-roasted, boiled in a little liquid, simmered in a lot of liquid, roasted directly over a fire, minced, roasted on spits and baked in an underground pit. In a method called *putapaka*, minced meat is flavoured with the vesavara spice mixture, wrapped in leaves and white flour or orange peel, covered with clay and cooked in a pit in the ground. Minced meat is formed into cones or other shapes, boiled and then fried. To make a dish called tanduram, meat marinated in spices is hung in a pit filled with burning charcoal. Boiled meat, milk and sugar are even made into a sweet dish, called ksiramrtam (milk ambrosia).

Fish is cooked in the same way as meat, but with one-quarter of the oil. After smearing the fish with asafoetida to remove the odour, it is dipped in a batter of chickpea flour, turmeric, ground ginger and coriander, and fried in mustard oil. Fish forcemeat can be a stuffing for both idli and mandaka. There are many recipes for broth, some made with buttermilk, meat and spices.

The longest chapter in the *Ksemakutuhalam* is devoted to edible plants – the leaves, flowers, fruit, stalks, bulbs and roots. A simple method of preparation is to sauté vegetables in oil with salt, asafoetida and cumin seeds, then add tamarind or buttermilk. The long list of suitable plants includes various varieties of gourd, Bengal quince, wood apple, myrobalan, bitter gourd (poetically described as resembling 'an emerald without and a coral within'), green Bengal gram, figs, plantain, cow peas and many with no English name. Green leafy vegetables include goosefoot, amaranth, cassia, spinach, fennel, fenugreek, black nightshade, purslane, jute leaves, black pepper leaves and safflower leaves. At one point the author inserts a whimsical dialogue between three leafy vegetables:

'I am of two kinds and am rich in all the six tastes. What is the use of other dishes when I am there?' In this manner the Indian spinach, mixed with rice, seems to smile proudly.

'Although single, I am of multiple tastes and I am scented by my own fragrance.' In this manner, Satapuspa (Indian fennel) seems to proclaim her victory.

'What is the use of limiting one's prosperity to oneself as Satapuspa is doing by scenting only herself with her fragrance? But I am not like that. I perfume the entire dining room with my fragrance.' Thus does Fenugreek rebuke the selfish Fennel.[22]

Aubergine (eggplant), a versatile ingredient, is indigenous to India. Late 18th or early 19th century,

But the author's favourite vegetable is the aubergine:

Fie on the meal that has no aubergine. Fie on the aubergine that has no stalk. Fie on the aubergine that has a stalk but is not cooked in oil and fie upon the aubergine that is cooked in oil without using asafoetida![23]

Aubergines are featured in sixteen recipes: for example, pieces are boiled with tamarind, then fried in ghee, coriander, ginger juice and turmeric; the flesh of the green aubergine is dipped in asafoetida-flavoured mustard oil and black pepper; fried in ghee with rice flour, grated coconut, black pepper and cardamom; and cooked in vesavara spice mixture, black pepper, asafoetida and buttermilk. One dish resembles the modern baigan bharta: a whole aubergine is cooked over high heat until it is soft, then mashed and mixed with mustard seeds, rock salt and yoghurt. Aubergine served with tamarind and sesame oil 'gives great pleasure, just as a maiden to her beloved'.

The book contains many recipes for sweet dishes and snacks. For sweets, the basic ingredients are ghee, sugar and milk products: khoya is made by boiling milk until it is thick, and chhana by separating milk with a souring agent and then straining it. Ground lentils, rice flour and white flour are other ingredients. Dough is extruded to make vermicelli-like strands called sev that can be made into laddu and other sweets. The most frequently used spices are cardamom and black pepper. Many sweet dishes are soaked in sugar syrup, as they are today. The repertoire of sweet dishes includes:

Laddus, small balls made from rice flour and yoghurt, white or wholewheat flour, ground vegetables, lotus seeds, coconut, lentils, even fish and meat. Sometimes they are composed of sev or little globules

Phenika (modern pheni, or vermicelli), a lightly fried multi-layered cake made from white flour or ground lentils, yoghurt and ghee

Vatikas (vadas), a dough of ground fermented lentils or white flour and yoghurt formed into various shapes (square, oblong or round) and deep-fried

Mandaka, disc-shaped wheat-flour cakes similar to the modern mandige. They can be mixed with cardamom, ghee, sugar and milk

Polika, a thin mandaka filled with lentils and jaggery

Lapsika, a porridge of white flour, ghee, sugar, cloves and black pepper

Ghrtapura (from Sanskrit *ghrta*, 'ghee'). Many varieties, made by cooking wheat or rice flour, khoya, mango, water chestnut and other ingredients with ghee and sugar, sometimes spiced with camphor and black pepper

Puri, a puffy bread made of chickpea and wheat flour flavoured with ajwain (small brown seeds that taste like thyme), asafoetida and cloves, and fried in ghee

Jalebi, a mixture consisting of two parts white flour and one part wheat flour and milk is fermented, then dripped through holes into hot ghee to form coils, which are then soaked in sugar syrup (of Arab origin, this may have been a borrowing from one of the Islamic courts)

Kapuranalika, white flour, ghee and water rolled into squares and fried in ghee to make polikas. They are wrapped around crystallized sugar to form tubes, fried in ghee and filled with camphor, ghee and sugar

Kasara, a mixture of sugar, white flour (or lotus-root or water-chestnut flour) and ghee is cooked, spread on to a pan smeared with oil, and cut into squares.

The final section of the *Ksemakutuhalam* describes drinks and other dishes that stimulate the appetite and increase energy. They include lemon or orange pulp mixed with sugar, pepper and cardamom; orange and sugar cooked in ghee, then cooled and mixed with milk; and various yoghurt drinks flavoured with rock salt, ginger and toasted cumin seeds. A recipe is given for the yoghurt dish sikharini (shrikhand), which is said to be especially nourishing for those who are 'languid after enjoying dalliance with intoxicated ladies'.

Jalebi, spirals of fried lentil batter soaked in sugar syrup,
is one of India's most popular street foods.

VIJAYANAGAR

In the south, a great Hindu kingdom called Vijayanagar came to rule
much of the Deccan. Its founder, Harihara I (ruled 1336–56), won
the support of powerful local landlords, built a huge army, conquered
local kingdoms and built a capital city, Vijayanagar, that at its height
was the largest or second-largest (after Beijing) city in the world with
a population of 500,000. Foreign travellers painted glowing pictures
of a rich, well-governed land and a capital city with elegant gardens
and broad streets lined with merchants' mansions. The port of Bharkal
linked Vijayanagar to China, the Middle East and Southeast Asia. The
countryside was fertile and extensively cultivated, but rainfall was scarce,
so the rulers built irrigation systems and lakes to collect rainwater.

The Portuguese traveller Domingo Paes, who visited Vijayanagar in
the early 1520s, compared the city favourably with those of his native
land:

> This is the best-provided city in the world, and is stocked with
> provisions such as rice, wheat, grains . . . and some barley and
> beans, mung dal, pulses, horse gram and many other seeds which

grow in this country and which are the food of the common people, and there is a large store of these and very cheap; but wheat is not so common as the other grains since no one eats [it] except the Moors (that is Muslims).[24]

Paes noted that the markets were full of quail, partridge, hares, mutton 'so clean and fat it looks like pork' and pigs so white and clean 'you could not see better in any country'. Every day carts brought loads of sweet and sour oranges, pomegranates, aubergines and other vegetables (but not, he notes, lettuce and cabbage as in Portugal), and limes that made those sold in Lisbon appear worthless. Ordinary people ate millet, and rice was the staple of the wealthy. Paes observed that while some people ate meat, the brahmins in charge of the temples ate neither meat nor fish nor anything that made a dish red, since that resembled blood. All classes of society consumed betel nut throughout the day (even though it stained their mouths red).

The last Vijayanagar rulers faced incursions from rival dynasties in the south as well as from the Portuguese, who were gaining an economic foothold in the region. In 1565 the empire was defeated by an alliance of Muslim rulers, who razed the city. Today all that remains are a few scattered ruins of buildings near the village of Hampi, which is a World Heritage Site. Meanwhile, a new power appeared in the north that was to establish one of the greatest Indian empires and bring cuisine to new heights: the Mughals.

NINE

The Mughal Dynasty and its Successors, 1526–1857

In North India, the power vacuum left by the disintegration of the Lodis, the last of the Delhi sultanates, was filled by a new dynasty called the Mughals (from the Persian word for Mongols). It was founded by Babur (1483–1530), a prince of the tiny kingdom of Ferghana in Central Asia, whose ancestors included Timur/Tamerlane and the Mongol leader Genghis Khan.

In 1526 Babur entered the Punjab with a small army at the invitation of a local ruler. He defeated the opposing armies at the battle of Panipat (the first time gunpowder was used in India), and proclaimed himself emperor of all Hindustan. Babur is one of history's most intriguing figures: a brave warrior who as a very young man fought hostile tribes in Afghanistan and founded a powerful dynasty, but also a talented Persian poet, a sensitive memoirist and a devotee and planter of gardens. He wrote in one of his couplets: 'Enjoy the luxuries of life, Babur, for the world is not going to be had a second time.'[1] Although his native language was Chagatai, a Turkic language, he was fluent in Persian and steeped in Persian culture.

Babur's birthplace, the Ferghana Valley (now part of Uzbekistan, Tadjikistan and Kyrgyzstan), was famous for its grapes and melons. He frequently interrupts his stories of battles and treachery to describe a delicious melon he came across in his wanderings. According to his translator Annette Beveridge, 'Babur's interest in fruits was not a matter of taste or amusement but of food. Melons, for instance, fresh or stored, form during some months the staple food of Turkistanis.'[2]

Babur's first encounter with Hindustan was a disappointment. In a famous passage in his memoirs, he wrote:

Harvesting the almond crop, from the *Memoirs of Babur* (*c.* 1590).

The emperor Babur supervising the laying out of the Garden of Fidelity
outside Kabul, *c.* 1590, watercolour and gold on paper.

Hindustan is a country of few charms. Its people have no good
looks; of social intercourse, paying and receiving visits there is
none; of genius and capacity none; of manners none; in handi-
craft and work there is no form or symmetry, method or quality;
there are no good horses, no good dogs, no grapes, muskmelons
or first-rate fruits, no ice or cold water, no good bread or cooked
food in the bazaars, no hot baths, no colleges, no candles, torches
or candlesticks.

On the other hand, Hindustan

is a large country and has masses of gold and silver. Its air in the
rains is very fine . . . Another good thing about Hindustan is that
it has endless workmen of every kind. There is a fixed caste for
every sort of work and for everything.[3]

A banquet being prepared for Babur and the royal princes, from the *Memoirs of Babur* (c. 1590).

Banquet being given for Babur, with roast goose at the centre, 1507, miniature.

Of all the fruit Babur encountered in Hindustan, the only one that appealed to him was the mango, although with the caveat that 'mangoes when good are very good, but as many as are eaten, few are first-rate.' He notes that they are usually plucked when green to ripen indoors, and are best made into condiments or preserved in syrup. Babur planted gardens wherever he went, and imported seeds and gardeners from Central Asia and Persia to grow melons, peaches, apricots, pistachios, walnuts and almonds. Dishes mentioned in his memoirs are lamb kebabs and chikhi, a porridge made from wheat-flour paste, meat, ghee, onions, saffron and aromatic spices.[4]

At parties, guests drank chaghir, a cider-like alcoholic drink made from apples, pears or grapes, imported from Kabul and Shiraz. But Babur regretted that he drank alcohol; in 1526, on the eve of an important battle, he pledged to renounce wine, emptied his flask on the ground and smashed his goblets. However, he continued to consume ma'jun, a paste of poppy seeds (opium), hashish seeds, walnuts, pistachios, cardamom, milk and honey.[5]

181

After defeating Ibrahim Lodi, the last of the Delhi sultans, Babur set up his court in Delhi. Wanting to try Hindustani dishes, he ordered that his predecessors' cooks be brought to him, and out of 50 or 60 kept four. Ibrahim Lodi's mother tried to murder him by enlisting one of the cooks to sprinkle poison on his meal of bread, hare, fried carrots and dried meat. The attempt failed. Babur died at the age of 47 in Agra. He was buried there, but his body was later moved to his beloved Kabul, to a place now called Babur Shah's Gardens.

After 1539 Babur's son Humayun (1508–1556) temporarily lost the kingdom to the Afghan invader Sher Shah Suri and, together with his Persian wife, sought refuge at the Safavid court in Persia, where Shah Tahmasp feted him in grand style. On hearing of Humayun's imminent arrival, the shah issued the following decree:

> Upon his auspicious arrival let him drink fine sherbets of lemon and rosewater, cooled with snow; then serve him preserves of watermelon, grapes and other fruits with white bread just as I have ordered. For this royal guest prepare each drink with sweet attars and ambergris; and each day prepare a banquet of five hundred rare and delicious and colorful dishes . . . O my son, on the day of his arrival give feast, tremendous and enticing, of meats and sweetmeats, milks and fruits to the number of three thousand trays.[6]

In 1555, with Shah Tahmasp's military help, Humayun regained his kingdom and took some of the shah's artists, poets, administrators and cooks with him. Persian became the language not only of culture but also of administration, a position it held until it was replaced by English in 1837. But Humayun reigned for only six months, and little is known about his culinary habits. He is said to have abstained from meat for several months when campaigning to regain his throne.

It was Humayun's son Akbar, considered one of India's greatest rulers, who was the chief architect of the Mughal Empire. By 1560 he had established his authority over the Gangetic Valley, and he eventually extended it to all of northern and western India, including Bengal, Kashmir, Gujarat and Baluchistan, as well as part of the Deccan Plateau. By war and matrimonial alliances with the Rajput princes, he brought all of Rajasthan under his control. In 1572 he annexed Gujarat, where he encountered the Portuguese, who had established trading posts along the coast.

Akbar divided the empire and its 100 million inhabitants into twelve provinces and smaller subdistricts. Each province was ruled by a viceroy or governor, known as a *subadar* or nawab (a word that came to signify a person of great wealth and importance). Their courts were miniature versions of that of the emperor in Delhi. Because the wealth of Mughal grandees reverted to the emperor on their death, lavish spending and high living became the order of the day. Poetry, painting, music and cuisine flourished.

During his long reign (1556–1605), Akbar won the support of his non-Muslim subjects by abolishing discriminatory taxes, appointing them to high posts in his administration, encouraging and patronizing Hindu culture, and marrying the daughters of Hindu Rajput kings (as well as a Christian Portuguese woman). Akbar banned the eating of beef at his court and avoided other foods that would offend Hindus and Jains. He invited Hindu, Muslim, Jain, Parsee and Jesuit scholars to explain their religions to him. Like his father, Humayun, Akbar visited the tombs of Sufi saints and welcomed Sufi holy men to his court.[7] He even tried to start a new religion called Deen-i-llahi that combined elements of different faiths.

Descriptions of the imperial cuisine are given in the *Ain-i-Akbari* (a detailed chronicle of Akbar's court by his prime minister Abu'l-Fazl ibn Mubarak Allami) and the accounts of European travellers.[8] The royal kitchen was a department of state reporting directly to the prime minister. Its enormous staff included a head cook, a treasurer, a storekeeper, clerks, tasters and more than 400 cooks from all over India and Persia. Food was served in gold, silver, stone and earthenware dishes, tied in cloths, inspected and approved by the head cook and tasted several times before being served. Ice, used for cooling drinks and making frozen desserts, was brought daily from the Himalayas by an elaborate system of couriers.

The kitchen commanded the finest ingredients from every part of the empire: regional and seasonal varieties of rice, butter from a certain town, duck and waterfowl from Kashmir. The palace chickens were fed by hand with pellets flavoured with saffron and rosewater, and massaged daily with musk oil and sandalwood. A kitchen garden provided a continuous supply of fresh vegetables and especially fruit, since, as Abu'l-Fazl wrote, 'His Majesty looks upon fruits as one of the greatest gifts of the Creator, and pays much attention to them.'[8] Akbar brought horticulturists from Central Asia and Iran to supervise his orchards. They cultivated many varieties of melons, peaches, apricots, walnuts, pistachios, pomegranates, almonds, plums, apples, pears, cherries, chestnuts and grapes.

The Catalan Jesuit priest Antonio Monserrate described the meals at Akbar's court:

> His table is very sumptuous, generally consisting of more than forty courses served in great dishes. These are brought into the royal dining hall covered and wrapped in linen cloths, which are tied up and sealed by the cook, for fear of poison. They are carried by youths to the door of the dining hall, other servants walking ahead and the master of the household following. Here they are taken over by eunuchs, who hand them to the serving girls who wait on the royal table. He is accustomed to dine in private, except on the occasion of a public banquet.[9]

In his chronicle, Abu'l-Fazl lists three categories of dish. The first were vegetarian dishes, called sufiyana, meant for the emperor's days of abstinence from meat. They included khushka, plain boiled rice; pahit, lentils cooked with ghee, ginger, cumin seeds and asafoetida; khichri, made of equal parts rice, mung dal and ghee; thuli, sweet, spicy cracked-wheat porridge (a dish eaten today in western India); chikhi, a dish described by Abu'l-Fazl as made from a fine paste of wheat flour, onions and spices dressed with various kinds of meat; badanjan, aubergine cooked with onions, ghee and spices; sag, green leafy vegetables; zard bir-inj, rice pudding flavoured with saffron; and various kinds of halwa.

Dishes in the second category were made with meat, served with rice or other grains. They include qabuli, a mixture of rice, chickpeas, onions and spices; qima pulao (the only mention of pulao), rice and ground meat; shulla (see recipe); bughra, meat, flour, chickpeas, vinegar, crystal-lized sugar, carrots, beet, turnips, spinach and fennel leaves; harissa, meat and cracked wheat; kashk, meat with crushed wheat, chickpeas and aromatic spices; halim, a porridge of meat, cracked wheat, turnips, carrots, spinach and fennel leaves; and sanbusa or qutab (a Turkic word still used in Azerbaijan for samosas, which Abu'l-Fazl notes can be made in twenty different ways – which unfortunately he does not describe).

The third category, meat dishes, included yakhni, a meat stock; musamman, stuffed roast chicken; dopiaza, meat prepared with large quantities of onions; dampukht, meat cooked slowly with aromatic spices in a pot with a sealed lid; qaliya, highly spiced meat with a thick gravy; malghuba, a soup made from lamb, vegetables, lentils and rice; biryan (from a Persian word meaning frying or roasting), prepared from a Dashmandi sheep (a town in Afghanistan), ghee, saffron, cloves, pepper and cumin seeds; and various kinds of kebab.

Abu'l-Fazl does not give cooking directions for any of these dishes; of biryan, he simply states that 'it is made in various ways'. But cooking techniques were no doubt very complex and labour-intensive. The dish murgh mussalam, for example, was made by removing the bones of a chicken so that it remained whole, marinating it in yoghurt and spices; stuffing it with rice, nuts, minced meat and boiled eggs; and baking it coated with clarified butter and more spices.

The names of the dishes reflect the diverse culinary influences. They come from Arabic (halim, harissa, halwa, sanbusa), Persian (kashk, shirbirnj, pulao, zard birinj, dampukht, bandijan) and Turkic (qutab, qima, boghra, shulla). But despite the Persian influence, some of the most characteristic features of Persian cuisine are missing, notably the combination of sweet and sour flavours and the addition of green herbs and fruit to meat stews (khoresht).

The Mughals' ethnic background left some mark on their cuisine. In the early seventeenth century the court included Uighurs, Chagatai Turks, Turkmens, Uzbeks and other groups from Central Asia. They were once herdsmen who moved around Central Asia with their flocks of sheep, goats and horses. According to the food historian Charles Perry, grains were an important part of their diet from the tenth century onwards as they moved west into grain-growing regions. Two of the dishes listed by Abu'l-Fazl may reflect this heritage: kashk, a porridge of crushed wheat and meat, and shulla, which came to refer to a rich dish based on boiled grain, preferably rice, enriched with whatever the host could afford to throw in to honour his guest.[10]

Wheat bread was part of every meal at Akbar's court. A large bread similar to modern naan was baked in an oven; a small, thin bread which sounds rather like the modern chapatti was cooked on an iron plate. (The seventeenth-century French traveller and writer François Bernier, who served as a physician to the Mughal royal family, admired many aspects of Indian life – but not its bread, which, he wrote, while occasionally good, 'can never be compared with the *pain de Gonesse* and other delicious varieties to be met with in Paris'. He attributed this inferiority to the poor quality of Indian ovens.[11]) Small plates of pickles (Abu'l-Fazl lists 30 kinds sold in the market), yoghurt and lime were served during meals.

Many recipes in the *Ain-i-Akbari* call for onion and ginger, but very few contain garlic. The main cooking medium was ghee, which was used in enormous quantities. (The recipe for khichri, for example, calls for equal amounts of rice, lentils and ghee.) The most frequently used spices were ginger, cinnamon, black pepper, cumin, cardamom, cloves, saffron and coriander. However, many of the spices sold in the market-place were *not* used in the royal dishes, including long pepper, dried ginger, aniseed, turmeric, kalonji (nigella), fennel, mustard seeds, black and white sesame seeds, tamarind and curry leaves. Perhaps these spices, key elements in the local cuisine, were still foreign to Central Asian and Persian taste.

Also missing are red chillies from the New World, since they had not reached North India by Akbar's time, although a reference to them can be found in a South Indian poem written in the first half of the sixteenth century.[12] Tomatoes and potatoes are likewise absent, but pineapples had reached the capital: Abu'l-Fazl notes that a single pineapple was sold in Delhi markets for the price of ten mangoes.

Another New World gift was tobacco, which was introduced by the Portuguese in the Deccan. A courtier brought tobacco to Akbar's court, together with a jewelled hookah. (The hookah may have been invented at Akbar's court by a Persian physician, Abu'l-Fath Gilani, who perhaps got the idea from a primitive version using a coconut shell as the base that had been used to smoke opium and hashish.[13]) Akbar apparently liked it, because tobacco-smoking became popular in the royal household, despite the disapproval of religious conservatives.

At around the same time, Shah Abbas banned smoking in Iran. The Mughal ambassador at the court was a chain-smoker, however, so the shah made an exception and wrote the following poem:

> The ambassador of our friend
> Is so fond of smoking
> I shall light up the tobacco market
> With the candle of my friendship.[14]

Coffee had reached India by the early seventeenth century, since it is mentioned by Edward Terry in 1617. It had probably been introduced

Shulla (from Ain-i-Akbari)

10 seers meat (1 seer = approximately 1 kg/2¼ lb)

3½ seers rice

2 seers ghee

1 seer chickpeas

2 seers onions

½ seer salt

¼ seer fresh ginger

2 dam garlic (1 dam = 20 g/¾ oz)

1 dam each round pepper, cinnamon, cardamoms
and cloves

Reconstructed directions

Melt the ghee in a pot and fry the meat, onions and garlic for five minutes over a medium heat. Add 360 ml (1½ cups) water, the salt, chickpeas and cinnamon. Simmer for ten minutes. Stir in the other spices, then add the rice and another 120 ml (½ cup) water. Simmer until the rice is cooked.

earlier than that by Arab traders (although a poetic legend attributes it to a Muslim holy man, Baba Budan, who brought seven coffee seeds back from Mecca in 1720). A poet at the court of Akbar's son Jahangir praised it with the following verse:

Coffee is pleasing to princes
The water of Khidr [a Muslim saint who is said to have
    discovered the water of eternal life] is concealed within;
In the gloomy kitchen filled with its smoke
The coffeepot seems like the source of life.[15]

Despite the opulence of the cuisine at his court, Akbar himself led an austere, even ascetic, existence, as Abu'l-Fazl wrote:

If his Majesty did not possess so lofty a mind, so comprehensive an understanding, so universal a kindness, he would have chosen the path of solitude, and given up sleep and food altogether; and even now . . . the question 'What dinner has been prepared today?' never passes over his tongue. In the course of 24 hours, his Majesty eats but once and leaves off before he is fully satisfied; neither is there any fixed time for this meal, but the servants have always things so far ready that in the space of an hour after the order has been given, a hundred dishes are served up.[16]

And elsewhere:

His Majesty cares very little for meat, and often expresses himself to that effect. It is indeed from ignorance and cruelty that, although various kinds of foods are obtainable, men are bent upon injuring living creatures, and lending a ready hand in killing and eating them; none seems to have an eye for the beauty inherent in the prevention of cruelty, but makes himself a tomb for animals. If his Majesty had not the burden of the world on his shoulders, he would at once totally abstain from meat; and now it is his intention to quit it by degrees, conforming, however, a little to the spirit of the age.[17]

A seller of zarda (flavoured tobacco) which is sometimes added to paan.
Tobacco was introduced by Europeans in the 16th century.

Akbar fasted regularly and gradually increased the number of days on which he did so. He did not impose his abstinence on his subjects, although it was his wish that people should refrain from eating meat during the month in which he came to the throne, so that the year would be an auspicious one.

Akbar's son Jahangir (ruled 1605–27) and grandson Shah Jahan (ruled 1627–58) preserved and slightly extended Akbar's empire. Jahangir built many palaces and mosques, planted gardens – including the famous Shalimar Bagh in Kashmir – and supported large ateliers of artists. Like his great-grandfather Babur, he was fascinated by the natural world and left behind descriptions of plants and wildlife. He honoured and emulated his father by ordering that no animals should be killed on Thursdays, the date of his accession, and on Sunday, the day of Akbar's birth, quoting his father, who said that on that day 'all animals should be free from the calamity of those of a butcherly disposition'.

Jahangir was very fond of khichri, especially a version he encountered in western India. In his memoirs he wrote:

> Of the food that is particular to the people of Gujarat, there is the bajra khichri, a mixture of split peas and millet boiled together. It is a kind of split grain which does not grow in any other country but Hindustan. It is cheaper than most vegetables. As I had never eaten it, I ordered them to make some and bring it to me. It is not devoid of flavour, and it suited me well. I ordered that on days of abstinence, when I partake of dishes not made of flesh, they should frequently bring me this khichri.[18]

Jahangir's memoirs also describe his battle with alcohol and how he reduced his consumption. Unlike his father, Jahangir also enjoyed meat, especially wild game. In an account of his visit to Jahangir's court, Edward Terry was surprised that instead of eating large joints of meat, as the English did, the Mughals cut it into small pieces and stewed it with 'onions, herbs, roots and ginger and other spices with some butter'. At one royal banquet, he was served 50 dishes; he particularly liked one of spiced venison with onions (dopiaza) and rice coloured in fantastic shades, including green and purple.

Shah Jahan (who built the Taj Mahal in Agra as a monument to his late beloved wife Mumtaz Mahal) was deposed by his son Aurangzeb (ruled 1658–1707), a religious man of ascetic leanings who reversed the prevailing policy of religious tolerance and cooperation. Aurangzeb was very puritanical and often fasted. He ate a mainly vegetarian diet and had a passion for fruit, especially mangoes. Tavernier, his doctor, wrote that as no animal food passed his lips, he became 'thin and lean, to which the great fasts that he keeps have contributed . . . he only drank a little water and ate a small quantity of millet bread'.[19] When he seized power, Aurangzeb imprisoned his father, but he offered to let him eat his favourite dish every day for the rest of his life. The prison cook advised Shah Jahan not to choose a complicated dish but to ask for dal, assuring him that he could make a different dish out of it every day of the year.

THE FOOD OF THE COMMON PEOPLE

Average Indians ate quite differently from their rulers. Agriculture was often at the mercy of the weather, and so food production was unreliable. The ambassador Sir Thomas Roe (1581–1644) wrote:

> The people of India live like fishes do in the sea – the great ones eat up the little. For first the farmer robs the peasant, the gentleman robs the farmer, the greater robs the lesser, and the king robs them all.[20]

The reports of European travellers indicate that poor people ate mainly vegetarian fare (as they did in much of the world at the time): rice boiled with green ginger, a little pepper and butter; bread made of a coarse grain (perhaps millet) baked on small round iron hearths; boiled lentils; and local fruit and vegetables.

There was a lively street-food scene in towns and cities. The Portuguese priest Friar Sebastien Manrique (1585–1669) was fascinated by the brilliantly lit bazaars of Lahore, where he saw

> a great number of occupied tents, or should I say cookshops; in some, only the roast flesh of various domestic and wild animals was sold. We saw other shops containing large spits bearing the meat of winged creatures such as fowls, capons, chickens, young pigeons, peacocks, doves, quails and other birds . . . [and] booths containing household utensils and brass vessels in which were sold the same kind of meat but different to the palate owing to varied seasoning. Among these dishes, the principal and most

substantial was the rich and aromatic Biring [*birinj*, meaning husked] rice. It is cooked in innumerable ways, and Persian Pulao [is] a dish composed of rice with meat and other ingredients or of rice and spice without meat.[21]

Three kinds of bread were sold in the market: a cheap paper-thin unleavened bread baked on a skillet and then on live charcoal (like chapatti); a more expensive bread that was as thick as a finger; and, for the wealthy, khejuru, a sweet bread made from wheat flour, a lot of ghee, poppy seeds and sugar.

The Decline of the Mughals and the Emergence of New Cuisines

At its height in 1700, the Mughal Empire covered 3.2 million sq. km (1.25 million sq. miles) and had a population of 150 million – a quarter of the world's population at the time. However, its decline began under Aurangzeb and accelerated after his death. Poor transportation and communications made control of such a vast territory difficult, and the regional governors had considerable autonomy. Another factor was the military victories of the Hindu Marathas under the leadership of Shivaji Bhosale (1627–1680) and his successors. At its peak, the Maratha Empire stretched from Tamil Nadu in the south to Peshawar in the north, and as far east as Bengal. The Marathas remained the dominant power in India until they were defeated by the British in 1817. The Rajputs, hereditary rulers of kingdoms in western India, regained some of their territory from the Mughals after Aurangzeb's death but also fell victim to the Marathas until they accepted British suzerainty in 1818.

A severe blow to Mughal rule occurred in 1738 when the Persian ruler Nadir Shah invaded India. He sacked Delhi, slaughtering tens of thousands of people and looting a great quantity of gold and jewels. His victory gave him control over much of Central Asia and Persia, but his empire quickly disintegrated after he was assassinated in 1747.

Other foreign powers were by this time making inroads into the subcontinent. The Portuguese, the Dutch, the French and the British filled the power vacuum left by the declining Mughals. By the early nineteenth century the Mughal Empire had ceased as an effective political organization, although it existed in name until 1857, when it was replaced by the British Crown. Meanwhile, the regional governors became in fact, if not in name, independent of the imperial court in Delhi. The main centres were Hyderabad in South India; Awadh in North India; Murshidabad in West Bengal; Lahore, now in Pakistan; and Kashmir. But many of the traditions of the Mughal court were preserved and enhanced at the courts of these various rulers, creating new cuisines that in some ways surpassed the old.

AWADH AND LUCKNOW

One of these provinces was Awadh (called Oudh by the British) in what is today Uttar Pradesh. Humayun had made it a province of his empire in 1555 under a governor known as the *nazim* or nawab, an honorific title. In 1719 the Persian adventurer Nazim Sa'adat Khan became the de facto independent ruler, and the position became hereditary. In 1753 Asaf-ud-Daula moved the capital to Lucknow, which came to rival Delhi as the cultural and culinary capital of North India and reached 'a level of splendour and sophistication scarcely paralleled in any other Indo-Islamic society'.[22]

These are the words of Abdul Halim Sharar (1860–1926), a journalist and historian who chronicled life in Lucknow in his book *Lucknow: Last Phase of an Oriental Culture*. He describes a vibrant syncretic culture that combined elements of North Indian Hindu and Muslim music, dance, clothing, painting and cuisine. A more colourful description was given by the twentieth-century art historian Stuart Cary Welch, who compared the city to 'an Indian mixture of [pre-revolutionary] Teheran, Monte Carlo and Las Vegas, with just a touch of Glyndebourne for good measure'.[23]

Gourmetship was prized not only by the nawab and his entourage but also by wealthy landowners and even middle-class and ordinary people. The affluent vied with one another over who could create the most complex dishes; chefs, called *rakabdar*, enjoyed a high status and salary. One of the nawab's cooks was paid 1,200 rupees a month, equivalent to perhaps £5,000 today. These cooks were much in demand in other parts of India, and disseminated Lucknavi cuisine to courts at Hyderabad and elsewhere. They would cook only small quantities for a few people, since they considered it beneath their dignity to produce large amounts of food, something that was the province of the *bawarchi* (ordinary cooks). Presentation was extremely important: dishes were adorned with dried fruit cut into the shape of flowers or edible silver leaf.

One of these cooks' special talents was to create dishes from unusual
ingredients or to make an entire meal from a single ingredient, a technique called *pehle* (riddle). For example, when a prince from Delhi who
was a well-known gourmet dined with the tenth and last nawab, Wajid
Ali Shah (1822–1887), he was served what he was told was a murabba, a
thick, highly spiced conserve made of fruit or vegetables. In fact, it was
a korma, a meat curry, but fashioned to look like a murabba. A few days
later the prince reciprocated by serving the nawab hundreds of dishes,
including pulao, korma, kebabs, biryani, chapattis and other breads – all
made of sugar, even the serving plates. One chef was famous for making
khichri from pistachios shaped like lentils and almonds cut to look like
grains of rice. Another chef specialized in making arvi ka salan, taro root
in a sour, spicy gravy. His only condition of employment was that he
be allowed to serve a different arvi ka salan twice a day all year round.
A Kashmiri dish that became popular in Lucknow was shab degh – a slow-
cooked stew of minced meatballs and turnip, its two main ingredients
impossible to tell apart.

Pulao and korma were favourite dishes of the aristocracy. Wealthy
epicures fed their chickens musk and saffron pills to scent their meat,
which was cooked to make a broth in which to simmer rice. Sharar writes
that in Delhi biryani was popular, but in Lucknow people preferred

A Lucknow resident and his wife at dinner.

Mughal Cuisine

The Oxford Companion to Food describes Mughal food as 'a blend of Persian and Hindu kitchen practices' featuring such dishes as pilaf (pulao), biryani, kebabs, kormas, koftas, tandoor dishes and samosas, and cream, almonds and rose-water as ingredients. Related are dishes containing the words *shahi* (royal), Akbar, Shah Jahan and the like in their names. The term 'Mughal', which was probably first used by enterprising restaurateurs to lend cachet to their dishes, has become a catchphrase for rich, generally meat-based dishes associated with Muslim cuisine of north India or Pakistan. However, the usage is somewhat inaccurate. Many of the dishes attributed to the Mughals existed earlier at the court of the Delhi sultans, and some (such as kebabs) had antecedents in indigenous cuisine. In addition, the Mughal emperors themselves, with their frequent fasts, avoidance of meat on certain days and love of khichri, were far from being either gourmets or gourmands (perhaps subconsciously hankering after the simple food of their Turkish or Mongol forefathers).

pulao. The difference between the two dishes has been the subject of much debate and discussion. Sharar offers the following distinction:

> To the uninitiated palate both are much the same but because of the amount of spices in biryani, there is always a strong taste of curried rice, whereas pulao can be prepared with such care that this can never happen. In the view of gourmets, a biryani is a clumsy and ill-conceived meal in comparison with a really good pulao.[24]

A hotly debated issue in Indian gastronomy is the difference between pulao and biryani. A lot has been written on this topic, much of it contradictory. Both dishes consist of long-grained rice dishes prepared with meat, poultry, fish, seafood and vegetables and sometimes they are almost impossible to tell apart. Moreover, there are a great many regional and local variations. There are few general distinctions: first, pulaos are usually an accompaniment to a meal whereas biryanis are the centre piece, accompanied by various side dishes. Second, pulao is a single-pot dish made by first sautéing the spices, meat and rice in oil, then adding a liquid and simmering until the liquid is absorbed. For biryanis, the meat and rice are prepared separately, then combined. The meat may be marinated with yogurt and spices or ground onions, ginger and ginger pastes, and spices, and the rice is parboiled. Layers of meat and rice are put in a pot, which is sealed and slowly cooked for hours. Finally, usually the spicing for pulao is simpler and milder than for biryanis.

Pulaos had poetic names, such as *gulazar* (garden), *nur* (light), *koku* (cuckoo), *moti* (pearl) and *chambeli* (jasmine). Chefs sought to transform pulaos into works of art. In one pulao, half of each grain of rice was coloured fiery red like a ruby, and the other half was white and sparkled like a crystal, so that together they resembled the seeds of a pomegranate. The apogee of the pulao-maker's art was a *moti* pulao made by beating 200 g (7 oz) of silver foil and 20 g (¾ oz) of golden foil into the yolk of an egg. The mixture was stuffed into the gullet of a chicken, which was lightly cooked. When the skin was cut with a knife, shining pearls appeared; they were mixed with the meat and the whole was mixed with rice.

Other chefs fashioned meat into the shape of small birds, which perched on the edge of the plates as if they were pecking at the rice. (A variation popular in Hyderabad was a large pie that contained small birds that flew away when the pie was opened – probably inspired by the nursery rhyme, since it was a favourite of British officials and their wives at state dinners.)

The province of Awadh was renowned for its bread. Leavened bread was baked in underground clay ovens (tandoors), while Hindus traditionally fried their unleavened bread in ghee. According to Sharar, this gave Muslim bakers the idea of adding ghee to their bread, which was cooked on a griddle – and so the paratha was born. (Some of Sharar's ideas, like this one, are fanciful and must be taken with a pinch of salt.) Delhi's bakers were famous for their parathas, which were made with equal amounts of ghee and flour. However, Sharar complained that when he lived in Delhi the parathas could only be eaten fresh; when cold they were like leather, because the ingredients were not well mixed.

Another bread Sharar claims originated in Lucknow, although it probably came from Persia (shirmal means 'washed with milk' in Persian), is shirmal, a unleavened bread made from a dough of white flour and sugar, baked in a tandoor and sprinkled with milk and saffron. It was supposedly invented by a vendor called Mahumdu, whose nihari (beef stew) was so famous that the wealthiest aristocrats patronized his stall. Served with shirmal, it became an essential dish at any celebration. A variation is bakharkhani, a multi-layered bread made with plenty of ghee and cooked on a grill.

THE COLLECTIVE NAME for the dishes served at a dinner or sent to others was *tora* (Persian for 'basket'). The custom of sending food to people's homes arose to include the women of the household, whose movements were restricted because of *purdah* (the custom of keeping women secluded and revealing their faces only to family members). At a minimum a *tora* included pulao; muzaffar, a sweet saffron-flavoured rice dish; mutanjan, meat, sugar and rice with spices; shirmal; safaida, a simple sweet rice dish; fried aubergine; shir birinj, a sweet dish of rice boiled in milk; korma, pieces of meat slowly braised in spices and a yoghurt or cream gravy; arvi (taro) cooked with meat; shami kebabs (ground meat and chickpea patties); and, as condiments, murabba, pickles and chutney.

The number of dishes reflected the host's status. The nawab's *tora* consisted of 101 dishes, each one said to cost 500 rupees. Although this custom may have originated at the Mughal court, Sharar comments that

Shirmal is often served with korma, a rich meat stew.

Shirmal, a speciality of Lucknow and Hyderabad, is a leavened bread made of white flour, milk and sugar, baked in the oven and flavoured with saffron.

he had never seen ceremonial observances in Delhi equal to those in Lucknow, which was (and still is) famous for its residents' exquisite and elaborate manners. The system of etiquette became popularly known as *pehle-aap* ('after you') because of its emphasis on lowering one's own importance and elevating that of others (a custom sometimes parodied in Bollywood films). In culinary matters, it extended to the most minor matter. When serving water to even the most lowly person, a servant would place the glass on a small tray, cover it and hand it to the guest with the utmost respect.

Lucknow was also famous for its sweets. Those sold to the general public were usually made by Hindu *moiras* (confectioners), while the

For the Love of Ghee

Ghazi ud Din Hadar, the seventh nawab of Lucknow (ruled 1814–27) loved parathas, and his chef would cook six each day using 4.5 kg (10 lb) of ghee for each one. One day the vizier (prime minister) asked the chef why he used so much ghee. He replied, 'Sir, I cook parathas.' The vizier asked to watch and was shocked when the chef threw the ghee away after cooking each paratha. He informed him that from now on he would receive only 900 g (2 lb) of ghee for each paratha. After a few days the *nawab* asked his chef what was wrong with the parathas. He replied, 'Your Majesty, I cook the parathas as the vizier has ordered.' The nawab sent for the vizier, who told him: 'Your Majesty, your people rob you right and left.' The *nawab* became angry and slapped him. 'What about you? You rob the whole monarchy and the entire country and think nothing of it. He only takes a little too much ghee for my meals.' The vizier repented, and never interfered with the chef again.[25]

upper classes enjoyed sweets made by Muslim confectioners (*halwais*). But Sharar comments that the standard of Hindu sweets on the whole was higher, and that the people who really appreciated sweet dishes were Hindus. The reason, he surmises, is that Muslims are meat-eaters and prefer salty food, whereas Hindus have a sweet tooth.

Sweets were both Indian and foreign in origin. According to Sharar, while the word halwa is of Arabic origin and came to India via Persia, tar halwa (also known as mohan bhog), a pudding-like sweet made with semolina, clarified butter and nuts and eaten with puris, is purely Hindu. The five most popular kinds of halwa are sohan, hard orange-coloured discs with nuts; papri, which is hard and dry; jauzi, soft and crumbly; habshi, soft and black; and dudhia, a steamed jelly-like sweet.

Much attention was paid to the production of malai, or cream. The milk was warmed in very shallow trays over a slow fire and the layers removed one by one and carefully stacked on top of each other, a technique similar to that used to make English clotted cream or Turkish/Central Asian kaymak.

Sharar does not mention two of Lucknow's best-known contributions to Indian cuisine: the *dum* (Persian for 'steam') style of cooking and the local kebabs. *Dumpukht* is a method of cooking a dish in a sealed pot. According to legend, in 1784 during a terrible famine Nawab Asaf-ud-Daula provided jobs for his people by building a great monument, the Bara Imambar, in Lucknow. Every day workers constructed it and every night they tore it down. Their food was cooked in giant pots sealed with dough and kept warm in huge ovens. One day the nawab sampled the food and liked it so much that he adapted the oven for use at court banquets.[26]

Kakori kebabs, a distinctive Lucknow kebab, are made from minced tendon from a leg of mutton, khoya (thickened milk), white pepper and a secret blend of spices. According to legend, it was invented by the nawab of Kakori, a town near Lucknow. Offended when a British officer complained that the kebabs served at dinner were coarse, he ordered his chefs to create a more refined, softer dish. Even more delicate are galawati (or galavat) kebabs made of very finely ground minced meat and cream, shaped into patties and fried in ghee, which were created for Nawab Wajid Ali Shah when he lost his teeth in his old age. The

Kakori kebabs, a Lucknow delicacy, are soft, sausage-shaped kebabs made from finely minced mutton, thickened milk and spices.

199

Hyderabadi Yakhni Pulao

Take half a seer or about 500g (1 lb) mutton, four or five whole onions, a piece of green ginger, two dried cassia leaves, eight corns of black pepper and 6 quarts (7 litres/14¾ pints) of water.

Boil these ingredients in an earthen vessel until 1½ or 2 quarts (1.5–2 litres/3–4 pints) of liquid remain.

Mash the meat with the liquor and strain the broth (yakhni).

Melt 450 g (1 lb) butter in a tinned copper vessel and fry the onions cut into long slices until they become reddish.

Remove the onions from the pan. In the remaining butter, fry a chicken that has already been boiled. Remove it and fry the dry rice in the butter.

As the butter evaporates, add the broth and boil the rice in it.

Put in 10 or 12 cloves, 10 or 12 peppercorns, 4 pieces of mace, 10 or 12 small whole green cardamoms, one dessert-spoonful of salt, a piece of sliced ginger and 2 dried cassia leaves.

When the rice is done, remove the coals from underneath the pot and put a few of them on the cover of the pot. If the rice is hard, add a little water and put in the fowl, so that it may imbibe the flavour. When serving, put the fowl on a dish and cover it with the rice, garnishing the latter with a few hard-boiled eggs cut in two and the fried onions.

Ja'far Sharif, trans. Gerhard Andreas Herklots, *Qanoon-e-Islam; or, The Customs of the Moosulmans of India* (London, 1832)

original version was said to contain more than 100 aromatic spices and flower essences.

In 1856 the British East India Company annexed Awadh and exiled Wajid Ali Shah to Matiabur on the outskirts of Calcutta, where he set up a mini-Lucknow. (This event was one of the sparks that in 1857 ignited the First War of Independence, also known as the Indian Mutiny.) Many cooks who had worked for the nawabs found work in wealthy homes or

Haleem, a dish of
Middle Eastern
origin, is a porridge
of grain and meat.

set up food stalls in Lucknow's old markets, where even today vendors sell shirmal, kebab and pulao.[27] Others moved with him to Calcutta and opened stalls and restaurants, perhaps contributing to a local tradition of excellent Muslim food.

HYDERABAD

Hyderabad, today the capital of Andhra Pradesh, was home to a vibrant, eclectic culture and cuisine under different Islamic dynasties. The region was annexed by Muhammad Tuqhlaq, but a revolt in 1347 by the governor led to the creation of the Bahmani sultanate, which extended across much of the Deccan. The Bahmanis, who claimed descent from Bahman, a legendary king of Iran, were patrons of Persian language, culture and cuisine.

In the early sixteenth century a Persian adventurer declared independence from the Bahmani sultanate and established the Qatb Shahi dynasty of Golconda. In 1581 one of his successors founded Hyderabad as his capital. In 1687 the Mughal emperor Aurangzeb conquered the region and made it part of the Deccan province. But in 1724 the viceroy Nizam Asaf Jah declared his independence and founded a dynasty known as the Nizams of Hyderabad. They ruled the kingdom until 1948, when it became part of independent India. Hyderabad was the largest of the Indian princely states, and for a time the Nizams were the richest men in the world, their wealth coming mainly from the diamond mines of Golconda.

The royal flag of Hyderabad featured a unique culinary symbol: a kulcha (a round, slightly leavened flatbread). According to legend, before leaving Delhi, Asaf Jah visited a Sufi holy man, who shared his meal with him. Asaf Jah ate seven kulchas, and, although pressed to take more, declined. The holy man then blessed him and told him that he and his descendants would rule the Deccan for several generations (which turned out to be the case).

The local cuisine incorporated many influences, since the city was at the crossroads of east and west, north and south. Although the rulers were Muslim, the majority of the population was Hindu, including many officials, and the Nizams supported the construction of Hindu temples. The local staple was rice; wheat parathas were eaten mainly at breakfast. The Persian influence remained strong, since the rulers in theory recognized the shah of Iran as their sovereign, and until the mid-twentieth century there was a sizeable Iranian community in Hyderabad. The palace guard were Arabs, mainly from Yemen, and their presence is said to account for the popularity of haleem (see below).

In the mid-eighteenth century a French soldier in Hyderabad wrote enthusiastically about the local food:

> There are dishes consisting of bread made à la manteque [with butter; probably paratha], stew and the liver of fowls and kids, very well dressed, but most renowned of all is the rice boiled with quantities of butter, fowls and kids, with all sorts of spicery . . . which we found to be very good and which refreshed us greatly.[28]

Like their Lucknow counterparts, the Nizams and their officials were gourmets who practised one-upmanship when it came to food. Every nobleman's house had its own speciality. Once when the nawab was invited to the home of a noble to taste his chutneys, he said he would accept if the meal consisted only of chutneys and bread. The host served more than 100 types of chutney.

A detailed account of the region's food customs is found in an unusual work commissioned by the East India Company: *Qanoon-e-Islam; or, The Customs of the Moosulmans of India*, published in London in 1832.[29] According to the author, Ja'far Sharif, a wealthy Muslim had three meals a day: a breakfast at 7 am of tea (probably green tea from China) and coffee with sweets; a midday meal of unleavened bread, soup, minced savoury meat, cream, vegetables and sometimes rice; and a dinner at 7 pm consisting of rice and dal or rice boiled with meat, meat and fish, and, at the end, yoghurt, mangoes or plantains. The three daily meals of middle-class people were less elaborate, while poor people ate two meals: a breakfast of millet bread at 11 am and rice and dal with a little ghee and chillies or onions in the evening.

According to Ja'far Sharif, there were at least 25 varieties of pulao, among them:

Babune, flavoured with chamomile
Korma, in which meat is cut into very thin slices
Mittha, 'sweet', rice, sugar, butter, spices and aniseed
Shahsranga, like the above but drier
Tarl, rice, meat, turmeric and butter
Soya, dill
Macchhi, with fish instead of meat
Imli, with tamarind
Dampukht, steamed; butter added when nearly cooked
Zarda, yellow, with saffron
Koku, fried eggs
Dogostha, two meats; very hot
Biryan, marrow, spices, limes, cream, milk
Mutanhan, meat, rice, butter and sometimes pineapple and nuts
Haleem, chickpea, wheat, meat, spices
Lambni, cream, nuts, crystallized sugar, butter, rice, spices
    (especially aniseed)
Jaman, jaman fruit
Titar, partridge
Bater, quail
Kofta, meatballs
Khari chakoli, meat, vermicelli, green lentils.

In addition to the standard roti, parathas and puri, local breads included godida, 'ox-eyed', and gaozaban, 'ox tongue' naans, so-called because of their shape; satparati roti, a cake made by layering seven thin breads, sprinkling them with butter and sugar and frying them in butter; laungchira, a bread shaped like a clove; andon ki roti, a white bread filled with eggs; gulguli, deep-fried balls of flour, sugar, yoghurt and spices; and roghandar, bread made with plenty of butter.

Around the same time, Dr Robert Flower Riddell, the superintending army surgeon at the court of the Nizam, wrote the *Indian Domestic Economy and Receipt Book* (1841), featuring recipes for dishes made at the Nizams' court, including salan, a curry-like meat or vegetable dish with a thinnish gravy.

A more recent description of court cuisine is given by Sidq Jaisi, a poet from Lucknow who lived at the Hyderabad court from 1931 to 1938. He describes his first meal at the court in the following way:

How can I describe each dish? Each grain of rice in the biryani seemed to be filled with ghee. The last dish consisted of almonds and cream. Bowls, each containing about 3 kilos of cream, were placed in front of each person. Another dish, similarly placed, contained almonds and pistachios. Those nuts were eaten with cream. The layer of cream was at least three to four fingers thick . . . The buffaloes whose milk was used to make this cream were fed on almonds and pistachios from morning to evening. I counted eleven bowls of cream that evening. That day the famed cream of Lucknow which I had tasted earlier at the table of the nobles of Awadh fell in my estimation.[30]

At the end of another meal, the servant brought five round wafers of sohan halwa, each weighing at least 20 kg (44 lb). These were shared among the guests together with the special cream.

As in Lucknow, there was a cult of making dishes that looked like something else. Khichri, for example, was composed of peeled almonds sliced thinly to resemble grains of rice and pistachios sliced to look like green lentils. Almonds, pistachios and lentils were mixed in equal measure and cooked slowly with either an equal or a double amount of ghee.

One writer prepared a list of more than 200 dishes that were served at the court in the early twentieth century: 112 main dishes, 76 sweet dishes and 33 chutneys and achars (pickles), including many that are standard in Hyderabad today, notably bagharay baigan, fried aubergines stuffed with spices in a sour gravy; chakhna, a spicy offal stew; dalcha, a tamarind-flavoured stew of mutton and lentils; tootak, baked pastries filled with panir and potatoes; salan ka mirch, green chillies or capsicum in gravy; murtabak, baked layers of minced meat, panir and eggs; double ka meetha (also called shahi tukra), a bread pudding with cream; khubani ka meetha, apricot purée with cream; gosha ka meetha, elephant ears (flaky pastry) with cream; ande ka halwa, a saffron-flavoured halwa made with eggs and milk; badam ki jaali, lacy almond rounds; haleem; and biryani.[31]

KASHMIR

Until the fourteenth century Kashmir was ruled by Buddhist and Hindu kings. In 1334, following devastating invasions by Tatar and Mongol tribes, Shah Mir, an Indian Muslim, seized power. He founded a dynasty that lasted until 1587, when Akbar conquered Kashmir and made it part of his empire. Kashmir, which the Mughals called Bagh i Khas (Garden of Elites), was their favourite place for rest and recreation. Kashmir's hundreds of orchards and gardens became a major supplier of grapes, melons, cherries and saffron to the Mughal court, carried by men in conical baskets.

Following Timur's invasion of North India in 1398, some 1,700 skilled woodcarvers, architects, calligraphers and cooks are said to have migrated from Samarkhand to Kashmir. Their descendants became a class of professional Muslim chefs called *wazas*, who are still engaged by both Hindu and Muslim families to prepare banquets, called *wazwans*,

Hyderabad is famous for its biryani.

Preparation for a *wazwan*: an elaborate Kashmiri feast with as many as 36 dishes.

to celebrate weddings, births and other important events. Dozens of male cooks headed by a master chef, the *vasta waza*, bring herds of sheep and goats and enormous cooking pots to the celebrants' home. The animals are slaughtered according to Muslim ritual and butchered on the spot.

A traditional *wazwan* consists of 36 courses, between 15 and 30 of which are meat. There are a few vegetable dishes, but dal is never served. According to the *wazas*, there are 72 parts to an animal and most of them will be cooked, including the organs. Guests are seated in groups of four and share the meal from a large metal tray. Many of the dishes have rich, often yoghurt-based sauces. Seven dishes are always present: rista (meatballs in a red gravy), rogan josh (lamb cooked in a thin, tomato-based sauce), tabak maaz (lamb simmered in a yoghurt sauce and then fried), daniwal korma (lamb roasted with yoghurt and flavoured with coriander), aab gosht (lamb cooked in thickened milk), marchwangan korma (chicken thighs in an onion-based gravy) and, at the end, gushtaba (meatballs in a spicy yoghurt sauce). Even Kashmiri *brahmins* (called *pandits*) eat lamb and goat (although not chicken, onions or garlic).

Today the cuisines of Lucknow, Hyderabad and Kashmir are considered by some to be the crowning glories of Indian Muslim haute cuisine.

Although the nawabs, maharajahs and other rulers lost their kingdoms and their official privileges in the twentieth century, their rich culinary heritage lives on in the kitchens of their descendants and a few top restaurants.

TEN

The Europeans, the Princes and their Legacy, 1500–1947

For centuries Europeans had sought a sea route to the Indian subcontinent. Spices were a great luxury, valued not only for their taste and medicinal properties but also as a way of showing off one's wealth. Until the fifteenth century the trade in spices had been controlled by Arab traders who shipped them across the Persian Gulf to Alexandria, from where Venetian merchants transported them across the Mediterranean.

Venice had taken over the maritime appendages of the Byzantine Empire and, despite a brief collapse of its spice business in the early sixteenth century caused by its wars with Turkey, it maintained its dominant role until the early seventeenth century, when the Dutch lowered the price to the point that spices brought via the Middle East were no longer competititive. According to Michael Krondl, the idea of going round Africa to reach the source of spices may have originated with Genoese merchants, although it was ultimately realized by the Portuguese.[1] King João II (1455–1495) made reaching Asia by sea a national priority and in 1492 Christopher Columbus set out to find a passage to India and instead stumbled on a new continent. In 1498 the Portuguese explorer Vasco da Gama rounded the Cape of Good Hope to reach Calicut on India's Malabar Coast, a thriving port where Arabs, Hindus and Chinese merchants had exchanged spices, cloth and luxury goods for centuries. In 1501 the maharajah of Cochin allowed da Gama to buy spices, and he returned to Portugal with seven ships full. As the Portuguese extended their empire to the western hemisphere and Africa, their trading posts became the hubs of a global exchange of plants – the so-called Columbian Exchange, which changed world cuisine profoundly.

Spice-seller and customer, *c.* 1830.

The Portuguese

The Portuguese conquests of the fifteenth and sixteenth centuries constitute a remarkable chapter in the history of empire. Throughout the
sixteenth century the Portuguese retained a dominant position in the
maritime trade of the Indian Ocean and an important share of the trade
east of the Strait of Malacca. At the heart of this mercantile empire was
India. The Portuguese even used the expression 'Estado da India' ('state
of India') to describe all their conquests between the Cape of Good
Hope and the Persian Gulf on one side of Asia, and Japan and Timor
on the other. At its height, the Portuguese Empire contained more than
40 forts and factories extending from Brazil to Japan.

In 1510 the Portuguese seized Goa from the sultan of Bijapur and
made it the capital of Estado da India. This was Europe's first base on
the Indian subcontinent – and the last to be relinquished, in 1961. They
also established trading posts along the Malabar Coast, on the island of
Sri Lanka and in Bengal. By 1560, with a population of 225,000, Goa

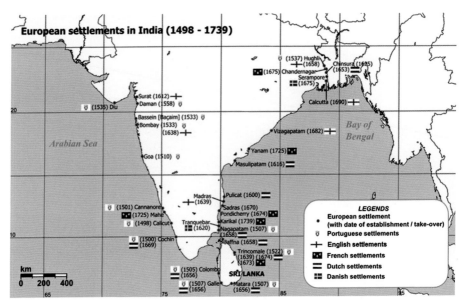

European settlements in India, 1498–1739.

was larger than Madrid or Lisbon. Along the southwest coast of India, almost every acre of land capable of growing spices was planted.

Unlike the British or the Dutch, who were mainly interested in making money and had little desire to change local culture, the Portuguese forcibly converted the inhabitants to Christianity. They brought the Inquisition to India and persecuted converts for following such 'heretical' customs as refusing to eat pork or beef, cooking rice without salt (a Hindu ritual custom) and wearing their traditional clothing. Growing a tulsi plant (a symbol of Lord Vishnu) was forbidden. Ironically, while such forced quasi-Westernization was going on, the Portuguese themselves lived much like Indians. They kept vast retinues of retainers and slaves, maintained harems, wore Indian clothes, chewed betel nut, drank arrack and hired Indian cooks.

In 1580 Emperor Akbar granted the Portuguese a charter to settle in a village on the banks of the Hooghly River, 40 km (25 miles) upstream from present-day Kolkata. It became a meeting place for vessels from other parts of India, China, Malacca and the Philippines. By 1670 at least 20,000 Portuguese and their descendants were living there. They dressed in the style of the local nawabs and 'made merry with dancing slave girls, seamstresses, cooks and confectioners'.[2] For servants and cooks, they took on Moghs from Sylhet and the Chittagong Hills, who for centuries had worked as deckhands and cooks on Arab ships trading with Southeast

Asia. They quickly learned their masters' culinary arts and became famous for their bread, cakes and pastries. The British later recruited them as seafarers and cooks, and today Sylhetis can be found running Indian restaurants in the United Kingdom and New York City.

One legacy of the Portuguese in India may be cheese, including India's only indigenous Western-style cheese, Bandel, a soft, smoky cow's-milk cheese still sold in Kolkata's New Market. It has been argued (by me, among others) that the Portuguese were responsible for the creation of chhana, the curds made by curdling milk, used in sandesh, ras goolah and many other famous Bengali sweets.[3] K. T. Achaya and others argue that this practice may have lifted an ancient Hindu taboo on the deliberate curdling of milk. However, *Manasolassa* and other works indicate that the technique was practised earlier (see chapters Seven and Eight). But this does not rule out the possibility that Portuguese cheese, which looks like chhana, was the specific inspiration behind Bengali sweets.

By far the most important Portuguese contribution to Indian and world cuisine was the so-called Columbian Exchange. The far-flung trading posts of the Portuguese and Spanish empires (Portugal was united with Spain between 1580 and 1640) became the hubs of a global exchange of fruit, vegetables, nuts and other plants between the western hemisphere,

Sculpture of a Portuguese nobleman with an Indian lady, 1540.

Custard apple (*sitaphal* in Hindi) was brought to India from the New World. Late 18th or early 19th century.

Africa, the Philippines, Oceania and the Indian subcontinent. To India, the Portuguese introduced potatoes, chillies, okra, papayas, pineapples, cashews, peanuts, maize, sapodilla, custard apples, guavas and tobacco.

A few writers have argued that maize, pineapple, sunflowers, cashews and custard apples grew in India even before the arrival of the Europeans. They point to more than a hundred carvings on temples in Karnataka built between the eleventh and thirteenth centuries that appear to depict these plants, and claim that the plants were either indigenous to India or came from very early contact between Indian and Meso-American civilizations. Those who disagree maintain that what is depicted in these sculptures is actually other fruit. It is to be hoped that DNA evidence will shed light on this controversy.[4]

The new plants were not all integrated into Indian cuisine at the same time. By the mid-sixteenth century three varieties of chilli (*Capsicum*) from various parts of the New World were recognized in India and were rapidly adopted as a substitute for black pepper, since they grew virtually wild. The appearance of the tomato (called *vilayati begun*, or 'foreign aubergine' in Bengali) cannot be precisely dated. In *Tomatoes in the Tropics*, Ruben L. Villareal writes that while the Spanish began introducing several agricultural commodities into the Philippines in 1571, it is possible that tomatoes had been taken from Spain to Asia much earlier, perhaps just a few years after the discovery of the Philippines by Ferdinand Magellan in 1521. Trade between the Philippines and China, Japan and India may have been responsible for the spread of tomatoes into those countries. The British, Dutch and French may also have introduced tomatoes into their Asian colonies.[5]

In 1832 William Roxburgh wrote in *Florica Indica*: 'Although [the tomato] is now very common in India, I suspect it is as little native as the common potato, which is now generally cultivated over India, even by the natives for their own use.'[6] The new arrivals became substitutes for ingredients that were already part of the cuisine. Potatoes were a replacement for indigenous tubers, and became an indispensable component of Indian food. (Bengalis are said to be the world's largest consumers of potatoes after the Irish.) The Sanskrit word for tubers, *alu*, is the word for 'potato' in many Indian languages, although Marathis use the Portuguese word *batata*.

Maize is prepared in various ways. Roasted on the cob, it is a ubiquitous street food. Corn kernels are an ingredient in curries in western India, while cornflour is used to make the national dish of Punjab, makki ki roti (corn bread). However, as the food historian Rachel Laudan points out, rarely were cooking techniques exchanged or borrowed; for example, the Meso-American technique of treating maize with an alkali in order to free the niacin was never adopted in India.[7] However they were introduced, all these products, especially tomatoes, chillies and potatoes, were assimilated to such a degree that it is now impossible to imagine Indian cuisine without them.

The Portuguese capital, Goa, became famous for its meat dishes, especially those using beef and pork. Classic Portuguese dishes were enlivened by the addition of spices: caldo verde, a potato and cabbage soup, was flavoured with ginger and black pepper; chicken xacuti contained a paste of roasted coconut, peanuts and spices, flavoured with vinegar; and the most famous Goan dish, vindaloo (from the Portuguese carne de vinha d'alhos, meat in wine and garlic), was turned into a sweet, sour and fiery hot pork curry. The authentic Goan version can be very dry, like a pickle, so that it can be taken on long journeys. The

Portuguese tradition of baking flourishes in pau, light oven-baked bread rolls; bibinca, a cake made by stacking layers of pancakes; and boliho de coco, little coconut cakes.

A valuable source of information about plants and ingredients in sixteenth-century India is Garcia de Orta's *Colóquios dos simples e drogas . . . da India* (*Colloquies on the Simples and Drugs of India*, 1563).[8] De Orta (*c.* 1501–1568) was a Portuguese Sephardic Jewish physician and naturalist who served as physician to the Portuguese viceroy of India for thirty years, and died in Goa. Written in the form of conversations between de Orta and a friend, each of the work's 59 chapters describes the origins, history and medicinal properties of a spice, drug or plant, including pepper, turmeric, banana, betel, bhang (cannabis), galangal and camphor.

De Orta noted the importance of turmeric as a medicine, especially for diseases of the eye and the skin. It was also used for colouring and seasoning food, and exported to Arabia and Persia. Bananas, which he called 'the figs of India', were roasted and served in wine with cinnamon, or cut in half, fried in sugar and sprinkled with cinnamon. They were also taken to Portugal as ships' provisions. De Orta mentions pineapples only in passing as a fruit native to the West Indies, but they were clearly known in India by this time. Of asafoetida he writes:

> The thing most used throughout India, all parts of it, is that Ass-Fetida, as well as for medicine as in cookery. A great quantity is used, for every Gentio [Hindu] who is able to get the means of buying it will buy it to flavour his food. The rich eat much of it . . . and he who imitates Pythagoras [a vegetarian]. They flavour the vegetables they eat with it; first rubbing the pan with it, and then using it as seasoning with everything they eat . . . The Moors [Muslims] eat it, but in smaller quantity and only as a medicine.[9]

De Orta goes on to say that while to him asafoetida has the nastiest smell in the world, the vegetables seasoned with it do not taste bad. He was fascinated by the widespread use of bhang, noting that his servants who took it said that 'it made them so as not to feel work, to be very happy and to have a craving for food' (adding that he never tried it himself).[10]

The glory days of the Portuguese Empire lasted little more than a century. The burden of maintaining such an extensive empire was too great for a nation of just over a million people. The Portuguese system of administering the spice trade was inefficient, and the viceroy in Goa disdained merchants, many of them converted Jews who fell victim to the Inquisition. Many Portuguese left Goa to seek their fortunes as mercenaries at various Indian courts. But the Portuguese association with India left its mark not only on the cuisine of India but also on that of Portugal. Ginger, pepper, turmeric, coriander, cinnamon, fennel, cloves, allspice and chillies are used to flavour Portuguese dishes, including caldeirada, a stew of fish and vegetables. Dashes of curry powder are often added to casseroles and soups in the remotest country kitchen.

THE DUTCH

In the late sixteenth century Jan Huyghen van Linschoten (1563–1611), a Dutch merchant, traveller and historian who lived in Goa, published a book on the Portuguese Asian trade and navigational routes that helped the British and the Dutch break the Portuguese monopoly on trade with the East Indies. The Dutch East India Company was founded in 1602 with a 21-year charter to carry out colonial activities in Asia. The merchants established themselves on the west coast of India and in Bengal. Kochi (formerly Cochin) was a major trading centre, and the Dutch influence is still visible in the architecture. In the early nineteenth century the Dutch exchanged their Indian possessions for British holdings in the East Indies (Indonesia), which henceforth became the focus of their mercantile and imperial ambition.

The Dutch brought slaves from India as well as Indonesia to work in their kitchens in South Africa, originally a provisioning port en route to India. They were the ancestors of the Cape Malays, famous for their delicious spicy cuisine. The Dutch presence was much more lasting in Sri Lanka, which they controlled from 1633 to 1792. There, their culinary legacy includes various dishes of Dutch origin, among them frikkadels (meatballs) and various sweets. The Burghers – people of mixed European (especially Dutch) and Sinhalese or Tamil descent – developed their own distinctive hybrid cuisine. However, the Dutch had little, if any, influence on the cuisine of India itself.

THE FRENCH

In 1664 Louis XIV founded the French East India Company to give France a seat at the spice table. French outposts were established on both coasts of India, and at one point France controlled the area between Hyderabad and Cape Comorin, at the very southern tip of the subcontinent. Its headquarters were in Pondicherry (today called Pudicherry), 160 km (100 miles) south of Chennai (Madras).

France and England went to war over control of South India, and while the French were temporarily victorious, in the long run the British prevailed. Napoleon wanted to use Egypt as a base to attack India, but the destruction of the French fleet in 1805 by Lord Nelson put an end to that scheme. By 1761 the French presence had been reduced to a few small settlements, which became part of independent India in 1954.

Still, even today Pudicherry has a French flavour. Older residents speak French, the policemen's uniforms resemble those of French gendarmes, and streets are named after French admirals and governors. The French government encourages cultural ties, and many French tourists visit the city. The local cuisine has a few dishes that may reflect the French legacy, including a stew called ragout, heavily flavoured with garlic and aromatic spices; dishes called rolls (lamb stuffed with minced lamb), which are served on New Year's Eve; meen puyabaisse (fish bouillabaisse) and Pondicherry cake, a rum-soaked fruitcake served at Christmas.[11] But, unlike in Britain, India left little mark on the way the French eat, perhaps because their own culinary tradition is so strong. Today there are a few Indian restaurants in Paris, but they are far outnumbered by those that serve North African cuisine. Some menus are like those of their British counterparts, heavy on North Indian dishes, while others (particularly those in the 10th arrondissement) serve mainly South Indian food.

THE BRITISH

On 31 December 1600 Elizabeth I of England granted a royal charter to the East India Company (popularly known as the Company), giving it a fifteen-year monopoly on trade with the 'Indies', defined as all the lands between the Cape of Good Hope and the Strait of Magellan. In 1618 a British ship landed at Surat, the principal port of the Mughal Empire. The following year this became the site of England's first 'factory' – a trading establishment at a foreign port. By 1647 the British had established 28 factories in India and gained access to the Mughal emperor. In 1665 the Portuguese viceroy handed over Bombay, with its excellent harbour, to the English as part of the marriage settlement of Charles II and the Portuguese princess Catherine of Braganza. In 1696 the emperor let the Company establish a new settlement in Bengal, called Fort William, which later became Calcutta.

As long as the Mughal emperors were able to enforce their authority, the activities of the foreigners were limited to trade. They exported cotton goods from Madras and Gujarat; silk, sugar and saltpetre from Bengal; spices from the Malabar Coast; and opium, which the Company forced upon the Chinese in exchange for tea. Profit margins of 25 per cent were regarded as moderate, and some merchants, known as *nabobs*, became fabulously wealthy. Moreover, officers of the Company's ships were allowed to trade on their own account, ensuring that English goods, including ham, cheese, wine and beer, were supplied to the British community in India.

Political instability from the mid-eighteenth century onwards led the Company to seek political power. It formed its own armies and began to meddle in local disputes. In 1757 the Company's British troops and their Indian allies defeated the forces of the Mughal viceroy at the Battle of Plassey, and secured permission to collect the Mughals' taxes in return for an annual tribute and for maintaining order. They subsequently installed puppet rulers in Bengal, Bihar and Orissa, and extended their control over Malabar and much of the west coast.

In the late eighteenth century the British government established a separate Administration and Civil Service to run India. They appointed governors in Madras (now Chennai) and Bombay (Mumbai) and a governor-general in Calcutta (Kolkata), which remained the capital of British India until 1905. In the second half of the nineteenth century the British annexed the Punjab, Nepal and Burma.

In 1857 North India went up in flames. After a mutiny of Indian regiments in Meerut, other Indian troops rebelled and slaughtered their British commanders and local British residents. The rebels set out for Delhi with the goal of restoring the Mughal emperor Bahadur Shah II to power. Dietary complaints played a role: the rumour was that the cartridges used by the army were greased with pork and/or beef fat, while news of the impending revolt was purportedly spread by the distribution of chapattis.

Ultimately the revolt failed and the reprisals were savage. This event – called the First War of Independence by Indians, and the Indian Mutiny by the British – had significant consequences. Emperor Bahadur Shah was exiled to Burma, and the reign of the Mughals came officially to an end. The Company was disbanded, and in 1858 the British Parliament transferred all its rights to the British Crown. In 1877 Queen Victoria was named empress of India.

From then until 1947, when India gained its independence, around 60 per cent of India's land area was under direct British rule, sometimes called the Raj. The rest of the subcontinent, the so-called Princely States, retained their rulers, who pledged obedience to Victoria and were more or less under the control of the British authorities.

BRITISH FOOD CUSTOMS

As the Portuguese had done before them, until the early eighteenth century British traders lived much like the local population: they spoke Indian languages, took Indian mistresses and wives, wore Indian clothes, smoked hookahs and ate Indian food. The prodigious meals at the British settlements, prepared by Indian, Portuguese and British cooks, were similar to those eaten by the Mughals and their local representatives, and featured rice pulaos and biryanis, dumpukht, chicken, khichri, chutneys and relishes, accompanied by shiraz wine from Persia, English beer or arrack.

According to David Burton in his chronicle of the food of the Raj, the first British settlers may not have considered the highly spiced cuisine of India very strange: 'In 1612, English cooking had itself barely emerged from the Middle Ages and was still heavy with cumin, caraway, ginger, pepper, cinnamon, cloves and nutmeg.'[12] The Indian dumpokhed chicken, stewed in butter and stuffed with spices, almonds and raisins, was very similar to an English chicken pie of the same period. Forks were still relatively uncommon in England, and the English scooped food into their mouths with pieces of bread – just as the Indians did. Even the custom of eating spices (paan) after a meal as an aid to digestion had its counterpart in voidee, the English custom of offering departing guests assorted spices and wine at the end of a banquet.

Not long after their arrival, the British opened taverns, often named after famous British pubs, where they sold wine, beer, rum, punch and local arrack, and also served suppers and cold collations. Punch, a popular drink from the mid-seventeenth century, was named after the Hindi word for 'five' because it contained five ingredients: arrack, rosewater, citron juice, sugar and spices. By all accounts, both men and women drank alcohol to excess. At a dinner in Calcutta in 1831, the 23 guests drank eleven bottles of wine, 28 quarts of beer, 1½ quarts of spirits and twelve bowls of punch, and 'would have drunk twice as much if not restrained', as Bishop Wilberforce complained.[13] A French count visiting India observed:

> If you are a Frenchman, you will be thunderstruck by the enormous quantity of beer and wine absorbed by these young English ladies, in appearance so pale and delicate. I could scarcely recover from my astonishment at seeing my fair neighbour quietly dispose of a bottle and a half of very strong beer, eked out with a fair allowance of claret, and wind up with five or six glasses of light but spirited champagne taken with her dessert.[14]

Stomach disorders were common, but were blamed on the climate, not on people's drinking habits or their heavily meat-based diet. A few

An East India Company civil servant and his wife breakfasting on fried fish, rice and Sylhet oranges, with servants in attendance, 1842.

European physicians pointed to the over-consumption of meat as inappropriate, and one regretted that the majority avoided eating local food 'from a kind of false bravado and the exhibition of a generous contempt for what they reckon the luxurious and effeminate practice of the country'.[15]

By the early nineteenth century Indianized habits among the British had become rarer. Company employees were forbidden to wear Indian dress or to take part in local ceremonies and festivals, while their children by Indian women were excluded from employment by the Company. Part of the blame falls on General Charles Cornwallis who, having recently been defeated at Yorktown, Virginia, wanted to make sure that a settled colonial class did not emerge in India to undermine British rule, as it had in America. Clothes began to follow London fashions, and Indian food, although still offered in punch houses and taverns, was no longer the norm. British wives replaced Indian mistresses, and these women, many of them neither well-educated nor adventurous, had no interest in exploring local culture or cuisine. As one writer put it:

> The Englishwoman fought against eating Indian food for more than one reason. Highly spiced food often upset her poor digestion and through ignorance she regarded Indian food as hot and unpalatable. It also gave her a sense of superiority to despise the food of the natives. French cuisine was considered fashionable and food cooked in wine was the last word in good taste.[16]

Curries were no longer acceptable dishes at dinner parties, although they were still served at lunch. Canned fish, cheese, jam and dried fruit from Europe became de rigueur, and were valued in part because they were hard to obtain. Dinner parties, an important part of social and official life, consisted of multiple courses of bland English food with joints, legs of lamb, great saddles of mutton and boiled chicken. In the novel *A Passage to India* (1924), E. M. Forster makes this clear:

> And sure enough they did drive away from the Club in a few minutes, and they did dress, and to dinner came Miss Derek and the McBrydes, and the menu was: Julienne soup full of bullety bottled peas, pseudo-cottage bread, fish full of branching bones, pretending to be plaice, more bottled peas with the

Queen Victoria with
Indian servants,
1897–1901,
chromolithograph.

cutlets, trifle, sardines on toast: the menu of Anglo-India. A dish
might be added or subtracted as one rose or fell in the official
scale . . . but the tradition remained: the food of exiles, cooked
by servants who did not understand it.

However, curries, kedgeree and mulligatawny soup continued to be served
at breakfast and lunch until the twentieth century. Common soldiers,
meanwhile, lived in appalling conditions on a diet of tough beef and raw
rum all year round.

Although she never visited India, Queen Victoria took her respon-
sibilities as empress seriously. She learned Hindustani, and during
the last decade of her reign insisted that curry be cooked every day for
lunch. At Osborne House on the Isle of Wight, one of Victoria's favourite homes, banquets were served by Indian waiters wearing showy
gold and blue uniforms in the ornate Durbar Room, decorated with
Indian motifs. Her grandson George v was especially fond of beef
curry served with Bombay duck (a small dried fish). Indian chefs were
employed in the palace kitchens to prepare such dishes as biryani, pulao,

> ### *India Pickle*
>
> To a gallon of vinegar one pound of garlick, and three quarters of a pound of long pepper, a pint of mustard seed, one pound of ginger, and two ounces of turmerick; the garlick must be laid in salt three days, then wip'd clean and dry'd in the sun; the long pepper broke, and the mustard seed bruised; mix all together in the vinegar, then take two large hard cabbages, and two cauliflowers, cut them in quarters, and salt them well; let them lie three days, and then dry them well in the sun.
>
> N.B. The ginger must lie twenty-four hours in salt and water, then cut small and laid in salt three days.
>
> Hannah Glasse, *The Art of Cookery Made Plain and Easy*, 1747

dal and dumpukht. The Swiss chef Gabriel Tschumi left behind an account of their activities. For religious reasons, they could not use the meat that came to the kitchens in the ordinary way, and so killed their own sheep and poultry. A special area was set aside for grinding spices between two large stones.[17]

Back in India, to help the *memsahibs* (British wives) cope with their new environment, including managing enormous contingents of servants, old hands at the expatriate life in India wrote domestic handbooks with menus and recipes, most of them for British and European dishes. Recipes for Indian dishes were relegated to separate chapters and were often referred to in derogatory terms. Flora Annie Steel (1847–1929), the co-author of one of the most famous handbooks, wrote in *The Complete Indian Housekeeper and Cook* (first published in 1888) that 'most native recipes are inordinately greasy and sweet.' Another writer called 'pellows' (pulaos) 'purely Hindoostanee dishes', some of which were 'so entirely of an Asiatic character and taste that no European will ever be persuaded to partake of them'. More sympathetic was Colonel Arthur Robert Kenney-Herbert (1840–1916), who wrote under the name Wyvern. In his *Culinary Jottings for Madras* (1878) he sought to give Indian curries the same care and attention as he did a classic French fricassee or blanquette.

Social contact between Indians and the British was limited to the princes and wealthy families, such as the Tagores in Calcutta and the

Tatas in Bombay, who made their fortunes acting as go-betweens. Despite this separation, the two cultures left lasting marks on each other's cuisine. The most obvious Indian legacy to Britain is curry. The word was not historically used by Indians, who called dishes by their specific names: korma, kalia, salan, rogan josh, and so on (in 1973 in her book *An Invitation to Indian Cooking* the celebrated Indian cookery writer Madhur Jaffrey wrote that the word 'curry' was 'as degrading to India's great cuisine as the term "chop suey" was to China's'). The word appears to have been first used in 1502 in a Portuguese travel account, and may come from the Tamil *karil*, signifying a watery sauce poured on rice. The British came to use this word for any dish of vegetables, meat or fish cooked in a spicy sauce. It has since gained respectability among Indians, and twenty years later Jaffrey herself called a book *The Ultimate Curry Bible*.

Another Indian contribution is kedgeree, a favourite British breakfast dish that is a variation of khichri, the rice and lentil dish beloved of the Mughal emperors. A British kedgeree is made with rice (no lentils), smoked fish and hard-boiled eggs. During Victorian and Edwardian times, kedgeree was a staple of English country-house breakfasts. As P. G. Wodehouse's character Bertie Wooster put it, 'We really had breakfast . . . fried eggs, scrambled eggs, fishcakes and kedgeree, sometimes mushrooms, sometimes kidneys.'[18] Other hybrids are mulligatawny – a spicy, rather thick meat soup that is a modification of a thin broth eaten in south India – and Worcester sauce, a popular condiment said to be based on an Indian recipe brought back to England by a governor of Bengal in the early nineteenth century. The popular condiment piccalilli was created by adding mustard to traditional chutney ingredients.

In the seventeenth century green tea imported from China to England by the Company was a popular drink among the wealthy, but its cost was becoming a drain on the British treasury. To break the Chinese monopoly, the British looked for another source, and discovered tea growing wild in northeastern India, where it had been used since time immemorial as a fermented pickle (as it is today in Burma and northern Thailand) and an infusion.[19] Using Chinese seeds and techniques of planting and cultivation, the government launched a tea industry in India by offering land in Assam to any European who agreed to grow tea for export. Tea cultivation spread to the Darjeeling area in the Himalayas, the Nilgiri Hills in the south, and Ceylon (Sri Lanka). The price in the

The Origin of India Pale Ale

In the late eighteenth century the owner of the Bow Brewery,
near the East India Company's docks in London, decided to
brew a specific kind of beer for export to India, using a pale
malt and plenty of hops, both known for their preservative
qualities. This helped to stabilize the beer during the long,
rough, hot journey to India. The combination produced
a beer with a distinctively bitter taste and excellent thirst-
quenching properties – a perfect drink for a hot climate and
spicy food. The beer, called Hodgson's, became very popular and was soon imitated by other brewers.[20]

United Kingdom dropped dramatically, and by the end of the century
black tea had become a mass drink in Britain.

It was the British who introduced tea-drinking to India, initially
to the Anglicized elite. Afternoon tea – with cakes and sandwiches,
and such Indian snacks as samosa and pakora – became an important
meal, especially in Calcutta. However, tea did not become a mass
drink in India until the 1950s, when the India Tea Board, faced with
a surplus of low-grade tea, launched an advertising campaign to popu-
larize tea, especially in the north, where the drink of choice was milk.
In this form, tea is typically boiled with milk and spices. This *chai* is sold
in little clay cups by millions of vendors on the streets and at railway
stations.

In South India, coffee is the drink of choice, especially at breakfast.
Although it had been grown earlier, the British built the first large-scale
plantations in the hills of Karnataka in the 1830s. By the end of the nineteenth century more than 100,000 ha (250,000 acres) of South India were
planted with coffee.

Another British contribution to India was beer. A popular beverage
among the English in India from the early seventeenth century, especially
porter and pale ale, it was originally imported, but in 1830 the first
brewery was set up in the Solon District of Himachal Pradesh (it is still
in operation). By 1882 there were twelve breweries in India.

Many vegetables originally grown by the British for their own use
were quickly assimilated into Indian cuisine, including cauliflower, orange
carrots, cabbage and spinach.

Another legacy of the British was the club: a members-only private institution for upper-class men. The first club in India was the Bengal Club in Calcutta, founded in 1827; it was followed by the Byculla Club in Bombay and the Madras Club (both 1833). These were gathering places for the British ruling elite, and at first tradesmen and Indians were barred. Delhi's Gymkhana Club, which opened in 1913, was a relative latecomer. (It used to be said that India was ruled from the Gymkhana Club.) Today every town of any size in India has its own club, while large metropolises have many.[21] Club dining rooms offer Indian, Western and often Chinese food.

The Bengal Club was famous for its omelettes, made with minced onions and chillies, which became a popular breakfast dish in India. The clubs were also known for their bars, offering whisky soda, beer and gin. When tonic water was invented in the 1860s and marketed as anti-malarial because of its quinine content, mixing it with gin led to the birth of the famous gin and tonic.[22] Gin mixed with lime juice made a gimlet, which may also have been invented in India.

ANGLO-INDIAN FOOD

In the early to mid-nineteenth century the term Anglo-Indian referred to British residents of India, but it later came to mean the descendants of official or unofficial unions between British men and Indian women, sometimes referred to as Eurasians. Certain jobs were reserved for these people, especially in the railways, and there were large communities in Calcutta, Bombay, Madras and other railway centres. After India gained its independence, many Anglo-Indians emigrated to Britain, Australia and Canada.

Most Anglo-Indians were Christians of various denominations, spoke English, wore European clothes and married within their community. They also had a distinctive cuisine, which incorporated dishes from all over the subcontinent as well as British and Portuguese foods, leading some to call it the first pan-Indian cuisine.[23] As Christians, they had no food taboos. Typical dishes were meat and potato curry, pepper water (a spicy beef soup), chicken jalfrezi (leftover meat in a dry sauce), dry fry (beef cooked with onions, tomatoes and spices), roast beef and many Goan dishes, including pork vindaloo, sorpotel, balchow (fried fish in a sweet-and-sour sauce), foogath (vegetables fried with onion, garlic and mustard seeds) and Western-style cakes. Christmas was celebrated with great

---

*The Maharajah of Sailana's Recipe
for Jungli Mans
(Wild Game Prepared During a Hunt)*

Heat some ghee or oil and add pieces of meat to it. Add salt and whole red chillies, and cook it for ten minutes. Add a little water now and then, making sure the meat neither fries nor boils. When tender, dry up the water and eat.

The author notes that he has deliberately avoided giving any weights or measures, as they are not available when one is stranded on a hunt.

From www.royalhouseofsailana.com

---

gusto, with a roast turkey or duck; the plum pudding was prepared weeks in advance.

THE PRINCES

Once the British had taken control of India from the Mughals, India's local and regional rulers entered into alliances, first with the Company and later with the government of India. In return for protection, they accepted Britain as a 'paramount power'. This meant that they retained their internal autonomy and the right to collect taxes, while handing over control of their external affairs to the British, who were represented at their courts by an advisor called a Resident. The British did not hesitate to depose rulers who resisted their control.

At the time of Independence in 1947, the 562 princely states covered around 40 per cent of the Indian subcontinent.[24] Some, such as Kashmir, Mysore and Hyderabad, were as large as European countries, while others were tiny, even consisting of a single village. Their hereditary rulers held different titles – Maharajah, Rajah, Rana, Rao, Maharana, Maharao, Nawab, Nizam, Gaekwad – but were collectively referred to as princes (a term preferred by the British, since there could be only *one* king or queen in the empire). Under the Indian Independence Act of 1947, the British relinquished their suzerainty and left the states free to choose to join independent India or Pakistan. Most acceded to India, while eight joined

Pakistan. A few states sought independence, notably Hyderabad, but it was forcibly annexed by India.

After Independence the princes were paid a pension by the government of India, called the privy purse. In 1971 Prime Minister Indira Gandhi abolished their titles and withdrew government support. Some, such as the maharani of Jaipur, became politicians; others turned their palaces into hotels, opened their collections as museums or supported programmes to conserve India's wildlife and heritage.

The British sought to instil Western values into the rulers by arranging British tutors for their children and sending them to Eton and Harrow, or to Indian preparatory schools along the same lines. They also encouraged those who could afford it to travel to Britain for such events as coronations and jubilees. (Occasionally this backfired. The maharajah of Indore, who ruled from 1926 to 1961, spent so much time abroad that the British Resident proposed that the Indore national anthem be 'Some Day my Prince will Come'.)

Some princes and princesses became glamorous society figures with residences in London and Paris. They patronized such establishments as the Savoy and the Ritz, and sent their cooks there for training. The maharani of Cooch Behar, Indira Devi (1892–1968), took her chef to Alfredo's in Rome so that he could learn to make pasta the way she liked it. Others were more conservative in their dining habits. When the maharajah of Baroda (1879–1939) visited Europe, he took his own cooks, groceries and two cows, while Madhao Singh I of Jaipur attended Edward VII's coronation in 1902 with four silver urns, each filled with 9,000 litres (19,000 pints) of water from the Ganges River, because of its reputed healthful properties. (The Mughal emperors are also said to have taken the water of the Ganges with them on their travels.)

The control exercised by the British left some princes with little to do, and so maintaining a luxurious lifestyle became a way of passing the time. It was also a sign of their authority and power: they had to live like kings to retain the respect and admiration of their subjects and their prestige among their peers. From the earliest contact with the Europeans, the wealthiest Indian rulers acquired rare and expensive goods from the West. This practice reached its apogee in the early twentieth century when some became patrons of the leading European manufacturers of luxury goods, ordering cars from Rolls-Royce, dinner services from Limoges and Spode, crystal from Baccarat and Lalique, and jewellery from Cartier. During the Great Depression of the 1930s, some of these companies survived solely on the orders of the maharajahs.[25]

Princely households had enormous staff and retinues, occasionally numbering in the thousands. Some servants were hired during famines as a way of providing employment; some were descendants of earlier generations of servants; while others came from other parts of India (notably Goa, which was famous for its cooks) or from Europe. Cooks specialized in vegetarian food, meat or fish, or even a single dish. Occasionally the preparation of a dish was divided among several cooks so that no one would know its secret. The royal kitchen at Mysore, one of the largest of the princely states, employed 150 chefs who cooked only vegetarian dishes and 25 who cooked non-vegetarian food. The latter were divided into Muslim and Hindu cooks. Another twenty brahmin cooks prepared food for religious ceremonies in a separate kitchen where no meat, fish, onions or garlic were allowed.

Life in the royal courts revolved around entertaining. Food played a role not just in celebrations, but also in diplomacy and politics, and princes competed to provide the most unusual and luxurious fare. A minimum of 51 dishes was de rigueur at parties at the Moti Bagh Palace in Patiala. At Hyderabad, at least twenty dishes had to be provided even if only two family members were dining, so that the cooks would not lose their skill. In some royal families, including those of Lucknow and Patiala, the men of the family supervised the cooking.

When British officials or other great princes were being entertained, the menus often consisted almost entirely of Western dishes. For example, when Sayajirao Gaekwad III of Baroda (ruled 1875–1939) held a dinner for Jivaji 'George' Rao Scindia of Gwalior (ruled 1925–61) at his Laxmi Vilas Palace in Baroda in 1910, the menu was entirely in French, as it would have been in aristocratic British society of the time. The menu featured almond soup, fish in a mayonnaise sauce, crème de volaille with truffles, lamb cutlets à l'Italienne, roast partridge breast with green peas, artichoke hearts with a demi-glace sauce, curry with rice, baked apples with cream and pistachio ice cream.

Some princes had extensive wine cellars. In a few royal houses, such as those of the Rajput states of Jamnagar and Chhota Udaipur, Indian food was rarely eaten. In others, breakfast was English while other meals were Indian. Christmas was a major celebration, and such British dishes as boar's head, game pie and plum pudding were served.

Menu of a
dinner given
by the Maharajash
of Baroda at his
Laxami Vilas Palace.

The royal tables also featured local dishes. In Kashmir, for example, vegetarian dishes such as guchchi pulao (mushroom rice), saak (Kashmiri spinach) and nadru (deep-fried lotus stems) are to this day served on silver *thalis* to the maharajah and his family. The royal family of the northeastern state of Tripura (the world's second-oldest continuous line, after the Japanese) dines on such dishes as chunga bejong (grilled pork served with bamboo shoots), maimi (sticky rice wrapped in a banana leaf and roasted in a hollow bamboo stem over a wood fire) and gudak (mashed vegetables with fish).[26]

Because hunting, or *shikar*, was a way of life for many princes, meat dishes played an important role at many courts. Jodhpur, for example, was famous for its barbecued and roast meat dishes cooked out in the open, including khud khargosh (rabbit cooked in an underground pit) and roast quail. A famous Rajasthani dish is lal maas, venison cooked with red chillies. However, the Wildlife Protection Act of 1972, which banned the hunting of wild animals, put an end to this princely pastime; these dishes nowadays are prepared with pork.

Another Rajasthani royal tradition that has been restricted is the production of strong spirits, called ashavs, made from local herbs, spices and fruit. They include kesar kasturi, a distillation of saffron, dry fruit, herbs, nuts, seeds, 22 spices, milk and sugar that is a speciality of Jodhpur, and jagmohan, a spirit made from dried fruit and 32 spices and herbs, once brewed for the rulers of Mewar. The production of such spirits was banned in Rajasthan in 1952, but in 2006 a special law was passed authorizing the production of so-called Heritage Liqueurs, which are popular with tourists.[27]

There were exceptions to the princely carnivorous lifestyle. From the twelfth century until Independence, Kerala was divided into three kingdoms: Kochi, Malabar and Tiruvithamcore, ruled by three different royal families, all vegetarian. To this day meals served in the *madapilli* (royal kitchen) of the Cochin royal family are unassuming, featuring dishes prepared with local ingredients by brahmin cooks.[28] The strictest regime is followed by the maharajahs of Benares (Varanasi), one of the sacred cities of Hinduism. Not only are they strict vegetarians who avoid onions and garlic, but also they are so orthodox that they cannot eat in the presence of other people, even their own family members. The current maharajah, Anant Narain Singh, eats only food prepared by a team of Bihari cooks, who accompany him on his travels to prepare his lonely meals.[29]

Because royals usually married other royals, dishes were often transmitted from one region to another. For example, the Jivaji Rao of Gwalior married a Nepali aristocrat, who introduced Nepali dishes into the Maratha kitchens; by the mid-1970s the kitchen at the Gwalior palace became as well known for its Nepali delicacies as for its Marathi ones.

Although the lavish royal lifestyle is to some degree a thing of the past, the royal families have played an important role in Indian cuisine by preserving traditional dishes in their homes and in restaurants, especially in the hotels into which their palaces were converted. Some have even become hoteliers or consultants. The Taj Group has restored several palaces and re-created princely dishes in its restaurants, most recently in Falaknuma Palace in Hyderabad, once home to the Nizams.

In recent years there has been a renewed interest in the lives and cuisine of India's royals, evinced by the publication of a lavishly illustrated and informative book *Dining with the Maharajahs: A Thousand Years of Culinary Tradition* (2012), parts of which were televised. An earlier work by Raja Dilip Singh Ji of Sailana, a small state in Madhya Pradesh, is considered one of the best Indian cookbooks ever written. Singh's grandfather began collecting, recording and even testing recipes from other royal houses, and his son published them to critical acclaim.

Mahatma Gandhi, the Freedom Movement and Food

Partly as a reaction against this princely indulgence, India's great political and spiritual leader, Mohandas Gandhi (1869–1948), advocated an austere lifestyle and diet. His ideas represent a combination of ancient beliefs with modern dietary theories.

The Indian National Congress (INC) was formed in 1885. It was a moderate group of mainly Western-educated professionals who passed resolutions on uncontroversial topics, such as opportunities for Indians in the civil service. By 1900 it had emerged as an all-Indian political organization. In 1906 the All-India Muslim League was founded to represent that community's interest. The partition of Bengal by the viceroy Lord Curzon in 1905 alienated both Hindus and Muslims, and intensified dissatisfaction with British rule.

The participation of Indian soldiers in the First World War – more than a million fought for the British Empire, and a great proportion died or were injured – economic depression and especially the massacre of unarmed civilians at Jallianwala Bagh in the Punjab in 1919 increased Indians' desire for more control over their own affairs. The INC changed from an elite political club to a mass organization. The government introduced reforms to give Indians a greater role in the government and civil service, but these were too little, too late, and by 1930 some people were demanding total independence from Britain.

Chakravarti Rajagopalachari, Motilalal and Jawaharlal Nehru, Vallabhbhai Patel and Subhas Chandra Bose (who advocated armed revolution) were significant members of the freedom movement, but Mohandas Gandhi, later known as Mahatma ('great soul'), emerged as the most prominent figure. His vision brought millions of ordinary Indians into the movement. The basis of Gandhi's movement was *satyagraha*, meaning 'insistence on truth' or 'force of truth'. It is based on the principle of *ahimsa*, non-violence or non-injury, which dates back to the sixth century BCE (see chapter Two). While Gandhi's religious beliefs were rooted in Hinduism, with a strong Jain influence, he maintained that all religions contain both truth and error, so that none was superior to another. He adopted the clothing style of the masses of rural India by wearing *khadi* (homespun cloth), urged Indians to rely on goods made in

Baz Bahadur, the last sultan of Malwa (1555 to 1562), and his queen Rupmati hunting.

India by Indians, and favoured small-scale agriculture and industry over large-scale industrialization.

Gandhi's beliefs about food are inseparable from his moral and political philosophy; indeed, it is impossible to think of another world political leader who is or was so concerned with food. His writings reflect traditional Indian religious and medical beliefs as well as the nutritional theories of the day.

Gandhi was born into a Vaishnav Hindu family on the coast of Gujarat, a region with a strong Jain presence. His family was vegetarian and his pious mother often fasted. When Gandhi was a teenager, a friend persuaded him to try meat. At the time there was a popular belief that the British owed their strength and dominance to their consumption of meat, and that if Indians followed suit, they could defeat the British and win independence. A popular Gujarati poem went:

> Behold the mighty Englishman
> He rules the Indian small,
> Because being a meat-eater
> He is five cubits tall.

> *Mahatma Gandhi's Recommended Daily Diet*
>
> 800 ml (2 lb/1½ pints) cow's milk
> 175 g (6 oz) cereal
> 75 g (3 oz) leafy green vegetables
> 150 g (5 oz) other vegetables
> 3 tbsp ghee
> 2 tbsp sugar
> Fruit according to taste and budget
> 2 litres (5 lb/½ gall.) water or other liquid

Even the great spiritual leader Swami Vivkenanda urged the eating of meat on the grounds that it was the only way to achieve robust health and prevent the abject surrender of the weak to physically stronger people. 'Which is a greater sin – to kill a few goats, or to fail to protect the honour of my wife and daughter?' he asked. 'Let those who belong to the elite, and do not have to win their bread by physical labour, shun meat.'[30]

In his autobiography, Gandhi described his first foray into meat eating:

So the day came. It is difficult fully to describe my condition. There were, on the one hand, the zeal for 'reform', and the novelty of making a momentous departure in life. There was, on the other, the shame of hiding like a thief to do this very thing. I cannot say which of the two swayed me more. We went in search of a lonely spot by the river, and there I saw, for the first time in my life, meat. There was baker's [English-style] bread also. I relished neither. The goat's meat was as tough as leather. I simply could not eat it. I was sick and had to leave off eating.

I had a very bad night afterwards. A horrible nightmare haunted me. Every time I dropped off to sleep it would seem as though a live goat were bleating inside me, and I would jump up full of remorse. But then I would remind myself that meat-eating was a duty, and so become more cheerful.[31]

Gandhi's friend began to cook special meat dishes for him and even arranged meals at a restaurant. Gandhi eventually overcame his reluctance (and his compassion for goats) and began to enjoy meat dishes. This went on for a year. Eventually, however, he was overcome with guilt and concluded that lying to his parents was worse than not eating meat. He decided that as long as they were alive, eating meat was out of the question.

In 1888 Gandhi left for England to study law. Before he went, his mother made him swear a vow before a Jain monk that he would never touch meat, alcohol or women. At first he subsisted on a diet of boiled vegetables and bread, until he discovered a vegetarian restaurant in London. There he bought a copy of the book *A Plea for Vegetarianism* (1886) by the British reformer Henry S. Salt, one of the first modern advocates of animal rights. The book outlines the moral reasons for being a vegetarian, including the inherent violence in eating meat and the non-violence that could be achieved from abstaining from it – ideas that Gandhi identified with the ancient concept of *ahimsa*. Now, rather than abstaining from meat because of his vow to his mother, he did so from moral conviction: 'The choice was now made in favour of vegetarianism, the spread of which henceforward became my mission.'[32] Gandhi joined the London Vegetarian Society and became a member of its Executive Committee.

In a speech entitled 'The Moral Basis of Vegetarianism', delivered to the society in 1931, Gandhi said that people who became vegetarians purely for health reasons usually failed because vegetarianism requires a moral basis as well as a practical one. Some vegetarians made food a fetish and thought that by becoming vegetarians they could eat as much cheese, lentils and beans as they liked – an approach that did not improve their health. The secret to remaining healthy, he said, is to cut down the quantity of one's food and reduce the number of meals.

In later life, when drinking goat's milk helped him to recover from a severe case of dysentery, Gandhi was forced to admit the necessity of adding milk to a vegetarian diet, since it provides a much-needed source of protein. Nonetheless, he called his inability to give up milk 'the tragedy of my life'. Gandhi accepted the consumption of eggs as long as they were unfertilized. Cereals should be ground and processed locally to avoid removing the nutritious pericarp. He recommended that green leafy vegetables and seasonal fruit be eaten every day, preferably raw. Milk and bananas, which are rich in starch, make a perfect meal.

Gandhi maintained that a certain amount of fat is necessary; the best is pure ghee, followed by freshly ground peanut oil. About 40 g (1½ oz) a day is necessary to meet one's bodily needs. Using more, especially to deep-fry puris and laddus, is a 'thoughtless extravagance'. Some sugar is needed – he recommended 25–40 g (1–1½ oz) a day – and more if sweet fruit is not available. But the undue preference given to sweet things in India is wrong, he said; in fact, to enjoy sweetmeats in a country where many people do not even get a full meal is equivalent to robbery.

'Food should be taken as a matter of duty – even as a medicine – to sustain the body, never for the satisfaction of the palate', Gandhi wrote, since pleasure comes from satisfying hunger.[33] He opposed the use of spices on the grounds that their only function is to please the palate. He also believed that they have no role in maintaining health, and that all condiments, even salt, destroy the natural flavour of vegetables and cereals. Likewise, tea, coffee and cocoa are not beneficial and can even be harmful.

For Gandhi, alcohol was beyond the pale because of the economic, moral, intellectual and physical harm it does to poor people (as well as, he noted, to some princes whose lives had been ruined by spirits). Gandhi advocated a total ban on the manufacture, sale and consumption of alcohol, a policy that is still in force in his native Gujarat and some other Indian states. (Gujarat even imposes the death penalty on those found guilty of making and selling bootlegged alcohol that leads to death.) Regarding tobacco, he quoted the Russian writer Tolstoy, who called it the worst of all intoxicants and noted that it was very expensive, smelly and dirty, especially when people spit. Gandhi's writing makes no mention at all of drinking urine, although some people believe that was part of his food philosophy.[34]

While Gandhi rigorously followed his own prescriptions, he was not dogmatic about imposing them on others. Prolonged experimentation and observation convinced him that there is no fixed rule for all constitutions, and that while vegetarianism, 'one of the priceless gifts of Hinduism', is highly desirable, it is not an end in itself. 'Many a man eating meat and [dining] with everybody, but living in the fear of God, is nearer his freedom than a man religiously abstaining from meat and other things, but blaspheming God in every one of his acts', he wrote in *Young India*.[35] Despite his affinity with the Jains, he did not hesitate to have insects or snakes killed if they invaded his ashram, nor did he find it necessary to avoid aubergines or potatoes, as Jains did.

One of Gandhi's main weapons in the fight for independence was fasting. He undertook seventeen fasts during his lifetime; the longest, to

Gandhi during his final fast at Birla House, New Delhi, in January 1948 to restore communal harmony.

stop communal rioting in 1943, lasted 21 days. This tactic has been adopted by others in India and abroad, most recently by the Indian anti-corruption fighter Anna Hazare.

Gandhi was also an assiduous defender of the protection of cows. He wrote:

> The central fact of Hinduism . . . is cow-protection. Cow-protection to me is one of the most wonderful phenomena in human evolution . . . Man through the cow is enjoined to realize his identity with all that lives. Why the cow was selected for apotheosis is obvious to me. The cow was in India the best companion. She was the giver of plenty. Not only did she give milk, but she also made agriculture possible . . . She is the mother to millions of Indian mankind. Protection of the cow means protection of the whole sub-creation of God. The ancient seer, whoever he was, began with the cow. The appeal of the lower order of creation is the gift of Hinduism to the world. And Hinduism will live so long as there are Hindus to protect the cow.[36]

236

Today many of the Indian states have cow protection laws, which forbid the transport and slaughter of cattle and in some cases the consumption of beef.

Whether Gandhi's views on food had a lasting effect in India is doubtful. The dietary changes accompanying economic growth have led to a rise in diabetes, high blood pressure and other 'diseases of affluence' – a topic reprised in chapter Twelve.

ELEVEN

An Overview of Indian Cuisine: The Meal, Cooking Techniques and Regional Variations

Throughout history the diet of most people in the world was limited to what was seasonally and locally available. This was especially true of India, with its vast territory and poor roads. Moreover, India is so climatically diverse that few plants and ingredients are available throughout the entire country. Even the common classification by regional or local cuisines – South Indian, Punjabi, Bengali, Hyderabadi and so on – does not begin to do justice to its diversity. It is no exaggeration to say that an example can be found to refute any statement made about Indian food. Despite its shortcomings, a regional survey is the most practical way of describing the diversity and richness of the subcontinent's cuisine.

THE MEAL

An Indian meal is centred on a starch, either rice or a grain. Nationwide, cereals provide 70 per cent of all the calories and protein consumed, although the percentage falls as income rises. In rice-producing regions (the northeast, South India, Uttar Pradesh), that is the staple grain, whereas in the wheat-producing north (including Punjab and Haryana) the staple is wheat, usually consumed as bread. In western India, so-called coarse cereals, such as millet and sorghum, were once staples, but they have largely been replaced by wheat.

The second major part of the diet is pulses (beans, peas and lentils). Together, grains and pulses provide the full complement of amino acids necessary for health. Vegetables, dairy products, spices, chutneys, pickles, fruit and sugar supply vitamins, minerals and trace elements. In many parts of India a meal ends with buttermilk or yoghurt, which is believed to aid digestion.

People living in Punjab, where dairy farming is widespread, consume seventeen times as much milk per capita as those in Odisha and twice as much as the national average. Heading the list in the consumption of oil and fat are Gujarat, the country's largest producer of oil seeds, and Punjab, where butter and ghee are eaten daily by those who can afford it. In the past other local oils were used – coconut oil in Kerala, mustard oil in West Bengal, sesame oil in the south – but today they are increasingly being replaced by vegetable and soy-bean oils.

Contrary to popular Western belief, there is evidence that a minority of Indians are vegetarian: the proportion was estimated by one survey as 25–30 per cent nationwide. Regionally, the proportion ranges from less than 6 per cent in Kerala, Orissa and West Bengal to 60 per cent or more in Rajasthan and Gujarat.[1] However, meat is expensive and most people cannot afford to eat it every day; even affluent people eat relatively little by Western standards. When meat is served, the portions are smaller than in the Western diet, where meat is often the centre-piece of a meal. On average, Indians obtain 92 per cent of their calories from vegetable products and only 8 per cent from animal products (meat, dairy and eggs).

Most middle-class Indians eat two main meals a day, supplemented by one or two smaller meals, including an afternoon tea and a light dinner. In rural areas, the main meals are a hearty breakfast or early lunch to prepare for the day's labour and a light dinner, perhaps supplemented with bread and snacks in the afternoon.

According to ancient Hindu dietary theory, every meal is supposed to include all six tastes in the following order: sweet, sour, salty, pungent, bitter and astringent. Today, most people are unaware of this theory, and the only meal at which all the tastes are experienced – except for the distinctly bitter – is a formal wedding banquet. Nonetheless, usually four or five tastes are present in an Indian meal. As in any country, a skilful cook tries to achieve a harmonious interplay of colours and textures. For example, if a meat dish has a thin gravy, the vegetables are served in a thick sauce, or a thin dal will be served with dry meat dishes, such as kebabs.

Indian meals do not normally have a sequence of courses. Everything arrives more or less at once, although certain dishes may appear at differ-ent times and remain on the table throughout the meal. According to the

Nobel Laureate Octavio Paz (1914–1998), once Mexico's ambassador to India:

> In European cooking, the order of the dishes is quite precise. It is a diachronic cuisine. . . . A radical difference in India, the various dishes come together on a single large plate. Neither a succession nor a parade, but a conglomeration and superimposition of things and tastes; a synchronic cuisine. A fusion of flavours, a fusion of times.[2]

A common method of serving food is on a *thali* – a round metal plate about 35 cm (14 in.) in diameter with slightly raised edges. Once used mainly in northern India, *thalis* are now popular throughout the country in homes and restaurants. Rice, bread and pickles are placed on the *thali* while dals, vegetable, meat and fish dishes, yoghurt and sweet dishes are served in small round metal bowls called *katoris*. The word *thali* may have originated in a ritual cooking pot, *sthali*, used in the Vedic kitchen to boil rice. *Thalis* can be made of silver and gold (for the wealthy), bronze, kansa (an alloy of copper, tin, zinc, iron and mercury) and even styrofoam, with indentations instead of bowls for large informal receptions. Certain metals are traditionally believed to have medicinal properties and to enhance digestion.[3] The word *thali* is also used to refer to a set meal in an Indian restaurant. In the south, food was traditionally

A *thali*, or metal tray, with small bowls is a traditional way of serving food.

A traditional way of serving a meal in South India and in South Indian
restaurants in Southeast Asia is on a banana leaf.

served on a banana leaf, although today that occurs mainly at festivals
and weddings.

The traditional way of eating Indian food is with one's right hand.
During the preparation of food, it is not touched or tasted by anyone else,
so in a way, the final act of preparation is left to the eater, who mixes
the rice or bread with the food and condiments to his or her liking. If
the food is too bland, the diner can add a little pickle or chilli; if too
spicy, some yoghurt. Eating is done with a circular movement of the
hands, as the diner gathers the rice with his fingertips or tears off a piece
of bread and then uses it to scoop up portions of the other foods. More
Westernized households use knives and forks.

Cooking Techniques and Equipment

Indian cooking tends to be technique-based and very labour-intensive.
The provenance and freshness of ingredients are less important than
in, say, Italian cuisine. In most households, cooking was traditionally
done by women. In a joint family, where the sons' wives lived with their
parents, the senior woman would supervise, aided by her daughters-
in-law. In brahmin households, women would start cooking only after
bathing, wearing cotton saris. Affluent households would employ cooks,

who were often men and, in orthodox households, brahmins. (In the olden days, cook was the second most common profession among brahmins, after priest). To avoid polluting the meal, no one was allowed to enter the kitchen or to touch the cook.

Indian kitchens are simple, even austere, by Western standards (although affluent urbanites are now starting to install 'designer kitchens'). Almost all cooking is done over a stove or burner. Traditional fuels were dried cowpats, charcoal, coke, twigs or wood shavings. The use of cow dung is an ancient form of recycling that also provides income for the people who collect, dry and sell it. Cowpats provide a gentle heat ideal for slow-cooking dishes with sauces and liquids, which are sometimes left overnight on hot coals. In middle-class households, the standard cooking device is a small hob (cooktop) with two burners fuelled by bottled gas (propane). It is amazing what elaborate feasts can be prepared on this simple piece of equipment. Pressure cookers, invented in France in the seventeenth century, are owned by three-quarters of all urban households in India. A sealed lid increases the air pressure, lowering the temperature at which water boils and significantly reducing the cooking time.

A technique that has no exact equivalent in Western cuisine is a combination of sautéing, stir-frying and stewing. The cook fries spices and a paste made from garlic, onions, ginger and sometimes tomatoes in a little oil until it is soft. Then pieces of meat, fish or vegetables are browned in the same oil. The next step is to add small amounts of liquid a little a time, while stirring. The amount of liquid added and the cooking time determine whether the dish will be wet or dry. Another uniquely Indian technique (called *chhauk*, *takar* or *bagar*) is the addition of spices fried in a little oil or ghee to a curry or dal after it has been cooked, imparting a delightful aroma.

One possible explanation for the prevalence of slow simmering and 'curries' is the institution of the joint family, where meals had to be prepared for many people at the same time. This would preclude stir-frying, for example, in which speed and freshness are important. Ovens and stoves, which are used for heating the home as well as for cooking, were not needed in India; thus, roasting is rare except in the far north.

Pickling, an ancient technique, is important in a hot climate. It is a way of preserving fruit, vegetables, meat or fish by impregnating them with acid, which discourages the growth of most microbes. This can be done either by adding the acid, usually vinegar, directly, or by soaking them in a strong salt solution, which encourages acid-producing bacteria to grow. Indian pickles can be sweet, sour, salty, cooling, hot or very hot indeed, and add another taste dimension to a meal.

The Indian *batterie de cuisine* is relatively small. In ancient times, pots and cooking utensils were made of earthenware and cleaned with ashes, earth and acidic or alkaline natural substances. Today they are made of metal. One of the most frequently used receptacles is a deep stainless-steel or cast-iron pot (*karahi*) with two handles and a flat or slightly concave bottom, used for shallow- and deep-frying. Rice and curry-like dishes with a liquid sauce are prepared in a straight-sided pan with a lid. The lid is saucer-shaped, so that live charcoal can be placed on it for certain dishes. A *tawa*, a flat, heavy iron griddle with a long handle, is used for roasting and preparing breads that require little or no oil. A slotted metal spoon is used for frying and draining, and a ladle for stirring. In Bengal, a large knife mounted on a wooden board, called a *bonti*, is used to cut up fish and large vegetables. South Indian and Gujarati kitchens have a variety of specialized devices for preparing steamed breads and snacks.

In some parts of India, the cook crushes spices, onions, garlic and herbs by pressing and rolling them with a small stone rolling pin on a large stone slab. In South India, a mortar and pestle is generally used. Modern cooks have electric grinders and blenders. Very large kitchens, such as those in a wealthy home or a restaurant, may employ a person whose sole job is to grind spices. Spices and flavourings are often ground early in the morning for the day's meals.

Kashmir

Jammu and Kashmir is India's northernmost state.[4] One of the largest princely states of British India, it was claimed after Independence by both India and Pakistan, and since 1972 it has been divided by a Line of Control. Two-thirds of the original territory comprises the Indian state of Jammu and Kashmir; the rest, called Azad Kashmir, is under Pakistani control. India and Pakistan have fought several wars over the region since the 1950s, and the economy of the state has been badly damaged by political unrest and the Kashmir earthquake of 2005. Of Jammu and Kashmir's 12 million residents, approximately 70 per cent are Muslims; the rest are Hindus, Sikhs and Buddhists. The population of Azad Kashmir is 4.5 million, mainly Muslims.

With its lush scenery and lakes, Kashmir was the favourite summer resort of the Mughal emperors. The legendary Vale of Kashmir produced an extremely rich bounty of fruit and vegetables. The lakes supply fish,

A kitchen in the home of an aristocrat in Lucknow.

water chestnuts and lotus roots, a delicacy. Nomadic herdsmen raise goats and sheep. Distinctive Kashmiri ingredients include saffron; small, sweet red shallots called *praan*; morels; wild asparagus; and a mild-flavoured red pepper called Kashmiri chilli. Mustard oil was the traditional cooking medium.

There are two schools of Kashmir cuisine: Hindu, sometimes called Pandit, and Muslim. While both groups eat meat (although the Pandits avoid chicken), the spicing is different. Hindus use yoghurt and asafoetida,

Women preparing lunch for a school in a Bengali village.

while Muslims flavour dishes with onions and garlic, both of which are avoided by Pandits.

Turnips are eaten raw, pickled, fried with spices and simmered in yoghurt, or cooked in a creamy gravy. Kashmir is one of the few parts of India where mushrooms are standard fare, particularly a local variety of morel. One of the most popular dishes is dum aloo, small boiled potatoes fried and simmered in a sauce of yoghurt and spices. Plain boiled rice accompanies everyday meals; feasts feature aromatic pulaos and biryanis.

Kashmir is famous for its rich meat dishes, served during the special banquets called *wazwan* (see page 205–6), which may consist of as many as 40 courses. The preferred meat is goat, the younger the better, and often marinated in yoghurt and spices and cooked with milk and cream to produce a rich, thick sauce. The standard Kashmiri drink is qehwa – green tea flavoured with saffron, cardamom and almonds and served from a samovar.

Uttar Pradesh

With a population of more than 130 million, Uttar Pradesh is India's most populous state. India's capital, New Delhi, is located within its borders. Situated on a large alluvial plain with a tropical monsoon climate, Uttar Pradesh is India's top wheat-growing state and a major producer of sugar cane, pulses, potatoes, livestock, dairy products, vegetables and fruit.

Around 82 per cent of Uttar Pradesh residents are Hindus, and 60 per cent are vegetarians. Meat is eaten by a large caste called kayasthas, the descendants of Hindus who served as administrators for the Mughals and then the British. A popular breakfast dish is halwa puri: puris (deep-fried wheat bread), carrot halwa, curried chickpeas and potatoes and pickles. A main meal typically consists of dal, wheat bread (puris, parathas or chapattis) and one or two seasonal vegetable dishes – cauliflower in winter, bitter gourd in summer. Non-vegetarians replace a vegetable dish with a meat curry.

Varanasi (formerly Benares), considered a holy city by Hindus, is distinguished by its vegetarian cuisine, cooked in ghee without onions and garlic, and its sweets, which are mostly made with khoya, the sticky solid made by boiling down whole milk. Other U.P. cities are famous for their sweets. Mathura, the birthplace of Lord Krishna, is known for its peda, a semi-soft round light-coloured sweet made from thickened milk flavoured with cardamom, nuts or saffron. Agra is home to the petha, a translucent soft sweet made of cooked ash gourd soaked in sugar solution. In contrast to the austere vegetarian food of Hindus, the food of Lucknow, the state's capital, is meat-centred and sumptuous, a legacy of the Awadhi court (see page 192–6).

The Northwest

The earliest evidence of farming and herding in South Asia, dating back to 7000 BCE, was found at Mehrgarh in the Pakistani province of Baluchistan, today home to Baluchis and other ethnic groups.[5] The terrain is rugged and barren, the food simple and unspiced. Bread is important, including tandoori roti; khameer roti, which is slightly leavened and baked in a special clay oven built into a wall; and kaak, a rock-hard bread made by wrapping dough around a hot stone and baking it on coals.

Kebabs are lightly seasoned with salt and coriander. The most popular dish is shorba, a soup often made with milk. Another distinctive food is quroot – milk curds that are fermented, salted and shaped into pebble-like balls that are dried in the sun. Sajii, a dish of Middle Eastern origin, is a whole lamb marinated and roasted over burning wood on a spit stuck in the ground. Sajii is traditionally served with kak. Meat is dried and salted, then boiled during the winter months. A common drink is green tea prepared with water infused with green cardamoms and cinnamon.

Until 2010 Khyber Patunkhwa, a province of Pakistan with a Pasthun majority, was called the Northwest Frontier Province. It came under British rule in 1849 after being part of Afghan and Sikh kingdoms. The food is similar to that of Baluchistan and is centred on meat. (According to a local proverb, even burnt meat is better than lentils.) Mutton or beef kebabs, lightly spiced, are very popular. The staple is bread, usually made from wheat flour (in some areas corn) and baked in a tandoor, a clay oven owned by many households. A village near the provincial capital, Peshawar, was the birthplace of India's most famous restaurateur, Kundan Lal Gujral, the creator of tandoori cuisine (see pages 282–3).

Sindh

Today a province of Pakistan, the region known as Sindh was part of the Indian historical mainstream for thousands of years, starting with the Indus Valley civilization.[6] At the time of Independence, around 25 per cent of the population were Hindus and Sikhs, including many business-people who emigrated to India and abroad.

In the arid Thar Desert only sorghum and millet grow, and these remain the staple among rural people. Vegetation is scarce, except in the irrigated Indus Valley region, where fruit and vegetables are cultivated. Rice and wheat grow in the northern and southern parts of the province. Seafood, especially prawns, and freshwater fish are important to the Sindhi diet. A popular fish is the bony palla (ilish, called hilsa in Bengal), which migrates up the Indus River. It is eaten grilled or fried, or filled with a masala paste and cooked over low heat or baked in hot sand. Fried fish with phulka, a puffy bread, is a typical breakfast.

Sindh has many distinctive breads and snacks, such as chanwaran jo atto, made from red rice; dho do, thick rotis prepared with masala and garlic paste; and bossari, a rich roti prepared with jaggery and ghee. The influence of the Arabs, who arrived in the seventh century, is apparent in the many varieties of halwa, some made with a sesame-seed paste as in the Middle East. Another Arab legacy may be mazoon (from the ancient name for Oman), a sweet of chopped nuts, spices and sugar syrup cooked in ghee.

Punjab and Haryana

The region known as the Punjab, which means 'five rivers', has long been the heartland of Indian agriculture. Following Independence in

1947, the British province of Punjab was divided between Pakistan and India, and in 1966 Indian Punjab was broken into three states on linguistic and religious grounds: the small mountain state of Himachal Pradesh; Haryana, with a Hindu majority; and Punjab, with a large Sikh population. On the other side of the border, the Pakistani province of Punjab has 91 million residents, more than half the country's population. Its capital, Lahore, is just 30 km (19 miles) from Amritsar, the capital of Indian Punjab.

Located on a fertile plain, the two Punjabs are the breadbaskets of India and Pakistan, producing wheat, barley, corn, chickpeas, sugar cane, rice, mustard and fruit and vegetables. Farming is more mechanized than elsewhere in India, and the poverty rates are the lowest of anywhere in the two countries. Dairy farming (of cows and buffaloes) is an important industry.

The food of the region is simple, robust and closely linked to the land. The region is sometimes dubbed 'the land of rotis' because the staple is bread, made from wheat or sometimes millet and corn. Seasonal vegetables, such as cauliflower, carrots, turnips, pumpkins and mustard greens, are an essential part of the diet. Somewhat paradoxically, in view of the region's high per-capita income, Indian Punjab also has a high proportion of vegetarians – 54 per cent. People in this region have a low rate of lactose intolerance and drink a lot of milk, flavoured yoghurt (lassi) and buttermilk.

Women in Gujarat preparing dishes from the flour of local millet.

The Sikhs

Some 18 million Indians are followers of Sikhism, a mono-theistic religion founded by Guru Nanak (1469–1539). Born a Hindu, he preached the doctrine of 'one God, the Creator, whose name was truth'. Between 1459 and 1708 his successors, called gurus, rejected the caste system, ritualism, asceticism and the worship of idols, and recognized the equality of the sexes and of all religions. Sikhs adopted five distinguishing symbols: the beard, the dagger, an iron bracelet, special underwear and the turban. A Sikh scripture, the *Adi Granth* or the *Granth Sahib*, is the focal point of Sikh places of worship, which are called *gurdwaras*. After the service, a *halwa* made of equal parts wheat flour, ghee and sugar is distributed to the worshippers.

There are few uniquely Sikh dishes: instead Punjabi Sikhs eat Punjabi food, and so on. Most Sikhs are not vegetarian, although they do not eat beef or animals that are not killed in accordance with Sikh law (called *jatka*: using a single stroke of a sword or axe to sever the head). Their sacred writings contain passages indicating that whether or not to eat meat should be a decision left to the individual. Sikh *gurdwaras* have a community kitchen, a *langar*, which provides free meals to all worshippers and visitors, even those from other religions. The food served there is always vegetarian, which makes it accessible to everyone.

Panir – farmer's cheese pressed under a weight and cut into cubes – is a characteristic ingredient in curries, often combined with peas and other vegetables. It can also be grilled on skewers. Sauces are made from onions, tomatoes, garlic and ginger fried in ghee, and spicing is straightforward, featuring coriander seeds, cumin seeds and red chillies. Rice is served mainly on special occasions. The thick, rich dals of the region are famous all over the subcontinent: in dal makhani, for example, black lentils, chickpeas, black-eyed peas or kidney beans are simmered for a long time over a slow fire and flavoured with spices and cream. Another famous Punjabi dish is mustard greens, sarson ka sag, served with a corn bread similar to the corn tortilla. Spicy chickpeas served

Lassi, a popular
yoghurt drink, was
traditionally sold
in clay pots.

with a slightly puffy fried bread is a popular street food and breakfast dish
called chole batura.

In Pakistani Punjab, meat – mutton (goat), chicken and beef – is
widely consumed by those who can afford it. Specialities include paye
cholay (cow's trotters with chickpeas), chargha (a whole chicken marinated
in lemon juice and deep-fried) and various kebabs.

Rajasthan

The state of Rajasthan was formed in 1947 by the union of more than
twenty princely states. The Aravalli mountain range divides the state
into the hilly southeastern region and the barren Thar Desert, one of
the hottest, driest regions in the world. However, thanks to the use of
irrigation, Rajasthan has become a major producer of millet, rapeseed,
mustard, barley, corn, certain spices and livestock. Around 90 per cent
of the population are Hindus and Jains.

Grain is ground into flour to produce some of the subcontinent's most delicious breads. A staple throughout western India is bhakri (also called dhebra), a round, flat unleavened bread that can be soft or hard in texture, made from coarsely ground flour and water. It was traditionally taken by farmers to the fields and eaten with chutney, chillies or pickles. Wheat is increasingly replacing the traditional grains of the region. Cooking oil and ghee are precious commodities among poor people, so bread is usually roasted in a heavy pan, and a little ghee added before serving.

Just under two-thirds of Rajasthani people are vegetarians. The most famous dish of the region is the ancient dal batti churma. The dal is typically made from five kinds of lentils cooked in ghee. Battis are wheat-flour balls roasted in coals until hard, then cracked open and eaten with ghee. Churma is coarsely ground wheat crushed and cooked with ghee and sugar. Lentils are omnipresent in dals and kadhis (spicy curries with yoghurt and chickpea flour) or ground into flour to make breads and snacks. A dough of chickpea flour, yoghurt and spices is rolled into long, thin strands that are boiled and dried to make gatta. They are prepared like vegetables. Sun-dried vegetables are also popular.

A group called Marwaris, traders by caste, originated in Rajasthan and, from at least the time of Akbar, migrated all over India. They are strict vegetarians (many are Jains) who avoid garlic and onions, but have developed a rich cuisine based on sun-dried vegetables, breads and many sweets.

The cuisine of the Rajputs, the hereditary rulers, relies heavily on meat, reflecting their caste (ksatriya) and their love of hunting. Quintessential Rajput dishes are sula, a smoked, grilled kebab traditionally made from wild boar, venison, quail and other game; wild boar and venison pickle; and safed maas, an aromatic white stew of meat prepared with yoghurt, coconut and cream.

Gujarat

The state of Gujarat, bordered by the Arabian Sea, Pakistan and several Indian states, was created in 1960 when the state of Bombay was divided by language into Gujarat and Maharashtra. Two-thirds of Gujaratis live in rural areas. A large minority are merchants and businessmen. Ninety per cent of the population are Hindus and 9 per cent Muslim.

The main crops are rice, wheat, millet, lentils, peanuts and cotton. Seventy per cent of the population are vegetarians – the highest proportion in India. This reflects the influence of the Jain community and the heritage of Mahatma Gandhi. Many Hindus do not eat eggs, onions or garlic. A standard flavouring is a paste of green chilli and ginger. Dishes are made with relatively little oil, and some are steamed. Sweet and sour is a popular flavouring, the sourness coming from the rind of the fruit kokum (*Garcinia indica*). Cooks often add a pinch of sugar to dals and vegetables dishes and serve them with a piece of jaggery and a piece of a sweet. Despite the state's long coastline, fish and seafood are rarely used in Gujarati cuisine. Distinctive vegetables include papri, a very long thin green bean; colocasia (arvi), the leaves of the taro plant; and many varieties of squash and yam.

Western Gujarat, or Saurashtra, is known for its dairy products, dry vegetable dishes and pickles. A famous local dish is undhio or oondhiya, a medley of sweet potatoes, aubergine, green beans, grated coconut and little dumplings made from chickpea flour and fenugreek leaves. The part of Saurashtra known as Kathiawar is particularly known for its robustly spicy cuisine.

Surat, the second largest city in Gujarat, is home to one of India's oldest Muslim communities, called Surtis, who have their own cuisine featuring many varieties of soups. Central Gujarat is the state's granary, and is distinguished by its breads, snacks and lentil dishes. Southern

Dhokla, a popular Gujarati farsan, or snack, are squares of steamed fermented rice and chickpea flour.

Khaman Dhokla (Gujarat)

150 g (2 cups) raw chickpeas
4 tbsp yoghurt
4 green chillies, finely chopped
2.5 cm (1 in.) piece of fresh ginger, finely chopped
¼ tsp turmeric
1 tbsp sugar
1 tsp bicarbonate of soda
4 tbsp oil
1 tsp mustard seeds
salt to taste
coriander leaves and fresh coconut, to garnish

Soak the chickpeas in water overnight. Drain and grind coarsely. Add the yoghurt, cover and leave to ferment for four hours.

Add the green chillies, ginger, turmeric, sugar and salt, and mix well.

Dissolve the bicarbonate of soda in 1 tbsp of the oil and add to the batter.

Lightly grease a flat metal plate (*thali*) with a 4 cm (1½ in.) rim and pour the batter into it. Cover and steam for 20 minutes. When cool, cut into squares and place on a serving plate.

Heat the rest of the oil and the mustard seeds in a small pan. When the seeds start to crackle, pour them over the dhoklas. Garnish with coriander leaves and coconut.

Gujarat is a fertile, well-watered region that produces plenty of green vegetables and fruit, including some of India's finest mangoes.

Afternoon tea is an occasion for enjoying Gujarat's delicious snacks called farsans. An emblematic Gujarati dish is dhokla, a steamed dish of fermented legumes. Gujarat has a long history of confectionary. Some sweets are milk-based; others are made from pulses, such as a sweet lentil-stuffed puri and halwa made from chickpea flour.

Maharashtra

The state of Maharashtra is the industrial powerhouse of India, and its capital, Mumbai, its commercial centre. The state is a major producer of oil seeds, peanuts, soy beans, sugar cane, turmeric, vegetables and grapes, the last of which are used in a rapidly growing wine industry. Fish and seafood are abundant along the 800 km (500 miles) of coast. Around 80 per cent of the population are Hindus, 10 per cent Muslims and the rest Christians and Parsis. The two largest Hindu castes are brahmins, who are vegetarians, and non-vegetarian Marathas. About 30 per cent of the state's population are vegetarian.

Maharashtrian cuisine is eclectic because of the state's location between north and south – both wheat and rice are staples – and its long contact with the Portuguese. Chillies, tomatoes, potatoes, peanuts, sweetcorn, sweet potatoes, green peppers, green beans, cashews, tapioca and papayas play a larger role in Maharashtrian cuisine than in many other parts of India.[7]

Another distinctive feature is the blending of sweet, salt, hot and sour flavours in a meal or even a single dish. As in Gujarat, sweets are eaten *during* the meal, not afterwards. Foods are placed in a strictly defined order on *thalis* or, at feasts, on banana leaves. There is little deep-frying or roasting; rather, dishes are lightly sautéed and steamed to retain their flavours. An emblematic and ancient Maharashtrian sweet is shrikhand, a soft pudding made from strained yoghurt with sugar, saffron, cardamom and other spices.

A common food among rural people is zunka bhakar: a porridge made from chickpea flour, onions and spices and a thick bread of sorghum or millet flour, with red chillies on the side and perhaps a dollop of butter on top. (In 1995 the Maharashtra state government set up a chain of stalls selling zunka bhakar for 1 rupee. The purpose was to provide employment and win political support.)

A coastal cuisine called Konkani features seafood, coconut, fruit and vegetables. Popular fish dishes are bombil, or Bombay duck, a small fish dry-fried until it is crisp and often served as an accompaniment to curries; and pomfret, which is eaten stuffed, grilled, fried or curried in a coconut sauce. Crabs, prawns, shrimp, shellfish and lobster are other popular foods.

A distinctive cuisine combining Indian, Persian and British influences is that of the Parsis, the descendants of Zoroastrians who came from Persia in the seventh century CE. The Parsi community in Mumbai was instrumental in the development of Indian industry and commerce. However, their numbers are rapidly declining, and in 2001 there were fewer than 70,000.

Parsis eat meat and fish, although they may avoid beef and pork out of respect for their Hindu and Muslim neighbours. Meat dishes are cooked Iranian style with vegetables, such as aubergines, potatoes, spinach and peas, and only lightly spiced. Chillies are used in moderation. The Iranian influence is also evident in the use of nuts, dried fruit and rosewater. The most famous Parsi dish, dhansakh, combines meat with as many as seven kinds of bean and lentil, pumpkin, aubergine, fenugreek leaves, onions, ginger, garlic, tamarind and spices.

Eggs are a popular breakfast dish – in the old days eating three or four a day was not uncommon – served over minced meat, fish, potatoes, cooked vegetables or bananas. Akoori is scrambled eggs flavoured with onions, garlic, coriander leaves and tomatoes and cooked in ghee. Most meals are accompanied by bread, pickles and chutneys. The Parsi community adopted many English dishes, including custard, cakes, puddings and stews.

A major event in the Parsi calendar is New Year, or Navroz, held at the time of the vernal equinox and observed by lavish feasting. Three sweet dishes, which probably came from Iran, are always served: ravo, a semolina and cream pudding flavoured with spices and rosewater; sev, fried vermicelli cooked in sugar syrup; and meethu dhai, or sweet yoghurt.

Parsis are supposed to observe four days of abstinence each month when they do not eat meat, although fish and eggs are acceptable. Meat is also supposed to be avoided during the eleventh month of the Parsi year. Meat is not eaten for three days after the death of a loved one; on the fourth day, the fast is broken with dhansakh.

In the nineteenth and early twentieth centuries a second wave of Zoroastrians emigrated from Iran; called Iranis, they opened small eateries, called Irani cafés, that serve biscuits and other baked goods, bread and butter, samosas and other Indian snacks, Parsi dishes and Iranian-style tea. They are, however, rapidly disappearing: in the 1950s there were 350 Irani cafés in Mumbai; only some 25 remain.

Goa

The tiny state of Goa was a Portuguese possession from the early sixteenth century until 1961.[8] About a third of the population are Roman Catholic, the rest mainly Hindu. The state is affluent, with less than 5 per cent of people living below the poverty line. The soil is sandy and there is little arable land, but there is plenty of fish, seafood, fruit, cashews and coconut. Meat plays an important role in Goan cuisine, including pork, chicken and even beef. Goan cooks are famous for their culinary expertise.

Goan cuisine is an amalgam of Portuguese, Indian and even British influences. Classic Portuguese dishes are adapted and enlivened by spices (see chapter Ten). A popular local beverage is feni, a distilled spirit from cashews first made by Portuguese monks.

Goans celebrate Christmas with great fanfare. Pork is a must for Christmas lunch, especially sorpotel, a hot-and-sour curry made from the meat, liver, blood and fat of a pig, flavoured with vinegar and spices. A traditional Christmas cake is bibinca, sixteen layers of egg yolk, flour and coconut milk batter that is baked and turned upside down. Other holiday delicacies are dodols, a soft jaggery fudge, and Western-style cakes called bols made from almond paste, semolina, sugar, eggs and brandy. Goa is also home to a lively carnival before Lent.

Madhya Pradesh

Madhya Pradesh is India's second-largest state, with more than 75 million inhabitants. The region was ruled by the Mauryans, the Mughals and the Marathas, but by the early eighteenth century had broken into several small kingdoms, which the British incorporated into the entity called Central Provinces. Nearly half of the state's population are vegetarian.

Central Madhya Pradesh is dominated by the Malwa Plateau, where the rich black soil allows the growing of sorghum, rice, wheat, coarse millet, peanuts, pulses, soy beans, cotton, linseed, sesame and sugar cane. The western region is much drier, and its cuisine resembles that of neighbouring Rajasthan. Typical dishes are bhutta ri kees, grated corn roasted in ghee and cooked with seasoned milk; and baati or bafla, a roasted ball of wheat flour. A sour kadhi is made from ground chickpeas and tamarind instead of yoghurt. Thuli is a sweet, porridge-like dish made of cracked wheat, typically eaten with milk or kadhi.

Tamil Nadu

India's four southern states – Tamil Nadu,[9] Karnataka, Andhra Pradesh and Kerala – are culturally, linguistically and gastronomically distinct from the rest of the country, although there are significant regional and local differences among them. The languages (called, respectively, Tamil,

Kannada, Telugu and Malayalam) belong to the Dravidian family and have their own scripts and vocabulary, albeit with many Sanskrit words.

Rice and lentils in all four states are the staples of the vegetarian cuisine that is consumed by most brahmins, with wheat playing a secondary role. Typical spices include mustard seeds, fenugreek, cumin seeds, asafoetida, curry leaves, red chillies and tamarind.

In 1947 the Madras Presidency became Madras State, comprising Tamil Nadu and parts of Andhra Pradesh, Kerala and Karnataka. The state was later divided along linguistic lines, and in 1969 Madras State was renamed Tamil Nadu, meaning 'land of the Tamils'. Its capital, Chennai (formerly Madras), was founded by the British as Fort St George in the seventeenth century. However, the British had relatively little influence on Tamil culture or cuisine. The state's population is 89 per cent Hindu, 5 per cent Muslim and 5 per cent Christian. An estimated 15 per cent of Tamils are brahmins, and most are vegetarian. The major crops are rice, millet, pulses, sugar cane, peanuts, onions, oil seeds and many vegetables. The Western Ghat mountains to the west are home to coffee and tea plantations.

Breakfast, an important meal, consists of idlis (soft, steamed discs) or dosas (flat, round, crispy crêpes fried in a little oil). The dough for both is made by soaking rice and black lentils and grinding them into a paste, which is then left overnight to ferment. Both are served with sambar – a thin, spicy lentil soup made from toor dal and sometimes vegetables – and coconut chutney, a paste of ground coconut, urad dal and spices. Dosas can also be made with semolina flour and/or filled with spiced potatoes (masala dosas). Dosas in Tamil Nadu are generally thicker and softer than the thin crispy ones favoured in Karnataka. Milakai podi, a powder made from ground lentils, spices and chillies, is sprinkled over rice.

Tamil lunches and dinners follow a set pattern, although within each course all the elements are mixed together. The first course consists of white rice, sambar and a vegetable dish, such as avial with a creamy coconut sauce or kootu, a thick stew of vegetables, boiled lentils and coconut. The vegetables are fresh and vary every day. Papadums (crispy lentil wafers) or vada, a deep-fried lentil bread that looks like a hole-less doughnut, may accompany the meal. The second course is of rice, rasam (a watery, hot-and-sour dal) and another vegetable. The meal ends with buttermilk or yoghurt. The standard drink is strong filtered coffee mixed with milk, reminiscent of French *café au lait*.

Toddy

A popular drink, especially in South India, toddy (from the Hindi word *tari*) is a beverage made from the fermented sap of the palmyra, date or coconut palm. The sap is extracted by a tapper and collected in a pot. The initial liquid is sweet and non-alcoholic, but fermentation starts quickly because of the presence of natural yeasts. Within two hours, it becomes a drink with up to 4 per cent alcohol content; longer fermentation yields a stronger, more acid version until finally it turns into vinegar. Sometimes spices are added for flavour. In Kerala and Karnataka, it is sold in toddy shops that also sell food. However, the production and sale of toddy is controversial, and state governments periodically try to prohibit it. Toddy is also used as a leavening agent in Kerala's appams and Goa's sanna, steamed breads made from rice flour and coconut milk. Boiling down toddy produces a variety of jaggery (gur).

Freshly made toddy bubbling in a clay jar.

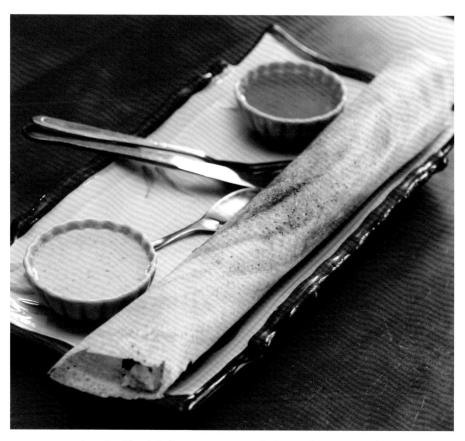

A staple of South Indian restaurants, masala dosa is a large crêpe made
of fermented ground rice and lentils with a spiced potato filling.

A non-vegetarian cuisine is enjoyed by the Chettinads or Chettiars,
a wealthy merchant community who made their fortunes trading with
Southeast Asia in the Middle Ages. Today they live in 75 communities
some 400 km (250 miles) south of Chennai. Their cuisine is known for
its hot, aromatic meat and seafood dishes, such as kozhambu, meatballs
in a creamy cashew-based sauce; meen kulambu, fish cooked in a thick,
aromatic tamarind sauce; and kozhi kuruma, chicken in an aromatic
sauce of coconut and almonds.[10]

Karnataka

The state of Karnataka was created in 1956 from the former princely state
of Mysore and the Kannada-speaking area of adjacent states. The state
capital is the centre of India's booming computer industry and the
fastest-growing city in Asia. It is known for its Western-style pubs and

restaurants. The state grows rice, mangoes, wheat, millet, coconuts, peanuts, oil seeds, wheat, coffee, tea, cashews and spices, especially peppercorns and cardamoms. Eighty-five per cent of the population are Hindus, 12 per cent Muslims and 2 per cent Christians. A third of the population is vegetarian. Generally, people consume equal amounts of rice, wheat and millet, especially in the north, where the food is similar to that of Maharashtra.

The food of Karnataka has been documented for nearly 1,000 years in such works as the *Lokopakara* and the *Supa Shastra*, and more recently by K. T. Achaya, who comes from Karnataka. An emblematic Karnataka dish is bisi bele bhat, an elaborate mixture of rice, lentils, vegetables, curry leaves and other spices that originated in an eleventh-century dish called ogara. Another ancient dish is the mandige, a large paratha made from wheat-flour dough flavoured with sugar and ground cardamom. An essential part of every festival is the local sweet mysore pak, small triangles with a fudge-like consistency, made from chickpea flour, ghee and sugar.

Coorg or Kodava, a lush, hilly region of coffee, spice and orange plantations in the Western Ghats, has a distinctive cuisine characterized by pork and chicken curries made with coconut milk; mushroom and bamboo-shoot stews; and breads, noodles and round dumplings made from rice.

The coastal region of Mangalore is famous for its spicy fish and seafood preparations and coconut sauces. Rice is eaten in many forms: as dosas, sannas (idlis fermented with toddy or yeast), kori rotis (a wafer-thin bread) and adyes, round dumplings made of ground rice and coconut milk.

Kerala

The small state of Kerala in the southwest corner of India was created in 1956 by combining several Malayalam-speaking regions.[11] Spices, notably cardamom and pepper, have been cultivated there from ancient times, and the state remains a leading exporter of spices, cashews and seafood. Kerala's lush landscape is covered with coconut groves, banana trees, rice paddies and vegetable gardens, while its 650 km (400 miles) of coastline and fresh and saltwater lagoons teem with fish and seafood. Cardamom, coffee and tea grow in the eastern highlands.

For all communities in Kerala the staple is rice, which is parboiled by soaking the paddy in water, then drying it before milling. Rice flour is used to make many distinctive breads, including wellayappam or appam (known as 'hoppers' in English). The dough is fermented with toddy and fried in a wok-like pot (called a *cheen-chetti*, literally 'Chinese pot', reflecting its origins) to make a disc-shaped bread with a soft centre and thin, crispy outside border. A popular breakfast dish, poottu, consists of ground rice and coconut steamed in a bamboo tube.

Fresh and sea fish and seafood are eaten by all communities. A quintessential Kerala dish is meen molee, a spicy fish stew with a coconut sauce that is also popular in Southeast Asia. Some attribute its origins to the historical ties between Kerala and Southeast Asia, and claim that the word *molee* comes from 'Malay'.

Two common Keralan ingredients are coconut, as we have seen, and tapioca. Tapioca was introduced to Kerala at various times but became widespread during a rice shortage during the Second World War. Its use has since declined, but cooked tapioca served with spicy fish is still a delicacy in southern Kerala.

Onam is the state festival of Kerala, celebrated by Hindus, Muslims and Christians in August or September. The festival celebrates the rice harvest and the memory of an ancient king, Mahabali, whose rule is thought of as a golden age. On the third day families or communities eat a vegetarian meal served on banana leaves.

Unlike many other parts of the country, Kerala was never under direct British rule. It has the highest literacy rate in India, and the lowest birth rate. Only 6 per cent of the state's population are vegetarian. Although 57 per cent of the people of Kerala (known as Malayalis) are Hindus, the state is home to sizable populations of Muslims (23 per cent) and Christians (19 per cent). The Muslims, called Moplahs or Mappilas (from a word meaning 'bridegroom'), are descendants of Arab traders who married local women. Their distinctive cuisine shows the influence of Western Asia, particularly Yemen. Typical dishes are harees (Arab *harissa*), a hearty wheat and meat porridge; erachi pathiri, minced mutton and whole eggs encased in wholemeal pastry; and Malabar biryani, flavoured with local aromatic spices. Although cinnamon, cloves and nutmeg are locally grown, they are used in moderation, and even black pepper is using sparingly. Traditionally, spices were confined to the preparation of Ayurvedic medicines for which Kerala is known.[12]

Kerala's Christian population is a mixture of Syrian Christians (who trace their origins back to St Thomas), Roman Catholics and other sects; they are largely non-vegetarian.[13] Seafood, chicken, eggs and beef

Idlis in Space

Dr K. Radhakrishnan, a scientist at the Indian Space Research Organization, has developed idlis, sambar and coconut chutney for astronauts to eat in space when India launches its first manned space mission in 2016. The idlis are heated with infrared radiation to a temperature of 700°C (1292°F) and then microwaved to remove the water, until each one weighs 12 g (about ½ oz). When soaked in hot water, they swell to 25 g (nearly 1 oz). Each pack contains ten little idlis, equivalent to three normal-sized ones. The sambar and coconut chutney are dried using infrared radiation.

Dr Radhakrishnan also spent a year and a half developing the Indian sweet rasgullas for space. The balls are freeze-dried and then vacuum-packed, while the syrup is dried to make a powder that can be dissolved in water. 'Rasgullas are ideal for space', he says. 'They have a beautiful texture that doesn't disintegrate easily like other sweets.' His main accomplishment is space yoghurt, which was created by pulsing short bursts of electricity through the yoghurt to render harmful microbes inactive while keeping the good bacteria alive. It may be no coincidence that Dr Radhakrishnan's father and uncle ran an Udupi restaurant in Mysore.

Sohini Chattopadhyay, 'The Space Idli Mission', *Open Magazine*, 9 June 2012.

are regularly eaten; pork and duck (now rather hard to find) are reserved for special occasions, such as weddings and Christmas. Many Catholics in Kerala fast by avoiding meat and even eggs for 25 days before Christmas. Cochin and other cities once had small but thriving Jewish communities, but they have virtually disappeared because of emigration to Israel.

Andhra Pradesh

One of India's largest states, Andhra Pradesh was created in 1956 to encompass the Telugu-speaking parts of South India and the former princely state of Hyderabad.[14] Ninety per cent of the state's population are Hindus and 8 per cent are Muslims, most of whom live in the city of Hyderabad, the state capital. The state also has a sizeable population of Scheduled Tribes (see pages 271–2). Andhra Pradesh is a major producer of rice, barley, millet, lentils, bananas, chillies, turmeric and black pepper. Although brahmins are strict vegetarians, other Hindu castes eat meat and fish, especially those living near the coast, and only 16 per cent of the state's population are vegetarian.

Three ingredients are essential in Andhra cuisine: tamarind, red chillies and gongura, the leaf of the roselle (hibiscus). A typical meal among the poor is gongura with boiled rice, or rice and a chutney of red chillies, garlic, salt and lime juice. A classic Andhra dish is gongura pachadi, a pickle of fried gongura, chillies and other spices. Tamarind imparts sourness to vegetable and rice dishes or is mixed with sugar and salt to make a drink. Its flowers and leaves are added to stews, its seeds are ground into flour, and its ripe fruit can be mixed with jaggery and eaten as a sweet. (When people in parts of Andhra Pradesh started to replace tamarind with tomatoes, entire villages began to suffer from fluorosis, a disease that causes permanent damage to and deformity of the bones. The drinking water proved to have high concentrations of fluorine, the effects of which are mitigated by tamarind.)

Andhra cuisine is reputed to be the hottest in India. According to a legend, there was once a severe famine in the area and all that grew were red chillies, which then became a staple of the local diet. The hottest chilli is called *koraivikaram*, which in Telugu means 'flaming stick'. A dry chutney is made by pounding these chillies to a fine powder and mixing it with tamarind pulp and salt. The state's most famous dish is a green mango chutney called *avikkai*, which is so hot that it has sent unsuspecting visitors to hospital.

The city of Hyderabad is renowned for its haute cuisine associated with the court of the Nizams (see chapter Nine). Hyderabadi biryani, known as kacchi biryani, is made by marinating goat meat in yoghurt, onions and spices, then layering it with partly boiled rice, milk, fried onions, saffron and cardamom, and cooking it in a sealed pot until the liquid has been absorbed. It is typically served with boorani (yoghurt with tomatoes or vegetables) or salan ki mirch, boiled green chillies or green peppers in a sauce of ground peanuts, coconut, tamarind, sesame seeds and spices. Nihari, a spicy meat stew (often made from tongue) cooked slowly overnight, is a local speciality, and is often served for

Preparing nihari, a rich dark meat stew that is cooked slowly overnight and often
eaten for breakfast by South Asian Muslims, especially during Ramadan.

breakfast. Another classic dish is haleem, a porridge of wheat, lentils and goat pounded until it is thick, cooked slowly and served with fried onions on top. It may be a variant of the Arabian harissa introduced by the Nizam's Arab (mainly Yemeni) palace guards in the nineteenth century. In 2010 Hyderabadi haleem was granted Geographical Indication Status (GIS), the first non-vegetarian dish in India to be so designated. To qualify as authentic it must be made with goat meat; the ratio of meat to wheat must be 10:4; the ghee must be laboratory certified as totally pure; and the dish must be cooked in a copper pot over firewood for twelve hours.

Bengal

The populous state of West Bengal borders Nepal, Bhutan, Bangladesh and the Bay of Bengal. Historically the region was part of the Mughal province of Bengal, and many Bengalis converted to Islam, especially in the east. Later parts of Bengal were ruled by the nawabs, the most important being the nawab of Murshidabad.[15] The British founded Calcutta in the late seventeenth century, and it remained the capital of British India until 1911. Calcutta was the most anglicized city in India, and the British influence permeated many aspects of life. The predominantly Muslim eastern part of Bengal became part of Pakistan as East Pakistan in 1947, but in 1971 the people of East Pakistan rebelled and formed the independent country of Bangladesh.

Linguistically, culturally and gastronomically, West Bengal and Bangladesh have much in common. West Bengal is 75 per cent Hindu and 23 per cent Muslim, with minorities of Christians and adherents of tribal religions. In Bangladesh, 85 per cent are Muslim, 15 per cent Hindu and the rest Buddhists or followers of indigenous religions. Only a very small proportion of Hindu Bengalis are strict vegetarians, and even brahmins relish fish (sometimes dubbed 'vegetables of the sea').

The land is fertile and well watered, and periodically suffers devastating floods. The main crop is rice, which is boiled, heated in a sand-filled oven and popped to make muri, a component of many street snacks. Wheat, chickpeas, potatoes, oil seeds, many varieties of gourd and squash, and tea grow here. Both West Bengal and Bangladesh are exporters of fish and seafood. The standard Bengali spice mixture is panchphoron ('five spices'), a mixture of fenugreek, nigella, cumin, black mustard, and fennel seeds. Mustard seeds are ground into a paste with water for use in curries, or ground into oil. All parts of a plant (leaves, stems, flowers and seeds) are used. A speciality of the region is rezala, mutton cooked slowly in yoghurt, milk, aromatic spices and green chillies.

Bengalis take food very seriously and are said to spend a larger portion of their disposable income on it than people elsewhere in India. Two hallmarks of Bengali cuisine are fish and sweets. (So great is the love of fish there that poor people will buy fish scales and add them to a dish to impart a fishy flavour.) Freshwater fish is considered desirable, while sea fish is not, with the exception of bhekti, a delicate cod-like fish. One reason for that is that some deep-sea fish have an unpleasant taste and can cause illness unless they are eaten extremely fresh.[16]

A favourite frying medium is mustard oil, since its pungency is believed to bring out the flavour of fish. The iconic Bengali dish is maacher jhol, a fish stew made by cutting fish (often carp) into large pieces, bones and all, frying it with spices and then simmering it with vegetables. The most coveted Bengali fish is hilsa, a shad-like sea fish that swims upriver to spawn, although when eating it careful attention must be paid to removing the myriad of tiny bones.

Remnants of the British Raj include cutlets (minced vegetables, meat, shrimp or fish breaded and fried); chops (minced meat coated with mashed potato and deep-fried); soufflés and omelettes; and the institution of afternoon tea, complete with cucumber sandwiches, cakes, salty snacks and tea prepared English-style (without spices).

A Hindu Bengali meal follows a definite progression of flavours, from bitter through salty and sour and ending with a sweet dish, often mishit doi, sweetened yoghurt. Bengalis are famous for their love of sweets. Income permitting, they eat sweets throughout the day: as dessert at the end of a meal; for afternoon tea; and as snacks. Sweets, especially sandesh, are an essential component of Bengali hospitality. Most sweets are made of sugar and curds (chhana).

Odisha

Odisha (formerly Orissa) is one of India's poorest states, with a sizeable tribal population.[17] More than 90 per cent of its population are Hindus, but only about 6 per cent are vegetarian. The cuisine shares many features with that of Bengal. A characteristic dish is ambul, fish cooked with dried mangoes. In the south the food is closer to that of South India, commonly using coconut, tamarind, red chillies and curry leaves. Odisha has a wide variety of sweet and savoury dishes, collectively called pitha,

Hilsa fish is an emblematic Bengali dish, famous for its many small bones.
In this version, the bones have been removed.

that are served on special occasions, including chakuli, crêpes made of rice, wheat or lentil flour, and manda, steamed dumplings.

Bihar

Once the centre of Indian civilization, today Bihar is one of the country's poorest states. Many landless farmers became labourers who migrated to Kolkata and other cities for work. Of the population, 82 per cent are Hindus and 15 per cent Muslims. Bihari food is rustic and simple. A staple of the diet is sattu, roasted chickpea flour. Labourers carry it to work tied in a knotted towel and mix it with salt and green chillies. Wheat, barley, corn and other grains are parched by being buried in sand, where they are heated by the sun.

Mustard oil is the traditional cooking medium. A standard meal consists of rice, dal and vegetables. A distinctive Bihari dish is litti – wheat and chickpea or lentil flour formed into balls, filled with ghee and deep-fried. It is served with chokha, mashed vegetables garnished with mustard oil, onions and chillies. Many Biharis emigrated to the Caribbean (especially Trinidad and Guyana) in the nineteenth century and took their food customs with them (see chapter Thirteen).

Assam

The state of Assam, known worldwide for its tea, takes its name from the Ahom, an ethnic Tai people who migrated from southwest China in the early thirteenth century and ruled the region until 1826, when the British annexed it.[18] In the 1970s sections of Assam were broken off to create the states of Nagaland, Meghalaya, Mizoram and Arunchal Pradesh, which have ethnic and tribal majorities. Around two-thirds of Assam's population are Hindu, 28 per cent are Muslim (including many immigrants from Bangladesh), and the rest Christian and adherents of tribal religions. Most Assamese are not vegetarians.

Certain features of Assamese food make it one of India's most intriguing cuisines. It is virtually alone in preserving the six basic tastes of ancient Hindu gastronomy, including alkalinity. An iconic Assamese dish is tenga, a slightly sour stew made by frying pieces of fish in mustard oil, then simmering them with fenugreek seeds, vegetables and lime juice. Another sour dish is made of fermented bamboo shoots. Sourness is counteracted by khar, a class of dishes with an astringent or alkaline taste. Today the alkalinity comes from baking soda, but it used to come from the ash of burnt banana-tree stems; this was also sprinkled on dal or vegetables. Rice is the staple, mustard oil the traditional cooking medium, and fish, especially carp and hilsa (as in Bengal), are much in demand. Assam has many versions of pitha, a sweet made from rice flour and sugar and associated with its harvest festivals or *Bihus*. Pitha can be filled with coconut, flavoured with sesame seeds or aniseed, or mixed with jackfruit pulp.

Other Northeastern States

The seven states in India's northeast – Mizoram, Nagaland, Arunchal Pradesh, Meghalaya, Tripura, Manipur and Sikkim (sometimes called the Seven Sisters) – are inhabited by a multitude of ethnic and tribal groups, some of them descendants of people who migrated centuries ago from Southeast Asia and south China, who speak Tibeto-Burman languages. Many are Christians because of long-standing missionary activity in the area. (The state language of Nagaland is English, which is why that is one of the official languages on Indian banknotes.) The people are mainly non-vegetarians and rice-eaters, preferring a sticky rice to the long-grained variety favoured in the rest of India.

Littis are bihari breads made of balls of dough filled with spiced sattu (roasted chickpeas).

Litti-chokha (balls of dough filled with sattu and served with mashed, spiced vegetables) is the iconic Bihari meal.

Wak Me-A-Mesang Pura (Pork with Fermented Bamboo Shoots), Meghalaya

500 g (1 lb) fermented bamboo shoots
1 kg (2 lb) pork with fat and bones
2 tsp finely chopped green chillies
2 tsp finely chopped fresh ginger
1½ tsp salt
Pinch of turmeric powder
75 g (½ cup) rice flour

Wash and drain the bamboo shoots.

Cut the pork into medium-sized pieces. Cook in a heavy pot over a low heat without oil or water for 25 minutes, stirring occasionally, until the water from the pork evaporates.

Add the bamboo shoots and 240 ml (1 cup) water; cook for a few minutes more.

Add the green chillies, ginger, salt and turmeric, and simmer until dry.

Stir in 480 ml (2 cups) more water and cook for 15 minutes, until the pork is tender.

Add the rice flour and cook for 15 minutes, until the sauce thickens.

Adapted from Hoihnu Hauzel, *The Essential North-east Cookbook* (New Delhi, 2003), p. 204.

In Nagaland, pork is a popular meat (as is dog – hence a saying that the Nagas eat everything with legs except tables and chairs). Very little cooking oil is used; food is usually boiled, steamed or roasted over an open fire. Bamboo shoots are an essential ingredient in curries and pickles. Rice and fish are wrapped in banana leaves and steamed. Flavouring comes from garlic, green onions, ginger and chillies. (One of the hottest chillies in the world, bhut jolokia, or ghost pepper, is grown in the region.) People in Tripura and Manipur dry and ferment small fish and use them in curries, sauces and pickles. Drinks are locally brewed from millet or rice. Fermentation is a common technique, and there is a wealth of fermented products across the region, including soy beans, bamboo shoots, yam and mustard leaves, fish and river crabs. In Nagaland, boiled soy beans are fermented for several days in a pot, smashed in a mortar and pestle, wrapped in a banana leaf and stored next to the fire, where they ferment again. (Similar preparations are found throughout Asia, including natto in Japan, chungkukjang in Korea and thua nao in northern Thailand.) Tea has grown wild in this area from ancient times. It was fermented and eaten as a vegetable, or boiled as a beverage that is still made by a tribe called the Konyaks in the high hills of Nagaland.[19]

In Mizoram, a *mithun* – a cross between a cow and a water buffalo – is killed in a ceremonial sacrifice and eaten in a communal feast. The cuisine of Arunchal Pradesh features many typically Tibetan dishes, including momos, a boiled dumpling stuffed with meat; dried yak cheese; and tsampa, a tea made from barley flour and yak butter that is churned to make a kind of thick soup.

SCHEDULED TRIBES

Nearly 9 per cent of India's total population are members of Scheduled Tribes, also called tribals or *adivasis* (Hindi for 'original inhabitants', since some are believed to be the descendants of the original people of the sub-continent, who were pushed back into the forests and the mountains).[20] More than 350 tribal groups speaking 100 languages live in India, in all states except Haryana and Punjab. The vast majority, 87 per cent, are in central and western India, including the 7.4 million Gonds and 5.5 million Bhils. In 2001 three new states were created to give the tribals their own states: Uttaranchal, Jharkhand and Chhattisgarh.

Tribals are the most deprived group in India in terms of income and access to education and healthcare. They have survived in the forests by hunting and fishing, gathering wild plants and practising shifting cultivation. With deforestation, they are becoming settled farmers, although their land is often very poor. Sometimes they barter wild cardamoms, resin, honey and other forest products for oil, rice, salt and cooking utensils. One source of protein is the rats that live in the rice fields; they are smoked out after the harvest and boiled or roasted. Red ants are ground to make a piquant chutney.

In Madhya Pradesh, the Gonds make a drink called sulfi from the sap of the sulfi tree. When first tapped it is mildly alcoholic, but after a day or two it ferments and thickens, and becomes more potent. Another drink, a clear spirit with a heady flavour, has been made from the flowers of the mahua tree from ancient times, and was even produced commercially by the British. Attempts are underway to revive its commercial production.

TWELVE

New Trends in Indian Food, 1947–Present

POST-INDEPENDENCE FOOD SECURITY

The world's worst recorded food disaster occurred in 1943. It is estimated that during the so-called Bengal Famine between 5 and 6 million people died of hunger and related diseases in eastern India. At first the famine was attributed to a shortfall in food production, but later the economist and Nobel Laureate Amartya Sen (who experienced the famine as a child) concluded that it was 'man-made', caused by government mismanagement and hoarding, and by a decline in real income, especially in rural areas.

After India gained its independence in 1947, food security was a priority of the new government. At the time 72 per cent of the population lived in rural areas. The first governments followed to some degree the Soviet model, based on central planning, the development of heavy industry and the centralization of food distribution, although farming remained in the private sector. Because agricultural production could not keep up with demand, India was a net importer of food throughout the 1950s.

Starting around 1950, a 'white revolution' was launched in dairy farming, called 'Operation Flood'. A network of village milk producers' cooperatives made modern technology and management techniques available to its members with a view to increasing milk production, enhancing rural income by eliminating middlemen, and ensuring fair prices for consumers. Today India is the world's largest milk producer (having surpassed the United States in 1998). More than 10 million farmers produce more than 20 million litres (42 million pints) of milk a day.

The subsequent 'green revolution' transformed India from an importer of food into one of the world's leading agricultural producers. Over the period 1966–77, programmes were implemented to expand farming areas and consolidate holdings; to promote double cropping; to open agricultural colleges based on the American land-grant model; to increase the use of fertilizer and insecticide; to expand irrigation; and to develop and use high-yielding varieties of seed, especially wheat and rice. By 1978 per-acre production had increased by 30 per cent.

Agriculture has continued to grow. Between 1961 and 2009 the production of wheat rose from 11 million tonnes to 80 million tonnes, while individual daily consumption increased sevenfold to about 58 kg (128 lb) per person per year. The consumption of millet and sorghum declined to a third of its initial level by the end of that period, but individual consumption of fruit, vegetables, milk and spices nearly doubled. Animal products still account for only about 9 per cent of a person's average daily consumption, compared with 28 per cent in the United States. The poultry sector has grown by an average of 10 per cent per year over the past decade, reflecting integrated farming methods and the use of hybrid varieties of chicken. Egg production has also risen dramatically, as has the consumption of ghee, which has nearly tripled since 1990.

At the same time, the number of poor people in India has risen in absolute terms. According to the World Bank, in 2010 around a third of India's population lived below the international poverty line income of u.s.$1.25 a day, while two-thirds lived on less than $2 a day. The poorest states are Bihar, Jharkhand, Madhya Pradesh and Chhattisgarh (all three of which have large tribal populations), and Uttar Pradesh. In recent years there have been reports that Indian farmers, burdened by low yields and debt, have been committing suicide at a rate much higher than the general population, especially in Maharashtra and Andhra Pradesh.[1]

India also ranks near the bottom on the Global Hunger Index developed by the International Food Policy Research Institute, notably in the proportion of underweight children under the age of five (43.5 per cent).[2] Although India's score has improved since 1990, the figure has not kept pace with its economic growth. People are malnourished not so much because of insufficient food production but because of waste and poorly managed storage and distribution.[3] Less than half of the grain picked up from government warehouses reaches Indian homes. As a consequence, the diet of the very poor is little different from what it was thousands of years ago: in the north, a chapatti made of flour and water with a little pickle and vegetable and, for the slightly more affluent, dal;

in the south, rice with pickle and sambhar; in the west, sattu, dried lentils with a chilli on the side. In July 2013 the government passed the National Food Security Bill in an attempt to eliminate hunger and malnutrition. It guarantees a subsidized allowance of 5 kg (11 lb) of grain each month very cheaply (for between 1 and 3 rupees, or 2–4 cents, per kg) to households that comprise half of the urban poor and 75 per cent of the rural population, and an additional allowance to extremely poor households.

To date, the only genetically modified (GM) crop grown in India is cotton, starting in 2002. In 2009 the government tried to introduce a GM aubergine, called Bt Brinjal, which carried a gene that made it resistant to insect attack, but when concerns were raised over its safety for animal and human consumption, the government imposed an indefinite moratorium on its cultivation. A panel of experts appointed by the Supreme Court recommended that all field trials of GM crops be halted for ten years. In May 2013 the National Biodiversity Authority of India (NBA) sued the biotechnology corporation responsible for Bt Brinjal, Monsanto, on the grounds that it had used local varieties of aubergine in developing the GM crop 'without prior approval of the competent authorities' or the consent of the hundreds of thousands of farmers who have cultivated these varieties for generations.

In 2009 India passed a law deeming all traditional medicinal herbs (as well as yoga postures) to be part of the nation's cultural heritage and therefore 'public property', and prohibited anyone from patenting them. The most prominent opponent of GM foods has been the ecologist Vandana Shiva. Her organization Navdanya, founded in 1987, focuses on 'conserving the biodiversity of our crops, promoting organic and non-violent farming, revalorizing indigenous food and food culture while preserving livelihoods'.[4]

LIBERALIZATION AND THE RISE OF THE MIDDLE CLASS

In 1991, faced with a balance of payments crisis, the Indian government decided to liberalize and globalize the country's economy. It opened India to international trade and investment, deregulated and privatized some sectors of the economy, and took control of inflation. Foreign capital poured in, exports and industrial production grew, inflation fell and the stock market boomed, and by 2007 India's GDP was growing at a rate of 9 per cent, leading the press to talk of India's economic miracle. (The growth rate has slowed somewhat since then.)

Since then, urbanization has increased (the proportion of Indians living in cities rose from 18 per cent in 1961 to 32 per cent in 2011) and an Indian 'middle class' has emerged, a subject much discussed in the media and by think tanks.[5] The definition of the middle class is problematic. The Indian government has defined it as consisting of two groups: 'seekers', who have a daily income equivalent to u.s.$8–$20 per person, and 'strivers', with a daily income of $20–$40. Using this definition, the Indian middle class represented nearly 13 per cent of all households in 2009–10, or 153 million people. Other estimates are lower, placing it at 75 million people, 60 per cent of whom live in urban areas. Some academics propose an even broader definition: a mindset in which people are optimistic about social and economic upward mobility for their children or a reasonable assurance of a steady income. A subset of this middle class are young Indian consumers with jobs in call centres, IT companies, international banks and consultancies, who are earning salaries beyond their parents' wildest dreams. Whatever the definition or the numbers involved, there is no doubt that such a class exists and that their affluence has led to changes in Indian eating patterns.

One of these changes is an increase in the consumption of meat, especially chicken. As noted earlier, only a minority of Indians are strictly vegetarian. Data is scanty, but a survey conducted in 2006 found that just 21 per cent of all households were entirely vegetarian.[6] Thirty-four per cent of Indian women are vegetarian, compared with 28 per cent of men, as are 37 per cent of people over the age of 55, compared with 29 per cent of people under the age of 25. Rather surprising is the fact that 3 per cent of Indian Muslims report themselves as vegetarians, as do 8 per cent of Christians, perhaps indicating how deeply rooted the vegetarian ethos is in Indian society.

Individual families may contain both vegetarians and meat-eaters, although those family members who eat meat often do so outside the home. The anthropologist R. S. Khare, who studied food habits within certain brahmin households in Uttar Pradesh, observed that an older orthodox person who initially ate only with members of his own caste might at some point start eating food outside the home, when travelling, if not in restaurants then in a *vaishnav bhojanalaya* (a North Indian establishment that serves vegetarian food prepared according to orthodox standards).[7] The next step might be to eat in a coffee shop or a sweetshop, places that are also vegetarian but where the caste or even religion of the cooks might be unknown.

The principle of 'Don't ask, don't tell' seems to prevail in such situations. Eating in a restaurant would be the final stage of departing from orthodoxy. Khare wrote: 'A modern restaurant represents a total refutation of the entire orthodox culinary and *jati* commensal rules that the tradition inculcates at the level of the domestic hearth. It is a clear opposition of principles.'[8]

Eating Out . . .

Until modern times, India did not have a tradition of public dining or a culture of restaurants (that is, places where diners could eat in relative comfort or luxury, choosing dishes from an extensive menu).[9] The norms of social life and the complex dietary prescriptions of the various law codes

Enjoying a morning snack at a streetside stand in Kolkata.

discouraged dining out. For most households, the only exceptions were festivals, wedding dinners, caste feasts and temples.

Nevertheless, since ancient times there have been taverns, public inns and shops that served cooked meat, snacks and sweets for travellers, students and, no doubt, housewives who did not feel like cooking. This tradition lives on in India's rich and vibrant street-food culture. An estimated 10 million people work in the street-food sector in India, including 300,000 vendors in Delhi and 130,000 vendors in Kolkata alone. Street food, which is often vegetarian, is usually made to order and eaten on the spot, since in a hot climate it is not safe to eat dishes that have been standing. Every city and region in India has its own special street foods: bhelpuri in Mumbai, kathi kebabs in Kolkata and chaat in northern India, for example. As transportation and communication improve and people move elsewhere in search of jobs, many of these foods have become universal.[10]

Food safety is a problem, because many vendors have no access to clean water or disposal facilities, and often cook and handle food with dirty hands. In 2007 the Delhi city government tried to ban the preparation of food at street stands, a move supported by India's High Court, but the order proved unenforceable and has not been implemented. Now street food is starting to move off the street, as it has done in countries like Malaysia and Singapore where government authorities have set up street-food courts with proper sanitation. Chains like Jumbo King in Mumbai and the Great Kabab Factory in various cities offer sanitized

A modern *dhaba* on the roadside near New Delhi.

The Dabbawallas of Mumbai

A unique Mumbai institution are the dabbawallas, or tiffin-box carriers, who pick up freshly made meals in lunchboxes from office workers' homes, usually by bicycle, deliver them to their workplaces by lunchtime, and return the boxes later in the day. The boxes are first delivered to a local railway station, where they are colour-coded, then delivered to other stations in Mumbai, re-sorted and carried to their destinations. Each day between 4,500 and 5,000 dabba-wallas deliver between 175,000 and 200,000 boxes for a small fee, and their punctuality and reliability are legendary. Today text messaging is sometimes used for booking.

Numbered dabbas (tiffin boxes) ready for delivery.

Mumbai's dabbawallas pick up freshly made meals in lunch boxes from office workers' homes and deliver them to their workplaces by lunch time.

Chicken Kiev
at Kolkata's
famous Mocambor
restaurant, which
has served
Continental food
since the 1950s.

versions of traditional dishes, and street-food courts are being installed in modern urban shopping centres.

Another descendant of the old food stalls are the *dhabas* – small wayside stands located on main roads, typically serving five or six dishes in large brass pots. Many also serve cups of a thick, milky tea sometimes called *nabbe mil chai* ('90 miles tea') in Hindi, signifying a beverage so strong that it will keep a lorry driver going for 90 miles. The first patrons of such stands were lorry drivers, but *dhaba* food has become fashionable among young urban Indians, and some have even gone upscale by adding walls, air-conditioning, tables and chairs, and printed menus.

In the south, travellers and people living away from home can take their meals at military hotels, which serve meat and egg dishes, or Udupi hotels (see chapter Five), which offer only vegetarian fare.[11] In an interesting twist, New York City now has several restaurants serving kosher south Indian food.

Western-style restaurants came to India in the late nineteenth century, not long after they appeared in Britain. In about 1890 Federico Peliti, an Italian confectioner, opened his eponymous restaurant in Calcutta, and it became a favourite lunch spot for the city's business community.

A restaurant in
Kolkata's famous
Chinatown.

After the First World War the Swiss Angelo Firpo opened Firpo's on
Chowringhee, Calcutta's main street. The menus of these restaurants
consisted mainly of Western-style dishes, plus a few quasi-Indian dishes
such as mulligatawny soup and curry. Flury's, a famous pastry shop on
Park Street, opened in 1927 and is still thriving. Their counterparts in
Bombay were Monginis, owned by Italian caterers; the Wayside, which
described itself as a 'pleasing English Inn, which is quiet and exclusive';
and Gourdon & Company, serving Continental food.[12] The patrons
of these establishments were Europeans or members of the anglicized
Indian elite.

Kolkata, once home to more than 80,000 mainly Hakka Chinese, also
had a thriving Chinese restaurant culture, which still lives on in the city's
Chinatown, Tengra. In recent years, an Indo-Chinese hybrid cuisine has
become one of India's most popular restaurant foods, characterized by
the use of hot red sauces and featuring such dishes as chicken corn soup;
Mongolian chicken, lamb or panir; and chilli chicken.

Restaurants serving high-quality Indian food in a pleasant family-
friendly setting came relatively late to India. The progenitor was Moti
Mahal, which opened near the Red Fort in New Delhi in 1947. Its founder,

The Inventor of Tandoori Chicken

Today, tandoori chicken, butter chicken and tandoori roti are staples of Indian restaurants around the world, but until the mid-twentieth century they were virtually unknown, even on the Indian subcontinent. They are the creation of one of India's most dynamic and innovative restaurateurs, Kundan Lal Gujral, the founder of India's most famous restaurant, Moti Mahal in Delhi.

Kundan Lal was born near Peshawar in the Northwest Frontier province of British India, a Hindu of Punjabi and Pathan origin. As a child he worked in Peshawar in a small catering shop that eventually became a restaurant called Moti Mahal (Pearl Palace). It specialized in kebabs baked in a tandoor, a large clay oven buried in the ground, accompanied by naan.

When India was partitioned in 1947, Kundan Lal and his family ended up in the Indian capital, Delhi, where he set up a small roadside café on Daryaganj near the Red Fort. He named it Moti Mahal, and found a tandoor-maker (a fellow refugee) who experimented with different designs until he came up with an above-ground version that would work in a restaurant kitchen.

To make the bland food of his region more palatable to Indian taste, Kundan Lal tried different spice mixtures until he settled on the blend that is still used in the restaurant today. Its secret recipe is said to contain ground coriander seeds, black pepper and a mild red pepper that gives tandoori chicken its characteristic red colour. Pieces of chicken and even whole chickens were marinated in this mixture and yoghurt, and roasted in the tandoor. To please palates used to richer sauces (and, some claim, to use up leftover tandoori chicken), he created butter chicken: pieces of roast chicken cooked in a sauce of tomato, cream and butter. Another Moti Mahal speciality was dal makhani, black lentils cooked slowly overnight and mixed with tomatoes, butter and fresh cream. Kundan Lal also served the breads of his region, including long, thick naans and Peshwari naan, filled with nuts and raisins.

Tandoori chicken was created by Kundan Lal, a refugee from Peshawar, in the late 1940s.

In the tradition of many great restaurateurs, Kundan Lal was a consummate showman, easily identified by his lambswool fez, curled moustache and courtly manners. The restaurant became a favourite of many politicians, including India's first prime minister, Jawaharlal Nehru, and his daughter Indira Gandhi, who as prime minister took many visiting VIPS there. An Indian official once told the visiting shah of Iran that coming to Delhi without eating at Moti Mahal would be like visiting Agra without seeing the Taj Mahal. The restaurant catered for many important events, including a state dinner for the visiting American First Lady Jacqueline Kennedy and the wedding reception of Nehru's grandson Sanjay Gandhi.

Kundan Lal opened branches in Delhi and Moosoorie, but remained a fixture at his original restaurant until the end of his days. His grandson Monish, who studied restaurant management, launched a company called Tandoori Trail, which now has more than 90 franchises acress India. Today Moti Mahal has countless imitators in India and throughout the world; and, in one of the ironies of gastronomical history, tandoori chicken is regarded as the quintessential Indian dish.[13]

> ## Millet: From Despised Grain to Nutri-Cereal
>
> Millet (a category that includes sorghum as well as finger, foxtail, proso, little, kodo and barnyard millets) is among the world's oldest crops, and in ancient times was the main staple in China and South India. Although India remains the world's largest producer of millet, today it is used mainly as lifestock fodder. Since the 1960s some 44 per cent of land once cultivated with millet has been lost. One reason for the grain's decline in popularity is that it is not as soft as wheat, takes longer to cook and needs to be cooked and consumed while fresh. Moreover, millet was traditionally the food of poorer people and the lower classes, while eating rice and wheat came to be identified with higher social status.
>
> Millet has recently been making a comeback, however. The Millet Network of India, an alliance of institutions,

Kundan Lal Gujral, was the virtual creator of the tandoori style of cuisine that has become a hallmark of Indian restaurants worldwide.

Many of the refugees who came to New Delhi in 1947 were Punjabis, who set up small businesses, including food stalls that did not require a lot of capital. Some expanded into small neighbourhood restaurants and eventually into more sophisticated establishments. The restaurant chains Kwality's and Gaylord's are well-known examples. Gaylord's originally served Western and Chinese food and later expanded their menus to include Indian dishes. A mainstay of their menus was Punjabi food with touches of South Indian and so-called Mughlai cuisine. This style of cooking was taught at the catering colleges set up by the Indian government in the 1960s. As the graduates moved into the workforce, they introduced it into five-star hotels, which in the 1970s and '80s became centres of dining and social activity for newly affluent city-dwellers.

Another important landmark was Karim's in Old Delhi, opened in 1913 by Haji Karimuddin, a descendant of cooks who worked for the Mughal emperors. Today the fourth generation of his family operates the restaurant, which has several branches. The founder's goal, which is stated on the menu, was 'to bring the Royal Food to the common man'.

farmers, nutritionists and food activists, is promoting the revival of millet, citing its environmental and nutritional benefits. For example, millets have much higher fibre, protein, mineral and calcium content than rice.

On World Heart Day, the International Crops Research Institute for the Semi-Arid Tropics called for India to prioritize a return to sorghum- and millet-based farming to help deal with rising lifestyle diseases. Millet is becoming fashionable among urban foodies in India and abroad because of its health benefits and perhaps a longing for 'authenticity'.

Information from the Millet Network of India, Deccan Development Society, *Millets: Future of Food and Farming*: www.swaraj.org/shikshantar/millets.pdf (accessed May 2014)

The menu features North Indian Muslim dishes such as biryani, kebabs, haleem, nihari and brain curry.

The past two decades have seen a proliferation of restaurants serving Western food, not just in major cities but also in smaller towns. Thai and Italian food, which offer many vegetarian options, are especially popular. American fast-food chains such as KFC (since 1995), McDonald's and Pizza Hut (both since 1996) and Ben & Jerry's ice cream (since 2013) serve dishes adapted to local tastes and habits. Instead of beef, menus feature such items as the Chicken Maharaja-Mac™, the McVeggie™ and the Veg Twister™. Indian companies followed suit by offering Indian fast foods. Takeaway meals, virtually unheard of in the early twenty-first century, have become very popular.

Until recently, few restaurants served regional dishes other than South Indian. Five-star hotel chains, notably ITC Hotels and Taj Hotels, were leaders in reviving and promoting regional cuisine. In 1977 ITC hired Imtiaz Qureshi, a chef and caterer from Lucknow, to upgrade their restaurants. He opened Bukhara, specializing in tandoori and Northwest Frontier dishes, and Dum Pukht, featuring traditional Lucknow specialities, both in the Maurya Sheraton in New Delhi. Restaurants in the Taj Hotels feature Rajasthani, Hyderabadi and various South Indian

A shop in Old Delhi serving kulcha, a Punjab speciality.

cuisines, and also host food festivals. Today in large cities the diner can find smaller restaurants specializing in Bihari, Chettinad, Kashmiri, Gujarati and other regional cuisines.

One of the most successful Indian chains, Oh! Calcutta, has branches in major cities serving classic Bengali dishes. Its founder, Anjan Chatterjee, a graduate of the Institute of Hotel Management and Catering, runs the Speciality Restaurants group, which also includes restaurants serving North Indian and Chinese food. Another chain, Punjabi by Nature, offers upscale Punjabi food. Enclaves like Hauz Khas Village in New Delhi have dozens of restaurants, ranging from fast food to Indian regional and European restaurants; Bangaluru (formerly Bangalore), the centre of India's high-tech and call-centre industry, is famous for its lively nightlife and varied restaurant scene. Many establishments have extensive wine lists and serve cocktails and 'mocktails', and patrons can rate restaurants on websites like zomato.com.

. . . AND DRINKING OUT

The Indian attitude towards alcohol has always been ambivalent. Despite the disapproval expressed in the *shastras*, there is evidence that alcoholic beverages have always been popular, and they were even prescribed by Ayurvedic physicians as a cure for certain conditions. Mahatma Gandhi opposed the consumption of alcohol on the grounds that it harmed the poor, and the Constitution of India, influenced by his thinking, imposed total prohibition in 1977. It lasted only two years, but the production and consumption of alcohol are still prohibited in several states, including Mizoram, Manipur and Gujarat. India also has some 'dry' holidays, including Gandhi's birthday.

Poor people make their own spirits from whatever is available: rice, palm sap, local fruit and vegetables. For middle-class men, the standard drink has always been whisky, which was introduced by the British, and today India is the world's largest importer of the spirit. (Middle-class women have traditionally confined themselves to fruit juice.) However, wine is becoming the beverage of choice for a small but enthusiastic group of both male and female urbanites. The consumption of wine nearly tripled between 2004 and 2020, although that growth is now levelling off. Import duties on foreign wines are very high, and currently about three-quarters of the supply is produced domestically.[14] Wine-drinkers come from the upper middle classes, who have greater exposure to foreign foods and higher disposable income. The fastest-growing market segment is women. One explanation is that wine, made from grapes, is not a major leap from fruit juice. Wine also has the reputation of a sophisticated drink, an indicator of higher status.

Big cities have wine clubs to teach aspiring connoisseurs, and there is even a magazine, *Sommelier*, devoted to wine. The dingy 'English wine shops' have been supplemented, albeit not totally replaced, by elegant establishments in shopping centres. Upscale restaurants have extensive wine lists, and in late 2012 India's first wine and tapas bar, Vinoteca, opened in Mumbai, serving Spanish-style tapas. Its owner, Rajeev Samant, a graduate of Stanford, left his job in Silicon Valley, California, to start Sula Winery, which produces some of India's most popular wines. Sula, Grover and Chateau Indage wineries together have more than a 90 per cent share of the market. Almost all domestic wine is produced in Maharashtra, particularly the Nasik region, where higher altitude and a cooler climate are ideal for growing grapes. A major obstacle to the increase in wine consumption is price. The duty on imported wine is 150 per cent, on top of which every state imposes its own taxes.

The growth of a food culture in India has been promoted by the media. While newspapers have always carried recipe columns, many now have lifestyle sections with restaurant reviews and articles on the latest culinary trends. A pioneer reviewer was Busybee, the pen name of a Parsi journalist, Behram Contractor (1930–2001), who for decades wrote the widely read column 'Busybee's Guide to Eating Out' for various publications.[15] In 2001 he and his wife, Farzan, started a magazine called *Upper Crust*, devoted to 'food, wine and the good life'. It runs articles on restaurants in India and abroad, interviews with chefs and serious gourmets, recipes and travel articles, and sponsors food and wine festivals.[16]

The number of cookbooks has proliferated since Arjun Appadurai wrote the article 'How to Make a National Cuisine: Cookbooks in Contemporary India' in 1988. Indeed, the role cookbooks played in increasing familiarity with regional cuisines has to a large degree been supplanted by cooking shows on India's many private television stations. Online, food blogs and many videos demonstrating the preparation of dishes are available.

The emergence of chef as a respected and respectable profession represents another significant change in India. In the past, with a few exceptions, chefs were regarded as little better than cooks or servants, and middle-class parents would be horrified if their children wanted to take up the profession (a scenario touched on in the film *Monsoon Wedding*, 2001). Today chefs are celebrities and entrepreneurs with their own blogs, television shows and travel series. Sanjeev Kapoor's programme *Khana Khazana* broadcasts to more than 500 million viewers in 120 countries, and he has launched his own food channel and product line. Amateurs and professionals compete for the title of Master Chef on televised competitions based on American and British models. The ultimate proof of the new status of the chef is the film *Cheeni Kum* (2007), in which the superstar Amitabh Bachchan plays a London-based chef who wins the heart of a glamorous younger woman.

HEALTH AND DIET

Another post-liberalization change is the proliferation of supermarkets that sell fresh fruit and vegetables, meat and fish, imported Western products (such as taco chips, French cheeses and Italian olive oil) and many prepared and packaged foods. Servants are becoming a thing of the past in middle-class households, and as more women enter the workforce, convenience foods are a necessity. Currently only 2 per cent of fruit and vegetables are processed into prepared foods, but the share is increasing.

The link between diet and health has always been central to the Indian food ethos. Growing prosperity among some segments of society, the availability of fast food, increased consumption of white rice, sugar and fats, and a decline in physical activity have led to an explosion of so-called lifestyle diseases: high blood pressure, coronary problems, obesity and type 2 diabetes.[17] Estimates of the number of diabetics in India range from 30 million to 65 million, and as many as 77 million people are classed as pre-diabetic. Type 2 diabetes is becoming common in rural as well as urban areas, and is even turning up in young children. The World Health Organization predicts that by 2015 the cost to India of diabetes and other non-communicable diseases could reach $236 billion.

This has led to a new concern with healthy cooking and eating. Celebrity chefs and the authors of cookbooks have begun to advocate low-fat, low-carbohydrate meals – not an easy proposition, since the traditional Indian diet is starch-based, sweets are very popular, and frying is a common technique. There has been a resurgence of interest in traditional grains, such as millet, as well as traditional Ayurvedic and Siddha cures.[18] Meanwhile, 'organic' and 'locavore' have become bywords among urban

A night fruit and vegetable market in New Delhi.

foodies, and the government has initiated various programmes to promote the production of organic crops, fruit and vegetables.

Researchers around the world, not just in India, are now investigating the health-giving properties of traditional Indian remedies. A search of the u.s. National Institute of Health's PubMed database in January 2013 found 2,143 articles on studies or trials that involved using Ayurvedic remedies to cure such diverse medical problems as diabetes, cancer, tuberculosis and even depression.

THIRTEEN

The Food of the Indian Diaspora

For thousands of years, Indians travelled to other parts of the world as traders, Buddhist monks, Hindu priests, labourers and, more recently, immigrants. Seals testify to the presence of merchants from the Indus Valley in the cities of Mesopotamia. In ancient and medieval times, merchants went to the Middle East, eastern and northern Africa, and Southeast Asia. Some went by sea to the Middle East, Sri Lanka and Indonesia, others by caravan along the great Silk Road that extended through Iran, Afghanistan and Central Asia all the way to China.

From the seventeenth century onwards, a few Indians trickled into South Africa, Britain and North America as slaves or servants.[1] However, massive emigration from the subcontinent began only in the 1830s with the introduction of the indentured labour system. In the late nineteenth century agricultural workers settled on the west coasts of Canada and the United States. Restrictive immigration policies in the early twentieth century, however, reduced the inflow of Asian immigrants to North America, Britain and Australia to a trickle, until the policies were amended in the 1960s and '70s.

Today, those of Indian, Pakistani and Bangladeshi origin constitute a diaspora of some 30 million people, a scale matched only by the Chinese.[2] Over the centuries they have developed their own distinctive cuisines that combine the dishes of their native regions with local ingredients and influences.

THE INDENTURED LABOUR SYSTEM

In August 1834 the British declared slavery illegal in the West Indies. The sugar plantations had been worked by African slaves; after regaining their freedom, most refused to continue this back-breaking, poorly paid work. The economic consequences for the owners of plantations, many of whom were politically well connected (including Prime Minister William Gladstone's father), appeared to be devastating, so the East India Company came to their rescue by recruiting workers from the poorer parts of India. These so-called indentured labourers signed contracts agreeing to work on a particular sugar estate for two terms of five years each, at the end of which the owner would pay for their passage back to India, or they could stay on and purchase land. When the French and Dutch abolished slavery in their overseas possessions in 1846 and 1873 respectively, the East India Company provided them with workers, as well.

Between 1834, when the first ship arrived in Guyana, and 1917, when the system of indentured labour was abolished, an estimated 1.4 million Indians left the subcontinent, including 240,000 to Guyana, 144,000 to Trinidad and 37,000 to Jamaica. Another destination was the island of Mauritius in the Indian Ocean, acquired by the British from the French in 1810. Some 500,000 Indians went there to work on the sugar plantations. Others went to the French colonies Réunion, Guadeloupe and Martinique, the Dutch-owned Suriname, and even the Danish island of Saint Croix.[3] The voyages lasted as long as eighteen weeks. The migrants' skimpy rations on-board ship consisted of a little rice and flour, preserved meat, dried fish, coconut and mustard oil, and a few seasonings, such as cumin, fenugreek, tamarind and salt. The cooking of meals often resulted in fires.

Most of the migrants came from the famine-ravaged rural areas of eastern Uttar Pradesh and western Bihar, and spoke a language called Bhojpuri. Around 10 per cent were from South India. The proportion of Hindus to Muslims was 85 to 15 per cent. Surprisingly, between a quarter and a third of the immigrants were women, often widows or women fleeing unhappy marriages. Unlike the African slaves, who were completely dispossessed of their identity, the Indians were allowed to practise their religion and customs, and a few brahmin priests and imams accompanied them. (The Trinidadian Nobel Laureate V. S. Naipaul is descended from one of these brahmin priests.) While some returned to India at the end of their tenure, most purchased plots of land and stayed. Today people of Indian origin constitute two-thirds of the population of Mauritius (the largest proportion outside the subcontinent), and around 40 per cent of Guyana, Suriname and Trinidad.

In 1852 the system was extended to Southeast Asia to supply Indian workers for the coffee, palm and rubber plantations there. Approximately 2 million people went to Malaya (now Malaysia) and another 2.5 million to Burma, mostly from South India. Most left Burma after the military coup in 1962. Starting in 1860, some 150,000 Indian workers went to South Africa and another 30,000, largely Sikhs from the Punjab, came to British East Africa (now Kenya and Uganda) to help build the railway into the interior of the country. Another group went to the sugar plantations of the island of Fiji.

The Caribbean
Trinidad and Tobago

An estimated 40 per cent of the population of this small island nation just off the coast of South America is of Indian origin; 38 per cent are Afro-Trinidadians and the remainder European, Chinese and Middle Eastern. On their arrival, immigrants received daily rations of rice, dal, coconut oil or ghee, sugar, salt, turmeric, onions and sometimes salted or dried fish. When their period of indenture was over, most of the workers bought land, formed villages and tried to settle down into their former way of life, cultivating rice, sugar and vegetables. Naipaul wrote that the indentured Indians managed to 'recreate an Eastern Uttar Pradesh village in Central Trinidad as if in the vastness of India'.[4] Because Trinidad and Tobago possesses large amounts of oil and gas, the country has never been as dependent on tourism as other Caribbean islands, and this may have helped to preserve cultural and culinary traditions. (The discovery of oil also contributed to the demise of Trinidad's sugar-cane industry.)

The India immigrants' regional origins explain some distinctive features of Trinidadian cuisine. Wholewheat flour is not used to make bread as it is in India, because the immigrants came from rice-consuming regions and the first flour they encountered on-board ship or in Trinidad would have been white flour supplied by the British. The savoury snacks sold on the streets and in small shops are very similar to those found in nineteenth-century Bihar: phulorie, deep-fried balls of ground, seasoned split peas; bara, a flatter, heavier version of phulorie; kurma, a sweet made of flour, sugar and clarified butter; sohari, cakes fried in a little butter; sweet-and-sour tamarind balls; and sahenna, green vegetables fried in lentil batter.[5] These snacks are usually served with sour mango sauce or spicy

Tomato Chokha (Trinidad and Guyana)

This breakfast dish is often eaten with sada (plain) roti.

450 g (1 lb) ripe tomatoes
1 small onion, diced
1 chilli, finely chopped
2 tsp vegetable oil
2 garlic cloves, crushed
salt, to taste

Grill the tomatoes until they are charred. Leave to cool, then remove the skins and mash the tomatoes until they are pulpy. Add the onion, salt and chilli.

Heat the oil in a small pan and briefly fry the garlic. Add it to the tomato mixture and mix thoroughly.

Sada Roti (Guyanese flatbread)

250 g (8¾ oz) plain flour
2½ tsp baking powder
¼ tsp salt
1 tsp sugar

green mango chutney. Another typical Bihari dish is chokha: vegetables, often potatoes, mashed with oil and chopped onion.

Curry is a common main course in Trinidad and Tobago. The chief spices – cumin, coriander, fenugreek and turmeric – are those used in a rural Bihari household. Because curry leaves, fresh coriander and mint were not grown in Trinidad, substitutes were found. Coriander was replaced with a local herb called shado(w) beni (*Eryngium foetidum*) that grows wild in drainage ditches. The chilli used in Trinidadian curries is the fiery scotch bonnet, so called because it looks like a little pleated bonnet. In place of the spinach-like greens called *sag* in India, Trinidadians (and Jamaicans) use callaloo, the leaf of the dasheen plant, a form of taro. Curries are accompanied by chutneys and sauces, such as mango kuchela, a mango and mustard oil pickle, and 'mother-in-law', a hot vegetable relish, and served with roti, a flatbread made from white flour.

1 tbsp finely chopped onion
1 green or red bird's-eye chilli, finely chopped
about 150 ml (5 fl. oz) lukewarm water
1 tbsp oil, ghee or butter, plus about 3 tbsp extra for
brushing

Mix all the ingredients to make a supple dough.

Shape the dough into a ball, then put it in an oiled bowl and cover with clingfilm. Leave to rest for 30 to 60 minutes. Re-knead the dough lightly, then divide into four pieces. Roll out each piece into a circle about 15 cm (6 in.) in diameter, dredging with a little flour if necessary.

Preheat a tawa (or a heavy griddle or frying pan). When the pan is hot, turn the heat down. Slap a roti on to it and let it cook until tiny brown spots appear on the bottom. Flip the roti over and allow the other side to cook. Brush with ghee or butter on both sides and keep wrapped in a tea towel until ready to eat.

From Gaitri Pagrach-Chandra, *Warm Bread and
Honey Cake* (Pavilion, London, 2009)

In Trinidad, the word *roti* means not just bread, but also a popular street food that has been called the country's national dish. A large, round wheat bread coated with ground yellow peas is wrapped around a meat, fish or vegetable curry, enclosed in waxed paper or foil and eaten on the move. Another popular street food is doubles, a sandwich composed of two pieces of turmeric-flavoured fried roti filled with curried chickpeas and topped with spicy chutneys and chilli sauce, similar to the Indian snack chole bhature. Other distinctive Trinidadian breads are buss-up-shut roti (named after a 'busted-up shirt'), a flaky roti torn into ragged pieces; dal puri roti, fried bread stuffed with spiced lentils; sada roti, a plain white bread often made at home; and oil roti, a flaky paratha.

Guyana and Suriname
Although they are in the northeastern corner of the South American continent, these two small countries are culturally and gastronomically

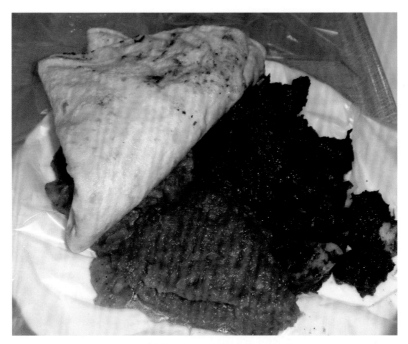

Dhalpuri roti is a Trinidadian bread filled with spiced yellow lentils
and served with curry, chickpeas and a sweet halwa.

part of the Caribbean. Guyana was a British colony until 1966, and
Suriname a Dutch colony from 1667 to 1975. Both were originally
sugar-plantation economies.

In Guyana, the largest ethnic group consists of people of Indian
origin (also known as East Indians), who make up nearly 44 per cent
of the population, followed by Afro-Guyanese at 30 per cent, people
of mixed heritage at 17 per cent, and indigenous people, Chinese and
Europeans at about 9 per cent. As in Trinidad, the food reflects the
regional origins of the immigrants. Bara and phulorie, made from chickpeas, are popular snacks that are eaten with hot pepper or mango sauce.
In Guyana, and in Trinidad, Hindus celebrate the festivals Holi (called
Phagwah) and Diwali. The sharing of traditional Indian sweets is part of
both celebrations.

Suriname is a melting pot of cultures and religions that includes
people of Indian origin (40 per cent), Creoles (people of mixed African
and native ancestry, 30–35 per cent), Indonesians (15 per cent) and
various minorities. After independence in 1975, around a third of the
population emigrated to the Netherlands, where today 350,000 Surinam-
ese (called Hindustanis) live. Typical dishes in Suriname include roti

Originally Guyanese peras were made from fresh milk boiled with sugar to make a firm product shaped into small balls. Later people began to use evaporated milk to produce a creamier flavour and softer texture and the shape gradually shifted from balls to flattened rounds or discs.

The Guyanese paratha is distinguished by its loose and flaky layers. As soon as it is removed from the tawa, the roti is flung into the air and caught with both palms in a clapping movement, a process repeated many times to separate the layers. This makes the roti very flexible, even after cooling, and therefore handy for scooping up curry.

made from white flour, often filled with potatoes or split peas; baras; phulorie; and samosas, often accompanied by Indonesian condiments.

Jamaica

About 40,000 Indians came to Jamaica between 1845 and 1917, but after their period of indenture ended they became dispersed among the general population. There was a much higher rate of intermarriage between communities in Jamaica than in Trinidad or Guyana, with the result that only 3 per cent of Jamaicans now claim Indian origin. However, the Indian impact on Jamaican food has been notable, especially in two of Jamaica's best-known dishes: patties and curry goat, the latter of which is served on festive occasions. It is prepared with commercially produced curry powder (which contains native allspice) and scotch bonnet chillies with a coconut-milk sauce. Patties – spiced minced meat in a dough pocket – are popular snacks not only in Jamaica but also among the Jamaican diaspora.

MAURITIUS

An island nation in the Indian Ocean, 800 km (500 miles) east of Madagascar and 4,800 km (3,000 miles) from India, Mauritius was colonized in turn by the Dutch, the French and the British, with the result that it is a linguistic and culinary melting pot. Today two-thirds of the population are of Indian origin; the rest are Franco-Mauritian or Chinese.

Mauritian cuisine is an intriguing mixture of African, Dutch, French and Indian ingredients and techniques. A curry may be made with octopus, or may combine venison and lilva beans (a slightly sweet and bitter bean popular in western India) or chicken and prawns. Vindaille (a word related to *vindaloo*) is prepared by marinating fresh tuna, octopus or other seafood in mustard, saffron, chillies, garlic, oil and vinegar. A popular Indian-Mauritian snack is dalpuri – fried Indian-style bread filled with curried lentils, rougaille (a spicy tomato-based sauce), chutneys and vegetable pickle.

FIJI

Nearly half the population of Fiji, an island nation in the South Pacific, is descended from 60,000 Indians brought by the British in the late 1890s to work on the sugar plantations. Fijian cuisine is a melange of

Melanesian, Polynesian, Indian, Chinese and Western elements. Fijian curries are made with breadfruit, yam, cassava, taro root and leaves, seafood and usually coconut milk. Flavourings include garlic, ginger, turmeric, coriander, fenugreek, cumin, soy sauce and chilli. A unique home-style curry is 'tinned fish' curry made with canned tuna, mackerel or salmon. From Fiji, curries and curry powder spread to Tonga, Samoa and other islands in the Pacific, where they are often served with boiled taro or breadfruit as the starch.

South Africa

In 1651 the Dutch East India Company established a settlement at the Cape of Good Hope to supply ships sailing between the Netherlands and the Dutch East Indies. The colonists built permanent settlements and brought slaves from Bengal, the Coromandel Coast and the East Indies to work on their farms and in their kitchens. The descendants of these workes became known as Cape Malays. (Malay was the lingua franca of trade.) Today, an estimated 180,000 Cape Malays live in South Africa, mainly in Cape Town.

Celebrated for their cooking skills, the Cape Malays were much in demand as cooks. The Indian influence is apparent in the popularity of biryani, dal, kebabs, puris, rotis, samosas and various curries (*kerries*) served with atjars (Indian-style vegetable pickles), fruit condiments, chutneys, sambals and rice.

In 1806 the British took over the Cape. They brought in 150,000 indentured labourers, most from rural South India. Lentils, beans, rice, flour rotis and mealie rice (crushed corn kernels boiled to look like rice) were dietary staples. The dried fish that was a ration on the labourers' transport ships also became part of their daily fare. From the 1880s onwards they were joined by Indian businessmen, traders and attorneys (including the young attorney Mahatma Gandhi). Many of these 'passenger Indians' came from Gujarat on India's west coast. They opened small restaurants and shops selling spices and Indian condiments.

The most famous Indo-South African dish is bunny chow, a meat curry served in a hollowed-out loaf of Western-style bread. One explanation of its name is that in Durban, Indian merchants were often called *banias*, their caste name. They opened small restaurants, which black South Africans could not enter because of apartheid; they could, however, be (illegally) served at the back door. An enterprising restaurateur got the

Deep-frying puris.

A hollowed-out loaf of bread filled with curry, bunny chow
originated in Durban, South Africa.

> ## A Decision to Emigrate
>
> When Kalloo was going on four years, a drought came. Last
> year's rice crop was bad, and now no rain for this year's
> crop to grow, and no money to buy food to eat. We should
> have planted bajra, millet, but again we hadn't, so we had to
> depend on the rice. I was the one cooking every day and I
> could see the rice getting less and less . . .
>
> I had to find work, but what work was there . . . in a
> village? So I took the last few handfuls of parched rice my
> mother-in-law had kept aside, and some sattva powder,
> from roasted channa, and tied them in two bundles. Then
> I picked up an extra sari, and walked with the child to the town
> of Faziabad [a city in Uttar Pradesh].
>
> And that was where I met the arkatiniya, the lady who
> recruited people to go with her as migrants. She met me
> on the street, just as I reached, and told me they were look-
> ing for labourers to go to a place called 'Chini-dad', a land
> of 'chini', sugar. In Chini-dad there were big estates where
> they made sugar. They wanted labourers to work the sugar-
> cane fields. She told me they were especially looking for
> women to go, and she promised me an extra advance if I
> signed up. Only one year there, she said, and then they
> bring you back. Plenty of money.
>
> From Peggy Mohan, *Jahajin* (New Delhi, 2007)

idea of hollowing out a small loaf of bread, pouring in curry, topping it
with Indian pickles and handing it over to the customer without cutlery.
The dish was named bunny chow, from *bania chow*.

EAST AFRICA

In 1888 the British established the Imperial British East Africa Company
to develop trade in the region, and later they created the Protectorate of
British East Africa, covering present-day Kenya and Uganda. In the late
nineteenth century 30,000 labourers were recruited from India to build
the Kenya–Uganda railway. They were followed by other Indian immigrants, including many Gujarati Hindus and Ismaili Muslims, who were

Kuku Paka (East Africa)

1 small onion, finely chopped
3 tbsp oil
1 kg (2¼ lb) chicken pieces, skin removed
1 medium tomato, finely chopped
½ tsp each crushed garlic, fresh ginger, ground cumin and
ground coriander
¼–1 tsp chilli powder, to taste
⅛ tsp turmeric powder
¼–1 tsp chopped fresh green chillies, to taste
1 tsp salt
480 ml (2 cups) water
90 g (3½ oz) unsweetened coconut cream
3 or 4 boiled eggs
3 boiled or fried potatoes
120 ml (½ cup) whipping cream
1 tbsp coriander leaves

Fry the onion in oil until soft.

Add the chicken, tomatoes, garlic, ginger, spices, chillies and salt.

Cook for two minutes, then add the water. Continue cooking over medium heat until the chicken is almost done.

Mix the coconut cream with 120 ml (½ cup) water and add to the mixture. The sauce should almost cover the chicken; add more water if needed.

Continue cooking until the chicken is done.

Add the eggs, potatoes, whipping cream and fresh coriander. Cook for two or three minutes and serve with parathas or rice.

Adapted from Noorbanu Nimji, *A Spicy Touch*
(Calgary, Alberta, 1986)

moneylenders, traders and owners of small shops, or *dukas*. By the mid-1960s some 360,000 people of Indian origin lived in East Africa, but most were forced to leave by the new nationalist government and, as holders of British passports, emigrated to Britain and Canada. With regime changes in Uganda and Kenya, some have returned and today run grocers and small stands selling samosas, curry and other Indian dishes. There are many Indian restaurants in large cities like Mombasa and Kampala.

A standard food of the railway workers was khichri with millet bread (rotli) and dal. Among the middle classes, a hybrid African-Indian cuisine developed, with many Indian dishes acquiring Swahili names. According to Yasmin Alibhai-Brown, who grew up in Kenya, 'African servants working for the Indians picked up much of the cooking, so that ghee and mchuzi have become part of the vocabulary of East African cuisine. How common is it today to stop at a wayside kiosk and ask for chapattis or samosas, kebobs or bhajias?'[6] Mchuzi is a curry made with tomatoes, coconut milk, tamarind and curry powder and accompanied by bananas and pickles, often made from the very hot bird's-eye chilli, called peri peri. *Mchuzi* is also the Swahili word for curry powder, which every household has on hand. Perhaps the most popular Kenyan-Indian dish is kuku paka, chicken in a coconut sauce.

PORTUGUESE AFRICA

From the sixteenth century onwards the Portuguese established colonies in what are today Angola, Equatorial Guinea, Madagascar, Mozambique and Zanzibar. They brought chillies, maize, tomatoes, sweet potatoes, cassava and the domesticated pig from the New World; salt cod from Portugal; and spices from their possessions in India. Both the Portuguese and the British brought Goans to their colonies, mainly as artisans and clerical workers. The Goan influence can be seen in the use of coconut milk as the sauce for many African dishes, especially those made with seafood. Curries, called *carils*, are popular dishes in Mozambique and Angola. According to Laurens van der Post, their curries tend to be 'either straightforward derivatives of the curries of India or pale imitations of those of South Africa, particularly Natal'.[7] The spicy chilli peri peri (also spelled *piri piri* or *pili pili*; the bird's-eye chilli) is grown throughout Africa and gives its name to a spicy Goan dish, usually made with chicken, that is popular in the United Kingdom.

SOUTHEAST ASIA

From ancient times, Southeast Asia held a crucial position on the trade routes between India and China. In the third century BCE Indian merchants brought not only spices and textiles, but also Hinduism and Buddhism, new forms of dance, sculpture and music, and Indian concepts of statecraft. So-called Hinduized kingdoms flourished in what are now Thailand, Vietnam, Cambodia and Indonesia until well into the eighteenth century. These traders may also have introduced tamarind, garlic, shallots, ginger, turmeric and pepper to the region, and disseminated such herbs as lemongrass and galangal from one area to another. In the eighth century Arab merchants took over the spice trade and converted many local people to Islam. They introduced kebabs, biryanis, kormas and other meat dishes from the Islamic world and may also have popularized the use of cloves, nutmeg and other local spices.

In 1602 the Dutch created the Dutch East India Company (Vereenigde Oostindische Compagnie or VOC), often considered to be the world's first multinational, to conduct trade and colonial activities in Asia. At its peak the VOC was far larger than the East India Company, and it eventually extended its control over all of present-day Indonesia (which, as the Netherlands East Indies, was a Dutch colony until it won its independence in 1945).

The British established Singapore in 1819 and later extended their control over the Malay Peninsula and Burma. By 1914 the French empire encompassed Indochina, present-day Laos, Cambodia and Vietnam. Only Thailand remained free from foreign occupation. Although there is a strong Indian influence on Thai culture and to some degree its cuisine, notably in Thailand's famous curries, few Indians migrated there, in contrast to other parts of Southeast Asia.

Malaysia and Singapore

In the nineteenth century 2 million Indian workers, mainly Tamils from South India and Sri Lanka, came to Malaysia and Singapore to work on the rubber and palm plantations. Indian civil servants also settled there. Today around two-thirds of Malaysia's 25 million people are Malay, 25 per cent Chinese and around 8 per cent Indian, predominantly Tamils. Singapore, which seceded from Malaysia in 1965, has a large Chinese majority and Malay and Indian minorities.

The main Indian culinary influence in the region is Tamil. A common sight in Kuala Lumpur are the banana-leaf restaurants, small establishments that serve idlis, dosas, vadas, sambars, rasams and other South Indian dishes on banana leaves.

Many street foods are of Indian origin. A local equivalent of an Indian stuffed roti is murtabak (from the Arabic word for 'folded'). Dough made from white flour is wrapped around spiced minced meat and beaten egg and folded into packets that are fried, cut into pieces and served with a curry sauce. Another popular street food is fish-head curry, supposedly invented by two Indian cooks in Singapore in 1964. Indian Muslims in Malaysia have developed a distinctive style of cooking called *mamak*, which includes such specialities as biryani and roti canai, a layered flatbread served with curry or stuffed fried eggs, onions, sardines, cheese, lentils and other ingredients. It is accompanied by a drink called teh tarik, or 'pulled tea': tea sweetened with condensed milk is poured into a glass several times from a mug held high in the air, which creates a froth – similar to the way coffee is made in South India.

Roti canai is an Indian-influenced sautéed bread that is a popular street food in Malayasia, Singapore and Indonesia. It is often served with a meat curry.

Other Southeast Asian Countries

One consequence of the French bringing labourers from their colonies in South India to Vietnam is the use of South Indian-style curry powders, made with chillies, turmeric and other spices. Popular dishes are chicken curry (cari ga), made with coconut milk, and beef curry (cari bo), which commonly contains bay leaves, cinnamon, onions, carrots and potatoes or sweet potatoes.

Burma (Myanmar), part of British India until 1948, consists of many ethnic groups, but the two greatest influences on its cuisine have been India and China. In the 1940s half of Rangoon's population was of Indian origin, but today Indians account for only 2 per cent. The Indian influence is apparent in Burmese samosas, biryanis, breads and curries, which incorporate Indian spices as well as lemongrass, basil leaves and fish sauce. Toasted rice, garlic, onions, lemongrass, banana heart, fish paste, fish sauce and catfish cooked in broth are combined to make the national dish, a Chinese-Indian-Burmese hybrid called mohinga, which is sold on the street.

BRITAIN

Indians first came to Britain as long ago as the late seventeenth century, mainly as servants or wives of returning East India Company men, or *nabobs*, who had made their fortune in India. The general term for Indian habits and customs as practised in England, chiefly London, was *nabobery*, and so-called Little Bengal grew up in the London districts of Marylebone and Mayfair. Just as the British had tried to re-create their homeland while they were in India, so they tried to recapture something of their life in India after returning home. Indian dishes were first served in the Norris Street Coffee House on Haymarket in 1733, but the first purely Indian restaurant was the Hindoostanee Coffee House. It was opened in 1809 at 34 George Street by an intriguing character named Sake Dean Mahomed (1759–1851), an Indian who served in the British Army and married an Irishwoman. It closed in 1833. In 1824 the Oriental Club was founded in the West End as a meeting place for ex-Company men. Its initial fare was French, but in 1839 it started serving curry. Today the Club continues the tradition by featuring a 'curry of the day' on its menu.

The first British cookbook to contain a recipe for curry was Hannah Glasse's *Art of Cookery Made Plain and Easy* (1747). Her first recipe was essentially an aromatic stew flavoured with peppercorns and coriander seeds, but in the edition of 1796 curry (powder) and cayenne pepper were added. From then on, curry recipes featured prominently in cookbooks throughout the English-speaking world, including the colonies. The first commercial curry powder was sold in 1784 by Sorlie's Perfumery Warehouse, and by 1860 curry paste, mulligatawny paste and chutney were being sold on a mass scale by Fortnum & Mason and Crosse & Blackwell. The one ingredient common to all these substances was turmeric powder. Other ingredients (in approximate order of frequency) were coriander seeds, cumin seeds, mustard seeds, fenugreek, black pepper, chillies, curry leaves and sometimes ginger, cinnamon, cloves and cardamom.

Another group of Indians who came to Britain were seamen, or *lascars*, recruited by the East India Company to serve on their ships, many of whom had jumped ship or were stranded in London. By the mid-nineteenth century there were more than 40,000 south Asians in Britain, and by the early twentieth century the number had grown to around 70,000, three-quarters of them *lascars*, the rest students. Many were from the Sylhet region, which had traditionally supplied cooks to the Portuguese and British, and some opened restaurants.

By 1920 there were a handful of Indian restaurants in London, including the Salut e Hind in Holborn and the Shafi in Gerard Street, and cafés in the East End, near the docks. In 1926 Edward Palmer, great-grandson of a Hyderabadi princess and an English lieutenant general, opened Veeraswamy's at 99 Regent Street, where it still operates. Palmer's restaurant tried to replicate the atmosphere of a British club in India, and the menu listed vindaloos, Madras curries, dopiazas, coloured pulaos and other popular dishes.

The Second World War was followed by a surge in immigration from Commonwealth countries, especially the Caribbean and the subcontinent, as people came to work in industry as part of the post-war reconstruction efforts. The creation of Bangladesh in 1971 generated a new wave, and these immigrants were joined the following year by South Asians expelled from East Africa. Immigration laws largely restricted further primary immigration, although family members of those already in the country were allowed to enter. According to the census of 2001, there were 2.3 million South Asians in the United Kingdom (including those of the second and third generations), 4 per cent of the total population; approximately half were of Indian origin, 750,000 Pakistani and 283,000 Bangladeshi.

To serve this growing population, companies such as Noon, Pathak's (later Patak's) and S&A Foods began to manufacture Indian spice mixtures and sauces, chutneys, pickles and other Indian products. Many immigrants opened restaurants, an industry that requires relatively little capital and a lot of inexpensive labour. Every large town and city in the UK has Indian restaurants, the most famous districts being London's Brick Lane and Birmingham's Broad Street. Their menus became standardized and served a hotchpotch of dishes from different regions. Curry became so popular that for a time it replaced fish and chips as the most popular takeaway food in Britain, only to lose its place again to fish and chips and Chinese food.[8]

NORTH AMERICA

The earliest Asian Indian immigrants arrived in America soon after the founding of the Jamestown colony in 1607. Some were sailors on the ships of the British East India Company; others were servants to wealthy British *nabobs* (some of whom moved to America after making their fortune in India).[9] Still others arrived as slaves, captured by Dutch or British traders. In the early eighteenth century 'East Indians' even outnumbered Native Americans in the Virginia census, and intermarriage was common between the two groups.

In the 1880s Bengali Muslim pedlars began coming to the United States to sell embroidered silks and other 'exotic' goods to a public that had a craving for all things Indian.[10] Their operations were centred in the New Orleans neighbourhood of Treme, and some married local African American women. Another group of Bengalis were seamen who after the Second World War jumped ship in American ports, especially New York. Many settled in Harlem, where they married Puerto Rican and African American women and opened halal butchers and small Indian restaurants.

Owing to immigration laws that excluded most non-whites, the country's Indian population remained very small: only around 3,000 people in 1930, many of them students living in New York City. By the end of the 1920s New York had half a dozen Indian restaurants, which were known for their fiery curries. The first significant wave of immigrants from the Indian subcontinent took place between 1900 and 1910, when more than 3,000 farmworkers, mainly Sikhs from the Punjab, came to the northwest coast and Canada. Anti-Asian sentiment drove them south to

Sacramento Valley in California, where they became successful farmers. After racial exclusion laws in 1917 ended immigration by 'non-whites', many married local Mexican women. Their community came to total 400 couples, and they became known as 'Mexican Hindus'.[11] Their cuisine combined elements of Mexican and Punjabi food. Rasul's El Ranchero in Yuba City, the last restaurant serving their dishes – including 'Hindu pizza' – closed in 2009.

In 1946 immigration laws were relaxed somewhat, and by 1965 around 6,000 Indians, mainly students, had entered the United States. In 1965 the old immigration quota system, which favoured people from 'white' countries, was replaced with one based on hemispheric quotas, with preference given to professionals and relatives of current citizens. In 1976 all regional quotas were abolished. Over the next decade hundreds of thousands of Indian professionals emigrated to the United States as part of the famous 'brain drain'.

By 2007 some 2.8 million people of South Asian origin lived in the United States. Of these, 1.5 million were born in India; the rest came from Pakistan, Bangladesh, the Caribbean and South Africa, or were second- or third-generation Asian Americans. The New York–New Jersey area alone is home to some 600,000 Asian Indians. The culinary needs of these new arrivals were met by grocers, restaurants and entire shopping districts, among them Jackson Heights in Queens, New York; 'Curry Hill' on Lexington Avenue in Manhattan; Devon Avenue in Chicago; Pioneer Boulevard in Los Angeles; Journal Square in Jersey City, New Jersey; and Hillcroft Avenue in Houston, Texas. As immigrants moved to the sub-urbs, so too did these establishments. Indian grocers such as Patel Brothers, headquartered in Chicago, opened branches throughout the country and eventually developed their own manufacturing and distribution networks.

While these stores originally sold spices, rice and other essential ingredients, their offerings have expanded to include ready-to-make and ready-to-serve products, including dishes in plastic pouches (usually vegetarian), frozen starters and appetizers, and fresh or frozen varieties of every bread imaginable. Today virtually every suburb and town has its own Indian grocers, while Indian products can also be found on the shelves of most supermarkets.

In the home, immigrants appear to combine Indian and Western eating patterns. A study by the sociologist Krishnendu Ray of Bengali households in the United States found that a typical breakfast is

Western-style, consisting of cereal and milk or toast (as it might be in a middle-class household in India), while lunch eaten outside the home is also Western, although many people do not eat beef. It is dinner that remains in the realm of 'tradition', although often with substitutions. It might consist of rice, dal and fish cooked with typical Bengali spices, or rice, croquettes made from turkey mince (instead of goat) and strawberry shortcake instead of a Bengali dessert. 'It is as if Bengalis have divided up the day into what they characterize as moments of "modernity" and moments of "tradition", both perceived as good and necessary in their separate places', wrote Ray.[12]

Canada's immigration policy also excluded non-whites until 1962, when the most blatantly racist provisions were overturned. In 1976 a new policy was adopted that based admission on education, employment skills, language abilities and family sponsorship. The Canadian census in 2001 reported more than 900,000 residents of Indian origin, 3.1 per cent of the entire population, including a sizeable number from Trinidad and Tobago and Guyana.

The Gulf and the Middle East

Ties between India and the Arab states in the Gulf and the Middle East have been strong since ancient times, as we have seen. Since the 1970s an estimated 3 million people from the subcontinent have moved to the Gulf States to work, most unskilled or semi-skilled workers. The majority are Muslim and over half are from Kerala. Many establishments exist to serve their needs, ranging from workplace canteens to small, inexpensive restaurants. For tourists and locals there are upscale Indian restaurants in such cities as Doha and Dubai. Kebabs, biryanis and tandoori chicken are popular everywhere. In Mecca, Indian and Pakistani restaurants serve food to pilgrims during the *hajj*. It is not uncommon for wealthy Arabs to have Indian cooks.

Since the creation of the state of Israel, most Indian Jews have migrated to Israel, which today has an estimated 70,000 residents of Indian origin. Large cities like Tel Aviv and Jerusalem have many Indian restaurants, some of them vegetarian, others serving meat but no dairy products to conform with kosher laws.

FROM VERY ANCIENT TIMES, India was part of a global culinary economy, adopting and absorbing ingredients, dishes, and techniques from virtually every part of the globe – Central Asia, the Middle East, Persia, Africa, China, the Western Hemisphere, Southeast Asia and Europe – and exporting its own culinary treasures and ideologies. This exchange has become even more pronounced in the twenty-first century, as people move freely between continents and boundaries between cuisines are dissolving.

Indian food in its many incarnations has become a world cuisine. One reason is a growing awareness of the virtues of a traditional Indian diet, especially the low consumption of meat, the abundance of fruit and vegetables, the centrality of grains and the use of spices, the medical benefits of which have been confirmed by science. Related is the growing popularity of vegetarianism, perhaps India's greatest gift to the world, for ethical, humane and health reasons. Food experts have identified a preference for spicier, 'hotter' food as one of the main consumer trends of the twenty-first century.

Timeline

NOTE: Because of the difficulty of assigning dates to early works
and events, some dates are approximate.

6500–2500 BCE	Mehrgarh culture (Baluchistan). Farming of barley, wheat, jujubes, grapes, pulses, dates; domestication of sheep, goats and cattle
3000–*c.* 1500 BCE	Indus Valley civilization. Urban civilization based on agriculture and trade. Main crops are wheat and barley. Diet includes chickpeas, lentils, meat, fish, buffalo milk, turmeric, black pepper and ginger
1700–1300 BCE	Indo-Aryan tribes migrate into Indo-Gangetic plain with their cows. Dietary staple is barley; later wheat and millet. Vedas are composed. Division of society into four castes
700–600 BCE	Ayurveda physician Susruta teaches in Benares
6th century BCE	Formation of sixteen *mahajanapadas*. Buddha (563–483 BCE) and Mahavira (540–468 BCE) establish Buddhism and Jainism, advocating non-violence (*ahimsa*) and abstinence from meat
c. 500 BCE	*Dharmasutras* composed
327 BCE	Alexander the Great invades India
316 BCE	Chandragupta founds Maurya dynasty
304–232 BCE	Emperor Ashoka advocates vegetarianism
300 BCE–100 CE	India, the wealthiest country in the world, exports pepper, spices and luxury goods to Rome, the Middle East and China
300 BCE–300 CE	Composition of *Mahabharata*
200–78 BCE	Invasion of North India by Central Asians, Bactrians and Greeks
200 BCE–200 CE	Composition of *Ramayana*; *Code of Manu* codifies behaviour, including dietary rules
200 BCE–400 CE	Indo-Scythian kingdom
180 BCE–10 CE	Indo-Greek kingdoms flourish
52 CE	St Thomas is martyred in South India

2nd century CE (est.)	Caraka writes treatise on Ayurveda
324–550 CE	Gupta Empire rules northern India; India's 'Golden Age'
c. 650 CE	Rajput dynasties emerge in Rajasthan; Parsis settle on west coast of India
712 CE	Muslim Arabs conquer Sindh
c. 400 BCE–1279 CE	South Indian dynasties
c. 400 BCE–1314 CE	Cheras
275–882 CE	Pallavas
543–1156 CE	Chalukyas
301 BCE–1279 CE	Cholas
756–1174 CE	Pala dynasty rules northern and northeastern India
c. 1017–25	Alberuni visits India
c. 1025	Composition of *Lokopakara*
1126–38	Reign of Somesvara III, author of *Manasolassa*
1206–1526	Central Asian dynasties establish Delhi sultanate. Introduce pulao, biryani, kebabs, samosas, halwa and other foods
1292	Marco Polo lands on Coromandel Coast
1336–1565	Vijayanagar Empire
1347–1527	Bahmani sultanate
1398	Timur (Tamerlane) invades northern India
1495–1505	*Ni'matnama* written at the court of the sultans of Mandu
1498	Vasco da Gama lands on west coast of India
16th century	Portuguese establish trading ports, capture Goa and establish Indian empire. Introduce tomatoes, potatoes, chillies, peanuts, pineapples, cashews and other New World plants
1526–1857	Mughal dynasty rules India. Court cuisine reaches new heights, although emperors are semi-vegetarian
1563	Garcia de Orta writes *Colloquies on the Simples and Drugs of India*
c. 1590	Abu'l-Fazl writes *A'in-i-Akbari*
31 December 1600	East India Company is chartered by Elizabeth I
1674–1817	Maratha Empire
17th century	Netherlands, Great Britain and France establish trading posts in India
1724	Nizam of Hyderabad declares independence from Delhi
1753–1856	Lucknow is culinary and cultural centre
1830–50	British establish tea plantations in Assam and Darjeeling and coffee plantations in South India. British returning home from India create curry powder and Worcester sauce
1857	First War of Independence (also known as the Indian Mutiny)

1858	Last Mughal emperor exiled. India comes under direct rule of the British Crown
1877	Queen Victoria named empress of India
1885	Indian National Congress formed
1890	Mahatma Gandhi joins London Vegetarian Society
1920–22	Mahatma Gandhi leads anti-British civil disobedience campaign
1947	Partition of India, independence from British rule as a dominion and creation of Pakistan. Tandoori chicken invented in Delhi
1966–77	Green Revolution boosts Indian agricultural production
1996	McDonald's opens its first restaurant in India
May 2000	India marks the birth of its billionth citizen

References

All translations are my own unless otherwise indicated.

Introduction

1 Although the subtitle of this book is *A History of Food in India*, it covers the historical food customs of the entire subcontinent: the Republic of India, the Islamic Republic of Pakistan and the People's Republic of Bangladesh. This part of the world has been called by many names, including south Asia, the subcontinent, the Indian subcontinent, the south Asian subcontinent, the Indo-Pak-Bangladesh subcontinent and Greater India. Because these terms may be politically charged or ambiguous (sometimes Nepal, Bhutan, Sri Lanka and even Afghanistan are included in south Asia, for example), I have chosen to use the word 'India' for the region. Food, like language, is not coterminous with political boundaries, and the six and a half decades since the region was politically divided are but a drop in the ocean of 6,000 years of common history. All three countries were part of three major empires – the Mauryan (316–184 BCE), the Mughal (1526–1857) and the British (1858–1947) – while India and Pakistan share a common heritage that goes back to the Indus Valley civilization.
2 Mark Twain, *Following the Equator: A Journey Around the World* (1897), chapter 43; available online at www.gutenberg.org.
3 Diana L. Eck, *India: A Sacred Geography* (New York, 2012), p. 82.
4 Arjun Appadurai, 'How to Make a National Cuisine: Cookbooks in Contemporary India', *Comparative Studies in Sociology and History*, XXX/1 (1988), pp. 3–24.
5 Carol Appadurai Breckenridge, 'Food, Politics and Pilgrimage in South India, 1350–1640 AD', in *Food, Society and Culture: Aspects in South Asian Food Systems*, ed. R. S. Khare and M.S.A. Rao (Durham, NC, 1986), pp. 21–2.

ONE: Climate, Crops and Prehistory

1 For a list of famines in India from the fifth century BCE to the eighteenth century CE, see R. C. Saxena, S. L. Choudhary and Y. L. Nene, *A Textbook on Ancient History of Indian Agriculture* (Secunderabad, India, 2009), pp. 112–16.

2 Dorian Q. Fuller and Emma L. Harvey, 'The Archaeobotany of Indian Pulses: Identification, Processing and Evidence for Cultivation', *Environmental Archaeology*, XI/2 (2006), pp. 219–44.

3 Food and Agriculture Organization of the United Nations: http://faostat.fao.org.

4 See, for example, Dorian Q. Fuller, 'Finding Plant Domestication in the Indian Subcontinent', *Current Anthropology*, LII/S4 (October 2011), pp. S347–D362. Available online at www.jstor.org. See also Fuller, 'The Ganges on the World Neolithic Map: The Significance of Recent Research on Agricultural Origins in Northern India', *Prāgadhāna* [Journal of the Uttar Pradesh State Archaeology Department], no. 16 (2005–6), pp. 187–206.

5 Dorian Q. Fuller et al., 'Across the Indian Ocean: The Prehistoric Movement of Plants and Animals', *Antiquity*, LXXXV/328 (2011), pp. 544–58: www.antiquity.ac.uk.

6 William Shurtleff and Akiko Aoyagi, 'History of Soy on the Indian Subcontinent', 2007: www.soyinfocenter.com; Ramesh Chand, *Agro-industries Characterization and Appraisal: Soybeans in India*, FAO Agricultural Management, Marketing and Finance Working Document 20 (Rome, 2007): www.fao.org.

7 See 'Rice's Origins Point to China, Genome Researchers Conclude', 3 May 2011: www.sciencenewsline.com; Xuehui Huang et al., 'A Map of Rice Genome Variation Reveals the Origin of Cultivated Rice', *Nature*, CDXC/7421 (2012), pp. 497–501.

8 'Mango – History', plantcultures.kew.org, accessed 28 June 2014.

9 K. T. Achaya, *A Historical Dictionary of Indian Food* (New Delhi, 2002), p. 84.

10 For papers on the health benefits of spices, search PubMed, the U.S. National Library of Medicine's database of articles from medical and biological science journals around the world, at www.ncbi.nlm.nih.gov. In January 2014 it contained over 6,200 references to turmeric and curcumin (one of the active ingredients in turmeric) alone, of which 2,400 related to cancer. See also Helen Saberi and Colleen Taylor Sen, *Turmeric: The Wonder Spice* (Evanston, IL, 2014).

11 Romila Thapar, *Early India: From the Origins to AD 1300* (Berkeley, CA, 2002), p. 57.

12 Genetic studies at Harvard University show that nearly all Indians are descended from mixtures of two ancestral populations. One, 'Ancestral North Indian', accounts for 40–80 per cent of the ancestry found in Indian genomes and is similar to that of western Eurasians, including Europeans, Middle Easterners and Central Asians. The other, 'Ancestral South Indian', is a distinct population not apparently related to any other of the world's populations. See David Reich et al., 'Reconstructing Indian Population History', *Nature*, CDLXI (24 September 2009), pp. 489–95, available at http://genetics.med.harvard.edu. Another DNA study has found that in about 2200 BCE Dravidian Indians travelled by ship to Australia, where they introduced cycad nuts (a common ingredient in the food of Kerala) and perhaps dingo dogs. See 'An Antipodean Raj', *The Economist*, 19 January 2013, pp. 77–8, available at www.economist.com.

13 Although it was once common to talk about a 'Dravidian' or 'Aryan' race, the equation of language with race is today considered spurious; indeed, the very concept of a unitary 'race' has been challenged, especially in the light of DNA analysis.

14 Frank C. Southworth, 'Proto-Dravidian Agriculture', www.upenn.edu, accessed 30 June 2014.

15 Dorian Q. Fuller and Mike Rowlands, 'Towards a Long-term Macro-geography of Cultural Substances: Food and Sacrifice Traditions in East, West and South Asia', *Chinese Review of Anthropology*, 12 (2009), pp. 32–3.

16 'India's "Miracle River"', *BBC News South Asia*, 29 June 2002, news.bbc.co.uk.

17 Jean Bottéro, *The Oldest Cuisine in the World: Cooking in Mesopotamia* (Chicago, IL, 2004).

18 Tarditionally the word 'curry' was used by Europeans, not Indians, who called dishes by their specific names: korma, rogan josh, molee, vindaloo etc. But today the word is often used by Indians as well for any dish with a gravy. For more information on the definition and origin of the word, see pp. 222 and 293; also Colleen Taylor Sen, *Curry: A Global History* (London, 2009).

19 Andrew Lawler, 'The Mystery of Curry', *Slate*, 29 January 2013, www.slate.com; Arunima Kashyap and Steve Weber, 'Harappan Plant Use Revealed by Starch Grains from Farmana, India', *Antiquity*, LXXXIV/326 (December 2010): www.antiquity.ac.uk; and Steve Weber, Arunima Kashyap and Laura Mounce, 'Archaeobotany at Farmana: New Insights into Harappan Plant Use Strategies', in *Excavations at Farmana: District Rohtak, Haryana, India, 2006–2008*, ed. Vasant Shinde, Toshiki Osada and Manmohan Kumar (Kyoto, 2011), pp. 808–82.

20 Jonathan Mark Kenoyer, *Ancient Cities of the Indus Valley Civilization* (Oxford, 1998), pp. 169–70.

21 Ibid., p. 164.

22 Ibid., p. 19.

TWO: The Age of Ritual, 1700–1100 BCE

1 See Colin Renfrew, *Archaeology and Language: The Puzzle of Indo-European Origins* (Cambridge, 1990). Also B. B. Lal, 'Aryan Invasion of India, Perpetuation of a Myth', in Edwin Bryant and Laurie Patton, *The Indo-Aryan Controversy: Evidence and Inference in Indian History* (London, 2005). An alternative theory, the 'Out of India' theory, is that the Indo-Aryans were indigenous to the Indian subcontinent and migrated north. This theory is not taken seriously by most academics, but it remains the subject of debate in some circles.

2 Two other Vedas, the *Yajur* and *Sama*, based on the *Rig Veda*, deal mainly with rituals. The *Atharva Veda* was composed somewhat later and contains charms, spells and some remedies to ward off disease or influence events. It is considered a precursor of Ayurveda. Unless otherwise noted, all quotations from the *Rig Veda* are from the translation by Ralph T.H.T. Griffith of 1896, available at www.sacredtexts.com.

3 For a modern re-enactment of a Vedic fire sacrifice, see videos on www.youtube.com.

4 See Emily Eakin, 'Holy Cow a Myth? An Indian Finds the Kick is Real', *New York Times*, 17 August 1992, pp. A13, A15; Herman W. Tull, 'The Killing that is Not Killing: Men, Cattle and the Origins of Nonviolence (Ahimsa) in the Vedic Sacrifice', *Indo-Iranian Journal*, 39 (1996), pp. 223–44; Ludwig Alsdorf, trans. Bal Patil, ed. Willem Bollée, *The History of Vegetarianism and Cow Veneration in India* (London, 2010); D. N. Jha, *The Myth of the Holy Cow* (London, 2004); and Ian Proudfoot, *Ahimsa and a Mahabharata Story: The Development of the Story of Tuladhara in the Mahabharata in Connection with Non-violence, Cow Protection and Sacrifice* (Canberra, 1987).

5 K. T. Achaya, *Indian Food: A Historical Companion* (New Delhi, 1994), pp. 104–5.

6 Wendy Doniger, *The Hindus: An Alternative History* (New York, 2009), p. 161.

7 Robert Gordon Wasson, *Soma: Divine Mushroom of Immortality* (New York, 1972), p. 316.

8 *The Rigveda*, trans. Stephanie Jamison and Joel Brereton (Oxford, 2014).

9 Achaya, *Indian Food*, p. 33.

10 'Lactose Intolerance by Ethnicity and Region', 23 February 2010: http://milk.procon.org.

11 The anthropologist Nicholas Dirks argues that caste as we know it today is not fundamental to Indian society, culture or tradition, but rather 'a modern phenomenon, that it is, specifically, the product of a historical encounter between India and Western colonial rule'. It is not that the British invented caste, which was always present and important in marriage and religious matters, but rather that before their arrival 'it did not seem particularly strikingly important or fixed'. The British used it as a means of systematizing India's diverse forms of social identity to facilitate their administration and justify colonial power. Nicholas B. Dirks, *Castes of Mind: Colonialism and the Making of Modern India* (Princeton, NJ, 2001). From the decennial census 1872 until 1932, caste became the primary subject of social classification. Questions about caste were restored in the most recent Indian census (2011), perhaps because of its new importance in politics.

THREE: The Renunciant Tradition and Vegetarianism, 1000–300 BCE

1 The idea that there was contact and cross-fertilization of ideas among these people is imaginatively explored in Gore Vidal's novel *Creation* (New York, 2002). The transmigration of souls (metempsychosis) was one of the doctrines of Pythagoras (580–495 BCE), who also advocated vegetarianism. Some claim that Pythagoras may have heard about Indian doctrines through Persian sources.

2 Ainslie T. Embree, ed., *Sources of Indian Tradition*, 2nd edn (New York, 1988), pp. 44–5.

3 Patrick Olivelle, 'From Feast to Fast: Food and the Indian Ascetic', in *Rules and Remedies in Classical Indian Law: Panels of the VIIth World Sanskrit Conference*, ed. Julia Leslie, vol. IX, (Leiden, 1987), p. 21.

4 For details about the ascetic lifestyle, including their food habits, see ibid.

5 Hanns-Peter Schmidt, 'The Origin of Ahimsa', in Ludwig Alsdorf, *The History of Vegetarianism and Cow Veneration in India*, trans. Bal Patil, ed. Willem Bollée (London, 2010), p. 109.

6 Romila Thapar, 'Renunication: The Making of a Counter-Culture?', in *Ancient Indian Social History: Some Interpretations* (New Delhi, 1978), pp. 56–93.

7 James Laidlaw, *Riches and Renunciation: Religion, Economy and Society among the Jains* (Oxford, 2003), p. 153. For a fuller description of Jain food customs, see Colleen Taylor Sen, 'Jainism: The World's Most Ethical Religion', in *Food and Morality: Proceedings of the Oxford Symposium on Food and Cookery, 2007*, ed. Susan R. Friedland (Totnes, Devon, 2008).

8 A Jain dinner organized by the author for a local food group was so popular that the attendees insisted on a repeat performance. For a collection of Jain recipes, see Manoj Jain, Laxmi Jain and Tarla Dalal, *Jain Food: Compassionate and Healthy Eating* (Germantown, TN, 2005).

9 The legality of this practice has been challenged since suicide is illegal under the Indian penal code. See W. M. Braun, 'Sallekhana: The Ethicality and Legality of Religious Suicide by Starvation in the Jain Religious Community', *Medicine and Law*, XXVII/4 (2008), pp. 913–24.

10 Sir Paul McCartney once wrote to the Dalai Lama to criticize him for eating meat. The Dalai Lama replied that his doctors had told him he needed it for his health, to which Sir Paul replied saying that they were wrong. 'Sir Paul McCartney's Advice to the Dalai Lama', *The Times*, 15 December 2008.

11 Patrick Olivelle, 'Kings, Ascetics, and Brahmins: The Socio-Political Context of Ancient Indian Religions', in *Dynamics in the History of Religions between Asia and Europe: Encounters, Notions and Comparative Perspectives*, ed. Volkhard Krech and Marion Steinicke (Leiden, 2012), p. 131.

12 Wendy Doniger, *The Hindus: An Alternative History* (New York, 2009), p. 256.

13 Rachel Laudan, *Cuisine and Empire: Cooking in World History* (Berkeley, CA, 2013), p. 73.

14 John Watson McCrindle, *Ancient India as Described by Megasthenes and Arrian* (Calcutta, 1877), p. 31.

15 Megasthenes may have divided Indians into seven castes in imitation of Herodotus, who categorized Egyptians as belonging to seven castes. From the time of Alexander the Great to as late as the nineteenth century, geographers and other writers drew analogies between ancient Egypt and India. McCrindle, *Ancient India*, p. 44.

16 Ibid., p. 99.

17 Quoted in Andrew Dalby, 'Alexander's Culinary Legacy', in *Cooks and Other People: Proceedings of the Oxford Symposium on Food and Cookery, 1995*, ed. Harlan Walker (Totnes, Devon, 1996), p. 82.

18 Ibid., p. 81.

19 Om Prakash, *Economy and Food in Ancient India*, Part II (New Delhi, 1987).

20 A. P. Nayak et al., 'A Contemporary Study of Yavagu (Prepared from Rice) as Pathyakalpana', *Ayurpharm: International Journal of Ayurveda and Allied Sciences*, I/1 (2013), pp. 9–13.

21 Prakash, *Economy and Food*, pp. 103–4.
22 V. S. Agrawala, *India as Known to Panini* (Calcutta, 1963), pp. 102–21.
23 'Kautilya's *Arthashastra*: Book 2: "The Duties of Government Superintendents"', trans. R. Shamasastry (Bangalore, 1915), available at www.sdstate.edu.
24 The mahua flower is edible and widely used by India's tribal groups to make a drink of the same name; the drink has become part of their cultural heritage.
25 Pankaj Goyal, 'Traditional Fermentation Technology': www.indianscience.org.

FOUR: Global India and the New Orthodoxy, 300 BCE–500 CE

1 Rachel Laudan, *Cuisine and Empire: Cooking in World History* (Berkeley, CA, 2013), p. 103.
2 Muziris, the exact site of which has never been found, is believed to have been destroyed in a great flood of the Periyar River in 1341. Puhar is thought to have been washed away by a tsunami in about 500 CE.
3 Jack Turner, *Spice: The History of a Temptation* (New York, 2004), p. 70.
4 Rohini Ramakrishnan, 'Connecting with the Romans', *The Hindu*, 24 January 2011.
5 Ibid.
6 Patrick Olivelle, trans., *Dharmasūtras: The Law Codes of Ancient India* (Oxford, 1999), p. xxxvii.
7 Ibid., pp. xlii–xliii.
8 *The Code of Manu* (first translated into English by William Jones in 1794) took on unprecedented status as an 'applied' legal document under early British rule. Even today the *Code* is one of the best-known Hindu texts, a fact underlined by its quotation in an episode of the popular American comedy programme *The Big Bang Theory*.
9 David Gordon White, 'You Are What You Eat: The Anomalous Status of Dog-Cookers in Hindu Mythology', in *The Eternal Food: Gastronomic Ideas and Experiences of Hindus and Buddhists*, ed. R. S. Khare (Albany, NY, 1992), p. 59.
10 Dharmasutra of Baudhayana, 3:32, in Olivelle, *Dharmasūtras*, p. 215.
11 Dharmasutra of Apastamba, 11:13, p. 52.
12 Patrick Olivelle, 'Abhaksya and Abhojya: An Exploration in Dietary Language', *Journal of the American Oriental Society*, CXXII (2002), pp. 345–54.
13 Mary Douglas, *Purity and Danger: An Analysis of Concepts of Pollution and Taboo* (London and New York, 2007), p. 67.
14 Louis Dumont, *Homo Hierarchicus: The Caste System and its Implications* (Chicago, IL, 1980), p. 141.
15 *The Code of Manu* contains only one reference to saliva: 'No expiation is prescribed for a man who drinks the saliva from the lips of a Sudra woman.'
16 According to the anthropologist R. S. Khare, the term 'orthodox' in food relations stands both for 'the ways of the forefathers that have "pastness", virtue and legitimacy and a nearness (even if assumed rather than real' and for 'textual, philosophical, and spiritual ideals'. Khare, *The Hindu Hearth and Home* (New Delhi, 1976), p. 48.

17 In the nineteenth century members of my husband's caste, vaidyas (medical doctors), petitioned the local brahmins to be allowed to eat in the same room as them during a festival rather than in a separate room.

18 M. N. Srinivas, *Religion and Society among the Coorgs of South India* (Oxford, 1952), p. 32.

19 M. N. Srinivas, 'Mobility in the Caste System', in *Structure and Change in Indian Society,* ed. Milton B. Singer and Bernard S. Cohn (Chicago, IL, 1968).

20 Quoted in Fa-Hien (Faxian), trans. James Legge, *A Record of Buddhistic Kingdoms* (Adelaide, 2014), chapter 16: http://ebooks.adelaide.edu.au.

21 'A Description of India in General by the Chinese Buddhism Pilgrim Hiuan Tsang', in *History of India*, vol. IX: *Historical Accounts of India by Foreign Travellers, Classic, Oriental and Occidental,* ed. A. V. Williams Jackson (London, 1907), pp. 130–31. I also used the translation by Thomas Watters, *On Yuan Chwang's Travels in India, 629–645 AD* (London, 1904), at www.archive.org.

22 Williams Jackson, *Historical Accounts*, pp. 138–9.

23 K. T. Achaya, *Indian Food: A Historical Companion* (New Delhi, 1994), p. 147.

24 I-Tsing (Yijing), *A Record of the Buddhist Religion as Practised in India and the Malay Archipelago*, trans. J. Takakusu (Oxford, 1896), pp. 40–44.

25 Hashi Raychaudhuri and Tapan Raychaudhuri, 'Not by Curry Alone: An Introduction to Indian Cuisines for a Western Audience', in *National and Regional Styles of Cookery: Oxford Symposium on Food History* (Totnes, 1981), p. 48.

26 Ibid., pp. 48–9.

27 H. N. Dubey, 'Agriculture in the Age of Sangam', in *History of Agriculture in India, up to c. 1200 AD*, ed. Lallanji Gopal and V. C. Srivastava (New Delhi, 2008), pp. 415–21.

28 Achaya, *Indian Food*, p. 45.

29 Quoted ibid., pp. 44–5.

FIVE: New Religious Trends and Movements: Feasting and Fasting, 500–1000 CE

1 Much has been written on this subject by Hindu and non-Hindu scholars. See, for example, K. M. Sen, *Hinduism* (London, 2005); Gavin D. Flood, *An Introduction to Hinduism* (Cambridge, 1996); Kim Knott, *Hinduism: A Very Short Introduction* (Oxford, 2000); and S. Radhakrishnan, *The Hindu View of Life* (London, 1927).

2 Sen, *Hinduism*, p. 29.

3 Today the best-known followers of Krishna outside India are members of the International Society for Krishna Consciousness (ISKCON), known popularly as the Hare Krishna movement, which was founded in New York in 1966. They follow a vegetarian diet and avoid onions and garlic.

4 Paul M. Toomey, 'Mountain of Food, Mountain of Love', in *The Eternal Food: Gastronomic Ideas and Experiences of Hindus and Buddhists*, ed. R. S. Khare (Albany, NY, 1992), pp. 117–46.

5 Paul M. Toomey, 'Krishna's Consuming Passions: Food as Metaphor and Metonym for Emotion at Mount Govardhan', in *Divine Passions: The Social Construction of Emotion in India*, ed. Owen M. Lynch (Berkeley, CA, 1990), p. 167.

6 Carol Appadurai Breckenridge, 'Food, Politics and Pilgrimage in South India, 1350–1640 AD', in *Food, Society and Culture: Aspects in South Asian Food Systems*, ed. R.S. Khare and M.S.A. Rao (Durham, NC, 1986), p. 68.

7 Alka Pande, *Mukhwas: Indian Food through the Ages* (Delhi, 2013), p. 70.

8 Manuel Moreno, 'Pancamirtam: God's Washings as Food', in Khare, *The Eternal Food*, p. 165.

9 Ibid., p. 149.

10 Roopa Varghese, 'Food in Indian Temples', *Indian Food Gourmet* (26 July 2008): www.indianfoodgourmet.com.

11 Stig Toft Madsen and Geoffrey Gardella, 'Udupi Hotels: Entrepreneurship, Reform and Revival', in *Consuming Modernity: Public Culture in a South Asian World*, ed. Carol Appadurai Breckenridge (Minneapolis, MN, 1995), p. 102.

12 These have been interpreted as inversions of the five products of the cow with which Hindus purify themselves (ghee, butter, milk, yoghurt and urine).

13 Arthur Avalon, trans., *Mahanirvana Tantra: Tantra of the Great Liberation* (1913), available at www.sacred-texts.com; 'Sugar Cane – Early Technology', www.kew.org, accessed 30 June 2014.

14 Diana L. Eck, *India: A Sacred Geography* (New York, 2012).

15 Kisari Mohan Ganguli, trans., *Mahabharata* (1883–96), part III, section 50, available at www.sacred-texts.com.

16 Cited in Indira Chakravarty, *Saga of Indian Food: A Historical and Cultural Survey* (New Delhi, 1972), pp. 24–5.

17 Padmini Sathianadhan Sengupta, *Everyday Life in Ancient India* (Bombay, 1950), pp. 547–8.

18 Ganguli, *Mahabharata*, part II, section 207, available at www.sacred-texts.com.

19 Trans. Ammini Ramachandran: http://peppertrail.com.

20 Ganguli, *Mahabharata*, part V, section 115.

21 Barbara Stoler Miller, trans., *The Bhagavad-Gita: Krishna's Counsel in Time of War* (New York, 1986), p. 138.

22 See, for example, Swami Vishnu-Devananda, *The Complete Illustrated Book of Yoga* (New York, 1988), pp. 204–19, and Swami Sivananda, *Kundalini Yoga* (Sivanangdanagar, India, 1991), pp. 8–11.

23 Arjun Appadurai, 'Gastropolitics in Hindu South Asia', *American Ethnologist*, VIII/3 (1981), pp. 494–511.

24 Joe Roberts and Colleen Taylor Sen, 'A Carp Wearing Lipstick: The Role of Fish in Bengali Cuisine and Culture', in *Fish: Food from the Waters: Proceedings of the Oxford Symposium of Food and Cookery, 1997*, ed. Harlan Walker (Totnes, Devon, 1998), pp. 252–8.

25 Moni Nag, 'Beliefs and Practices about Food During Pregnancy', *Economic and Political Weekly* (10 September 1994), pp. 2427–38.

SIX: Food and Indian Doctors, 600 BCE–600 CE

1 Cakrapanidatta, quoted in Dominik Wujastyk, *The Roots of Ayurveda: Selections from Sanskrit Medical Writings* (London, 2001), p. 8.
2 Ken Albala, *Food in Early Modern Europe* (Westport, CT, 2003), p. 216.
3 Manu claimed that physicians were ambasthas, born of a brahmin father and a vaisya mother.
4 *The Sushruta Samhita: An English Translation Based on Original Sanskrit Texts*, trans. Kaviraj Kunja Lal Bhishagratna, 3 vols (New Delhi, 2006).
5 See, for example, Tina Hesman Saey, 'Gut Bacteria May Affect Cardiovascular Risk', *Science News*, 4 December 2012: www.sciencenews.org; and Susan Young Rojahn, 'Transplanted Gut Bugs Protect Mice from Diabetes', MIT *Technology Review*, 21 January 2013: www.technologyreview.com.
6 Quoted in K. T. Achaya, *Indian Food: A Historical Companion* (New Delhi, 1994), p. 76.
7 Francis Zimmermann, *The Jungle and the Aroma of Meats: An Ecological Theme in Hindu Medicine* (Berkeley, CA, 1987), p. 116.
8 The origin of the word 'jungle'. In the late eighteenth or early nineteenth century the word acquired its present-day meaning of forest or tangled wilderness. See Henry Yule and A. C. Burnell, *Hobson-Jobson: A Glossary of Colloquial Anglo-Indian Words and Phrases, and of Kindred Terms, Etymological, Historical, Geographical and Discursive* (London and Boston, MA, 1985), p. 470.
9 Large herds of antelope once roamed northern India, but following Independence in 1947 a massacre took place (comparable to those in the 1880s on the American prairie) when the regulations abolishing hunting with rifles, considered a form of colonial oppression, were abolished. Hunters roamed the countryside at night, and India's antelope population was virtually exterminated. Today it survives in a few sanctuaries. Zimmermann, *The Jungle*, p. 58.
10 Kṣēmaśarmā, trans. R. Shankar, *Kṣēmakutūhalam: A Work on Dietetics and Well-being* (Bangalore, 2009), p. 115. This is another example of the depth of ancient wisdom. The ghee-making process concentrates the conjugated linoleic acid (a cancer fighter and atherosclerosis preventer) of the butter, making ghee healthier than butter. The process also changes the fat profile so ghee is more robust, with a longer shelf-life and higher smoke point. Ghee does not go rancid and therefore is healthier than butter. Dr Kantha Shelke, personal communication.
11 An attempt to launch a urine-based soft drink called *gau jal* ('cow water') in 2009 was abandoned. (See Dean Nelson, 'India Makes Cola from Cow Urine', *The Telegraph*, 11 February 2009.) Far from being an ancient Indian practice, drinking one's own urine as a therapy gained currency only in the 1940s, when the British naturopath John W. Armstrong published a book claiming that the practice could cure most diseases. The practice gained worldwide publicity when India's prime minister Morarji Desai said in an interview that drinking his own urine had cured his piles and that urine

therapy was the perfect medical solution for the millions of Indians unable to afford medical treatment. See Prasenjit Chowdhury, 'Curative Elixir: Waters of India', *The Times of India*, 27 July 2009.

12 Kṣēmaśarmā, trans. R. Shankar, *Kṣēmakutūhalam*, pp. 417–18.

13 Aparna Chattopadhyay, 'Studies in Ancient Indian Medicine', post-doctoral thesis, Varanasi, India, 1993, pp. 75–82.

14 Wujastyk, *The Roots of Ayurveda*, p. 42.

15 Quoted in ibid., pp. 202, 206.

16 Quoted in ibid., p. 204.

17 In 1742 Benjamin Franklin wrote in *Poor Richard's Almanack*, 'After Fish, Milk do not Wish.' Eating milk and fish together was believed to cause skin diseases, including leprosy. However, there is no clinical evidence that this is true. See Eric Silla, 'After Fish, Milk Do Not Wish: Recurring Ideas in a Global Culture', *Cahiers études africaines*, xxxv/144 (1996), pp. 613–24.

18 Robert E. Svoboda, *Ayurveda: Life, Health and Longevity* (New Delhi, 1993), pp. 118–20.

19 Caroline Rowe, 'Thalis of India', in *Food and Material Culture: Proceedings of the Oxford Symposium on Food and Cookery, 2013*, ed. Mark McWilliams (Totnes, Devon, 2014), pp. 264–71.

20 See, for example, Swami Vishnu-Devananda, *The Complete Illustrated Book of Yoga* (New York, 1988), pp. 204–19, and Swami Sivananda, *Kundalini Yoga* (Sivanangdanagar, India, 1991), pp. 8–11.

21 For a detailed study of food practices among North Indian brahmins, see R. S. Khare, *The Hindu Hearth and Home* (New Delhi, 1976).

22 While water boils at 100°C (212°F), the smoking point of oils (the temperature at which they start to burn) ranges from 121°C (250°F) to as high as 270°C (520°F). Ghee has a high smoking point of 190°C (375°F) compared with 121°C (250°F) for unclarified butter.

23 A. L. Basham, 'The Practice of Medicine in Ancient and Medieval India', in *Asian Medical Systems: A Comparative Study*, ed. Charles Leslie (New Delhi, 1998), pp. 19–20.

24 A suggested alternative derivation is that the Unani system comes from Yunnan province in China, perhaps because of similarities between Chinese and Indian medicine, including the hot–cold dichotomy.

25 A search of the United States National Institute of Health's PubMed database in January 2013 found 2,143 articles on studies or trials that involved applying Ayurvedic remedies to such diverse medical problems as diabetes, cancer, tuberculosis and even depression. See www.ncbi.nlm.nih.gov.

SEVEN: The Middle Ages: The *Manasollasa, Lokopakara* and Regional Cuisines, 600–1300 CE

1 Arjun Appadurai, 'How to Make a National Cuisine: Cookbooks in Contemporary India', *Comparative Studies in Sociology and History*, xxx/1 (1988), pp. 3–24.

2 Ibid., pp. 12–13.

3 The only English translation, by Dr (Mrs) P. Arundhati (New Delhi, 1994), is more of a paraphrase than a translation and contains inconsistencies, misspellings and mistranslations. I enlisted the help of Jessica Navright, a Sanskrit scholar and graduate student in the South Asian Department, University of Chicago, who retranslated many unclear passages using the version of *Mansasollassa* published in Gaekwad's Oriental Series, vols I, II and III (Baroda, India, 1939). She also provided many useful comments and background information.

4 A passage in the *Manasolassa* (1.4v: 45–52) contains a list of forbidden foods, including carrot, onion and garlic and the meat of tigers, crows, monkeys, lions, elephants, horses, parrots, hawks and 'all village animals and birds'. However, some of the recipes in the book use these ingredients. The list was probably inserted to pay lip service to the rules laid down for proper Hindu dietary habits.

5 K. T. Achaya, *A Historical Dictionary of Indian Food* (New Delhi, 2002), p. 61.

6 *Oggarane* means 'spice' in modern Kannada, and a popular cooking show is called *Oggarane Dabbi*, or 'spice box'.

7 The first mention of the idli is in a tenth-century Kannada work, but rice was not part of it until the thirteenth century. See Achaya, *A Historical Dictionary of Indian Food*, p. 61.

8 Kishori Prasad Sahu, *Some Aspects of Indian Social Life, 1000–1526 AD* (Calcutta, 1973), p. 34.

9 Quoted ibid., p. 42.

10 *Gazetteer of the Bombay Presidency*, vol. I, part 1, p. 531.

11 Taponath Chakravarty, *Food and Drink in Ancient Bengal* (Calcutta, 1959), p. 6.

12 'The Charypada', available at www.oocities.org, accessed 1 July 2014.

13 France Bhattacharya, trans. Radha Sharma, 'Food Rituals in the "Chandi Mangala"', *India International Centre Quarterly*, XII/2 (June 1985), pp. 169–92.

14 Ibid., pp. 188–9.

15 Om Prakash, *Economy and Food in Ancient India* (New Delhi, 1987), pp. 358–9.

16 Marco Polo, *The Travels* (London and Harmondsworth, 1974); see also Namit Arora, 'Marco Polo's India', *Kyoto Journal*, LXXIV (June 2010), available at www.shunya.net.

17 Achaya, *A Historical Dictionary of Indian Food* (New Delhi, 2002), p. 97.

EIGHT: The Delhi Sultanate: *Ni'Matnama, Supa Shastra* and *Ksemakutuhalam*, 1300–1550

1 For a description of Muslim feasts in India, see Christopher P. H. Murphy, 'Piety and Honor: The Meaning of Muslim Feasts in Old Delhi' in *Food, Society and Culture: Aspects in South Asian Food Systems*, ed. R. S. Khare and M.S.A. Rao (Durham, NC, 1986), pp. 85–119.

2 Christopher P. H. Murphy, 'Piety and Honor: The Meaning of Muslim Feasts in Old Delhi', in *Food, Society and Culture*, pp. 98–100.

3 K. Gajendra Singh, 'Contribution of Turkic Languages in the Evolution and Development of Hindustani Languages', at www.cs.colostate.edu, accessed 9 July 2014.

4 Much of the following description comes from Iqtidar Husain Siddiqi, 'Food Dishes and the Catering Profession in Pre-Mughal India', *Islamic Culture*, LIV/2 (April 1985), pp. 117–74, and Kishori Prasad Sahu, *Some Aspects of Indian Social Life, 1000–1526 AD* (Calcutta, 1973).

5 The word derives from the Arabic *shariba*, 'to drink'. Related English words are sherbet, sorbet, syrup and shrub (a drink popular during the American colonial era).

6 Muhammad ibn al-Hasan ibn Al-Karim (the scribe of Baghdad), *A Baghdad Cookery Book: The Book of Dishes*, trans. Charles Perry (Totnes, Devon, 2005), p. 78.

7 Siddiqi, 'Food Dishes and the Catering Profession', pp. 124–5.

8 According to Charles Perry, personal communication, the earliest reference to shorba (which in Persian signifies a dish cooked with salt water) is in the *Kitab-Al-Tabikh*, a tenth-century Arab cookbook, which describes how the dish was prepared for a sixth-century Persian king. The meat was boiled lightly, removed from the water (which was thrown away) and then cooked with fresh water, salt, cinnamon and galangal.

9 The culinary term for this is *betel quid*, a phrase related to the word cud, meaning something that is chewed for a long time. *Paan* comes from the Sanskrit word *parṣa*, 'feather' or 'leaf'. A synonym is *tambula*, which refers to both betel leaf and the quid itself.

10 In October 2013 the Indian government banned the manufacture and sale of *gutka* and chewing tobacco, citing the health risks and economic cost. India has one of the highest rates of oral cancer in the world, and it is the leading cause of cancer deaths among men.

11 Quoted in Muzaffar Alam and Sanjay Subrahmanyam, *Indo-Persian Travels in the Age of Discoveries, 1400–1800* (Cambridge, 2007), p. 75.

12 Quoted in Siddiqi, 'Food Dishes and the Catering Profession', p. 130.

13 Quoted in Sahu, *Some Aspects of Indian Social Life*, p. 63.

14 Iqtidar Husain Siddiqi, *Perso-Arabic Sources of Information on the Life and Conditions in the Sultanate of Delhi* (New Delhi, 1992), p. 115.

15 Shahzad Ghorasian, personal communication.

16 Henry Yule and A. C. Burnell, *Hobson-Jobson: A Glossary of Colloquial Anglo-Indian Words and Phrases*, 2nd edn (London, 1986), p. 710.

17 The word *gharib* can mean either 'foreign' or 'humble, poor'. Although the translator uses the first meaning, the second seems more appropriate in the context.

18 Many of the recipes were tested by modern homemakers, who noted that the instructions were clear and easily followed and the food not difficult to cook in the present context. Many items are part of Karnataka cuisine today, including roti, mandige, dosa made with different grains, and vada. Madhukar Konantambigi, trans., *Culinary Traditions of Medieval Karnataka: The Soopa Shastra of Mangarasa III*, ed. N. P. Bhat and Nerupama Y. Modwel (Delhi, 2012), p. 107.

19 Kṣēmaśarmā, trans. R. Shankar, *Kṣēmakutūhalam: A Work on Dietetics and Well-being* (Bangalore, 2009).
20 Ammini Ramachandran, private communication.
21 Kṣēmaśarmā, *Kṣēmakutūhalam*, p. 171.
22 Ibid., pp. 225–7.
23 Ibid., p. 192.
24 Quoted in Robert Sewell, *A Forgotten Empire (Vijayanagar): A Contribution to the History of India* (London, 1900), p. 237.

NINE: The Mughal Dynasty and its Successors, 1526–1857

1 Quoted in Salma Husain, *The Emperor's Table: The Art of Mughal Cuisine* (New Delhi, 2008), p. 29.
2 Babur (Zahiru'd-din Muhammad Babur Padshah Ghazi), *Babur-Nama: Memoirs of Babur*, trans. Annette Susannah Beveridge (New Delhi, 1989), vol. I, p. 3.
3 Ibid., vol. II, pp. 517–18.
4 Knives and spoons were apparently in use at the time. A chronicler wrote of one of Babur's dinner parties: 'A piece of fish was kept in the dish of Sherkhan [one of his courtiers] but Sherkhan, finding difficulty in tackling it, cut it into small pieces with a knife and then ate them with a spoon.' Kishori Prasad Sahu, *Some Aspects of Indian Social Life, 1000–1526 AD* (Calcutta, 1973), p. 33.
5 Opium had reached India by the twelfth century from West Asia, and was initially used as medicine. The first record of its cultivation dates from the fifteenth century. The Mughals made it a state monopoly, which was later taken over by the British. In the sixteenth century it became an important article of trade between India and China and other countries. By the seventeenth century the use of opium became more common among all classes as a replacement for alcohol, although it was banned by Emperor Aurangzeb. See S. P. Sangar, 'Intoxicants in Mughal India', *Indian Journal of History of Science*, XVI/2 (November 1981), pp. 202–14.
6 Quoted in Joyce Pamela Westrip, 'Some Persian Influences on the Cooking of India' in *Proceedings of the Oxford Symposium on Food and Cookery, 1984*, ed. Tom Jaine (Totnes, Devon, 1985), p. 74.
7 The Islamic sect called Sufism began in Iraq in the second half of the seventh century as a reaction against what some saw as the growing worldliness of Muslims. Its antecedents were a group contemporary with the Prophet, called *Ahi al-suffa* (People of the Bench) because of their practice of remaining in the mosque all day and night in devotion. Sufis embraced poverty, abstinence from worldly pleasures and intensive fasting as a method of self-discipline, purification and opening the soul to God. While not strictly vegetarian, they maintained the sense that eating meat could be deleterious to spirituality. A thirteenth-century Sufi master wrote: 'Be careful of your diet. It is better if your food be nourishing but devoid of animal fat.' Valerie J. Hoffman, 'Eating and Fasting for God in Sufi Tradition', *Journal of the American Academy of Religion*, LXIII/3 (1995), pp. 465–84. For a contemporary discussion of Islam and vegetarianism, see http://islamicconcern.com.

8 Abu'l-Fazl ibn Mubarak Allami, *The Ain i Akbari*, trans. H. Blochmann [1873] (New Delhi, 1989). Abu'l-Fazl himself was described as having an extraordinary appetite, consuming 22 sers (about 45 kg/99 lb) of food each day. He was murdered under the orders of Akbar's son Salim, who was jealous of his influence.

9 J. S. Hoyland, trans., *The Commentary of Father Monserrate, sj, on his Journey to the Court of Akbar* [1591] (London, 1922), from an excerpt at www.columbia.edu.

10 The word *kashk* and its cognates (including *kishik, keshk*) denote a very wide range of dishes found throughout the Middle East, Egypt and Central Asia, involving either a sour milk product or fermented barley or, more generally, requiring complex preparation. See Françoise Aubaile-Sallenave, 'Al-Kishk: The Past and Present of a Complex Culinary Practice' in *A Taste of Thyme: Culinary Cultures of the Middle East*, ed. Sami Zubaida and Richard Tapper (London, 2000), pp. 105–39. The word *shulla* had its origin in various Mongolian and Turkic languages, where it appears as *shilen, shilan, shölen, shülen, shilen* and so on, plus various forms without the 'n'. Charles Perry, private communication.

11 Michael H. Fisher, ed., *Visions of Mughal India: An Anthology of European Travel Writing* (London and New York, 2007), p. ix.

12 K. T. Achaya, *A Historical Dictionary of Indian Food* (New Delhi, 2002), p. 43.

13 Willem Floor, 'Tobacco', *Encyclopaedia Iranica*, 20 July 2009, www.iranicaonline.org/articles/tobacco.

14 Quoted in Annemarie Schimmel, *The Empire of the Great Mughals: History, Art and Culture* (London, 2004), p. 194.

15 Quoted in ibid., p. 193.

16 Abu'l-Fazl, *The Ain i Akbari*, p. 59.

17 Ibid., p. 64.

18 *The Tuzuk-i-jahangiri; or, Memoirs of Jahangir*, trans. Alexander Rogers, ed. Henry Beveridge (London, 1900), p. 419, available at http://archive.org.

19 Achaya, *A Historical Dictionary of Indian Food*, p. 162.

20 Ibid., pp. 162–3.

21 Quoted in Chakravarty, *Saga of Indian Food*, p. 73.

22 Abdul Halim Sharar, *Lucknow: The Last Phase of an Oriental Culture*, trans. E. S. Harcourt and Fakhir Hussain (Delhi, 1994), p. 13.

23 Quoted in William Dalrymple, *White Mughals: Love and Betrayal in Eighteenth-century India* (London, 2002), p. 266.

24 Sharar, *Lucknow*, p. 157.

25 Ibid., p. 159.

26 For an analysis of the dish and the legend, see Holly Shaffer, 'Dum Pukht: A Pseudo-Historical Cuisine', in Krishnendu Ray and Tulasi Srinivas, *Curried Cultures: Globalization, Food and South Asia* (Berkeley, CA, 2012), pp. 110–25.

27 See Mukul Mangalik, 'Lucknow Food, Streets, and Bazaars', 16 May 2007: www.gourmetindia.com; also Margo True, 'Fragrant Feasts of Lucknow', *Saveur*, 78 (October 2004), pp. 56–72.

28 Quoted in Michael H. Fisher, ed., *Visions of Mughal India: An Anthology of European Travel Writing* (London and New York, 2007), p. ix.

29 Ja'far Sharif, ed. and trans. Gerhard Andreas Herklots, *Qanoon-e-Islam, or, The Customs of the Moosulmans of India; Comprising a Full and Exact Account of their Various Rites and Ceremonies, from the Moment of Birth Till the Hour of Death* (London, 1832).

30 Sidq Jaisi (pen name of Mirza Tassaduz Hussain), *The Nocturnal Court, Darbaar-e-Durbaar: The Life of a Prince of Hyderabad*, trans. Narendra Luther (New Delhi, 2004), p. 12.

31 Ibid., p. xxxv.

TEN: The Europeans, the Princes and their Legacy, 1500–1947

1 Michael Krondl, *The Taste of Conquest: The Rise and Fall of the Three Great Cities of Spice* (New York, 2007), p. 116.

2 Minakshie Das Gupta, Bunny Gupta and Jaya Chaliha, *The Calcutta Cook Book: A Treasury of Over 200 Recipes from Pavement to Palace* (New Delhi, 1995), p. 148.

3 Colleen Taylor Sen, 'Sandesh: The Emblem of Bengaliness', in *Milk: Beyond the Dairy, Proceedings of the Oxford Symposium on Food and Cookery, 1999*, ed. Harlan Walker (Totnes, Devon, 2000), pp. 300–308.

4 See, for example, Carl Johanssen, 'Pre-Columbia American Sunflower and Maize Images in Indian Temples: Evidence of Contact between Civilizations in India and America', *NEARA Journal*, XXXII/1 (Summer 1998), pp. 164–80; and Johanssen, 'Considerations of Asian Crops Indicate Longstanding Transoceanic Pre-Columbian Contacts', *Epigraphic Society Occasional Paper*, XXV (2006), pp. 5–12. A more radical version of this theory holds that there was even earlier contact between South America, the Pacific Islands, Indonesia and India, and that the ancient Indians were the origins of the ancient civilizations of the New World. This is based on depictions of what appear to be Hindu deities and animals (such as the elephant) in Aztec and Mayan ruins, and similarities in social, religious and political structures and, of course, food – the tortilla/chapatti similarity is cited as a prime example. See Chaman Lal, *Hindu America?* (Bombay, 1941).

5 Ruben L. Villareal, *Tomatoes in the Tropics* (Boulder, CO, 1980), p. 56.

6 William Roxburgh, *Flora Indica: or, Descriptions of Indian Plants*, ed. William Carey, vol. 1 (Serampore, India, 1832), p. 565.

7 Rachel Laudan, 'Why 1492 is a Non-Event in Culinary History', 16 December 2009: www.rachellaudan.com.

8 Garcia de Orta, trans. Sir Clements Markham, *Colloquies on the Simples and Drugs of India* (London, 1913).

9 Ibid., pp. 44–5.

10 For an interesting account of the history and role of bhang in India, see Dominik Wujastyk, 'Cannabis in Traditional Indian Herbal Medicine', in *Ayurveda at the Crossroads of Care and Cure: Proceedings of the Indo-European Seminar on Ayurveda Held at Arrábida, Portugal, in November 2001*, ed. Anna Salema (Lisbon, 2002), pp. 45–73.

11 Lourdes Tirouvanziam-Louis, *The Pondicherry Kitchen: Traditional Recipes from the Indo-French Territory* (Chennai, 2012).

12 David Burton, *The Raj at Table: A Culinary History of the British in India* (London, 1993), pp. 3–4.

13 Henry Hobbs, *John Barley Bahadur: Old Time Taverns in India* (Calcutta, 1944) p. 127.

14 Ibid., p. 35.

15 Jayanta Sengupta, 'Nation on a Platter: The Culture and Politics of Food in Colonial Bengal', in Krishnendu Ray and Tulasi Srinivas, *Curried Cultures: Globalization, Food and South Asia* (Berkeley, CA, 2012), p. 74.

16 Eleanor Bobb, *The Raj Cookbook* (Delhi, 1981), p. 10.

17 Shrabani Basu, *Victoria and Abdul: The True Story of the Queen's Closest Confidant* (London, 2011), pp. 129–30.

18 Quoted in Burton, *The Raj at Table*, p. 84.

19 Caroline Rowe, 'Fermented Nagaland: A Culinary Adventure' in *Cured, Fermented and Smoked Foods, Proceedings of the Oxford Symposium on Food and Cookery, 2010*, ed. Helen Saberi (Totnes, Devon, 2011), pp. 263–77.

20 Alan Pryor, 'Indian Pale Ale: An Icon of Empire' in *Global Histories, Imperial Commodities, Local Interactions*, ed. Jonathan Curry-Machado (New York, 2013), pp. 38–57. For a slightly different account, see Martyn Cornell, 'Hodgon's Brewer, Bow and the Birth of IPA', *Brewery History*, 111 (2003), pp. 63–8.

21 For a list of Indian clubs, see 'List of India's Gentlemen's Clubs', http://en.wikipedia.org, accessed 30 June 2014.

22 Kal Raustiala, 'The Imperial Cocktail', *Slate* (28 August 2013): www.slate.com.

23 See Patricia Brown, *Anglo-Indian Food and Customs* (Delhi, 1998).

24 For a full listing of the princely states, see http://princelystatesofindia.com and 'List of Indian Princely States', http://en.wikipedia.org, accessed 30 June 2014.

25 Anna Jackson and Jaffer Amin, eds, *Maharaja: The Splendour of India's Royal Courts* (London, 2009).

26 Neha Prasada and Ashima Narain, *Dining with the Maharajas: A Thousand Years of Culinary Tradition* (New Delhi, 2013), *passim*.

27 Government of Rajasthan, Integrated Excise Management System, 'Heritage Liqueur': https://rajexcise.gov.in.

28 Ammini Ramachandran, *Grains, Greens and Grated Coconuts: Recipes and Remembrances of a Vegetarian Legacy* (Lincoln, NE, 2007), pp. 142–3.

29 Digvijaya Singh, *Cooking Delights of the Maharajahs: Exotic Dishes from the Princely House of Sailana* (Bombay, 1982). Manju Shivraj Singh, *A Taste of Palace Life: Royal Indian Cookery* (Leicester, 1987). Another book of recipes by a member of the Indore royal family and his American wife is Shivaji Rao Holkar and Shalini Devi Holkar, *Cooking of the Maharajas: The Royal Recipes of India* (New York, 1975).

30 S. Vivekenanda, *Patrabali Letters*, 5th edn (Calcutta, 1987), quoted in Jayanta Sengupta, 'Nation on a Platter', in *Curried Cultures: Globalization, Food and South Asia*, ed. Krishnendu Ray and Tulasi Srinivas (Berkeley, CA, 2012), p. 85.

31 Mohandas K. Gandhi, *Autobiography: The Story of my Experiments with Truth*, trans. Mahadev Desai (New York, 1983).

32 Ibid., p. 43.
33 M. K. Gandhi, *Key to Health*, trans. Sushila Nayar (Ahmedabad, 1948).
34 Gandhi's grandson Arun Gandhi denies that his grandfather followed this practice.
35 *Young India*, 10 June 1921.
36 *The Mind of Mohatma Gandhi: The Complete Book*, p. 118, at www.mkgandhi.org.

ELEVEN: An Overview of Indian Cuisine: The Meal, Cooking Techniques and Regional Variations

1 K. T. Achaya, *Indian Food: A Historical Companion* (New Delhi, 1994), p. 57.
2 Quoted in Krishnendu Ray, *The Migrant's Table: Meals and Memories in Bengali-American Households* (Philadelphia, PA, 2004), pp. 28–9.
3 Caroline Rowe, 'Thalis of India', in *Food and Material Culture: Proceedings of the Oxford Symposium on Food and Cookery, 2013*, ed. Mark McWilliams (Totnes, Devon, 2014), pp. 264–71.
4 Geeta Samtani, *A Taste of Kashmir* (London, 1995); Shyam Rani Kilam and Kaul Kilam, *Culinary Art of Kashmir: A Cook Book of all Popular Kashmiri Dishes* (New Delhi, n.d.), available at www.ikashmir.net; M.S.W. Khan et al., *Wazwaan: Traditional Kashmiri Cuisine* (New Delhi, 2007). For an overview of the debate on GM foods in India, see Michael Specter, 'Seeds of Doubt', *New Yorker*, 25 August 2014, pp. 46–57.
5 Shanaz Ramzi, *Food Prints: An Epicurean Voyage through Pakistan: Overview of Pakistani Cuisine* (Karachi, 2012), pp. 7–11.
6 Ibid., pp. 101–4, and Aroona Reejhsinghani, *The Essential Sindhi Cookbook* (New Delhi, 2004).
7 Kaumudi Marathé, *The Essential Marathi Cookbook* (New Delhi, 2009); Hermalata Dandekar, *Beyond Curry: Quick and Easy Indian Cooking Featuring Cuisine from Maharashtra State* (Ann Arbor, MI, 1983).
8 Maria Teresa Menezes, *The Essential Goa Cookbook* (New Delhi, 2000); Mridula Baljekar, *A Taste of Goa* (London, 1995).
9 The bible of Tamil cooking is S. Meenakshi Ammal's *Cook and See* (*Samaithu Par*) (Madras, 1991). It was first self-published by the author in Tamil in 1951 to teach young brides how to cook traditional vegetarian Tamil dishes. In 1972 it was translated into English with the traditional Tamil measurements (ollocks, palams) converted to metric units. See www.meenakshiammal.com.
10 Alamelu Vairavan, *Chettinad Kitchen: Food and Flavours from South India* (New Chennai, India, 2010).
11 K. M. Mathew, *Kerala Cookery* (Kottayam, India, 1964); Vijayan Kannampilly, *The Essential Kerala Cookbook* (New Delhi, 2003); and Ammini Ramachandran, *Grains, Greens and Grated Coconuts: Recipes and Remembrances of a Vegetarian Legacy* (Lincoln, NE, 2007).
12 Ramachandran, *Grains, Greens and Grated Coconuts*, p. 56.
13 Lathika George, *The Kerala Kitchen: Recipes and Recollections from the Syrian Christians of South India* (New York, 2009).

14 Bilkees I. Latif, *The Essential Andhra Cookbook with Hyderabadi Specialties* (New Delhi, 1999).

15 Minakshie Das Gupta, Bunny Gupta and Jaya Chaliha, *The Calcutta Cook Book: A Treasury of over 200 Recipes from Pavement to Palace* (New Delhi, 1995); and Chitrita Banerji, *Life and Food in Bengal* (New Delhi, 1993).

16 Joe Roberts and Colleen Taylor Sen, 'A Carp Wearing Lipstick: The Role of Fish in Bengali Cuisine and Culture', in *Fish: Food from the Waters: Proceedings of the Oxford Symposium of Food and Cookery, 1997*, ed. Harlan Walker (Totnes, Devon, 1998), pp. 252–8.

17 Laxmi Parida, *Purba: Feasts from the East: Oriya Cuisine from Eastern India* (New York, 2003).

18 Hoihnu Hauzel, *The Essential North-East Cookbook* (New Delhi, 2003).

19 Caroline Rowe, 'Fermented Nagaland: A Culinary Adventure' in *Cured, Fermented and Smoked Foods, Proceedings of the Oxford Symposium on Food and Cookery, 2010*, ed. Helen Saberi (Totnes, Devon, 2011), pp. 263–77.

20 Colleen Taylor Sen, 'The Forest Foodways of India's Tribals' in *Wild Food: Proceedings of the Oxford Symposium on Food and Cookery 2004*, ed. Richard Hosking (Totnes, Devon, 2006), pp. 285–90.

TWELVE: New Trends in Indian Food, 1947–Present

1 P. Sainath, 'Farmers' Suicide Rates Soar Above the Rest', *The Hindu*, 18 May 2013.

2 International Food Policy Research Institute, '2012 Global Hunger Index', 2012, at www.ifpri.org.

3 Vikas Bajaj, 'As Grain Piles Up, India's Poor Still Go Hungry', *New York Times*, 7 June 2012.

4 Navdanya, *Bhoole Bisre Anaj: Forgotten Foods* (New Delhi, 2006), foreword. *Navdanya* means both 'new gift' and 'nine seeds' in Sanskrit, a reference to the nine ancient grains and lentils of India. For an overview of the debate on GM foods in India, see Michael Specter, 'Seeds of Doubt', *New Yorker*, 25 August 2014, pp. 46–57.

5 See Rukmini Shrnivasan, 'Middle Class: Who are They?', *Times of India*, 1 December 2012: www.timescrest.com; and Christian Meyer and Nancy Birdsall, 'New Estimates of India's Middle Class: Technical Note', November 2012: www.cgdev.org.

6 Y. Yadav and S. Kumar, 'The Food Habits of a Nation', *The Hindu*, 14 August 2006.

7 R. S. Khare, *The Hindu Hearth and Home* (New Delhi, 1976), pp. 244–63.

8 Ibid., p. 246.

9 Compare this with Sung China (960–1279 CE), where a restaurant culture flourished. The capital cities Haifeng and Hangchow were home to hundreds of elegantly decorated restaurants serving regional delicacies and alcoholic beverages in both private rooms and commonal dining areas. Their patrons were wealthy merchants and officials who valued connoisseurship and

experimentation: 'Mobile, experimental, and egalitarian in temper, little influenced by dietary taboos, they brought about the creation of a Chinese cuisine', writes Michael Freeman in 'Sung', in *Food in Chinese Culture: Anthropological and Historical Perspectives*, ed. K. C. Chang (New Haven, CT, 1977), p. 175.

10 For a more comprehensive description of Indian and world street food, see Bruce Kraig and Colleen Taylor Sen, *Street Food Around the World: An Encyclopedia of Food and Culture* (Santa Barbara, CA, 2013).

11 In Indian English, the word 'hotel' denotes 'any establishment, even a roadside stall, open to all and serving meals'. Nigel B. Hankin, *Hanklyn-Janklyn; or, A Stranger's Rumble-Tumble Guide to Some Words, Customs, and Quiddities Indian and Indo-British* (New Delhi, 1992), p. 88.

12 For a history of restaurants in Mumbai, see Frank F. Conlon, 'Dining out in Bombay', in *Consuming Modernity: Public Culture in a South Asian World*, ed. Carol Appadurai Breckenridge (Minneapolis, MN, 1995), pp. 90–127.

13 Colleen Taylor Sen and Ashish Sen, 'In Delhi, it's the Moti Mahal', *Christian Science Monitor* (5 October 1988), and Monish Gujral, *Moti Mahal's Tandoori Trail* (Delhi, 1994).

14 See USDA Foreign Agricultural Service, *Wine Market Update 2012*, Report no. IN2162, 24 December 2012, and Western Australia Trade Office – India, *Indian Wine Industry Report*, January 2012.

15 See www.busybeeforever.com, accessed 30 June 2014.

16 See www.uppercrustindia.com, accessed 30 June 2014.

17 See 'Diabetes in India', www.diabetes.co.uk, and Mark Bergen, 'No Answers in Sight for India's Diabetes Crisis', *Time*, 12 May 2013.

18 See, for example, Sheela Rani Chunkath, 'Easy Herbal Route to Tackle Diabetes', *New Indian Express*, 9 December 2012: http://newindianexpress.com.

THIRTEEN: The Food of the Indian Diaspora

1 There is evidence that some were slaves. See Francis C. Assisi, 'Indian Slaves in Colonial America', *New Indian Express*, 16 May 2007: www.indiacurrents.com.

2 See the report *The Indian Diaspora* published by the Indian Government in 1994, at http://indiandiaspora.nic.in.

3 Earlier the French had recruited artisans and other workers from their Indian colonies.

4 V. S. Naipaul, *An Area of Darkness* (London and Harmondsworth, 1968), p. 30.

5 See the chapter on food in G. A. Grierson, *Bihar Peasant Life* [1885] (Delhi, 1975).

6 Yasmin Alibhai-Brown, *The Settler's Cookbook: A Memoir of Love, Migration and Food* (London, 2008), p. 103.

7 Laurens van der Post, *African Cooking* (New York, 1970), p. 124.

8 'Fish and Chips Crowned the UK's Favourite Takeaway', *The Sun*, 12 October 2012: www.thesun.co.uk.

9 Every Englishman received a 20-ha (50-acre) land grant for each worker or servant he 'imported' to the colony. See 'The Geography of Slavery in Virginia', project compiled by Thomas Costa, Professor of History, University of Virginia's College at Wise: www.vcdh.virginia.edu/gos.

10 For a study of these Bengali immigrants and their descendants, see Vivek Bald, *Bengali Harlem and the Lost Histories of South Asian America* (Cambridge, MA, 2013).

11 See Karen Leonard, *Making Ethnic Choices: California's Punjabi Mexican Americans* (Philadelphia, PA, 1991), and Leonard, 'California's Punjabi Mexican Americans', 1989, at www.sikhpioneers.org.

12 Krishnendu Ray, 'Indian American Food', in *The Oxford Companion to American Food and Drink*, ed. Andrew F. Smith (Oxford, 2007), p. 317.

Select Bibliography

Achaya, K. T., *Indian Food: A Historical Companion* (New Delhi, 1994)
——, *A Historical Dictionary of Indian Food* (New Delhi, 2002)
Agrawala, V. S., *India as Known to Panini* (Calcutta, 1963)
Allami, Abu'l-Fazl al Mubarak, *The Ain i Akbari*, trans. H. Blochmann [1873]
    (New Delhi, 1989)
Alsdorf, Ludwig, *The History of Vegetarianism and Cow Veneration in India*,
    trans. Bal Patil, ed. Willem Bollée (London, 2010)
Appadurai, Arjun, 'How to Make a National Cuisine: Cookbooks in
    Contemporary India,' *Comparative Studies in Sociology and History*, XXX/1
    (1988), pp. 3–24
——, 'Gastropolitics in Hindu South Asia', *American Ethnologist*, VIII/3 (1980),
    pp. 494–511
Asher, Catherine B., and Cynthia Talbot, *India before Europe* (Cambridge, 2006)
Auboyer, Jeannine, *Daily Life in Ancient India from Approximately 200 BC to 700
    AD*, trans. Simon Watson Taylor (London, 1965)
Babur (Zahiru'd-din Muhammad Babur Padshah Ghazi), *Babur-Nama: Memoirs
    of Babur*, trans. Annette Susannah Beveridge (New Delhi, 1989)
Basham, A. L., 'The Practice of Medicine in Ancient and Medieval India',
    in *Asian Medical Systems: A Comparative Study*, ed. Charles Leslie
    (New Delhi, 1998), pp. 18–43
——, *The Wonder that was India: A Survey of the History and Culture of the
    Indian Sub-continent before the Coming of the Muslims*, 3rd revd edn
    (Kundli, India, 2004)
Bhishagratna, Kaviraj Kunja Lal, ed. and trans., *The Sushruta Samhita*
    (Delhi, 1916); available at http://chestofbooks.com
Burnett, David, and Helen Saberi, *The Road to Vindaloo: Curry Cooks and Curry
    Books* (Totnes, Devon, 2008)
Burton, David, *The Raj at Table: A Culinary History of the British in India*
    (London, 1993)
Chakravarty, Indira, *Saga of Indian Food: A Historical and Cultural Survey*
    (New Delhi, 1972)
Chakravarty, Taponath, *Food and Drink in Ancient Bengal* (Calcutta, 1959)

Chandra, Satish, *History of Medieval India, 800–1700* (Hyderabad, 2007)

Chattopadhyay, Aparna, 'Studies in Ancient Indian Medicine', post-doctoral thesis, Varanasi, India, 1993

Chavundaraya II, *Lokopakara* [*c.* 1025], trans. Valmiki S. Ayangarya (Secundabad, India, 2006)

Church, Arthur Herbert, *Food-grains of India* (London, 1886)

Collingham, Lizzie, *Curry: A Tale of Cooks and Conquerors* (Oxford, 2006)

Cunningham, Alexander, *The Ancient Geography of India* [1871], (New Delhi, 2006)

Dalrymple, William, *White Mughals* (London, 2003)

De Orta, Garcia, *Colloquies on the Simples and Drugs of India*, trans. Sir Clements Markham (London, 1913)

Dirks, Nicholas B., *Castes of Mind: Colonialism and the Making of Modern India* (Princeton, NJ, 2001)

Disney, Anthony R., *Twilight of the Pepper Empire: Portuguese Trade in Southwest India in the Early Seventeenth Century*, 2nd edn (New Delhi, 2010)

Doniger, Wendy, *The Hindus: An Alternative History* (New York, 2009)

Douglas, Mary, *Purity and Danger: An Analysis of Concepts of Pollution and Taboo* (London and New York, 2007)

Dumont, Louis, *Homo Hierarchicus: The Caste System and its Implications* (Chicago, IL, 1980)

Dundas, Paul, *The Jains*, 2nd edn (London, 2002)

Eck, Diana L., *India: A Sacred Geography* (New York, 2012)

Embree, Ainslie T., ed., *Sources of Indian Tradition*, 2nd edn (New York, 1988)

Fisher, Michael H., ed., *Visions of Mughal India: An Anthology of European Travel Writing* (London and New York, 2007)

Food and Agriculture Organization of the United Nations: http://fao.faostat.org

Gibb, H.A.R., trans. and ed., *The Travels of Ibn Battuta* (New Delhi, 2006)

Goody, Jack, *Cooking, Cuisine and Class: A Study in Comparative Sociology* (Cambridge, 1996)

Gopal, Lallanji, and V. C. Srivastava, eds, *History of Agriculture in India, up to c. 1200 AD* (New Delhi, 2008)

Grierson, George A., *Bihar Peasant Life* [1875] (Delhi, 1975)

Gupta, Shakti M., *Plants in Indian Temple Art* (New Delhi, 1996)

Hussaini, Mohammad Mazhar, *Islamic Dietary Concepts and Practices* (Bedford Park, IL, 1993)

Jackson, Anna, and Amin Jaffer, ed., *Maharaja: The Splendour of India's Royal Courts* (London, 2009)

Jaffrey, Madhur, *A Taste of India* (New York, 1985)

——, *Madhur Jaffrey's Ultimate Curry Bible* (London, 2003)

Jones, Constance A., and James D. Ryan, *Encyclopedia of Hinduism* (New York, 2008)

Kalra, J. Inder Singh, *Prashad: Cooking with Indian Masters* (New Delhi, 2006)

Keay, John, *The Honourable Company: A History of the English East India Company* (London, 1993)

——, *India: A History* (New York, 2000)

Karan, Pratibha, *Biryani* (Noida, 2009)

Kenoyer, Jonathan Mark, *Ancient Cities of the Indus Valley Civilization* (Oxford, 1998)

Khan, M.S.W., et al., *Wazwaan: Traditional Kashmiri Cuisine* (New Delhi, 2007)

Khare, R. S., *Culture and Reality: Essays on the Hindu System of Managing Foods* (Simla, India, 1976)

——, *The Hindu Hearth and Home* (New Delhi, 1976)

——, ed., *The Eternal Food: Gastronomic Ideas and Experiences of Hindus and Buddhists* (Albany, NY, 1992)

——, and M.S.A. Rao, ed., *Food, Society and Culture: Aspects in South Asian Food Systems* (Durham, NC, 1986)

Klostermaier, Klaus K., *A Concise Encyclopedia of Hinduism* (Oxford, 1998)

Knott, Kim, *Hinduism: A Very Short Introduction* (Oxford, 2000)

Konantambigi, Madhukar, trans., *Culinary Traditions of Medieval Karnataka: The Soopa Shastra of Mangarasa III*, ed. N. P. Bhat and Nerupama Y. Modwel (Delhi, 2012)

Kraig, Bruce, and Colleen Taylor Sen, *Street Food Around the World: An Encyclopedia of Food and Culture* (Santa Barbara, CA, 2013)

Kṣēmaśarmā, trans. R. Shankar, *Kṣēmakutūhalam: A Work on Dietetics and Well-being* (Bangalore, 2009)

Laudan, Rachel, *Cuisine and Empire: Cooking in World History* (Berkeley, CA, 2013)

Leslie, Charles, *Asian Medical Systems: A Comparative Study* (New Delhi, 1998)

Liu, Xinru, *Ancient India and Ancient China: Trade and Religious Exchanges, AD 1–600* (Delhi, 1988)

McCrindle, John Watson, *Ancient India as Described by Megasthenes and Arrian* (Calcutta, 1877)

Manu, *The Law Code of Manu*, trans. Patrick Olivelle (Oxford, 2009)

Mintz, Sidney Wilfred, *Tasting Food, Tasting Freedom: Excursions into Eating, Culture and the Past* (Boston, MA, 1996)

Nandy, Ashis, 'The Changing Popular Culture of Indian Food: Preliminary Notes', *South Asia Research*, XXIV/2 (March 2004), pp. 9–19

Navdanya, *Bhoole Bisre Anaj: Forgotten Foods* (New Delhi, 2006)

Olivelle, Patrick, 'From Feast to Fast: Food and the Indian Ascetic', in *Rules and Remedies in Classical Indian Law: Panels of the VIIth World Sanskrit Conference*, ed. Julia Leslie, vol. IX (Leiden, 1987), pp. 17–36

——, 'Food in India: A Review Essay', *Journal of Indian Philosophy*, XXIII/367–80 (1995)

——, trans., *Dharmasūtras: The Law Codes of Ancient India* (Oxford, 1999)

——, 'Abhaksya and Abhojya: An Exploration in Dietary Language', *Journal of the American Oriental Society*, CXXII (2002), pp. 345–54

Ovington, J., *A Voyage to Surat in the Year 1689*, ed. H. G. Rawlinson (London, 1929)

Pande, Alka, *Mukhwas: Indian Food through the Ages* (Delhi, 2013)

Prakash, Om, *Food and Drinks in Ancient India: From Earliest Times to c. 1200 AD* (Delhi, 1961)

——, *Economy and Food in Ancient India* (New Delhi, 1987)

——, *Cultural History of India* (New Delhi, 2005)

Prasada, Neha, and Ashima Narain, *Dining with the Maharajas: A Thousand Years of Culinary Tradition* (New Delhi, 2013)

Ramachandran, Ammini, *Grains, Greens and Grated Coconuts: Recipes and Remembrances of a Vegetarian Legacy* (Lincoln, NE, 2007)

Ray, Krishnendu, and Tulasi Srinivas, *Curried Cultures: Globalization, Food, and South Asia* (Berkeley, CA, 2012)

Raychaudhuri, Hasi, and Tapan Raychaudhuri, 'Not by Curry Alone: An Introduction to Indian Cuisines for a Western Audience', in *National and Regional Styles of Cooking: Oxford Symposium on Food History* (Totnes, 1981), pp. 45–56

Ramzi, Shanaz, *Food Prints: An Epicurean Voyage Through Pakistan: Overview of Pakistani Cuisine* (Karachi, 2012)

Rowe, Caroline, 'Fermented Nagaland: A Culinary Adventure,' in *Cured, Fermented and Smoked Foods, Proceedings of the Oxford Symposium on Food and Cookery, 2010*, ed. Helen Saberi (Totnes, Devon, 2011), pp. 263–77

Roxburgh, William, *Flora Indica; or, Descriptions of Indian Plants*, ed. William Carey, vol. 1 (Serampore, India, 1832)

Roy, Nilanjana S., ed., *A Matter of Taste: The Penguin Book of Indian Writing on Food* (New Delhi, 2004)

Sahu, Kishori Prasad, *Some Aspects of Indian Social Life, 1000–1526 AD* (Calcutta, 1973)

Sastri, K. A. Nilakanta, *A History of South India: From Prehistoric Times to the Fall of Vijayanagar*, 4th edn (Oxford, 2009)

Saxena, R. C., S. L. Choudhary and Y. L. Nene, *A Textbook on Ancient History of Indian Agriculture* (Secunderabad, India, 2009)

Schimmel, Annemarie, *The Empire of the Great Mughals: History, Art and Culture* (London, 2004)

Sen, Colleen Taylor, *Food Culture in India* (Westport, CT, 2004)

—, *Curry: A Global History* (London, 2009)

Sen, Kshitimohan, *Hinduism* (London, 1991)

Sengupta, Padmini Sathianadhan, *Everyday Life in Ancient India* (Bombay, 1950)

Sewell, Robert, *A Forgotten Empire (Vijayanagar): A Contribution to the History of India* (London, 1900)

Sharar, Abdul Halim, *Lucknow: The Last Phase of an Oriental Culture*, trans. E. S. Harcourt and Fakhir Hussain (Delhi, 1994)

Sharif, Ja'far, *Qanoon-e-Islam; or, The Customs of the Moosulmans of India; Comprising a Full and Exact Account of their Various Rites and Ceremonies, from the Moment of Birth Till the Hour of Death*, ed. and trans. Gerhard Andreas Herklots (London, 1832)

Siddiqi, Iqtidar Husain, 'Food Dishes and the Catering Profession in Pre-Mughal India,' *Islamic Culture*, LIV/2 (April 1985), pp. 117–74

Somesvara III, *Royal Life in Mānasôllāsa*, trans. P. Arundhati (New Delhi, 1994)

The Sushruta Samhita: An English Translation Based on Original Sanskrit Texts, trans. Kaviraj Kunja Lal Bhishagratna, 3 vols (New Delhi, 2006)

Svoboda, Robert E., *Ayurveda: Life, Health and Longevity* (New Delhi, 1993)

Thapar, Romila, *Early India: From the Origins to AD 1300* (Berkeley, CA, 2002)

Thieme, John, and Ira Raja, *The Table is Laid: The Oxford Anthology of South Asian Food Writing* (New Delhi, 2007)

Titley, Norah M., trans., *The Ni'matnāma Manuscript of the Sultans of Mandu: The Sultan's Book of Delights* (London and New York, 2005)

Upadhyaya, Bhagwat Saran, *India in Kālidāsa* (Delhi, 1968)

Wolpert, Stanley, *A New History of India*, 6th edn (New York, 2000)

Wujastyk, Dominik, *The Roots of Ayurveda: Selections from Sanskrit Medical Writings* (London, 2001)

Yule, Henry, and A. C. Burnell, *Hobson-Jobson: A Glossary of Colloquial Anglo-Indian Words and Phrases, and of Kindred Terms, Etymological, Historical, Geographical and Discursive* (London and Boston, MA, 1985)

Zimmermann, Francis, *The Jungle and the Aroma of Meats: An Ecological Theme in*
Zohary, Daniel, Maria Hopf and Ehud Weiss, *Domestication of Plants in the Old World: The Origin and Spread of Domesticated Plants in Southwest Asia, Europe, and the Mediterranean Basin*, 4th edn (Oxford, 2012)

Zubaida, Sami, and Richard Tapper, eds, *A Taste of Thyme: Culinary Cultures of the Middle East* (London, 2006)

Acknowledgements

I took on this project with enthusiasm, not realizing how challenging it would prove to be. Writing my previous book for Reaktion, *Curry: A Global History*, I was faced with a surfeit of books on the subject. For this book the problem was the opposite. Why the history of Indian food has been so neglected is a mystery, but I'm grateful to my publisher, Michael Leaman, for suggesting that I try my hand at writing one.

I owe a great debt to various people who helped me, although of course any mistakes and omissions are entirely my own. My husband, Ashish Sen, read the manuscript several times, translated passages, and made many excellent comments and suggestions. Professor David Gitomer reviewed several chapters, tactfully pointing out my errors. I once again owe an enormous debt of gratitude to Helen Saberi for her always perceptive comments and encouraging words, and to Bruce Kraig for his thoughtful review. Professor Marcia Harmansen, Peggy Mohan, Charles Perry, Mary Isin, Shahrzad Ghorasian, Jayant Sukhadia, Dr Kantha Shelke and Ammini Ramachandran generously shared their expertise. Special thanks to my friends in India, Mamta Chandra, Vivek Batra, Bappa and Anu Ray, Mridula and Prakash Seth, V. P. Rajesh, Peggy and Dinesh Mohran, Suresh Hinduja and Chef Shaun Kenworthy. And, despite the omnipresence of the Internet, librarians remain the researcher's greatest resource. I owe a great debt to Carol Worster of the Gas Technology Institute, James Nye of the University of Chicago and Catherine Wilson of the Chicago Public Libraries.

Since my first visit in 1972, I've been to India fifteen times and travelled around the country. One of my inspirations and models was my late mother-in-law, Arati Sen, a prominent journalist and food writer. However, much of my experience with Indian food comes from my long residence in Chicago. My husband and I live within walking distance of Devon Avenue, North America's most concentrated South Asian shopping and dining area and a constantly changing kaleidoscope of ethnicities and establishments. Our friends in many communities have invited us to share their meals, participate in their festivals and attend their houses of worship, providing a range of culinary experiences that would be difficult to experience so readily in India itself. To them especially I owe thanks.

Photo Acknowledgements

The author and publishers wish to express their thanks to the following sources of illustrative material or permission to reproduce it:

Ampersandyslexia: p. 160; Bigstock: pp. 13 (Europeanpix), 90 (A K Choudhury), 177 (masoodrezvi), 240 (smarnad), 250 (oysy); The British Library: pp. 19, 59, 61, 67, 162, 166, 167, 219; © The Trustees of the British Museum, London: pp. 71, 71, 96, 98, 115, 180, 181, 209, 221; Charles O. Cecil/Alamy: p. 100; Corbis: p. 236 (Bettmann); Ezralalsim10: p. 69; Getty Images/TUSEEF MUSTAFA/AFP: p. 206; © harappa.com: pp. 25, 29, 31; Charles Haynes: p. 142; iStockphoto: pp. 21 (Alatom), 24 (RileyMaclean), 75 (iannomadav), 141, 259 (danishkahn), 205 (Manu_Bahuguna), 252 (ShashikanDurshettiwar), 283 (jason5yuan), 300 bottom (Paul_Brighton); Kalamazadkhan: p. 296; Gunawan Kartapranata: p. 305; Vinay Kudithipudi: p. 258 Los Angeles County Museum of Art/LACMA: pp. 103, 232; Luis Wiki: p. 210; Miansari66: pp. 149, 201; The Museum of Fine Arts, Houston/MFAH: p. 107; New York Public Library: p. 229; Gaitri Pagach-Chandra: pp. 297 top, 297 bottom; PHGCOM: p. 74; Jorge Royan: p. 188; Ashish Sen: pp. 22, 88, 267, 269, 277; Colleen Taylor Sen: pp. 129, 134; Anilrisal Singh: pp. 20, 144, 145 bottom, 157 top, 161, 193, 196, 197, 199, 244, 264, 286, 289, 300; Victoria & Albert Museum, London: pp. 35, 66, 89, 136, 174, 212; Werner Forman Archive: p. 211 (Schatzhammer of the Residenz, Munich).

Index

Note: This index lists only the most important or historical references to a topic. It does not include references to common food items, such as dal and ghee, which each would have hundreds of entries.

Pages which contain illustrations are noted in *italics*; pages with recipes are in **bold**.